THE JEREMY COLLIER
STAGE CONTROVERSY
1698-1726

JEREMY COLLIER A.M.

THE JEREMY COLLIER STAGE CONTROVERSY
1698-1726

*A Dissertation Accepted by the Faculty of the Graduate
School, Marquette University, in Partial Fulfill-
ment of the Requirements for the Degree
of Doctor of Philosophy.*

BY

SISTER ROSE ANTHONY, S.C.

Benjamin Blom
New York

First published 1937
Reissued 1966, by
Benjamin Blom, Inc., New York 10452
Library of Congress Catalog Card No. 66-12286

Printed in U.S.A. by
NOBLE OFFSET PRINTERS, INC.
NEW YORK 3, N. Y.

To

The dearest people in the world

My Father and Mother

TABLE OF CONTENTS

CHAPTER VIII

CHAPTER IX.

**Entered for record. I have not seen the pamphlet.

CHAPTER X

CHAPTER XI

**Entered for record. I have not seen the pamphlet.
***2nd ed. of *The Occasional Paper, Number IX,* 1698.

**Entered for record. I have not seen the pamphlet.

PREFACE

The topic suggested for my dissertation was originally "The Literary Disputes of the Restoration." Consultation with Professor Allardyce Nicoll of Yale University, with Doctor A. L. Bouton and Doctor A. S. Borgman of New York University, and particularly with Doctor Ronald S. Crane of the University of Chicago convinced me that that topic was too broad. In consequence, I decided upon one dispute of the Restoration, the controversy resulting from Jeremy Collier's attack in 1698 upon the immorality and profaneness of the English stage. I was encouraged in this decision not only by the faculty at Marquette University but by Doctor Bouton and by Doctor Crane. It was Doctor Crane who suggested that I limit my field to 1698-1726 and these are the limits I have chosen.

The outline drawn up in the beginning required me

1. to ascertain Collier's motives for attacking the stage;
2. to analyze the five anti-stage pamphlets to which Collier subsubscribed his name;
3. to assemble—chronologically if possible—and to analyze the replies which these pamphlets evoked;
4. to note the influence of the 1694 Caffaro-Bossuet Controversy in France upon the Collier Controversy in England;
5. to augment the existing Collier bibliographies.

A year of intensive study in the Newberry Library in Chicago has enabled me to amplify my original plan by securing new material relevant to disputed topics as likewise to make certain contributions to knowledge in the field of my subject. Under the first heading I have collected data clarifying somewhat the disputed authorship of *A Vindication of the Stage*, of *The Occasional Paper, Number IX*, of *The Antient and Modern Stages survey'd*, of *A Defence of Dramatick Poetry*, of the "Supplemental Pamphlet," and of *A Letter to a Lady Concerning the New Play House*. Under the second, I have attempted to prove that Collier is the author of the following six anonymous stage-attacks which appeared between 1698-1726: *A Letter to Mr. Congreve on his Pretended Amendments*, 1698; the Preface to the English Translation of J. Bossuet's *Maximes et réflexions*, 1699; *A Representation of the Impiety and Immorality of the English Stage*, 1704; *The*

Theatre-Royal, 1718; *The Occasional Paper, Vol. III, Number IX, Of Plays and Masquerades,* 1719; and *The Conduct of the Stage Consider'd,* 1721. I have likewise offered proof that he partook actively in the stage-attack up to 1721 even though scholars have previously been of the opinion that his *Farther Vindication,* 1708, was the last attack which he made, and, lastly, that the disputed "lost *Supplemental Pamphlet"* is the actually existing pamphlet, "*A Representation of the Impiety and Immorality of the English Stage.*

I have intentionally given detailed anaylses of pamphlets and frequent quotations from them. My reason was threefold: first, many of the pamphlets are so exceedingly rare that I believed detail and quotation might prove interesting to scholars and helpful to future students of the Collier Stage-Controversy; second, because detailed analysis of many of the pamphlets has not been given by previous Collier students there was a necessity to acquaint myself and my reader with the substance of these pamphlets. In some cases previous Collier critics mention the pamphlets as being for or against the stage; in others they give an occasional quotation but they do not transcribe sufficient data to acquaint the readers with the style of the pamphleteers or with their method of argumentation. In the third place, I hoped to sift from the pamphlets the important topics used in attack of the stage and those used in vindication, and to show the sequence of these attacks and replies. I am confident that a great amount of literature on the controversy published between 1698-1726 has been lost; I am convinced, too, that the topic is so vast that I have scarcely gotten beneath the surface. Even though I have spared neither time, effort, nor money to secure the available pamphlets either in the original or as photostats, I have been obliged to delay to a future date the analysis of some of them. Too, pertinent data recently located in the British Museum as well as repeated instances of the unreliability of early periodicals for establishing the exact date of first appearance of pamphlets are factors which may warrant a future change in the chronology which I have adopted.

Appreciation for the courtesy and scholarly help extended to me in various ways during the past year demands grateful acknowledgment. I owe special thanks to the graduate faculty at Marquette University but especially to the scholarly counsel of Doctor Edward A.

Fitzpatrick, Dean of the Graduate School, of Doctor George E. Vander Beke, of Doctor William M. Lamers, of Doctor William Dehorn, and of Doctor James M. Purcell. Upon Doctor Purcell has fallen the onerous task of supervising and criticizing my work. He has been patient and helpful in advising, and generous in giving his valuable time. A simple "Thank You" expresses inadequately my gratitude to him.

I am indebted to scholars at universities other than my own who have proved themselves sympathetic with my difficulties even though I in soliciting their help had no claim to their time. To Doctor Crane, Professor of English at the University of Chicago am I especially obligated, for without his advice and the kindness with which he placed at my disposal his great knowledge of this period, my work would lack much of whatever virtue it may possess. I hope I have to some extent warranted his help by the production of a satisfactory piece of research. However, great as is my indebtedness to Doctor Crane, he can in no sense be held responsible either for my faults in method or for my errors in judgment.

To Mr. George B. Utley, Director of the Newberry Library, and to his courteous and efficient staff I acknowledge favors too numerous to recount. Every service within the power of the staff to grant me was cheerfully and generously given. I enjoyed for one year the privilege of a cubicle and the advice of Mrs. Gertrude L. Woodward, custodian of the rare books at the Newberry. She has been particularly helpful because of her wide acquaintance with the books relevant to my study. Likewise do I thank Mr. L. Raney, Director of the Library at the University of Chicago, Miss Catherine Hall and Mrs. R. Emerson, assistant librarians of the University libraries, Miss Mary Marshall and Miss Margaret Lawler of the Marquette Library. I must make acknowledgment, also, to the librarians of Library of Congress, of the Harvard College Library, of the Library of Haverford College, and of the Wren Library of Texas University for their generous loans of rare and valuable books. But to the members of my community, the Sisters of Charity of Cincinnati, and especially to Mother General Mary Regina, am I deeply grateful for help and encouragement.

In conclusion permit me to assume full responsibility for whatever faults my dissertation may possess, though I hope these will be found to be few and in no way to invalidate my conclusions.

THE JEREMY COLLIER STAGE CONTROVERSY 1698-1726

CHAPTER I.

BIOGRAPHY OF JEREMY COLLIER

Foreword

Of the several biographies of Jeremy Collier which are extant, mention should be made of that of Reverend William Hunt,[1] of S. Austin Allibone,[2] and of Andrew Kippis.[3] Besides these there are three other sources of information of Collier's life which deserve attention because they stress Collier's life as a nonjuror and because we derive from them abundant information concerning the important role played by Collier in political and religious controversies of the Restoration and of the early eighteenth century. The first of these latter studies both in time and importance is that of Thomas Lathbury published in 1852 as a Preface to his nine-volume edition of Collier's *Ecclesiastical History of Great Britain.* In developing Collier's controversial career, however, Lathbury places notable emphasis upon the quarrels of Collier as a Nonjuror, as a Defender of James II, and as the Absolver, but he does not exhaust the topic of *Collier the Stage-Reformer.* Prior to 1852 Lathbury had published in the *History of the Nonjurors* much biographical data of Collier but here, also, he stresses the political and religious angles of the controversies. However, from no other biographer have we such copious information not only concerning Collier's consecration as bishop in 1713 by Hickes and his two Scottish assistant-bishops, Campbell and Gadderer, but also concerning his leadership in a schism which flourished in the Anglican Church in the second decade of the eighteenth century. Probably from no other source can we gain

---

[1] *D. N. B.,* IV, 797-803.

[2] S. Austin Allibone, *Critical Dictionary of English Literature,* I, 408-410.

[3] Andrew Kippis, *Biographia Britannica,* IV, 12-20. Lathbury, however, says of Kippis' *Life of Collier;* "Few persons will regard Dr. Kippis as an unprejudiced or an impartial witness in the case." J. Collier, *Ecclesiastical History of Great Britain,* I, Preface, p. xix.

such accurate information concerning Collier's political leanings and his views of the "Four Usages."

Besides Lathbury's "Life of Collier" we have that of Canon Overton who in 1902, published a splendid dissertation on *The Nonjurors,* and among the various biographies given there we find eight pages on Jeremy Collier's life.[4] Then, too, Henry Broxap in his excellent work *The Later Nonjurors* published in 1924, has given us detailed information concerning Collier not only in his role as leader of the Nonjurors but also in the activity with which he conducted the controversy on the "Four Usages." Broxap tells us that the authorities for his work are the collection of papers and the correspondence of Doctor Thomas Brett, the various Edinburgh MSS. in the possession of the Scottish Bishops, and the eleven-volume edition of *Remarks and Collections of Thomas Hearne.*

In addition to the religious and political controversies of which Collier was the instigator and on whose leadership their life depended, we have in his attack upon the stage in 1698 the beginning of a controversy which agitated the stage-poets, evoked a barrage of pamphlets and resulted in much lampooning and satire with Collier as the victim. This angle has not been overlooked by biographers other than those mentioned above. Beljame, in his volume *Le Public et Les Hommes De Lettres, 1660-1744,* published in 1897,[5] has given masterful treatment of the subject, and, in addition, has contributed an extensive bibliography of Collier, Congreve, Vanbrugh, Dryden, Dennis, etc., as well as of the stage-war from 1698-1726. Then, too, Dr. Johnson's sketch of the controversy as given in the *Life of Congreve*[6] as well as that of Macaulay,[7] of Hazlitt,[8] of Krutch,[9] of Johannes Ballein,[10] and of Taylor[11] gives, in one way or another, its author's views of Collier's anathemas thundered against the stage and the stage-poets and of the replies which they evoked. The analysis given by Ballein is critical and his references to contemporary attacks are comprehensive, yet he does

---

[4] Canon Overton, *The Nonjurors,* pp. 121-129.
[5] A. Beljame, *Le Public et Les Hommes de Lettres, 1660-1744,* pp. 244-260.
[6] Samuel Johnson, *Lives of the Poets,* ed. by Chalmers; X, 260-261.
[7] Lord Macaulay, *Essays, Critical, Historical and Miscellaneous,* IV, 393-404.
[8] William Hazlitt, *Lectures on the English Comic Writers,* pp. 172-175.
[9] Joseph W. Krutch, *Comedy and Conscience after the Restoration,* pp. 88-192.
[10] Johannes Ballein, *Jeremy Collier's Angriff auf die englische Bühne.*
[11] D. Crane Taylor, *William Congreve,* pp. 106-145.

not include a bibliography. However, none of the students above mentioned suggested that Collier was in the ranks against the stage-poets as often anonymously up to 1708 as when he heralded his identity by the customary signature "Jeremy Collier, M. A.," nor have they hinted that he very often directed the guns and supplied the ammunition in the war on the stage waged between 1698 and 1721.

PART 1

Life of Jeremy Collier

Jeremy Collier was born on September 23, 1650, at Stow Qui, in Cambridgeshire. Both his father and grandfather were clergymen. His grandfather resided at Yeadow near Bradford in the County of York; his father, whose name also was Jeremy, spent a great portion of his life at Ipswich. He is said to have been possessed of a liberal education and was known as "a linguist and some-time Master of the Free-school at Ipswich, in the County of Suffolk."[12] His mother was Elizabeth Smith, also a native of Stow Qui, in which place the family was held in considerable honor.

Young Jeremy was educated by his father at Ipswich until his removal to Cajus College, Cambridge, on April 10, 1669. The lad was an earnest student; native ability joined to diligent application gave him the reputation among his fellow-students of being a scholar of no mean attainments. In 1672-1673 he received the degree of B. A., and in 1676 that of M. A. He was ordained deacon in September, 1673, and priest in February, 1677.[13]

As a priest he officiated for some time at the palace of the Countess Dowager of Dorsett at Knowle in Kent whence he removed to a small rectory at Ampton near St. Edmundbury, in Suffolk. For six years he held this benefice but resigned it and in 1685 came to reside in London where for some little time after he was lecturer at Gray's-Inn. "But the Revolution coming on, the public exercise of his function became impracticable."[14] From Collier's own testimony we learn that he could not exercise the functions of his ministry because of his refusal

---

[12] Andrew Kippis, *Biographia Britannica*, IV, 12.
[13] Jeremy Collier, *An Ecclesiastical History of Great Britain, Chiefly of England . . . With a Life of the Author, Embracing a View of His Opinions, and Those of the Nonjurors as a Body. By Thomas Lathbury*, I, ii.
[14] The principal facts quoted above were given by Collier himself. Kippis, *Biographia Britannica*, IV, 12.

to take the oath of allegiance to William and Mary. It was this refusal, moreover, which ostracized him for the rest of his life from that society which was his by right of birth, education, and ministry. Concerning the controversy between the juring and the nonjuring clergy which was waged at this time we have our most extensive and impartial account from Lathbury who tells us that it was Burnet who fired the gun that aroused Collier's fighting blood and which prompted him to encounter his political antagonist in a pamphlet battle. Burnet in his *An Inquiry into the Present State of Affairs* had portrayed James II as a "Deserter of the Crown." He had written:

> "A Kings deserting his People, and withdrawing both his Person and his Seals, by which the Peace, Justice and Order of the Nation are preserved, does certainly warrent them to look to their own safety and preservation; and when they are obliged to do this by ways and methods that are inconsistent with his authority, and that are so many Crimes if they stood still under any engagements to him, then they must be considered as acquitted from all their ties to him."[15]

The stigma of "Desertion" with which this statement branded James II fired Collier to caustic retaliation. He replied with *The Desertion Discussed*, "the first direct attack upon the principles of the Revolution." The pamphlet in question is in the form of a twelve-page "Letter to a Country Gentleman," the letter being divided into thirty-three articles. With characteristic pugnacity the author addresses his correspondent:

> "Sir, I Don't wonder to find a Person of your Sense and Integrity so much surpriz'd at the Report of the Throne's being declared Vacant, by the Lower House of the Convention."[16]

He states emphatically that a *Parliament* and a *Convention* are two very different things and that the latter for want of the king's writs and concurrence has no share in the legislative power. He very systematically refutes Burnet's contention

> "That when a King withdraws himself and his Seals, without naming any Persons to represent him, the Government is certainly laid down and forsaken by him."[17]

---

[15] Burnet, *William and Mary Tracts*, XII, 5.
[16] J. Collier, *The Desertion Discuss'd* found in *William and Mary Tracts*, XII, 134.
[17] *Ibid.*, p. 5.

This refutation is in the form of three statements which urge that James's flight was not abdication. It asserts:

> 1. "His Majesty, before withdrawing, had sufficient Grounds to make him apprehensive of Danger, and therefore it cannot be called an Abdication; 2. That the leaving any Representatives behind him was impracticable at this Juncture; 3. That we have no Grounds, either from the Laws of the Realm, or those of Nature, to pronounce the Throne void, upon such a Retreat of the King."[18]

One may easily imagine the grave offence which an article of this kind gave at a time when allegiance to William and Mary was being warmly advocated. From the tone of *The Desertion Discuss'd* one may infer that Collier would have been satisfied with a regency and with the Prince of Orange as Regent. Lathbury confirms this inference:

> "It cannot be supposed that a regency would not have preserved the Church and the liberties of the people. The bishops and the clergy had no wish to see King James restored to power but they conceived that every purpose connected with the safety of the country would have been answered by a regency. The schism would thus have been prevented; Sancroft and his brethren would have cordially concurred in such a settlement; and the peace of the Church would have been unbroken."[19]

Shortly after Collier's publication, Edmund Bohun, Esq., replied with *An Answer to the Desertion Discuss'd*. This, together with other answers, proved that Collier had antagonized those in authority; the answers also substantiate the fact that after the government was settled he was seized and committed as a close prisoner to Newgate. However he was at length discharged without being brought to trial.[20] Nothing daunted by his incarceration Collier emphasized his non-

---

[18] *Ibid.*, pp. 135-136.
[19] Thomas Lathbury, *History of the Nonjurors*, p. 33. Of the important role played by Sancroft we read: "It was Sancroft that drew up the petition to King James respecting the Declaration of Indulgence; Sancroft who first propounded the Regency Scheme; Sancroft who set the example of declining the oath of allegiance to William and Mary; Sancroft who, in a sense, established the Non-Juring communion; Sancroft who was mainly responsible for continuing the succession of the non-juring Episcopate." Overton, *The Nonjurors*, pp. 33-34.
[20] Andrew Kippis, *Biographia Britannica*, IV, 13. Edmund Bohun had published on April 1, 1689, *The History of the Desertion* containing an account of all the proceedings connected with the Revolution. This is found in *William and Mary Tracts*, XXVII, 1-134.

juring principles and his break with the government by publishing a series of pamphlets attacking the authorities.[21]

On November 8, 1692, Collier together with Newton, another non-juror, was apprehended and imprisoned in consequence of a visit to Romney Marsh where they were suspected of going that they might communicate with the exiled king. As no evidence was found against them they were admitted to bail.

> "So strict, however, were Mr. Collier's principles that he had not long been at liberty, before he began to question the consistency of his own conduct in giving bail; upon which he went before the Lord Chief Justice Holt, surrendered in their discharge and was committed to the King's Bench Prison; but upon the application of some of his friends to that most upright and impartial Judge, he was discharged in a week or ten days."[22]

During his brief term in prison he wrote as a defence of his conduct *The Case of Giving Bail to a Pretended Authority Examined,* dated from the King's Bench, November 23, 1692. Soon after this he wrote *A Perswasive to Consideration Tendered to the Royalists Particularly to Those of the Church of England,* 1693, and a pamphlet of extraordinary bitterness entitled *Remarks upon the London Gazette.*[23]

We hear very little of Collier's proceedings from 1691-1692 to 1696. In 1696, however, Collier together with Cook and Snatt became unenviably prominent by reason of their attending to the scaffold and absolving two men, Sir John Friend and Sir William Perkins, who were condemned to death for being implicated in the "Assassination Plot." The conduct of the three clergymen gave great offence; in consequence, Cook and Snatt were imprisoned at Newgate, and Collier upon absconding, was outlawed. However, conflict with the government seemed only to fortify Collier for further battles, for he published

---

[21] The titles of these pamphlets are found in Andrew Kippis, *Biographia Britannica,* IV, 13. We read that the Doctor Sherlock to whose case of allegiance Collier referred in his eighth pamphlet, *Dr. Sherlock's Case of Allegiance Considered* was one of the most conspicuous of those who took the oath after a resistance of several months. In order to vindicate himself for taking it he published his *Case of Allegiance Due to Sovereign Powers.*
[22] *Ibid.,* IV, 13.
[23] *D. N. B.,* IV, 798.

in 1696 *A Defence of His Absolution Given to Sir William Perkins at the Place of Execution.*[24]

Heated by the argument and instigated to further replies by answers received, he published on April 21 his *Vindication.* To this Collier adds a Postscript; it is dated four days later and refers to an answer to his publication of April 9. Following close upon this, Collier fortified his position still further by publishing on May 20 *A Reply to the Absolution of a Penitent, according to the Directions of the Church of England,* and, on July 1, *An Answer to the Animadversions on two Pamphlets lately published by Mr. Collier.* Both of the last mentioned pamphlets are subscribed by the letters J. C., but they do not show title-pages or a printer's name. Lathbury suggests as a reason for this either that Collier feared his retreat might be discovered or that the printer refused to give his name lest he be brought into trouble with the government.[25]

In 1697 Collier published Parts I and II of *Essays Upon Several Moral Subjects.*

> "They were written upon religious, moral, and entertaining subjects, with such a mixture of learning and wit, and in a style so easy and flowing, that notwithstanding the prejudice of party which could not but be strong against him, they were generally well received, and have run through many editions since."[26]

In the spring of 1698 Collier published *A Short View,* his attack upon the stage. In it he censures profaneness and immorality generally, but deals most sharply with contemporary writers who are guilty of these offences. He gives his blows unsparingly. Neither the popularity, wit, nor prestige of an author provide shelter for profaneness, im-

---

[24] S. Austin Allibone, *A Critical Dictionary of English Literature and British and American Authors,* I, 408. The *Defence* is dated April 9.

[25] J. Collier, *Ecclesiastical History,* I, xi, note.

[26] Andrew Kippis, *Biographia Britannica,* IV, 15. A very interesting article by Edmund Freeman appeared in the *Philological Quarterly,* VII, 17-26, January, 1928. The article bears the title "Jeremy Collier and Francis Bacon" and calls attention not only to the wide acquaintance of Collier with Bacon's *Essays,* but it suggests that Collier adopted Bacon's aphoristic style and that he has in several of his essays, taken over titles, e.g., "Of Friendship," "Of Riches," "Of Envy" etc., and that he has occasionally relied upon Bacon for certain phrases. In the case of the essay "Of Friendship" he has been indebted to him for several paragraphs.

morality, or abuse of the clergy.[27] Dryden, D'Urfey, Wycherley, Congreve, Vanbrugh—all feel the smart; of these, Congreve, Vanbrugh, and D'Urfey resent it. John Oldmixon in his *History of England* tells us, however, of the popularity of the pamphlet despite the ire of the poets:

> "His Book had a great run, and with many aton'd for the Crime he had been guilty of, in giving Absolution to impenitent Traytors; the Religious part of the Town cry'd it up, and some of the wealthy ones rewarded him, particularly a Presbyterian, Sir Owen Buckingham, an Alderman of London, and Member of Parliament for Reading, sent him 20 guineas."[28]

A moment's reflection upon the nature of the attack and upon the results accruing from it will convince the reader of the indomitable courage of the clergyman, and of his conviction of the justice of his cause. There is contemporary evidence to prove that to stigmatize the playwrights was equivalent to casting opprobrium upon the town.[29] Moreover, Colley Cibber asserts that Mr. Congreve was then in such high reputation as an author that besides his profits from the play, *Love for Love,* he was offered a whole share in the theatre.[30] He states, also, that the actors of the period were popular and were held in very high repute:

> "No stage at any one Period, could show thirteen Actors, standing all in equal Lights of Excellence, in their Profession."[31]

Besides Cibber's reference to Congreve's popularity we have Baker's statement of the esteem entertained for Wycherley:

> "On the appearance of his first play, he became acquainted with several of the first-rate wits, and likewise with the Dutchess of Cleveland, . . . Villiers, Duke of Buckingham, had also the highest esteem for him, . . . King Charles likewise showed him signal marks of favor; and once gave him a proof of his esteem."[32]

---

[27] For a discussion of opinions concerning the motives of the attack, cf. pp. 16-25; for Collier's acquaintance with play-lore, cf. pp. 225-7.

[28] J. Oldmixon, *History of England During the Reign of Queen Anne*, III, 192.

[29] John Dennis, *The Usefulness of the Stage*, pp. [7-8].

[30] Colley Cibber, *An Apology for the Life of Mr. Colley Cibber, Comedian, and Late Patentee of the Theatre-Royal. With an Historical View of the Stage During His Own Time*, p. 161.

[31] *Ibid.*, p. 143.

[32] D. E. Baker, *Biographia Dramatica*, I, 475.

In addition let it be said that Collier in attacking the wits of his day laid himself open to counter-attack and lampooning and to the certainty of being the victim of venomous tongues. It is not to be wondered at, therefore, that wounded and infuriated feelings produced immediate replies. D'Urfey, Congreve, Vanbrugh, Gildon, Dennis—all looked to their laurels. Congreve retorted with his *Amendments of Mr. Collier's False and Imperfect Citations,* and Vanbrugh published *A Short Vindication of the Relapse and the Provoked Wife.* D'Urfey in his Preface to the *Campaigners* gave a verbose vindication of the stage, and, in addition to exculpating himself, stepped to the assistance of his fellow-dramatists. Gildon in his Preface to *Phaeton,* Dennis in his *The Usefulness of the Stage,* and the anonymous authors of *A Vindication of the Stage, A Defence of Dramatick Poetry* and *A Farther Defence*— all allied themselves as opponents of Collier.

Occasionally a defender stepped to the fore who either openly or anonymously took the side of Collier against the stage-poets. We have in *A Letter to Mr. Congreve on his Pretended Amendments,* in the *Animadversions,* and in *The Stage Condemned* three examples of such anonymous defences of Collier. One of them, a *Letter to Mr. Congreve,* bears every mark of being the product of Mr. Collier's pen; I have attempted to prove this in conjunction with my analysis of the pamphlet.[33]

Another interesting anonymous pamphlet appearing shortly after the publication of the *Short View* is *The Occasional Paper Number IX, Containing Some Considerations about the Danger of Going to Plays.* It is generally ascribed to Richard Willis although I believe that it has the collaboration of Collier. My reasons for this statement are given at length in the analysis of this pamphlet.[34]

The flood of retaliating pamphlets which the *Short View* evoked heated further the fighting blood of Collier and undauntedly he replied in November, 1698, by the publication of his *A Defence of the Short View of the Profaneness and Immorality of the English Stage, etc. Being a Reply to Mr. Congreve's Amendments, etc., And to the Vindication of the Author of the Relapse.* It was not to be expected that one who had vindicated and re-vindicated himself on the occasions of "The

---

[33] pp. 113-125.
[34] pp. 82-89.

Desertion" and "The Absolution" would allow his opponents the last word. So, in his *Defence,* Collier, though formally addressing Congreve and Vanbrugh, pays his caustic respects to the minor vindicators.

The controversy waxed during 1698 and 1699. Oldmixon tells us in 1698 that the poets were a little awed at first, but that this awe soon wore off and in their plays, prologues, and epilogues the stage-poets were making this attempt to reform them the sport of what wit they had.[35]

A fact that should not be ignored in outlining Collier's activity in the stage-controversy between 1698-1708 is his connection with the translation of Bossuet's *Maximes et réflexions* which appeared in 1699. This connection has not generally been noted by Collier bibliographers. In addition to the evidences which the Preface bears to Collier's authorship, there is a statement substantiating this authorship found in Arber's *Term Catalogues,*[36] and another statement pertaining to the translation made by Collier in his *Defence.*[37]

Many authors—some of them anonymous—published other attacks on the stage, and some published other vindications. One of the most important of the vindications of 1699 was that of James Drake who produced *The Antient and Modern Stages Survey'd, or, Mr. Collier's View of the Immorality and Profaneness of the English Stage Set in a True Light. Wherein some of Mr. Collier's Mistakes are rectified, and the comparative Morality of the English Stage is Asserted on the Parallel.* Collier, however, was convinced of the justice of his cause and scorning the kind intentions of Mr. Drake to "rectify his mistakes" proceeded to make ready for a third charge. In 1700 he replied by a *Second Defence of the Short View . . . Being a Reply to a Book Entitul'd, The Antient and Modern Stages Survey'd, etc.*

During the following four years the controversy waned in vigor. In addition to a *Second Defence* Collier published in December, 1703, his *Dissuasive from the Playhouse,* and in January, 1704, his *Representation of the Impiety and Immorality of the Stage.* This latter anonymous pamphlet has not been previously ascribed to Collier but I am

---

[35] J. Oldmixon, *History of England,* III, 192.
[36] III, 159. Cf. also *Biographia Britannica,* IV, 18, for evidence that Collier not only wrote the Preface but translated the work.
[37] J. Collier, *A Defence of the Short View,* p. 134. Cf. also, pp. 157-162 of the present work.

convinced that it is his work. I have stated my reasons for my conviction in my analysis of the work.[38]

In June, 1704, there was published his second edition of the *Dissuasive* to which is added *A Letter by Another Hand*. It is of interest to note that not only in the *Dissuasive* and in the *Representation* but also in the *Occasional Paper* the ever-recurring theme is the necessity for combating the profaneness and immorality of the stage not in arguments given verbosely as in the *Short View* but in brief compass. It is reasonable to suppose, therefore, that Collier realized that his first work against the stage had lost much of its effectiveness because of its length, because of its tedious references to the ancient Greek and Latin poets and because of its detailed analysis of the opinion of the Fathers. In these three works, the identical opposition is waged against the profaneness and immorality of the stage and in almost the identical arguments, but we note that many of the unpopular elements have been omitted.

The period of temporary calm was broken in 1707 by Filmer who published his *A Defence of Plays*. Forthwith Collier again stepped into the arena with his reply, *A Farther Vindication of the Short View of the Profaneness and Immorality of the English Stage. In which the Objections Of a late Book, Entitul'd, A Defence of Plays, are Consider'd*, 1708. It is curious to note that Collier in his *Defence, A Second Defence,* and *A Farther Vindication* does not omit one word of censure in the title of the *Short View*. He seemed never to tire of emphasizing to those who refuted his views just what his opinion was of the profaneness and immorality of the English stage. His interest in a cause that advanced morality gave an impetus to his literary activity.

It has generally been conceded that Collier's *Farther Vindication* published in reply to Filmer's *A Defence of Plays*, ended his open participation in the stage controversy. There are those who believe that Collier had the better part of the argument:

> "Mr. Collier acquitted himself with so much force and vivacity that the most considerable of his antagonists were oblig'd, not only to quit the field of battle, but to confess that they were vanquished."[39]

---

[38] pp. 194-209.
[39] Andrew Kippis, *Biographia Britannica,* IV, 15.

Samuel Johnson also is of the opinion that Collier's castigation proved effective, for he tells us that "at last comedy grew more modest, and Collier lived to see the reward of his labors."[40] Even Mr. Henry T. Perry who spoke in 1925 of the age "which prides itself on having done away with moral barriers"[41] expresses his satisfaction that the finest examples of English Comedy are now recovering from the effects of their [Collier's and Macaulay's] disapproval, and are receiving again unprejudiced attention, thereby intimating that Collier had given a telling blow to Restoration Comedy.

The fight against profaneness and immorality did not cease, however, with the publication of Collier's *Farther Vindication*. Arthur Bedford donned the armor against the stage-poets and at a very early period in the controversy appeared in the ranks. Although he did not stand on Collier's political platform he certainly stood shoulder-to-shoulder with him on moral issues, and, until 1726, he together with William Law, W. Bulstrode, Josiah Woodward, and J. Field coked their guns and fired occasionally against the stage and into the ranks of the stage-poets. Collier was not absent from the firing line; of this I am convinced. Knowing Collier's tenacity of purpose, his fearlessness, and his controversial nature one does not suppose that he would, for instance, overlook such a direct thrust at himself and Bishop Hickes as was accorded when Cibber published, in 1717, *The Non-Juror;* neither is it likely that he would fail to lash the "pernicious consequences of masquerades." That he did not overlook either *The Non-Juror* or "Masquerades" I have attempted to show in my article on *The Theatre-Royal, 1718*[42] and on the *Occasional Paper, Vol. III, Number IX, Of Plays and Masquerades, 1719,*[43] both of which were published anonymously, it is true, but both of them bearing conclusive evidence of the authorship of Collier. In addition to these two pamphlets, we have another truly Collierian one published in 1721 entitled *The Conduct of the Stage Consider'd* which proves that Collier's interest in the stage-controversy had not abated in the least. This pamphlet though anonymous argues in favor of the authorship of Collier, and is, as far as I can determine, the last extant evidence of his participation in the war

---

[40] Samuel Johnson, *The Lives of the English Poets,* ed. by Chalmers, X, 260.
[41] Henry T. Perry, *The Comic Spirit in Restoration Drama,* p. 10.
[42] pp. 251-257.
[43] pp. 264-268.

against the stage-poets.[43a] However, native ability and diligence joined to energy and zeal gave birth to many literary productions other than those directed against the stage-poets, the germ of which lay in the erudite mind of the author. Note the following: *Essays upon Several Moral Subjects,* Vol. I, 1697, Vol. II, 1705, Vol. III, 1709, and the *Great Historical, Geographical, Genealogical and Poetical Dictionary,* 1701. This last is a translation, with additions, of Moreri's *Great Historical, Geographical, Genealogical and Poetical Dictionary.* In 1705 Collier published *A Supplement* to his *Dictionary* and in 1721 an *Appendix.*[44] He published in 1701 a translation of *Marcus Aurelius Antoninus,* in 1702 a Preface to S. Parker's Translation of Cicero's *De Finibus,* in 1708 the first volume of his great work *An Ecclesiastical History of Great Britain,* and in 1714, Volume II. Of this *History* Bishop Warburton in his *Directions to a Student in Theology* is said to have made the remark:

> "There are only two writers of the genuine History of our Church who deserve the name of historians, Collier and Fuller."[45]

In 1715 Collier published *An Answer to some Exceptions in Bishop Burnet's Third Part of the Reformation . . . with a Reply to . . . Bishop Nicholson,* and in 1717, *Some Remarks on Dr. Kennet's Second*

[43a] Cf. pp. 268-279.

[44] We read in Thomas Hearne's *Remarks and Collections,* I, 38, an article which is of value in its bearing upon the *Supplement* of Collier's *Great . . . Dictionary:*

"Mr. Collier's *Geographical and Historical Dictionary* gave but very little satisfaction to the subscribers upon Account of it's being several sheets less than was promised; besides the unaccurateness of divers particulars. Upon which he publish'd a Supplement with a design to correct the Faults, and satisfy for the Defects and omissions thereof. But this being done in hast there are still abundance of faults and more omissions. So that 'tis far from being a perfect work, it being requisite that a thing of this Nature should be undertaken by a set of men of great Industry and Knowledge, to procure Materials not only from Authors but from such Places where 'tis to be supposed are preserved any Evidences which may give light into the Life of any Great Man." (This excerpt occurs for August 29, 1705.)

[45] S. Austin Allibone, *A Critical Dictionary of English Literature,* I, 410. It is interesting biographically to note that in Collier's *Defence,* p. 138, we find the author deferring a more detailed refutation of Dennis' *The Usefulness of the Stage* because of "some urgent business." That this business was "for the press" we learn in the Preface to his *Second Defence* published in 1700. It is obvious that Collier was at this period deeply engrossed in his *Dictionary* and in his *Translation of Marcus Aurelius Antoninus*—both published in 1701.

and Third Letters. In the same year he became involved in another controversy which was precipitated by his *Reasons for Restoring some Prayers and Directions as they stand in the Communion Service of the First English Reformed Liturgy.* Three times he defended his work from the attacks of those who opposed him. In 1718 he published his *Defence of the Reasons,* and later in 1718 he published *A Vindication of the Reasons and Defence,* Part I, while in 1719 he published Part II of this pamphlet and also *A Further Defence.* His defences and vindications display all the vigor of a controversialist who had been well drilled in the art of attack.

In 1718 he published, possibly in conjunction with others, *A Communion Office;* in 1725 *Several Discourses Upon Practical Subjects,* and in 1726, the year of his death, *God Not the Author of Evil.*[46]

Because of certain views expressed in his *History* and, furthermore, because of his strong nonjuring tendencies as well as of his adherence to the "Usages" Collier was accused of holding "Romish" convictions. Concerning these as manifested in his *Ecclesiastical History* Bishop Burnet says:

> "I shall say no more of that work [*Ecclesiastical History*] . . . but that there appeared to me quite through the second volume, such a constant inclination to favour the popish doctrine, and to censure the reformers, that I should have had a better opinion of the author's integrity, if he had professed himself not to be of our communion, nor of the communion of any other Protestant Church."[47]

Another interesting article concerning the Catholic views of Collier is to be found in an article written anonymously and entitled *Mr. Collier's Desertion Discussed: or the Offices of Worship in the Liturgy of the Church of England Defended: against the bold attacks of that gentleman, late of her Communion, now of his own.* The author, himself a nonjuror, positively charges Collier with popery and

> "with setting up as the head of a new schism, and 'so by unsuspected ways' leading his sequacious disciples, by degrees at last into the communion of the Church of Rome. At least it seems to me, that he has his conscience so disposed, as perhaps

---

46 *D. N. B.,* IV, 802-803.
47 Bishop Burnet, *History of the Reformation of the Church of England,* III, vi.

his Library might be; at that end Papists, and at that Protestants, and he comes in the middle, as near one as the other."[48]

Concerning the restoration of certain "Prayers and Directions as they stand in the Communion Service of the First English Reformed Liturgy, compiled by the Bishops in the Second and Third Years of King Edward VI" Collier, the chief manager of the controversy, declared in 1717 that he was in favor of the following four "Usages:"

> "1. the addition of a little water to the wine in the celebration of the Lord's Supper; 2. the petition for the faithful departed in the prayer for the Church militant; 3. the prayer for the descent of the Holy Ghost on the sacramental elements; 4. the oblatory prayer, which followed the prayer of consecration in King Edward's First Liturgy."[49]

Mr. Lathbury asserts that the controversy which ensued over the "Four Usages" resulted in the display of much learning; that the tracts on the controversy form a volume of considerable size and that every page displays the learning and research of the authors. He claims that though the "Usages" were innovations of the Anglican Church since 1552 and that though it was unwise in the nonjurors to introduce them, nevertheless, they were harmless in themselves and cannot be charged with popery. He states, besides, that Collier together with the other Nonjurors has rendered a great service to theological literature by the publication of pamphlets remarkable for learning, zeal and a keen knowledge of divinity.[50]

---

[48] T. Lathbury, *History of the Nonjurors*, p. 289. It would be interesting for a Catholic theologian to trace the Catholicity of Collier not only in his advocacy of the "Four Usages," but also in his Jacobitical principles, and in his advocacy of the union of the Greek and Latin Churches. Concerning the last-mentioned topic let it be remembered that Lathbury records that in 1716 the nonjuring Bishops proposed union with the Greek Church. Spinckes, Campbell, and Collier drew up the proposals, put them into Greek ,and delivered them to the Archbishop of Thebais. The proposals consisting of twelve parts had for their object "A concordate betwixt the orthodox and Catholic remnant of the British Churches, and the Catholic and Apostolic Oriental Church." There are appended twelve points in which both groups agree and five in which they do not agree; and the plea is for re-consideration of the points of disagreement. The proposals were eventually sent to the Patriarch of Alexandria to be communicated to the four Eastern Patriarchs. Before the return of the answer from the Patriarch a breach had occurred among the Nonjurors, hence the project came to naught. T. Lathbury, *History of the Nonjurors*, pp. 310-318.

[49] J. Collier, *An Ecclesiastical History*, I, xxiv.

[50] J. Collier, *An Ecclesiastical History, Preface*, xxx-xlvii.

The question of Collier's two marriages is quite generally disregarded by biographers. However, Broxap mentions them, and there is, besides, information regarding them to be found in the Brett *Manuscripts* as well as in Hearne's *Diary*. From the *Manuscripts* we learn the following:

> "I take it ill that I was not apprized of it [the death of Collier] that I might have attended him to his grave as I did his first wife."[51]

From the *Diary* of Thomas Hearne we have the information not only concerning the second marriage of Collier but of his poverty at the time of his death:

> "Last Tuesday [April 26, 1726] died at London the Rev. Jer. Collier, a Man of excellent Parts and Learning, and great Integrity, he being a Nonjuror, and deprived of what he had at the time of the wicked Revolution. He was a Cambridge Man, and ought therefore to be reckoned among the famous Worthies of that University. He writ and published many Books, some of which are about the Stage, An Historical and Geographical Dictionary, a Church History of Britain, Essays, etc."[52]

During the last years of his life Collier's health was undermined by frequent attacks of the "stone." Sometimes his afflictions were very severe but throughout his trials his spirit was serene. His last work *God Not the Author of Evil* published just a short time before his death is free from the tincture of controversy which is evident in so many of his other works. He died on April 26, 1726, and was buried in the Churchyard of St. Pancras.[53]

PART 2
Collier's Motives in Attacking the Stage

It is natural to question the motives which prompted Collier to write his *Short View*, and, were it not for the several statements which he himself makes, we could do nothing more than conjecture the purpose he had in attacking the stage. However, with the clue which these

---

[51] *Brett MSS.*, VI, 127. The statement is taken from a letter of Campbell to Brett, written April 30, 1726. The Thomas Brett mentioned here had been consecrated by Collier, Spinckes, and Hawes in 1716. T. Lathbury, *History of the Nonjurors*, p. 248.

[52] Thomas Hearne, *Remarks and Collections*, IX, 125.

[53] Andrew Kippis, *Biographia Britannica*, IV, 19-20.

statements give we are able to determine that he intended to write against the stage-poets and the play-houses both of which were, in his opinion, largely responsible for debauching the age:

> "Being convinc'd that nothing has gone farther in Debauching the Age than the Stage Poets, and the Play-House, I thought I could not employ my time better than in writing against them."[54]

Moreover, he informs us that he intends to do all that he can to stem the tide of immorality,

> " 'Tis my business rather to kill the *Root* than *Transplant* it."[55]

To brand the age as debauched, and the stage-poets and the play-house as largely responsible for the condition of affairs was daring, to say the least, on Collier's part. Before beginning an analysis of the quarrel which was precipitated by the publication of the *Short View* let us search for a corroboration of Collier's indictment of the age and of the stage and stage-poets.

Contemporary evidence tells us that the loose morals of the times were, for others than Collier, a cause of alarm. Narcissus Luttrell (1657-1732), the patient compiler of a chronicle of contemporary events[56] informs us that during February, 1698, the month prior to the publication of the *Short View,* much concern had been manifested by king and parliament at the prevalence of profaneness and immorality, and that, in consequence, active measures had been proposed for

---

[54] Jeremy Collier, *A Short View,* Preface, p. i.

[55] *Ibid.,* p. 3.

Just what he meant to imply by "killing the root" may be ascertained from a statement which he made in the Preface of the *Defence* published a few months later. Here he attempts to vindicate himself for having attacked in the *Short View* what he considered the moral, the literary, and the dramatic remissnesses of the stage-poets:

"Those who Paint for Debauchery, should have the Fucus pull'd off, and the Coarseness underneath discover'd. . . . Some of the Stage-Advocates pretend my Remarks on their Poetry are forreign to the Business. On the contrary, I conceive it very defensible to disarm an Adversary, if it may be, and disable him from doing Mischief." J. Collier, *A Defence of the Short View, Preface,* p. ii.

[56] N. Luttrell, *A Brief Historical Relation of State Affairs from September, 1678 to April, 1714,* 6 Vols.

their suppression.[57] For Thursday, February 10, 1697-1698, Luttrell makes this entry:

> "The Commons . . . ordered an addresse to his majestie to suppress prophaneness and immorality and Socinian books."[58]

Between this and March 5 three other entries of a similar nature are to be found in Luttrell's work, while on March 5, (until recently considered as the date of Collier's publication of the *Short View*), the following interesting item appears:

> "The justices of peace of Middlesex have made an order that the constables goe to all publick houses, to caution them to observe his majestie's proclamation against prophanesse."[59]

An interesting item appears in one of the extant contemporary periodicals, *The Post-Man and the Historical Account*. This was a sheet published three times a week in London, and in it there appears under the issue of "Saturday March 19, to Tuesday March 22, 1698" the following Advertisement:

> "This following was delivered to the King the 15th instant: An Humble and Hearty Thanksgiving to Almighty God For His great mercy to this Nation, in that he hath put it into the Heart of his servant William, to send forth such a Proclamation wherein his utter Dislike, and Hatred is shewed against all manner of Wickedness:
> At the reading of which, there was not only a rejoicing in some, that had mourned for the vile abominations of the People; but also a hearty Prayer, that the Lord would reward the King a Thousand fold, for the great Uprightness of his Heart therein . . . "
>
> March 10, 1698   John Pennyman.

Not only do Luttrell and *The Post-Man* testify to the vices of the times but some of the very stage-poets who felt themselves incriminated by Collier's attack acknowledge that the age is debauched, that the stage contributes to the debauchery, and that the abuses need correcting. Charles Gildon whose *Phaeton* appeared in 1698 declares that no

---

[57] *Ibid.*, IV, 342-349.
[58] *Ibid.*, p. 342.
[59] *Ibid.*, p. 352.

one would be more glad to see all the indecencies driven from the English Stage than he himself.[60]

Thomas D'Urfey, a loquacious champion of the stage and stage-poets, says that the title-page of *The Short View* is not only fair and engaging but that the work itself is illustrated with many weighty and just censures upon the immorality of the stage and upon the licentious writings of the stage-poets for some years past.[61]

Motteux, the author of *Beauty in Distress,* received from the Anglican Divine whom he had consulted regarding the lawfulness of writing plays, the following statement:

> "Upon reflecting on the present Management of our Theaters, on the Actions, Humors, and Characters which are daily represented there, which are for the most part so lewd and Immodest, as to tend very much to the debauching the Youth and Gentry of our English Nation; I might very well diswade you from giving any Countenance to such unmanly Practices; by offering any of your Works to the service of the Stage.
>
> "But tho the Theatrical Representations are become an Offense and Scandal to most, yet I am not of their Mind, who think Plays are absolutely unlawful."[62]

The anonymous author of *A Vindication of the Stage,* in commenting upon "Mr. Collier's Book against the Stage," states that the arguments were cried up as invincible, and that all the precise old folk in Staffordshire—some of them who perhaps had never seen a play in their lives—joined in a loud out-cry against the wickedness of the stage.[63]

Even Congreve whose comedies had been so caustically attacked by Collier admits that his reply, the *Amendments,* is undertaken not to defend the corruptions of the stage but to do himself a necessary right.[64] And Mr. Dennis in a clever reply to the *Short View* informs us that had Mr. Collier attacked only the corruptions of the stage he, far from blaming him, would have publicly returned him thanks. Then follows a significant statement:

---

[60] Charles Gildon, *Phaeton: or, the Fatal Divorce, A Tragedy.* Preface, p. ix.
[61] Thomas D'Urfey, *The Campaigners: or, The Pleasant Adventures at Brussels,* Preface, p. 2.
[62] Peter Motteux, *Beauty in Distress, Preface,* p. ix.
[63] Anonymous, *A Vindication of the Stage With the Usefulness and Advantages of Dramatick Representations,* p. 3.
[64] William Congreve, *Amendments,* p. 3.

"For the abuses are so great, that there is a necessity for reforming them; not that I think that with all its corruptions the Stage has bebauch'd the people: I am fully convinc'd it has not. . . . But this is certain that the corruptions of the Stage hinder its efficacy in the reformation of manners."[65]

It is more than a coincidence that Collier's attack should have made its appearance at the time when king, parliament, and chroniclers were anathematizing the loose morals of the age. Were Collier not so completely out of royal favor, it would be easy to believe that his services had been engaged in the cause. But in view of the fact that Collier had been in the royal displeasure ever since his publication of *The Desertion Discuss'd* and because he was living the life of an outlaw since his refusal to deliver himself up to the authorities in consequence of the censure received from his *Defence of the Absolution,* such a supposition is out of the question. Whether or not Collier hoped by his pamphlet to be reinstated in the royal favor cannot be asserted. That King William was pleased with it and granted him in consequence the privilege of " Nolle prosequi" is a matter of record.[66] Notwithstanding this general recognition of theatrical evils which prompted Collier to attack the stage, many of the stage-poets ascribed to him unworthy motives in writing the *Short View,*—motives of avarice, sensuality, and policy.

Tom Brown, in his 3-act Comedy, *The Stage-Beaux toss'd in a Blanket: or Hypocrisie Alamode,* professes to expose "A Pretending Scourge to the English Stage" in a true picture of Jerry whom he describes in the Dramatis Personae as

"A Pert, Talkative, Half-witted, Coxcomb, vain of a very little Learning, always swims with the Stream of Popular Opinion, a great Censurer of Men and Books, always Positive, seldom or never in the Right, a Noisie Pretender to Vertue, and an Impudent Pretender to Modesty, a Hypocrite, and a false Zealot for Religion, and sets up for a Reformer of the Stage, of a Sagacious Nose, in finding out Smut or Obscenity; a wonderful Artist at extracting Prophaneness out of all things that fall into his Hands; a profess'd Enemy of the Stage, tho' a Frequenter of it; once thought a Divine but for Reasons best known to himself, he has cast aside his Gown for the Vanities of a Beau

---

[65] John Dennis, *The Usefulness of the Stage,* Introduction, p. 3.
[66] *D.N.B.* IV, 799. (rep. 1921-2).

Wigg and Sword; Vain, Proud, Ill-natur'd, and incapable of Conversion."[67]

Among the vicious characteristics and base motives imputed to Collier for writing *The Short View* Brown enumerates his lewdness of mind;[68] his desire to stir up the criminal curiosity of the people who, in consequence, will purchase immoral plays and thus enrich the booksellers;[69] his desire for money;[70] his ambition to disguise a false reason and a false thought in a brisk expression;[71] his desire manifested especially in his *Defence* to achieve not truth but victory; his purpose, to amuse the fancy, not to inform the judgment; his quarrel, to gratify personal spleen;[72] his failure as a playwright;[73] and, finally, his desire to justify himself with the world,—this in consequence of his embarrassment at having had his picture shown deformed in the various comedies, not to himself, but to everyone else.[74]

Congreve, too, has his criticism of the motives of Collier. He suggests that the *Short View* was instigated by the devil inasmuch as its author bellows with *fury and madness*.[75] In another passage he asserts that Collier, apprehensive of being shown on the stage in his true colors, attempts to prove that his priesthood exempts him from any correction which the drama might make of him.[76] He entertains the same idea as Brown that Collier's scourging of obscenity in plays was dictated by lewdness and caprice[77] and, in addition, asserts that

"The corruption of a rotten Divine is the Generation of a sowr Critick."[78]

D'Urfey, Vanbrugh, and the anonymous author of *A Vindication of the Stage* also believe that Collier had questionable motives in writ-

---

[67] T. Brown, *The Stage-Beaux*, p. xii.
[68] T. Brown, *The Stage-Beaux toss'd in a Blanket*, p. 26.
[69] *Ibid.*, p. 26.
[70] *Ibid.*, p. 27, p. 34. Brown refers to Collier's receipt of 50 pounds for the *Short View*, p. 27.
[71] *Ibid.*, p. 32.
[72] *Ibid.*, pp. 31-34.
[73] *Ibid.*, p. 8.
[74] *Ibid.*, p. 3.
[75] William Congreve, *Amendments*, pp. 34-35.
[76] *Ibid.*, p. 59.
[77] *Ibid.*, pp. 80-81.
[78] *Ibid.*, p. 26.

ing the *Short View*. D'Urfey insinuates both duplicity[79] and personal corruption: "The Pulpiteer may be tainted as well as the Poetaster."[80] Vanbrugh asserts that "the rancor of his venom, the stretch of his injustice . . . and the extremity of his folly"—all may have had a turn in evoking Collier's attack.[81] The author of *A Vindication of the Stage* says:

> "His Dwelling so long on the Subject of Debauchery, argues something of Delight and Pleasure in the case."[82]

This author, too, refers to the influence which the "Fifty Pounds" had upon Collier.[83]

John Dennis imputes to Collier the desire to deceive others: "I have industriously endeavour'd not to err, tho I verily believe that Mr. Collier industriously endeavour'd to err, as far as he thought it might be consistent with the deceiving of others."[84]

A careful examination of the vindications referred to above convinces the reader that Collier's motives were always construed as the worst. The vindicators invariably descended to coarse personalities and accused the clergyman not only of indecencies in his private life but of unholy deeds in his career in the ministry. On the other hand, it is curious to observe how tenaciously these same vindicators clung to their own laurels, and how anxious they were to appear upright in the eyes of the world.[85]

So much for the motives ascribed to Collier by his opponents. It would be unfair not to give Collier the credit of opinions advanced by those who claimed to be impartial in their views. Says the author of *The History of the Works of the Learned*:

---

[79] Thomas D'Urfey, *The Campaigners*, Preface, p. 2.
[80] *Ibid.*, p. 4.
[81] John Vanbrugh, *A Short Vindication of the Relapse and the Provok'd Wife*, p. 73. Vanbrugh here adds:
   "For sure there cannot be a greater [Folly], than for a Man of his Coat, at the very Instant he's declaiming against the Crimes of the Age, to lay himself so open, to be hit in the most Immoral Blot of Life, which that of Slander undisputably is."
[82] Anonymous, *A Vindication of the Stage*, p. 6.
[83] *Ibid.*, p. 3.
[84] John Dennis, *The Usefulness of the Stage*, p. 4.
[85] John Vanbrugh, *A Short Vindication*, p. 3; Anonymous, *A Vindication of the Stage*, p. 3; T. D'Urfey, *The Campaigners*, Preface, p. 1; William Congreve, *The Amendments*, pp. 1-3.

"When a Man sets himself against open, barefac'd and tolerated Wickedness, he must expect a great Many Opposers. *Vice* will keep its stand as long as possible, and the *Vicious*, when advis'd to change their Course of Life are too apt to fling into their Friends Face, that ill-natur'd and unmannerly saying, *Physician, Heal thy Self*. This is what Mr. Collier, and several others, who have aim'd at the Reformation of Men's Manners, have experienc'd."[86]

The Reviewer of Collier's *Essays Upon Several Moral Subjects,* Part III, does not fail to eulogize the author:

"It raises Mr. Collier's Character, that he employs his Pen in Defence of Vertue and Religion, in a Loose and Sceptical Age, whilst others of his Gown indulge themselves so far, in their private Resentments, as to throw Oil into the Flames of our Publick Contentions."[87]

But when an opponent praises the candor of a man's life the praise has added value; it lessens the sting left by the censure of an age. This we find to be true in the praise of Edmund Bohun who, as the famous antagonist of Collier in the controversy of 1689 to 1693 over the question of the "Desertion of James" and the "Oath of Allegiance to William and Mary" says of the character of his adversary:

"The Author of it [*The Desertion Discuss'd*] is my Acquaintance, and a Person for whom I have a great Esteem, both on the account of his Profession, and of his personal Worth, Learning and Sobriety; so that I cannot believe he had any ill design in the Writing or Publishing of it . . . I have the same design for the main that he had, viz. the Honour of the Church *England,* and the Safety of Government, and especially our Monarchy."[88]

Too, Father Courbeville, S.J., who translated into French the *Short View of the English Stage* (1715), speaks of Collier with all possible marks of admiration and esteem.[89]

In his *Life of Congreve,* Samuel Johnson has tersely given us his opinion of Collier's motives in writing the *Short View*. Granted that Johnson lived a generation after Collier, nevertheless, he wrote his

---

[86] *The History of the Works of the Learned,* II, 106.
[87] *Ibid.,* VI, 667.
[88] Edmund Bohun, *An Answer to the Desertion Discuss'd,* p. 146.
[89] Andrew Kippis, *Biographia Britannica,* IV, 20.

Life of Congreve at a time when contemporary evidence could supply much information. If we recall that between his tenth and twentieth years the echoes of the stage controversy were still to be heard; that within those years were published Bedford's *A Serious Remonstrance,* Law's *The Absolute Unlawfulness of the Stage-Entertainment Fully Demonstrated,* the anonymous *Law Outlaw'd,* and Dennis' *The Stage Defended,* we are more likely to evaluate that opinion at its proper worth. Besides, Johnson while a student at Oxford (1727-30) not only read but was profoundly affected by William Law's *Serious Call to a Devout Life.*[90] This work, supplementing, as some affirmed, Collier's works against the stage was published two years after Collier's death. A consideration of these facts gives, then, an added significance to Johnson's statement:

> "Collier, a fierce and implacable Non-Juror . . . published
> *A Short View* . . . I believe with no other motive than religious
> zeal and honest indignation."[91]

Then, too, when a man's general principles are upright they should be permitted to speak in his favor. The fact that Collier according to the dictates of his conscience supported publicly the claims of King James—an act which necessitated his quitting his preferment;[92] that he refused on conscientious grounds to take the oath of allegiance to William and Mary in consequence of which he could expect to spend the remainder of his days in poverty and seclusion, whereas by complying he might have retained his post and lived in comfort and plenty;[93] that he delivered himself up to imprisonment, preferring it to freedom when freedom could be purchased only by giving bail, and when giving it meant acknowledging the supremacy of the court;[94] that, after the indictment issued against him by the Court of the Queen's Bench in 1696 in consequence of his absolution of Friend and Perkins, he preferred to spend the remainder of his life under a sentence of out-

---

90 *D. N. B.,* X, 922.
91 Samuel Johnson, *The Lives of the English Poets,* edited by Chalmers, XXI, 260.
92 Jeremy Collier, *An Ecclesiastical History of Great Britain,* Preface by Thomas Lathbury, I, iii.
93 Thomas Lathbury, *History of the Nonjurors,* p. 109.
94 J. Collier, *An Ecclesiastical History,* I, vii.

lawry rather than to recognize the authority of the court;[95]—all of these facts, I say, should be borne in mind when forming an opinion of the motives which prompted Collier to write *The Short View,* and undoubtedly they lead one to believe that these motives were honest and sincere.

---

[95] *Ibid.,* I, ix-x.

CHAPTER II

AN ANALYSIS OF JEREMY COLLIER'S
"A SHORT VIEW OF THE IMMORALITY AND PROFANENESS
OF THE ENGLISH STAGE:
TOGETHER WITH THE SENSE OF ANTIQUITY
UPON THIS ARUGMENT"

Foreword

One of the most important publications of 1698 is *A Short View of the Immorality, and Profaneness of the English Stage, Together with the Sense of Antiquity upon this Argument,* by Jeremy Collier, M. A. It is important not only in its bearing on the stage-poets whose reaction to its censure was manifested in such divers ways, but important in so far as it affected contemporary and later comedy.

The title-page as well as the pamphlet itself bears evidence of the courage and pugnacity of the author. Very few appreciate just what was implied when Collier in 1698 attacked the stage for its profanity and immorality. The attack was equivalent to his hurling a dart at the profligacy of the Stuart dynasty which during the preceding decade he had upheld so valiantly and for which he had suffered the deprivation of all the worth-while things that life had to offer. It was, besides, an invitation for satire and lampooning from the vindictive natures not only of those whom he had attacked—Dryden, D'Urfey, Wycherley, Congreve, and Vanbrugh,—but likewise from those who felt called upon to vindicate plays, players, and playwrights. Just how the various poets received the *Short View* I shall attempt to show in the following pages. Suffice it to say here that the pamphlet was printed for Keble, Sare, and Hindmarsh in 1698. There has been some conjecture as to the exact date of its publication. In regard to this it is of interest to note that to the Preface there is subscribed "Mar. 5, 1697/8," and that up to 1931 this date was generally accepted. However, Mr. D. C. Taylor, in the Prefatory Note to his *William Congreve* asserts that "among the more obvious additions" to literature that he makes in his work, the establishing of the exact date of the *Short View* is one. In a subsequent statement we read:

> ". . . Collier's *Short View* was published on Thursday, April 21, 1698, six weeks later than has hitherto been supposed. The announcement of the first edition appears only in the *Flying Post* for Tuesday, April 19, to Thursday, April 21, 1698 . . . Critics have invariably assigned the first issue of the *Short View* to March because the preface to the first edition was dated March 5, 1698."[1]

Mr. Taylor's statement becomes more significant in view of the fact that Edward Arber assigns the publication of the *Short View* to Easter, 1698.[2]

However, I do not accept—neither do I reject—the date. I do not accept it on the evidence of the *Flying Post,* the authority on which Mr. Taylor bases his statement. My reasons for refusing to date the original appearance of books and pamphlets on the evidence contained in the periodicals of the times, I have explained in the "Foreword" to Chapters III-VI, pp. 58-60. I do not accept it on the authority of E. Arber because his statement is unsubstantiated. Consequently, until it is possible to collect more evidence concerning the date of publication of the *Short View* it is best to leave the subject open for discussion.

PART 1
The Immodesty of the Stage

Collier in his Introduction to the *Short View* very tersely outlines not only the topics which he intends to discuss but the vices that he will scourge in the chapters that are to follow:

> "Their [the stage-poets'] *Liberties* in the Following Particulars are intolerable, viz. Their *Smuttiness* of *Expression;* Their *Swearing, Profainness,* and *Lewd Application of Scripture;* Their Abuse of the Clergy; Their making their *Top Characters Libertines,* and giving them *Success* in their *Debauchery.* This Charge, with some other Irregularities, I shall make good against the *Stage* . . . And first, I shall begin with the *Rankness,* and *Indecency* of their *Language.*"[3]

---

[1] D. C. Taylor, *William Congreve,* p. 111.

[2] Edward Arber, *Term Catalogues,* III, 66.

[3] Jeremy Collier, *A Short View,* p. 2. It is important to note that the spelling, punctuation, capitalization, and italics vary in different editions of the same work. I have endeavored to use first editions wherever they were available.

Indecency of language, then, is to receive the first blast, and the stage-poets guilty of its use are to be given the first lashes of the reformer. Not all the stage-poets, however, does Collier chastise in his *Short View;* he selects those, seemingly, who are best able to defend themselves, viz., Wycherley, Dryden, Congreve, Vanbrugh, D'Urfey. For some reason best known to himself he does not attack women dramatists; he does not even mention Mrs. Behn who was certainly entitled to his ire. Neither does he refer to the plays of Mrs. Manley, Mrs. Pix, and Mrs. Trotter. This point is brought out by Mr. Taylor who says: "Nor was the controversial parson out to make war on women."[4] On several occasions Collier mentions Otway's *Orphan* for the purpose of rebuke,—Otway had been dead since 1685—but he does not mention the plays either of Etherege who had died in 1691, or of Shadwell who had died in 1692.

It is interesting to conjecture just why Collier directed his attack when he did, as he did, and at whom he did. The reason why Collier attacked the stage in the spring of 1698 I have discussed above.[5] The manner of his attack may perhaps be traced to his native pugnacity, his inherent hatred of impiety, immorality, and abuse of the clergy, and his characteristic desire to display his learning. The fact that Collier attacked the greatest and most popular wits of his day may, perhaps, be due to his fearlessness, and to his desire to have his work receive immediate attention not only by the audiences but by the playwrights themselves and by the authorities. His leniency with the women dramatists may be attributed to a certain gallantry and to consideration of them, both of which qualities are evident throughout his anti-stage works.

Collier first attacks Wycherley. He is not caustic; in fact, there is evident a tone rather of disappointment than of anger in his accusation. He arraigns for censure the characters which are most guilty of indecency of language—and these only from *The Country Wife* (1673), and *The Plain Dealer* (1674).[6] Wycherley's *Love in a Wood* (1672), and *The Gentleman Dancing-Master* (1673) though deserving of castigation, escape it. Throughout, there is a certain consideration for the aged play-wright and an expression of regret that his God-

[4] D. C. Taylor, *William Congreve*, p. 130.
[5] 16-26 pp.
[6] J. Collier, *A Short View*, p. 3.

given talents had not been used to better purpose. Collier laments that
a poet who can at his pleasure afford his Muse a more befitting dress,
should let her appear coarse and slovenly out of poverty; should permit her to be offensive for lack of necessaries.[7]

Collier next points the accusing finger at Dryden, Congreve, and
Vanbrugh, stating that in their plays from which he is citing, viz., *The
Mock Astrologer, The Spanish Friar, Love Triumphant, The Double
Dealer, The Old Batchelour, Love for Love, The Relapse,* and *Don
Sebastian,* there is a large collection of debauchery—debauchery "so
adorned" that its purpose is plainly "to engage the fancy, to fasten
upon the memory, and to keep up the charm from languishing;"[8]
debauchery so vicious, that it can have no alternative but to stain the
imagination, to awaken folly, and to weaken the defences of virtue.[9]

After a warning to young people not to entertain themselves with
lewd descriptions, especially when depicted by a master-artist, Collier
states that not only is the indulgence of such a liberty likely to raise
those passions which cannot be discharged without trouble nor satisfied without a crime, but that it is, besides, all scandal and meanness;
that it degrades human nature, sinks reason into appetite, and breaks
down the distinction between man and beast.[10] He brands indecency
in language as a fault in behaviour as well as in religion; he accuses
writers who make use of it as constrained thereto either by barrenness
of fancy, by a vicious imagination, or by convenience. He censures it
particularly when used among and before women and questions why a
conversation which disobliges so much in every-day affairs should entertain upon the stage. Either an indecent conversation pleases ladies or
it does not please them. For a stage-poet to suppose the first, grossly
reflects upon the ladies' virtue; to suppose the second is an admission
that he is designing to entertain them with their own aversion.[11]

Collier then proceeds to heap additional abuse upon the writers of
comedy previously mentioned because he finds them guilty of making
women speak indecently and he adds that even the writers of tragedy
are occasionally guilty of the same fault. To substantiate his statement

---

[7] *Ibid.,* p. 4.
[8] *Ibid.,* pp. 4-5.
[9] *Ibid.,* p. 5.
[10] *Ibid.,* pp. 5-6.
[11] *Ibid.,* pp. 7-8.

he cites Otway as having failed in this respect in his play *The Orphan*. He regrets, also, the strange lengths in the history of love which occur in *The Spanish Friar* and states that to bring women to listen to such misbehaviour is violence to their native modesty and a misrepresentation of their sex.[12] To prove that modesty is the character of women Collier quotes Rapin and Euripides; and, in addition, he states his regret that Shakespeare did not set Ophelia "a swimming a little sooner," inasmuch as he intended to let her sully her reputation before her death and to discover the rankness of her breath.[13] He very pointedly avows that in four ways[14] modern poets are guilty of making their characters indulge in indecent language:

First, they often represent their women characters either as *silly* or as *mad* for the purpose of enlarging their liberty or screening their impudence. To substantiate his argument he points to *Don Quixote, The Relapse,* and *Love for Love,* and thence launches into an eloquent eulogy of modesty many touches of which suggest that Collier was well acquainted with Portia's speech on "The Quality of Mercy:"

> "Modesty is the distinguishing Virtue of that Sex, and serves both for Ornament and Defence: Modesty was design'd by Providence as a Guard to Virtue; And that it might be always at Hand, 'tis wrought into the Mechanism of the Body. 'Tis likewise proportioned to the occasions of Life, and strongest in Youth when Passion is so too. 'Tis a Quality as true to Innocence, as the Sences are to Health; whatever is ungrateful to the first, is prejudicial to the latter . . . The Tumult of the Blood and Spirits and the Uneasiness of the Sensation, are of singular Use."[15]

Secondly, the stage-poets are so inconsiderate of their audience that they frequently do not give so much as the refuge of a double meaning to fly to, but compel their characters so to speak that either ribaldry or nonsense must be accepted. Furthermore,

---

[12] *Ibid.,* pp. 8-9.
[13] *Ibid.,* p. 10.
[14] N. B. Collier enumerates *five* ways, but his second citation viz., the representation of "single Ladys, and Persons of Condition, Under . . . Disorders of Liberty," *Short View,* p. 12, belongs to the chapter on "Immorality Encouraged by the Stage" to which chapter I have taken the liberty to transfer it.
[15] *A Short View,* p. 11.

"The Matter is so Contrived that the Smut and Scum of the
Thought rises uppermost; And like a Picture drawn to Sight,
looks always upon the Company."[16]

Thirdly, the Prologues, Epilogues, and Dedications are, in the
highest degree, guilty of indecency of language. Collier states that
here, if ever, the ladies should be used with respect and the measures
of decency observed in their regard. However, he finds that "here we
have Lewdness without Shame or Example: Here the *Poet* exceeds himself."[17] With characteristic bluntness he scathes the custom of choosing
women to give the prologues and epilogues and of calling upon them
to deliver to the audience "such Strains as would turn the Stomach of
an ordinary Debauchee, and be almost nauseous in the Stews,"[18] from
which he witheringly remarks of the stage-poets:

"This is the Desert he regales the Ladys with at the Close of
the Entertainment: It seems He thinks They have admirable
Palats. Nothing can be a greater Breach of Manners then such
Liberties as these. If a Man would study to outrage *Quality* and
Vertue, he could not do it more Effectually."[19]

His fourth point is that the Christian Religion within whose influence the poets live and under whose precepts they are forbidden to
indulge in the remotest tendencies to evil or in the follies of conversation—this it is which renders indecency of language most insufferable.
It is a religion which obliges *even* up to sobriety of thought and which
makes detestable and a subject of aversion those things which under
the cult of heathenism might have passed for raillery and entertainment.[20] Collier then in proof of his contention, lists a long line of
authorities—Plautus, Terence, Aeschylus, Sophocles, Euripides, Aristophanes,—and all are praised for their comparative reserve in conversation.[21] From ancient Rome and Greece he passes to England, "To
our own Times" in his effort to convict the modern stage-poets of
indecency of language and of a greater share of guilt inasmuch as
they live in an age when Christianity is exerting its influence, and
here in the attitude as well as in the style we detect the influence of

16 *Ibid.*, p. 12.
17 *Ibid.*, p. 13.
18 *Ibid.*, p. 13.
19 *Ibid.*, pp. 13-14.
20 *Ibid.*, p. 14.
21 *Ibid.*, pp. 15-50.

Thomas Rymer.[22] Collier praises for their modesty Ben Jonson, Fletcher, Beaumont, and Corneille, but the mighty Shakespeare he dismisses peremptorily with the statement "he is too guilty to make an Evidence."[23]

The chapter is concluded by a tirade against the "superlatively scandalous" condition of the English stage—a stage whose liberties, according to Collier, are greater than those of all times and all countries; a stage which is in reality a world of vice found out and nurtured with all imaginary industry. However, Collier has not exhausted his rage against indecency in language in the chapter set aside for the purpose. There are evidences throughout the remaining pages that the poet's liberties had branded themselves upon his brain and were not to be endured. Here and there he scourges the vice under the term "smut" and each lash given falls upon one or other of the stage-poets on whom his initial attack had been made. Here and there the censure he utters is so caustic that it aroused the stage-poets to ally themselves in counter-attack and to fight for two decades with that weapon often mightier than the sword—the pen.

PART 2

The Profaneness of the Stage

Without waste of words Collier opens his attack upon the stage for its profaneness and upon the stage-poets for their share in popularizing cursing and swearing, in ridiculing religion, and in burlesquing the Scriptures. His onslaught is vitriolic, and yet the chapter gives evidence that the author has developed his theme according to a pretty well-defined outline. There are, however, instances in which we find his zeal for the cause betraying his common sense, and his "warmth under provocation,"[1] being fanned into the flame of erroneous criticism. According to Collier the charges of dramatic profaneness may be viewed as falling into two divisions: cursing and swearing, and abuse of Religion and Scripture.[2] Briefly, he passes over the subject of cursing:

---

[22] Thomas Rymer, *A Short View of Tragedy;* pp. 86-159.
[23] J. Collier, *Short View,* pp. 50-54.

[1] J. Collier, *A Short View,* p. 80. Collier had said when speaking of profaneness "I can't forbear expressing myself with some warmth under these Provocations." p. 80.
[2] *Ibid.,* p. 56.

"What is more frequent then their wishes of Hell, and Confusion, Devils and Diseases, all the Plagues of this World, and
the next, to each other?"[3]

But on the subject of swearing Collier waxes eloquent. He asserts
that the offence should be viewed from three distinct angles,viz., from
that of "Fact,"[4] from that of "Law,"[5] and lastly, from that of "Manners."[6] From the viewpoint of fact, i.e. the actuality and the frequency
of the offence, Collier gives his views under three headings: those who,
in general, are guilty of the offence; their reasons for swearing; their
manner of swearing. Concerning those who varnish their conversation
with swearing, he observes:

" 'Tis used by all Persons, and upon all Occasions: By Heroes,
and Paltroons; by Gentlemen, and Clowns."[7]

And concerning their reasons for swearing he tells us:

"Love, and Quarrels, Success and Disappointment, Temper,
and Passions, must be varnish'd, and set off with *Oaths* . . . It
[swearing] stands up in the room of Sense, gives Spirit to a
flat Expression, and makes a Period Musical and Round. In
short, 'tis almost all the Rhetorick, and Reason some People are
Masters of."[8]

Their manner of swearing he gives in detail:

"Sometimes they mince the matter; change the letter, and keep
the Sense, as if they had a mind to steal a Swearing, and break
the Commandment without Sin. At another time the Oaths are
clipt, but not so much within the Ring, but that the *Image and
Superscripion* are visible."[9]

Collier says that Congreve has given us in the *Old Batchelour,
Double Dealer,* and *Love for Love,* instances of the above looseness,
while D'Urfey in *Don Quixote,* and Vanbrugh in *The Provok'd Wife*
and in *The Relapse* are particularly rampant and scandalous.[10] Characteristically, Collier then weighs in the scales of his judgment the Mod-

[3] *Ibid.,* p. 56.
[4] *Ibid.,* pp. 56-57.
[5] *Ibid.,* pp. 57-58.
[6] *Ibid.,* p. 59.
[7] *Ibid.,* p. 56.
[8] *Ibid.,* p. 56.
[9] *Ibid.,* p. 57.
[10] *Ibid.,* p. 57.

erns against their literary ancestors and, as usual, finds the Moderns wanting. Shakespeare and Ben Jonson are not guilty of profanity from the parson's view-point, while Beaumont and Fletcher, he points out, permit only profligate persons to swear, and then not with impunity.[11] Inasmuch as swearing is an offence, Collier indicates that it violates both the divine and the civil law. As a violation of the former he asserts

"what can be more Insolent and Irreligious, than to bring in God to attest our Trifles, to give Security for our Follies, and to make part of our Diversion?"[12]

As a violation of the latter, he points out that the law, framed in the reign of James I and known as "3d, Jac. 1 cap. 21" is expressly against the Playhouse[13] and if well executed, would either mend the poets or sweep the box.

Collier's spirit of gallantry manifests itself in this as on other occasions and he states that swearing is an ungentlemanly as well as an unchristian practice; that inasmuch as the "ladies" constitute a considerable part of the audience even civil atheists will forbear the liberty.[14]

Having thus discoursed of cursing and swearing Collier attacks the stage-poets' "Abuse of Religion and Holy Scripture" and to substantiate his charges he arraigns the guilty plays of four of the Moderns: Dryden, Otway, Congreve, and Vanbrugh.[15] So severely is Valentine's luckless remark "I am Truth" set upon that the replies it evoked caused controversial echoes to be heard in the Preface to *Phaeton,* in the *Amendments,* in *A Letter to Mr. Congreve,* in the *Animadversions,* and in *A Defence of the Short View.*[16]

Collier cannot forbear comparing what he calls the profane liberties of the Moderns with the usual reserve of the Ancients; in consequence, he calls to the witness-stand the plays of the Romans and the Greeks and he finds that the Ancients "run less often on the rock"

---

[11] *Ibid.,* p. 57.
[12] *Ibid.,* p. 58.
[13] *Ibid.,* pp. 58-59.
[14] *Ibid.,* pp. 59-60.
[15] *Ibid.,* pp. 60-79.
[16] C. Gildon, *Phaeton,* Preface, p. x.; W. Congreve, *Amendments,* p. 55; Anonymous, *A Letter to Mr. Congreve,* p. 12; Anonymous, *Animadversions,* p. 57; J. Collier, *A. Defence,* p. 63. Collier's censure of "I am Truth" occurs in *S. V.* p. 83.

than do the Moderns. He concludes his attack on the profaneness of
the English Stage by his customary climax couched in the usual staccato questions of which a single page affords us eleven successive
examples and of which I append four:

> "Have we not a clearer Light to direct us, and greater Punish-
> ments to make us afraid? Is there no Distinction between Truth
> and Fiction, between Majesty and Pageant? Must God be
> treated like an Idol . . . ? Are these the Returns we make Him
> for his Supernatural Assistance?[17]

The chapter which Collier devotes to attacking the profaneness of
the stage breathes forth the sincerity of its author; there is no questioning the fact. Neither can we doubt that the stage-poets, many of them,
were seriously guilty of the charge of profaneness and deserving of
every stroke of the reformer's lash. However, one cannot help wishing
that Collier had not read into some of the expressions a profanity which
the authors never intended; that he had used greater discrimination in
selecting his evidence; and that where the poets intended no profaneness, he had written with less impetuosity and less heat.

The forty pages given to rebuking the stage-poets for their profaneness do not exhaust Collier's zeal, however. We find throughout the
remainder of the pamphlet frequent indications that his anger has not
subsided; we see frequent outbursts of wrath when the name of God or
the interests of religion are slighted or ridiculed, and in the concluding pages of his *Short View* we find that he casts a last loving glance
at the Ancients for the purpose of comparing their reverence and respect for the Deity with the profanity of the Moderns and that he
sounds the climax when he says:

> "As for their [the Moderns'] . . . horrible Profaneness, and
> Blasphemies, there's nothing in *Antiquity* can reach them."[18]

---

[17] J. Collier, *Short View*, p. 95.
[18] *Ibid.*, p. 280.

PART 3

The Clergy Abused by the Stage

To evaluate correctly Collier's chapter on "The Clergy Abused by the Stage," it is necessary to analyze the opinion which the Viewer himself held of the dignity and the function of the priesthood. This opinion is stated clearly in the fifth of his *Essays Upon Several Moral Subjects* published in 1697, the essay itself being entitled "The Office of a Chaplain."[1] Collier evidently wished the reader of the *Short View* to acquaint himself with this essay, for, in the conclusion of the chapter "The Clergy abused by the Stage,"[2] he refers the reader to the treatise which, he asserts, fully proves that any ill treatment accorded the clergy, whether they be chaplains or not, is an outrage upon the whole Order.[3]

In the Preface to the essay in question as well as in the essay itself Collier portrays a rugged strength of character and an unflinching disregard of public opinion. He shows himself to be in embryo "Collier, the stage reformer." He states bluntly that the thoughts he is suggesting to the reader are given according to the norms of justice:

> "*If the Plainness of* what Follows *disgusts the sober Reader I am sorry for it. 'Tis a Circumstance which could not be declined without Prejudice to the* Subject. *The oversmoothness of an Argument, is apt to abate the Force. You must give it a Point to make way for Passage . . . And when the Case requires it, no man blames the Doctor for preferring the Cure to the Palate.*"[4]

He contends that the clergy are entitled to respectful treatment and that unless they receive it, both the office and the function suffer:

> "So that when a Man is Maim'd in his Credit, or burlesq'd in his Office, he must not expect to do any great Execution . . . To entertain a contemptible Opinion of any Person, cramps his power, and disables his Friendship, and puts him under a mighty disadvantage of doing any Good."[5]

---

[1] J. Collier, *Essays*, I, 161-215.
[2] J. Collier, *Short View*, p. 139.
[3] Concerning "chaplains" Collier states in the *Short View* p. 139, "'tis Objected that the *Clergy* in *Plays* are commonly *Chaplains*, And that these *Belonging* to Persons of Quality, they were obliged to represent them servile and submissive."
[4] J. Collier, *Essays*, I, p. 165.
[5] *Ibid.*, p. 168.

He unswervingly holds that civil magistrates have no power to create bishops, priests, or deacons; that it is not within the power of Parliament to make their conditions servile inasmuch as it cannot take away a power which it did not give, and that the Church is a Society distinct from the State and independent of it:[6]

"The Constitution of the Church is founded in the Appointment of Christ, in that Commission which he gave the Apostles and their Successors, and consequently does not derive its Authority from any Earthly Power."[7]

Collier gives equally clear statements concerning the respect which chaplains have a right to demand. From his essay we learn that he looked upon a chaplain as a clergyman in private employ,[8] and this opinion Collier further emphasizes in the *Short View* when he asserts that an outrage to the individual churchman is an outrage to the whole Order without regard to any particular office.[9] He argues that a chaplain is not in any way a servant in the house in which he resides,[10] and that he is entitled to his salary and diet without, in any way, compromising his independence.[11]

Collier apparently had misgivings that his motives for championing the clergy against the stage-poets would be misunderstood. He observes in the *Short View* by way of justification:

"There is no Vanity in necessary Defence. To wipe off Aspersions, and rescue Things from Mistake, is but bare Justice: Besides, where the Honour of God, and the Publick Interest are concern'd, a Man is bound to speak."[12]

In order to make his statement more explicit Collier argues by way of analogy. He insists that a man who has a king's commission is bound in honour and conscience to discharge his trust:

"To let it suffer under Rudeness is to betray it. To be tame and silent in such cases, is not Modesty but Meanness, Humility obliges no Man to desert his Trust; To throw up his Privilege,

---

[6] *Ibid.*, pp. 189-190.
[7] *Ibid.*, p. 189.
[8] *Ibid.*, p. 171.
[9] J. Collier, *Short View*, p. 139.
[10] J. Collier, *Essays*, p. 180.
[11] *Ibid.*, p. 174.
[12] J. Collier, *Short View*, p. 137.

and prove false to his Character. And is our Saviours Authority inferior to that of Princes?"[13]

It was Collier's opinion that the clergyman derived his dignity from the seal of his office; he further believed that whether juring or non-juring, the difference was only political, and that a man's politics in no way reflected upon the character of the calling which elevated him to the Ministry of the Gospel. In consequence of this opinion Collier asserts:

> "the *Clergy* deserve none of that Coarse Usage which it [the stage] puts upon them. I confess I know no *Profession* that has made a more creditable Figure, that has better Customs for their Privileges, and better Reasons to maintain them."[14]

It was from the above considerations that Collier assumed the right to rescue the clergy from the mal-treatment of the poets. He begins his attack on the stage-poets for their abuse of the clergy by inquiring into the reasons which prompt them to mistreat not only the *character* and the *individual,* but the *business* of the sacred office.[15] His conclusions are in no way complimentary to the poets. He asserts that because the clergy perpetuate religion, keep up the interests of virtue, curb vice, and awaken conscience, the poets consider them "no small Rub" in their way, and wish in consequence to be rid of them. In so far as they are looked upon as the messengers of heaven and the supports of government, in so far as they enjoy their old pretentions to credit and authority, just in that degree, Collier says,

> "the *Stage* must decline of Course, and Atheism give Ground, and Lewdness lie under Censure, and Discouragement. Therefore that Liberty may not be embarrass'd, nor Principles make Head against Pleasure, the *Clergy* must be attack'd, and rendered Ridiculous."[16]

He goes on to affirm that there are two requisites for a person to be represented fairly and without disservice to his reputation: he must not be ill used by others, and he must not be made to play the fool himself.[17] However, the stage-poets practice the reverse of both these methods, Collier asserts, and that in order to be assured of the success

---

[13] *Ibid.,* p. 137.
[14] *Ibid.,* p. 138.
[15] *Ibid.,* p. 97.
[16] *Ibid.,* pp. 97-98.
[17] *Ibid.,* p. 98.

of their diabolical plans, they strain their invention and malice and overlook nothing in ill nature or ill manners to gain their point.[18]

Collier, without equivocation, calls to task six of his contemporaries who have been guilty of abuse of the clergy—Dryden, Wycherley, Otway, Congreve, Vanbrugh, D'Urfey. He points out instances in the plays of each where the poet has mistreated the character and the function of the Order[19] and he acidly remarks:

> "These *Poets* I observe, when They grow lazy, and are inclined to Nonsence, they commonly get a Clergy-man to speak it. Thus they pass their own Dulness for Humor, and gratifie their Ease, and their Malice at once . . . Thus we see how hearty these People are in their Ill Will. How they attack Religion under every Form, and pursue the Priesthood through all the Subdivisions of Opinion."[20]

The treatment which the ancient poets and dramatists accorded their priests is given detailed attention for the purpose of showing the scandalous liberties taken by modern playwrights. Again, Collier runs the gamut of the Ancients and again he finds them in every respect superior to the Moderns. After giving detailed attention to the general regard which the clergy have commanded in all ages and from all peoples with the exception of the English stage-poets in the latter half of the seventeenth century, Collier gives a triple argument which is meant to convince the reader that the clergy have a right to regard and fair usage. He declares that they should be respected

> "I.   *Because of their Relation to the Deity,*
> II. *Because of the Importance of their Office,*
> III. *Because they have prescription for their Privilege. Their Function has been in Possession of Esteem in all Ages, and Countries."*[21]

In the conclusion of the chapter on the abuse of the clergy Collier, as if in anticipation of the censure which he would reap from the stage-poets by defending the clergy, upholds the ministry against the numerous and malicious thrusts which it was experiencing. We note that he fights ever to uphold the dignity, the character, and the function of

---

18 *Ibid.,* p. 98.
19 *Ibid.,* pp. 98-200.
20 *Ibid.,* pp. 109-110.
21 *Ibid.,* p. 127.

the priesthood; that he wages his warfare that the sacred ministry be
not despised; that he spares no effort to secure respect for the person
of God's anointed. He was not unmindful of the human element in the
ranks; neither did he forget that a Judas was numbered among Christ's
own Twelve:

> "I grant Persons and Things are not always suited. A good *Post*
> may be ill kept, but then the Censure should keep close to the
> Fault, and the Office not suffer for the Manager. The *Clergy*
> may have their Failings sometimes like others, but what then?
> The *Character* is still untarnish'd. The *Men* may be Little, but
> the *Priests* are not so. And therefore like other people, they
> ought to be treated by their best Distinction."[22]

PART 4

Immorality Encouraged by the Stage

Collier levels his aim, in his fourth onslaught, at the stage-poets
who "make their Principal Persons Vitious, and reward them at the
end of the Play."[1] In order to realize Collier's vehemence in censuring
the stage-poets for encouraging immorality it is necessary to understand
the spirit which emanates from the writer. From the very first pages
of the Preface to the *Short View,* Collier gives evidence of his high
regard for "Right Principles" which play so important a part in moral
rectitude. His experience in the ministry has made him too well acquainted with human nature to deny *"that people should check their*
Appetites, *and balk their* Satisfactions, *they don't know why."*[2] He
knows full well that when fear and shame are taken away, and

> "when Profit and Liberty lie on the same side, and a Man can
> Debauch himself into Credit, what can be expected in such a
> case, but that Pleasure should grow Absolute, and Madness
> carry all before it?"[3]

He refuses to believe that any one will trouble himself with Conscience *"if 'tis only* a Bugbear, *and has nothing in't but* Vision, *and
the Spleen."*[4] It is his opinion that the stage-poets are greatly to blame

---

[22] *Ibid.,* p. 139.

[1] J. Collier, *A Short View,* p. 140.
[2] *Ibid.,* Preface, p. iii.
[3] *Ibid.,* p. 141.
[4] *Ibid.,* p. ii.

for the immorality of the age; he asserts that they first strike at Religion in order to destroy the principles which induce persons to practice virtue and that when these principles are destroyed they more easily record a complete victory in debauchery.

> "*It seems* Lewdness without Atheism *is but* half of their Business . . . *To make sure work on't, there's nothing like* Destroying *of Principles; . . . For to have* no Good Principles *is to have no* Reason to be Good."[5]

A survey of contemporary English drama convinces him that the stage

> "cherishes those Passions, and rewards those Vices, which 'tis the business of Reason to discountenance . . . . 'Tis the most effectual means to baffle the Force of Discipline, to emasculate peoples Spirits, and Debauch their Manners. How many of the Unwary have these *Syrens* devour'd? And how often has the best Blood been tainted, with this Infection?"[6]

Regarding in this light the effects of the stage on the morals of the people, it is not surprising that Collier broke the vials of his wrath upon the heads of the offending stage-poets. He begins "Chapter Four" by depicting the "native appearances" between virtue and vice. Virtue, he tells us, has all the sweetness, charm, and grace imaginable, while vice resembles a post ill-carved into a monster and looking "both foolish and frightful together."[7] As long as the eye can discern the differences between the two, as long as the mind is awake and the conscience goes true, there need be no fear of deception. But if culprits

> "endeavour to blot the Distinctions, to rub out the Colours, or change the Marks, [they are] extremely to blame . . . . When Vice is varnish'd over with Pleasure and comes in the Shape of Convenience, the case grows somewhat dangerous; for then the Fancy may be gain'd and the Guards corrupted, and Reason suborn'd against itself."[8]

A close inspection of the favourable treatment which the stage-poets accord vicious characters convinces Collier that their design is not only to put lewdness into a thriving condition but to treat it with ceremony and respect; and when this is accomplished it is easy "to

---

[5] *Ibid.*, pp. ii-iii.
[6] *Ibid.*, p. 287.
[7] *Ibid.*, p. 140.
[8] *Ibid.*, pp. 140-141.

confound the Understanding, to fortifie the Charm, and to make the Mischief invincible."[9] The best proof of this contention is found in the manner in which the wits of the day treat their "men and ladies of breeding," and with this in mind, Collier attacks Dryden, Wycherley, Congreve, Vanbrugh, and Otway. Again he analyzes their plays and again he finds that one or another of them is guilty of ridiculing marriage, "of idealizing debauchery, and of rewarding an Atheistical Bully with a lady and a fortune." He hotly declares that both the men and ladies of quality are degraded by the poets; that comedy generally ridicules learning, industry, and frugality; that rich citizens are often represented as misers and cuckolds, and that the Universities are portrayed as "Schools of Pedantry."[10]

The condition of society, the lamentable part which comedy has played in debauching morals, and the light regard which the *Mock Astrologer* entertains concerning crimes committed in comedy[11]—all these considerations evoke from Collier deep-mouthed sarcasm:

> "And how stands the matter in Comedy? . . . There is nothing but a little Whoring, Pimping, Gaming, Profaneness, etc. And who could be so hard hearted to give a Man any Trouble for This? Such Rigours would be strangely Inhumane! A *Poet* is a better natur'd Thing I can assure you."[12]

Apparently Collier is fearful lest his readers fail to penetrate his sarcasm; fearful lest they take from his words the idea that crime *is* trivial so he follows up his thrust at the *Mock Astrologer* by a reproach in which Religion points an accusing finger at Dryden.

> "Is Dissolution of Manners such a Peccadillo? Does a Profligate Conscience deserve nothing but Commiseration? And are People damn'd only for *Humane Frailties?* I Perceive the Laws of Religion and those of the *Stage* differ extreamly!"[13]

After a lengthy discussion of critical principles, Collier passes on to a survey of "courtship" as portrayed by the English stage-poets and to stating his reflections of the decency and decorum with which they

---

[9] *Ibid.,* p. 141.
[10] *Ibid.,* pp.   141-145.
[11] *Ibid.,* p. 155. In his Preface to this play Dryden had remarked concerning crime in *Comedy* as contrasted with that of *Tragedy:* "There the *Faults are the sallies of Youth and the Frailties of Human Nature."*
[12] *Ibid.,* pp. 155-156.
[13] *Ibid.,* p. 156.

treat not only the women but the quality of both sexes. *The Spanish Friar, The Country Wife, Don Sebastian,* and *The Relapse* afford good examples of how *women* are affronted by "Persons of Figure," how their sex is degraded and how, occasionally, ladies are obliged to abuse themselves in order to render their discourse more probable.[14]

The Double Dealer, The Relapse, The Provok'd Wife, The Plain Dealer, Don Sebastian, Love Triumphant, Don Quixote,—these plays Collier cites as examples of the quarter which the English Stage affords to persons of quality.[15]

> "They [the stage-poets] dress up the *Lords* in Nick Names, and expose them in *Characters* of Contempt. *Lord Froth* is explain'd a *Solemn Coxcomb;* And *Lord Rake,* and *Lord Foplington* give you their Talent in their Title."[16]

Before Collier leaves the subject of "immorality as encouraged by the English Stage" he gives a few extra blows to the dramatic reputation of Dryden, D'Urfey, and Vanbrugh in the chapters devoted to *Amphytrion, King Arthur, Don Quixote,* and *The Relapse.*[17] He attempts to prove to the reader that adequate chastisement of the culprits is impossible as it would be out of order to quote in detail the lewd sentences which deserve castigation. In fact, so brazen, Collier asserts, is the effrontery shining forth in modern comedy that

> "Our *Stage-Poets* seem to fence against Censure by the excess of Lewdness; And to make the overgrown size of a Crime, a Ground for Impunity. As if a Malefactor should project his Escape by appearing too scandalous for Publick Tryal. However, This is their Armour of Proof, this is the Strength they retreat to. They are fortified in Smut, and almost impregnable in Stench, so that where they deserve most, there's no coming at them."[18]

In conclusion, he points out that these very stage-poets who destroy the "Principles of Good and Evil," these very men who would make

---

[14] *Ibid.,* pp. 170-173.
[15] *Ibid.,* pp. 173-175.
[16] *Ibid.,* p. 173.
[17] *Ibid.,* pp. 177-232.
[18] *Ibid.,* p. 179.

us believe that their design is "Virtue and Reformation," will scarcely combat vice successfully, for

> "as the Matter is manag'd, the Correction is much worse than the Fault. They laugh at *Pedantry* and teach *Atheism,* cure a Pimple, and give the Plague. I heartily wish they would have let us alone. To exchange Virtue for Behaviour is a hard Bargain. Is not plain Honesty much better than Hypocrisy well Dress'd?"[19]

PART 5
Collier's Principles of Literary Criticism

A careful perusal of the *Short View* convinces the reader that Collier has woven into his attack on the profaneness and immorality of the English Stage a net-work of dramatic and literary criticism. The title-page acquaints the reader with the author's intention to give *A Short View of the Immorality and Profaneness of the English Stage, Together With the Sense of Antiquity upon This Argument*; this, and this only. It does not indicate his design to discuss the purpose of literature, or the unities, or to treat of propriety and impropriety of manners —both poetic and moral. It does not state his plans to give the differences between comedy and tragedy, or to expound the literary theories of Rapin, of Ben Jonson, of Thomas Rymer; neither does it intimate that the modern stage-poets are to be judged by any save *moral* standards. It does not hint that he intends to discourse on style, on poetic justice, on wit, on probability in a play, and on the Chorus in Comedy. Rigid adherence to his topic would, undoubtedly, have given Collier greater claim to scholarship. However, my purpose is not to estimate his rank among scholars; it is rather to analyze the *Short View,* and, in consequence of digressions, it becomes necessary to analyze how far and in what manner the author has wandered.

As a prelude to my discussion of Collier's principles of literary criticism let me point out that when Collier acquaints the reader with his intention of giving a "Sense of Antiquity Upon the Argument" he is elaborating upon a pet theme of his. He invariably compares the Moderns with the Ancients and just as invariably chooses the latter as superior both in morality and in literary ability. Contemporary records

---

[19] *Ibid.,* pp. 286-287.

suggest a cause for this interest of Collier in the relative value of the ancient and modern writers; they attribute it to the Bentley-Boyle and to the Temple-Wotton Controversies. As the *Short View* was composed and published within the half-decade of the dispute, it is not a matter of surprise that the controversial echoes of the quarrel between the Moderns and the Ancients are heard in it. As mentioned above,[1] Collier's retirement in 1688 from the public exercise of his clerical duties had given him leisure for study, and his outlawry in 1696 had further increased his opportunities. These facts, added to a natural propensity for study and to a nature that delighted in controversy might well account for his being widely read in the quarrel of the Ancients and Moderns. And Collier's sympathy for the Ancients is not hard to understand inasmuch as such eminent personages as Thomas Rymer and René Rapin—to whose literary principles Collier often proudly refers— championed the cause of the Ancients.[2]

From the opinion which Collier entertained of the Ancients as opposed to the Moderns (and because of the abundance of the material the matter can only be touched upon), let us see what opinion he held of the "Purpose of Literature." The topic "The Purpose of Literature" was likewise a controversial one at the time but of much more ancient origin than the quarrel of the Ancients and the Moderns. Some critics there were who held that the purpose of literature was twofold, instruction and delight; others maintained that the purpose was only delight, while still others affirmed that the sole purpose was instruction.[3] Inasmuch as comedy and tragedy are types of literature it is evident that Collier in divulging his opinions on the "Ends of Comedy and Tragedy," was really arguing the age-old question of the "purpose of literature."

---

[1] pp. 3-7.
[2] In 1674, Thomas Rymer had published—with an elaborate preface in support of his views—an English translation of Rapin's *Reflections on Aristotle's Treatise of Poesie*. In 1692 there appeared Rymer's *A Short View of Tragedy* in which were caustic reflections on "Shakespeare and other Practitioners of the Stage." Then, too, Rapin, though he had died in 1689, was noted for his critical works on the Ancients. His works were published in 1706 in two volumes under the title of *The Whole Critical Works of Monsieur Rapin Newly Done into English by Several Hands*.
[3] J. Collier, *A Short View*, p. 157.

In the opening sentence of the *Short View,* Collier makes clear that he believes the purpose is preeminently to instruct:

> "The business of *Plays* is to recommend Virtue, and dis-
> countenence Vice; To show the Uncertainty of Humane Great-
> ness, the suddain Turns of Fate, and the Unhappy Conclusions
> of Violence and Injustice: 'Tis to expose the Singularities of
> Pride and Fancy, to make Folly and Falsehood contemptible,
> and to bring everything that is Ill under Infamy, and Neglect."[4]

He quotes as authorities of his opinion Monsieur Rapin who in his *Reflections* voices the judgment of Aristotle and of Horace.[5]

By quoting from Ben Jonson's Dedicatory Epistle of *The Fox* to the effect that the principal end of poesy is "to inform Man in the best Reason of Living" Collier further substantiates his opinion that the purpose of literature is to instruct.[6] With caustic emphasis he refutes Dryden who in the *Mock Astrologer* has asserted that the chief end of comedy is delight and that if instruction has anything to do in comedy, " 'tis no more than its secondary end: For the business of the Poet is to make you laugh." Declares Collier:

> "To laugh without Reason is the Pleasure of Fools, and against
> it, of something worse. The exposing of Knavery, and making
> *Lewdness* ridiculous, is a much better occasion for Laughter.
> And this with submission I take to be the End of *Comedy.*

---

[4] *Ibid.,* p. 1. Although in the above quotation Collier refers broadly to plays, his subsequent arguments center most frequently upon comedy inasmuch as his attack was leveled chiefly at the modern writers of comedy, and his censure was aimed directly at their looseness in depicting both the characters and the plot of comedy.

[5] *Ibid.,* p. 157.

We find Rapin's statement expressed in the following words:

"It is not easily decided what the Nature, and what precisely is the End of this Art, the Interpreters of Aristotle differ in their Opinions. Some will have the End to be Delight, and that 'tis on this Account it labours to move the Passions, all whose motions are Delightful, because nothing is more sweet to the soul than Agitation . . . . However, the principal End of Poesie is to profit; not only by refreshing the Mind, to render it the more capable of the ordinary Functions, and by assuaging the troubles of the soul with its Harmony, and all the Elegancies of Expression; But furthermore, by purging the Manners with wholesome instructions, which it professes to Administer to Human kind . . . " René Rapin, *Reflections on Aristotle's Treatise of Poesie,* II, 141-143.

[6] *Ibid.,* p. 159.

And therefore it does not differ from *Tragedy* in the End, but in the *Means*. Instruction is the principal Design of both."[7]

Other critical principles which Collier discusses at length are propriety and impropriety of the "Manners of the Stage . . . with respect to Poetry and Ceremony,"[8] poetic justice—a literary virtue which he finds much abused by the modern stage-poets,[9] the nature of pleasure,[10] the stage-poets' versification and diction;[11] and he agrees with Dryden who in the Preface to *Albion and Albanius,* declares that if the gods were to speak upon the stage their "Expressions should be Lofty, Figurative, and Majestical."[12] He agrees, too, concerning the observations which that poet makes of "probability" and of "wit," but waxes sarcastically eloquent on the quixotism of D'Urfey and upon his lack of precision in diction.[13] He is a warm advocate of the observance of the

---

[7] *Ibid.,* pp. 156-157. From the above quotation Dryden's position on the purpose of comedy is likely to be misunderstood. To avoid misunderstanding, the reader must take into consideration the whole of the context from which this quotation was wrested. In fairness to Dryden I quote from the Preface to *Mock Astrologer:*
"Thus tragedy fulfils one great part of its institution; which is, by example, to instruct. But in comedy it is not so; for the chief end of it is divertisement and delight: and that so much, that it is disputed, I think by Heinsius, before Horace's "Art of Poetry," whether instruction be any part of its employment. At least I am sure it can be but its secondary end: for the business of the poet is to make you laugh: when he writes humour, he makes folly ridiculous: when wit, he moves you, if not always to laughter, yet to a pleasure that is more noble . . . . This being then established that the first end of comedy is delight, and instruction only the second; it may reasonably be inferred, that comedy is not so much obliged to the punishment of faults which it represents, as tragedy . . . . But, lest any man should think this to make libertinism amiable, or that I cared not to debase the end and institution of comedy, so I might thereby maintain my own errors, and those of better poets, I must further declare, both for them and for myself, that we make not vicious persons happy, but only as Heaven makes sinners so; that is, by reclaiming them first from vice." *Dramatic Works* ed. by Scott and Saintsbury, III, 248-249.

[8] J. Collier, *Short View,* pp. 165-170; pp. 218-219.

[9] *Ibid.,* pp. 152-164.

[10] *Ibid.,* p. 160. Collier's inquiry concerning pleasures becomes significant in the after-light of Dennis' *The Usefulness of the Stage,* 1698, and of his later Preface to *An Essay on the Operas after the Italian Manner,* 1706. In both these treatises, Dennis dwells extensively on the topic "pleasure." The inquiry is likewise significant in the light of Caffaro's letter prefixed to Motteux's *Beauty in Distress* in which the author refers to Aristotle's *"Eutrapelia* whose business 'tis to set just bounds to our Pleasure." That Collier was acquainted with this letter I have pointed out below. pp. 53-6.

[11] *Ibid.,* p. 226.

[12] *Ibid.,* p. 186.

[13] *Ibid.,* p. 185; pp. 206-7.

unities, acidly censuring those authors who fail to observe them;[14] and in his attack on Vanbrugh's *The Relapse,* he gives his opinions concerning "plot." He asserts that in the contrivance of a plot the poet should be ingenious; that he should give to it certain touches of conduct and certain extraordinary strains of invention; that he should surprise the audience by an admirable and unexpected outcome. He adds:

> "And all this Finess must work by gentle degrees, by a due preparation of *Incidents,* and by Instruments which are probable. 'Tis Mr. *Rapins* remark, that without probability, *every Thing is lame and Faulty.*"[15]

So convinced is Collier that the outcome must not exceed the force of belief that he asserts:

> "To produce effects without proportion; and likelyhood in the Cause, is Farce, and Magick, and looks more like Conjuring than Conduct."[15a]

There are evidences in the *Short View* that Collier paid attention to such dramatic topics as "consistency in character portrayal," "titles of plays that are mis-nomers," "the moral of plays," "the power of music over an audience," "uniformity between the chorus and the acts," "the nature of the prologue and the epilogue," "style," etc.[16] His statements concerning the effect which airy and galliardizing tunes have upon an audience as well as his abhorrence of prostituting so noble an art as music to so base a thing as a play are interesting in that they show him to have given time and study to music, and in that they point the way to Bedford's *The Great Abuse of Musick,* 1711.

Before concluding the present section I desire to call attention to the personal opinion which Collier entertained of certain of the Moderns. As was previously indicated Collier singles out for castigation six contemporary poets and their plays. Of these six, Wycherley, Dryden, Otway, Congreve, D'Urfey, and Vanbrugh, Collier for some reason best known to himself, treats Wycherley with the greatest deference. He takes for correction but two of his plays, and when he refers to them

---

[14] *Ibid.,* pp. 228-9; p. 188; p. 170.
[15] *Ibid.,* p. 212.
[15a] p. 212.
[16] *Ibid.,* pp. 209-228; pp. 234-235; pp. 278-280; pp. 149-150; p. 13; p. 28; p. 30; p. 113; pp. 206-7; p. 107.

his censure is not abusive. Although the Viewer is acknowledged an adept in the use of sarcasm and satire he does not indulge in it at Wycherley's expense. We find no coarseness or raillery where the Plain Dealer is concerned. If justice compels him to lash the *Country Wife* and the *Plain Dealer* kindly feeling tempers the smart:

> "I'm sorry, the Author should stoop his Wit thus Low, and Use his Understanding so unkindly . . . He can afford his Muse a better dress when he pleases."[17]

On one occasion Collier even appeals to Wycherley to support a critical statement.[18]

To Dryden, Collier applies the lash with all the rigour of outraged patience. The nine plays that he singles out for censure he treats ruthlessly. In several instances, too, Prefaces, Dedications, and Poems are handled wtih a temerity that defies reply. Yet, notwithstanding Collier's severity with "Dryden the stage-poet" he gives repeated proofs of his respect for "Dryden the literary critic." He not only heeds Dryden's literary pronouncements but he frequently makes them a norm by which he judges other critical opinions. We occasionally hear him remark, "Mr. Dryden, to do him right;"[19] or "I grant Mr. Dryden clears himself of this imputation,"[20] and again, "If, as Mr. Dryden rightly defines it."[21] On three occasions Collier refers to Dryden's *Essay of Dramatick Poesy*[22] and in each reference he regards Dryden's opinion as authoritative. Frequently he takes Dryden to task for certain statements in his Epistles Dedicatory. We have instances of it in that of *King Arthur,*[23] of *Aurenge-Zebe,*[24] and of *Juvenal and Persius.*[25] To Otway's *Orphan* Collier refers four times,[26] and in three of these instances Monimia, a "Topping Lady" is guilty of offending in speech, and in the fourth instance, the young soldier, Chamont, is guilty of treating the clergy disrespectfully. However, Collier's references are

---

[17] *Ibid.,* pp. 3-4.
[18] *Ibid.,* p. 175.
[19] *Ibid.,* p. 67; p. 92.
[20] *Ibid.,* p. 108.
[21] *Ibid.,* p. 175.
[22] *Ibid.,* p. 126; p. 153; p. 175.
[23] *Ibid.,* p. 189; p. 194.
[24] *Ibid.,* pp. 66-67.
[25] *Ibid.,* pp. 69-71.
[26] *Ibid.,* p. 9; p. 62; p. 100; p. 146.

not caustic: he merely states his grievances against the deceased author
and then wields his lash in another direction.

For D'Urfey, Collier shows no deference either as a critic or as a
dramatist. Throughout the *Short View* (exclusive of Chapter V) he
rarely mentions *Don Quixote*; when he does, it is for castigation. However, he sets aside a section of Chapter V for D'Urfey in order to "consider him in a word or two by himself,"[27] and here he gives the author
some telling strokes. We can get a definite idea of the Viewer's mean
opinion both of *Don Quixote* and of D'Urfey from the following:

> "Were I the author, I would discharge my Muse unless she
> prov'd kinder. His [D'Urfey's] way is rather to cultivate his
> Lungs,and Sing to other Peoples Sense: For to finish him in a
> word, he is *Vox, et praeterea nihil.* I speak this only on Sup-
> position that the rest of his Performances are like These."[28]

Collier's wrath in regard to Congreve seems to have been kindled
upon the altar of some private grievance. Of the poet's four plays then
extant, Collier attacks each; his abuse is oftentimes coarse and his criticism vulgar. Guesses have been hazarded as to the reason for Collier's
violent dislike of Congreve. One interesting conjecture of the cause of
this dislike is given by the anonymous author of *Some Remarks Upon
Mr. Collier's Defence.* He declares:

> "All my Acquaintance that discourse this Matter, are con-
> vinced Mr. *Collier* has a particular Pique against Mr. *Congreve*;
> nay, some will go farther, and guess the Cause; perhaps there
> may be Lines of that Author's that vex the *Non-Juror* more than
> all the smutty jests he has pickt up; Lines that Mourn the Royal
> *Pastora*; Heroick Lines, that sound the Glory of our Monarch.
> From this sweet Poetry they judge his Gall is raised; which
> being gorged and full, overflows, nor spares the dead or living,
> Friends and Foes, the bitter Deluge reaches and bespatters
> all."[29]

Congreve himself was aware that the Reverend Gentleman

> "would have poison'd me, but he overdosed it, and the Excess
> of his Malice has been my Security."[30]

---

[27] *Ibid.,* p. 196.
[28] *Ibid.,* p. 208.
[29] Anonymous, *Some Remarks Upon Mr. Collier's Defence of his View of the
English Stage,* p. 17.
[30] W. Congreve, *Amendments,* p. 94.

Vanbrugh at the time of the publication of the *Short View* was the author of *The Relapse,* of *Aesop,* and of *The Provok'd Wife.*[31] Of these, the first and last come under Collier's displeasure. That he entertained a contempt for Vanbrugh's dramatic ability is evident from statements scattered throughout the chapter given to criticizing *The Relapse.* He refers to Vanbrugh's plays only in terms of deepest sarcasm and contempt. For example, when Sir Tunbelly in *The Relapse* gives undue scope to his wit, Collier satirically calls the author to task:

"Now to what purpose should a Fools Coat be embroider'd? Besides, I don't perceive the *Relapser* was in any Condition to be thus liberal . . . . And when a *Poet* is not overstock'd, to squander away his wit among his *Block-heads,* is meer Distraction. His men of Sense will smart for this prodigality."[32]

and when Vanbrugh in his preface makes a wretched apology for his abuse of the clergy Collier suggests that he take his play to *Samourgan* where

". . . 'Tis likely he might find Leisure to lick his *Abortive Brat* into shape; And meet with proper Business for his Temper, and Encouragement for his Talent."[33]

Collier's frequent coarseness and vulgarity have occasioned harsh criticism. That a clergyman should employ such expressions as he contemptuously hurled at Congreve, that he should collect the nauseous phrasings of D'Urfey, that he should indulge in offensive raillery at the expense of Dryden and of Vanbrugh—all these facts have caused not only readers of the *Short View,* but students of the comic dramatists of the Restoration to regard him with contempt and resentment. If Collier needs vindication for the quality of his abuse, I can but say that his vitriolic sentences were the outcome of a temper maddened by what he considered indecency and profanity; that the liberties which many of the stage-poets took with morality and religion provoked the stage-reformer to such a degree that his nobler sense was distorted. Occasionally, too, these liberties blunted his judgment, and, as a consequence,

---

[31] C. Gildon, *The Lives and Characters of the English Dramatick Poets,* pp. 143-145.

[32] J. Collier, *Short View,* p. 224.

[33] *Ibid.,* p. 232. Collier explains by a marginal note that Samourgan is "An Academy in Lithuania for the Education of Bears."

we find him magnifying the poets' defects of profanity and disrespect of the clergy. This, certainly, is to be lamented. On the other hand he had many occasions for *just* anger and for *just* censure, and where the occasions were just, it would have been impossible for one of Collier's temperament to hold his peace. It would have been impossible for a person of his honesty to speak of filth in terms of rose petals, or to picture a dunghill as a garden of lilies.

PART 6

Opinions of the Pagans, of the Church, and of the State Concerning the Stage

With apparent satisfaction Collier breaks away from his task of presenting the disorders of the English Stage and enters without waste of words upon that pet theme of his, viz., presenting to the reader "A Short View of the Sense of Antiquity," to which he proposes to add some authorities from modern sources. Collier makes the sweeping assertion that he will accumulate testimony to prove that plays have generally been looked upon as the nurseries of vice, as the corrupters of youth, and as the grievance of the country which tolerates them.[1] He arranges his evidence under three heads: (1) that of the most cele-brated heathen philosophers, orators, and historians, and of men most noted for consideration, sense, learning, and figure; (2) that drawn from the Laws and Constitutions of Princes; and (3) that taken from the Church records, from the Fathers, and from the Councils.[2]

He proves from antiquity and from modern sources his argu-ment for the abolition of the theatre and proceeds further to anathematize the stage by giving the opinion which the Church has voiced both in her councils and in single authorities during the first five hundred years of her existence. Of Councils he quotes six, viz., the first and second Councils of Arles, the third Council of Carthage, the Council of Illiberis, the Second Council of Chaalon, and lastly, one which Collier very inacurately refers to as "another African Council."[3] Of the single authorities quoted as evidence of the hostility of the primitive Church against plays, there are nine: Theophilus, Tertul-

---

[1] J. Collier, *Short View,* p. 23.
[2] *Ibid.,* p. 233.
[3] *Ibid.,* pp. 250-251.

lian, Clement of Alexandria, Minutius Felix, St. Cyprian, Lactantius, St. Chrysostom, St. Jerome, and St. Augustine.[4] Of the nine: Tertullian is quoted most extensively, while St. Cyprian, St. Chrysostom, and St. Augustine come in second for the amount of deference which Collier gives to their writings on the subject.

That Collier was influenced by the opinions of the ancient Fathers of the Church is evident from the nature and the number of quotations he gives from them. He professed, however, to discover this influence only for the first 500 years. Had he built up his evidence to a later date including the half-decade 1690-1695, he would undoubtedly have mentioned the clergymen Bossuet and Caffaro as well as the controversy in which they engaged. This controversy, with its series of stage pamphlets, was evoked by the letter of Caffaro which had been published by Boursault in January, 1694, as a preface to his *Piéces de Théatre*. To this letter, likewise, is traceable a frequent echo found both in the anti-stage works of Collier and in the replies which these works called forth.[5] A detailed analysis of the French controversy and of its influence upon Collier would be both impossible and impracticable here. I shall give Caffaro's letter more detailed analysis in my discussion of Motteux's *Beauty in Distress* because in its preface Caffaro's letter is transcribed.[6] In the present instance, however, I shall trace only the

---

[4] *Ibid.*, pp. 252-276.

[5] J. B. Bossuet, *Correspondance*, ed. by Urbain and Levesque. VI, 256. Inasmuch as Urbain and Levesque (VI, 257) not only call attention to the storm which Caffaro's letter excited, but give the titles of the most important pamphlets written in reply to Caffaro, I shall state them:
1. J. B. Bossuet, *Maximes et réflexions sur la comédie.* This treatise was published in August 1694, and in it Bossuet develops the opinions which he had stated in his letter to Caffaro on May 9, 1694.
2. *Réponse à la lettre d'un théologien défenseur de la comédie* (par Lelevel) ;
3. *La Refutation d' un écrit favorisant la comédie.* (par le S. de La Grange, Victorin) ;
4. *La Lettre d'un docteur de Sorbonne* (J. Gerbais) *à une personne de qualité sur le sujet de la comédie;*
5. *Le Discours sur la comédie* (par le P. Le Brun, de l' Oratoire) ;
6. *Decision faite en Sorbonne touchant la comédie* (le 20 mai 1694), *avec la Réfutation des sentiments relâchés d' un nouvean théologien,* par l' abbé L [aurent] P [égurier] ;
7. *Sentiments de l'Eglise et des Pères sur la comédie opposés à ceux de la lettre du P. Caffaro* (par P. Coustel).

[6] P. Motteux, *Beauty in Distress,* Preface, pp. [ix-xxvi].

influence which the references and statements made by Caffaro in his letter have exerted upon the *Short View*.[7]

Of the *heathen* authorities whom Collier mentions in support of his views against plays, Caffaro had mentioned two—Aristotle and Seneca—as *favoring* them. One of these, Aristotle, Caffaro quotes as being the authority for St. Thomas when in the second part of the *Summa* he proposes the question as to what should be thought of sports and diversions. The answer which the Angelic Doctor makes and upon which Caffaro's arguments are based, is in favor of liberty. He states that if diversions be moderate, not only are they not sinful but they are in some measure good and conformable to that virtue which Aristotle had styled "Eutrepelia," i.e., having the business to set just bounds to pleasure.[8]

Of the nine Fathers mentioned by Collier, Caffaro had mentioned seven, and it is interesting to note that in several of these, there is the echo of refutation to Caffaro. For example, Caffaro had quoted Tertullian as mentioning the silence of the Scriptures in regard to the lawfulness of being present at plays:

> "We no where find that we are as expressly forbidden in Scripture to go to the *Circus* and *Theatre* . . . as we are forbidden to worship Idols, or the being guilty of Murder, Treason and Adultery."[9]

Collier on the contrary, quotes the same Tertullian to prove the converse of the proposition:

> ". . . he [Tertullian] goes on, some peoples Faith is either too full of Scruples, or too barren of Sense. Nothing will serve to settle them but a plain Text of *Scripture*. They hover in uncertainty because 'tis not said as expressly thou shalt not go to the *Play-House,* as 'tis thou shalt not Kill."[10]

---

[7] Francisco Caffaro was descended from one of the most illustrious families of Messina. The year of his birth is not certain; his prominence dates from the early 1690's when, as a Theatin priest in France, he wrote on matters of Divinity, and on the lawfulness of the stage. *Enciclopedia Italiana Di Scienze, Lettere ed Arti. Publicata Sotto L'Alto Patronato Di S. M. Il Re D'Italia,* VIII, 257. Because Caffaro was a member of the Theatin congregation he is frequently referred to in the controversy simply as the "Theatin."

[8] P. Motteux, *Beauty in Distress,* Preface, p. xi.

[9] *Ibid.,* p. x.

[10] J. Collier, *Short View,* p. 254.

Caffaro urges St. Cyprian as authority for the statement:

" . . . Reason is to be heard where Holy Writ is Silent."[11]

and again Collier attempts to take the evidence from the same Father and apply it to the converse of the statement. He says:

"this Father [St. Cyprian] argues against those who thought the *Play-House* no unlawful Diversion because 'twas not Condemned by express *Scripture*. Let meer Modesty (says he) supply the *Holy Text*."[12]

Under the guidance of the Angelic Doctor, Caffaro argues that concerning those plays against which St. Chrysostom, Tertullian, St. Cyprian, St. Jerome, and St. Augustine had fulminated, we are to abhor their excesses and that, besides, we are bound in conscience to shun those plays which are guilty of excesses.[13] In addition, he states that St. Augustine's opinion coincides with that of St. Thomas on the lawfulness of diversion:

"In short, I would have you take care of your self, for 'tis the part of a Wise Man, sometimes to unbend his Mind which is too intent upon his Business."[14]

Both Caffaro and Collier cite the 3rd council of Carthage in its condemnation of blasphemy. The former strives to bring home the fact that the blasphemy at the ancient shows was one of the excesses which caused the Council to condemn as blasphemers those players who participated in the performance;[15] while the latter quotes the same Council in defense of his views that because plays are guilty of blasphemy they should be forbidden:

"Such sort of Pagan *Entertainments* [*Publick Shews*, or *Plays*] being forbidden all the *Laity*. It being always unlawful for all Christians to come amongst *Blasphemers*."[16]

Other topics of a similar nature engage the attention of both critics. Upon one subject, however, they entertain the same opinion, viz., on

[11] P. Motteux, *Beauty in Distress*, Preface, p. xi.
[12] J. Collier, *Short View*, pp. 261-262.
[13] P. Motteux, *Beauty in Distress*, Preface, p. xi.
[14] *Ibid.*, p. xi.
[15] *Ibid.*, p. xv.
[16] J. Collier, *Short View*, p. 250.

the comparative freedom from "excesses" of the French theatre. Besides, both critics discuss whether players are to be regarded as infamous. Of this Caffaro, quoting Baldus, asserts:

> "The Players who act in a modest way either to divert themselves or please others, and who commit nothing against good Manners, are not to be reputed infamous. You perceive then according to this Commentator, that the Infamy falls only on those who act infamous Plays."[17]

Collier quotes Didacus de Tapia, a Spaniard, to substantiate the opposite view, namely, that players are excommunicated and that in consequence they are not to be admitted to the Sacrament even though their performance be productive of some good.[18]

It is with the opinion of Didacus that Collier closes his evidences. He closes it deliberately and without modification: "My conclusion is, Let nobody go to the Infamous *Play-House.*" And, lest the condemnation fail to strike home Collier concludes with several thunderbolts of his own devising:

> "In short: Nothing can be more disserviceable to Probity and Religion than the management of the *Stage*. It cherishes those Passions, and rewards those Vices, which 'tis the business of Reason to discountenance. It strikes at the Root of Principle, draws off the Inclinations from Virtue, and spoils good Education: 'Tis the most effectual means to baffle the Force of Discipline, to emasculate peoples Spirits, and Debauch their Manners."[19]

He reaches a climax by his customary series of staccato questions:

> "How *many* of the Unwary have these *Syrens* devour'd? And how often has the best Blood been tainted, with this Infection? What Disappointment of Parents, what Confusion in Families, and what Beggary in Estates have been hence occasion'd?"[20]

He pursues these questions with his customary pessimistic rejoinders concerning the progress of the moral malady, the hopelessness of a cure, and the patients' scorn of religion to effect it:

---

[17] P. Motteux, *Beauty in Distress,* Preface, p. xx.
[18] J. Collier, *Short View,* pp. 275-276.
[19] *Ibid.* p. 287.
[20] *Ibid.,* p. 287.

"The Feavour works up toward Madness, and will scarcely endure to be touch'd. And what hope is there of Health when the *Patient* strikes in with the Disease,, and flies in the Face of the *Remedy*. Can Religion retrieve us? Yes, when we don't despise it. But while our Notions are naught, our *Lives* will hardly be otherwise . . . You may almost as well feed a Man without a Mouth, as give Advice where there's no disposition to receive it,"[21]

and in the arguments we learn Collier's attitude toward the playhouse, the stage-poets, and plays; we perceive his prejudice and his reasons for it—subjects which were to form the ever-recurring theme of his later anti-stage pamphlets.

---

[21] *Ibid.*, p. 288.

REPLIES EVOKED BY THE SHORT VIEW
APRIL 30—NOVEMBER 10, 1698
CHAPTERS III-VI

Foreword

As far as is possible to do it I shall deal chronologically with the replies to the *Short View*. The best sources for securing this chronology are the pamphlets themselves and the periodicals of the time. However, it is important to point out that the book notices and announcements appearing in these pamphlets and periodicals are oftentimes very fallible guides for arriving at the dates of initial appearances of books. Not only is the wording of the announcement frequently misleading in this respect, but the intermittent appearance of the announcement is likely to lead one astray. To illustrate both points by a single example. *The Post-Man* for February 15, 1698, contains the following Advertisement:

> "There is now published: An Italian Voyage: or, a Compleat Journey through *Italy,* in two parts with the Characters of the People and the description of the Chief Towns, . . . by *Rich Lassel,* Gent. The second Edition with large Additions, by a Modern Hand. Printed for *Rich. Wellington,* and are to be sold by *Bernard Lintot* at the Cross Keys . . ."

Then, the next ten issues of *The Post-Man* do not contain the above announcement, but on March 10, the identical notice again appears under a slightly different caption:

> "This day is published, An Italian Voyage, or a Compleat Journey through Italy, in two parts, . . ."

Now it is evident that one who had not read the advertisement for February 15 would conclude that the Second Edition of *An Italian Voyage* appeared for the first time March 10. Obviously, one of these statements is not true. Consequently, it behooves the student of eighteenth century literature to view these periodical announcements circumspectly, checking them constantly with other sources of information.

There is evidence that book notices have frequently mislead scholars who attempt to determine the chronology of pamphlets. For instance, both Mr. E. Gosse and Mr. D. Crane Taylor on the authority of extant periodicals fail to agree on the dates they assign for the initial appearance of several replies to the *Short View*. Mr. Gosse, in his *Life of Congreve*[1] asserts that shortly after *Phaeton* appeared (and he ascribes the publication of *Phaeton* to the month of April), Motteux's *Beauty in Distress* and D'Urfey's *The Campaigners* were published. Mr. Taylor, on the contrary, gives the date for *Beauty in Distress* as June 20, 1698, and for the *Campaigners* as July 9th.[2] Again, Mr. Gosse stating as his authority *The Post-Man* for May 26, asserts that Edward Filmer published on that date *A Defence of Dramatic Poetry*[3] while Mr. Taylor on the authority of *The Post-Boy* gives the date as June 2.[4] Obviously, announcements were repeated verbatim in both periodicals in successive issues as long as the publisher believed that he had a market for his publication. Sometimes, too, the announcement appeared before the book was actually put on sale. This is found to be the case in *The Character of a Trimmer* announced in *The Post-Man* for Jan. 13, 1698.

It is significant to note in a study of the replies to Collier's *Short View* that of the five living stage-poets whom Collier so severely attacked, only three—Vanbrugh, Congreve, and D'Urfey attempted a vindication of themselves. One—Dryden—stated on several occasions his reaction to the clergyman's lash, but his demeanor is, for the most part, submissive. Wycherley, so far as we can ascertain, gave no direct reply. There is *A Vindication of the Stage* published anonymously,

---

[1] Edmund Gosse, *Life of Congreve*, p. 113.

[2] D. Crane Taylor, *William Congreve*, p. 128. There is a statement made by the anonymous author of *A Letter to A. H.* which has bearing upon the publication of *Beauty in Distress*. It reads: " . . . for what'er Effect it [the *Short View*] has had on Mr. *Vanbroug* and *Congreve;* Motteux and Guildon resent it to the last degree." Consequently, we may infer that *Beauty in Distress* was published shortly after *Phaeton,* and before *A Short Vindication of the Relapse*. It is safe to assume, too, that it was published before the anonymous *A Vindication of the Stage,* May 17, because the author, apparently well aware of the progress of the controversy and of minute details of it, does not refer to this pamphlet.

[3] Edmund Gosse, *op. cit.,* p. 114. The genesis of *The Post-Man* is interesting. Walter Graham in his *The Beginnings of English Literary Periodicals* does not mention the work. However, the *British Museum Catalogue,* Periodical Publications, p. 590, states that it appeared first under the title *An Account of the Publick Transactions in Christendom.* August 11, 1694. Then it was continued as *An Historical Account of the Publick Transactions in Christendom,* August 18, 1694. No issues were published between Sept. 8, 1694 and May 4, 1695. Then it was continued as *The Post-Man And The Historical Account,* Oct. 22, 1695-Jan. 2, 1701.

[4] D. Taylor, *op. cit.,* p. 125. *The Post-Boy with Foreign and Domestick News* was begun June 1, 1695 and was continued intermittently to Nov., 1710. *The British Museum Catalogue,* Periodical Publications, p. 973.

and ascribed by Professor Gosse to Wycherley, but the authorship is disputed by other scholars. The remaining of the sextet of attacked stage-poets was Otway whose play *The Orphan* was censured by Collier under each of his four accusations. Otway, however, had in 1685, passed to a land where there is no further opportunity for vindication, and inasmuch as no critic formally championed his work, his play remains unvindicated. But more of this in the analyses which are to follow.

CHAPTER III
The Replies of April and May

1. Charles Gildon: *Phaeton*, Preface, April 30.
2. P. Motteux: *Beauty in Distress*, Preface. (Shortly after April 30.)
3. J. Dryden: Epistle to Motteux for his Play, *Beauty in Distress*.
4. Anonymous: *A Letter to A. H. Esq.* (Before May 17.)
5. Anonymous: *A Vindication of the Stage*, May 17.
6. Meriton: *Immorality, Debauchery, and Profaneness Exposed to the Reproof of Scripture*, May 19.
7. Anonymous: *The Occasional Paper, Number IX, Containing Some Considerations about the Danger of Going to Plays*, May 21.
8. Anonymous [E. Filmer]: *A Defence of Dramatick Poetry*, May 26.

Following close upon the publication of *A Short View* appeared Gildon's *Phaeton* with three pages of its preface devoted to a castigation of Collier. Motteux's *Beauty in Distress* with its preface of the famous Caffaro Letter together with Dryden's "Poetical Epistle," and the anonymous *Letter to A. H. Esq.* appeared shortly after. Not quite three weeks later was published *A Vindication of the Stage*. Both Gildon and the anonymous author of *A Vindication* admit that they are only tentatively answering the charges of Collier. Meriton's work is entered in my bibliography merely for record; I have been unable to secure the pamphlet. *The Occasional Paper* is a vindication of Collier and a brief restatement of the arguments given in the *Short View* against immodesty, profanity and abuse of the Scriptures, and immorality. *A Defence of Dramatick Poetry* is an attempt of a loquacious author to refute Collier's attack of plays and playwrights and to match Collier's display of learning with a display equally as flashy.

1.

The words of the *Short View* proved rapier thrusts to playwrights other than the attacked poets. Their stigma branded not only the stage in general but comedy and the wits in particular, and immediately stage-champions came to the fore to avenge the insult. Although the first blow of Collier's lash had been given to Wycherley he is not the first to reply. Many expected that he, well known for his plays and extremely popular in some circles for *The Plain Dealer*[5] would retaliate in the out-spoken manner for which his dramatic style was noted. We have evidence of this in "A Letter, In Answer to some Queries," where we read:

> "When Mr. C. made so vigorous an Attack upon our Stages, as shook the Foundation; what was the Reason, in so desperate a Juncture (when the whole Posse of *Parnassus* was expected up in Arms) that only the Minor Poets appear'd? Where was the Mighty W-------?"[6]

Others looked to Dryden for a withering rejoinder. D'Urfey declares:

> "I could have wish'd one who is best able, and whose admirable Genius and Skill in Poetry would have been remarkably service-able, had drawn his Pen to defend the Rights of the Stage, tho he had own'd the loosenesses of it, and had ventured the being presented for it; . . ."[7]

However, the month of May arrived and according to extant records none of the wits attacked by Collier had attempted a vindication. The first reply with which we are acquainted is that of Charles Gildon[8] who, in the conclusion of his Preface to *Phaeton: or, The Fatal Divorce* comes forward as an adversary of Collier and introduces himself thus:

---

[5] David E. Baker, *Biographia Dramatica*, I, 475-6.

[6] J. Collier, *Dissuasive*, 2nd ed., to which is added "A Letter written by an-other Hand; in answer to some Queries . . . "

[7] T. D'Urfey, *The Campaigners*, Preface, p. 3.

[8] Although *Phaeton* is anonymous the authorship is claimed by Charles Gildon who, in his completion of Langbaine's *Lives and Characters of the English Drammatick Poets*, states of his anonymous works (and among them he lists *Phaeton*): "His name, without his Consent, was omitted in the Impres-sions of the Plays." pp. 174-5.

*"Since the Conclusion of the foregoing Preface, I have met with
a Book, call'd a* Short View of the Immorality and Profaneness
of the English Stage, *etc. by* Jeremy Collier, A.M."[9]

The "foregoing preface" to which the author refers is about nine
pages in length and was written, as he tells us, to acquit himself of
"one of the greatest *Duties* of Mankind, that of *Gratitude* to a *Dead
Hero, and living Friend."*[10] However, Collier's *Short View* appearing
before his work was printed, Gildon appends to the preface two and
one-half additional pages—pages of "Reflections" concerning the attack
on the immorality and profaneness of the stage.

He begins very bluntly by admitting the indecencies of the English
stage as well as his own satisfaction could they be eliminated. He lays
a heavy hand on "this younger *Histrio-Mastix*,"[11] and assures his reader
that even though his present vindication of the poets and the stage is
incomplete, he will during the coming summer finish his defence by
divulging in "Vindication of the Stage, . . . all the Abuses, and Absurdities this Author [Collier] is guilty of."[12] He makes further reference to the "Vindication" he has in mind, when toward the end of the
preface he invites Collier to define

> "his Terms in the front of his book. Which I desire he may
> do before I publish mine in Vindication of the *Stage* against
> Mr. *Pryn,* and Mr. *Collier;* in which I question not, but I shall
> make evident that The Wit of Man can invent no way so effica-
> cious, as Drammatick Poetry, to advance *Virtue* and *Wisdom,*
> and the Supream duty of an *English man* (next the Love of
> God which is always supream) the love of our Country, a Les-
> son I shall particularly Recommend the *Stage* for to Mr. *Col-
> lier."*[13]

He cites the chapter-headings of "this furious gentleman" as he
calls Collier and replies very briefly and very weakly to Collier's first
accusation, i.e., to the rankness and indecencies in the language of the
English stage poets. This response is nothing more nor less than a re-

---

[9] C. Gildon, *Phaeton,* Preface, p. ix. The play is a five-act tragedy dedicated to
the Right Honourable Charles Montague and was printed for Abel Roper
at the Black-boy over against St. Dunstans Church in Fleetstreet. It appeared
according to *The Post Boy* about April 30, 1698.
[10] *Ibid.,* p. i.
[11] *Ibid.,* p. ix.
[12] *Ibid.,* p. ix.
[13] Ibid., *Preface,* p. xi.

gret that he has not with him the plays to which Collier's references are made, and, with the general remark that the indecencies are very likely goblins of his own forming, he passes on to refuting Collier's chapter on profaneness.

The Viewer's charges under this heading are, in the opinion of Gildon, not only nonsensical and unfounded, but unjust to the stage-poets in question. Although he omits a discussion of Collier's evidence against "cursing," he nevertheless expends time and energy in upholding Congreve and Vanbrugh under the charges of swearing and abuse of the Scriptures. In a brief prelude to his discourse on the afore-mentioned vices, he acidly remarks:

> "I grant this Gentleman is no *Friend* to *Oaths,* yet his *Zeal* should not transport him out of his *Princely* Wits, or make him run into such a Whimsie in *Etymology* as a certain fellow did in *Pedigre,* to derive himself from King *Pepin. Dipper, diaper; Napkin, Nepkin; Pipkin, King Pepin,* as foolishly Extravagant as this seems, Mr. *Collier* is more so through great part of his Charge against our *Stage* which to impartial Judges must seem very Innocent, when its professed Enemy is driven to the wretched Necessity of fixing forged Crimes upon it."[14]

Concerning the stage-poets' abuse of the clergy, Gildon has little to say. If the stage is abusing the character of the English Clergy whom the author lauds for its piety and learning, then the practice should be abandoned. However, Gildon asserts that Collier, because of his political tendencies, has no right to appear in the ranks of those who would correct the abuse:

> "he of all Men living, is the most unfitting Man to appear their [the clergy of the Church of England's] Champion, who has made it his endeavours to make much the greater part of that *Venerable Body* pass for a company of *perjured,* and *Mercenary Times-servers. But of this more hereafter.*"[15]

More briefly does the author dismiss the subject of immorality. He comes, merely, to the rescue of the ladies and of persons of quality with whom, he asserts, Collier has awkwardly tried to insinuate him-

---

[14] *Ibid.,* p. x.
[15] *Ibid.,* p. xi. Note that Gildon in his Preface to *Phaeton* as well as subsequent disputants refers contemptuously to Collier's non-jurancy and to his absolution of Friend and Perkins.

self but whom he has branded with infamy—infamy defined as "want
of honesty and understanding." He questions Collier's "Notion of
Words," and requests him to prefix a glossary to the *Short View* so
that misinterpretations of his meanings may be avoided.[16]

That Gildon intends to fulminate against Collier and to vindicate
the stage and the stage-poets during the coming summer is evident from
reiterated statements to that effect found in the Preface[17] where he lists
the topics upon which he will enlarge: all the abuses and absurdities
this author [Collier] is guilty of (p. ix.) ; the proof that Collier is
guilty of a greater immorality, profaneness, and blasphemy than all, or
at least, a greater part of the authors whom he has arraigned for the
same sins (p. xi.) ; the vindication of the stage against Mr. Prynne and
Mr. Collier (p. xi.) ; the eminent piety and learning of the clergy of
the Church of England, and Mr. Collier's unfitting character to appear
as their champion (p. xi) ; and, finally, the efficacy of dramatic poetry
to advance virtue, wisdom and patriotism (p. xi). He insists that it is
because of lack of space in the present preface that he is prevented
from discovering *all* the abuses and absurdities of which the Viewer is
guilty. "I have no room in this Place to show all the Abuses, . . . but
I reserve most of them for a work I have long design'd, and which I
resolve to conclude some time this summer."[18] And again, "I have not
room here . . . but I do not doubt in my answer to prove . . . "[19] and I
have neither Room nor Leisure now to examine his Charge on the
Stage, . . . But of this more hereafter."[20]

I especially mention these general characteristics of the Preface to
Phaeton so that in our analysis of *A Vindication of the Stage* which is
believed by some scholars to be the promised vindication, the reader
may determine whether or not the same author wrote both treatises.

2.

Soon after the appearance of Collier's *Short View* and The Preface
to C. Gildon's *Phaeton* there was published *Beauty in Distress. A Tragedy As it is Acted at the Theatre in Little Lincoln-Inn-Fields. By His*

---

[16] *Ibid.,* p. xi.
[17] *Ibid.,* pp. ix-xi.
[18] *Ibid.,* p. ix.
[19] *Ibid.,* p. xi.
[20] *Ibid.,* p. xi.

Majesty's Servants. The book was printed for Daniel Brown and Richard Parker, and according to the *London Gazette* appeared on June 20, 1698. But from a statement found in *A Letter to A. H. Esq.,* however, we learn that the book was published before Vanbrugh's vindication, and it is upon this authority that I have placed the pamphlet among the May replies to the *Short View.* The author of *Beauty in Distress* is Peter Motteux who, in addition to writing the Epistle Dedicatory, inserts "The Preface," "The Poet's Character of Himself," "A Letter from a Divine of the Church of England, . . . concerning the Lawfulness and Unlawfulness of Plays," a "Poetical Epistle from John Dryden," as well as a "Prologue" and an "Epilogue."[21] All the above-mentioned items are interesting, but the discourse on the lawfulness and the unlawfulness of plays is particularly so, inasmuch as its nucleus is the famous "Caffaro Letter" which had aroused such a storm of controversy in France in 1694.[22] A detailed analysis of the letter as well as of the historical, theatrical, and literary background of it has been made by M. Barras in his scholarly treatise *The Stage Controversy in France from Corneille to Rousseau.*[23] Barras has graphically portrayed the conditions under which the Caffaro letter was published, as well as those under which it was retracted. He tells us that as a result of his letter Caffaro suffered from ecclesiastical censure in consequence of which he was not only deprived of his preferment but was forbidden the confessional and the pulpit.[24] Barras traces to its source Bossuet's attack on Caffaro and informs us that the fiery Frenchman a few months later, in publishing his *Maximes et réflexions sur la comédie* refutes the Theatin's favorable attitude toward the theatre, and asserts among other things that the priest had either read the Fathers carelessly or had interpreted them incorrectly.[25]

A careful reading of the original letter convinces one that Caffaro

---

[21] P. Motteux, *Beauty in Distress*, pp. i-xxxi. The title-page gives the following announcement of the Letter: "With a Discourse of the Lawfulness and Unlawfulness of Plays. Lately written in French by the Learned Father Caffaro, Divinity Professor at Paris, Sent in a Letter to the Author By a Divine of the Church of England."

[22] Reference has already been made to the Caffaro-Bossuet Controversy, see above, pp. 53-4.

[23] pp. 111-129.

[24] *Ibid.,* p. 121.

[25] *Ibid.,* p. 122.

had attempted to "use reason where Holy Scripture is silent;"[26] that he had followed uncompromisingly the guidance of St. Thomas and that he had agreed with him both upon the advisability of unbending the mind which is too intent upon business, and upon enjoying the diverting words and actions which are not immoderate.[27] Throughout, Caffaro emphasizes the fact that what the Fathers so rigorously condemned in the theatre were the excesses committed there;[28] he deduces from the arguments of St. Thomas that players who are employed in an occupation which affords men an honest recreation are not in a state of sin provided

> "they neither speak nor act anything which is unlawful; mix nothing that is sacred with Profane, and never act in a prohibited time;"[29]

and that those who attend plays and give moderate pay to the performers, or assist them are not only guilty of no sin, but, on the contrary, are performing an act of justice, inasmuch as they are giving them the reward of their labor.[30] He states that plays, taken in themselves, and independent of any other circumstances, good or bad, ought to be reckoned among the number of things purely indifferent.

Consistent reasoning on the part of Caffaro ends only by a reiteration of his first statement that provided there be no "excess" in dramatic representations, there is no harm in them. In answer to a supposed objection from rigid reformers who would likely allege that since plays mention ambition, jealousy, revenge, and hatred, they are prone to arouse the passions of youth who will give rein to their real passions by seeing feigned ones on the stage, Caffaro states:

> "A fine Speech this for a rigid Declaimer, but not sound enough for an equitable Divine! Is there no difference, think ye, between an Action or a Word which may by accident raise the Passions, and those which do it in reality?"[31]

---

[26] *Beauty in Distress,* p. xi.

[27] *Ibid.,* p. xi.

[28] *Ibid.,* p. xiii ff.

[29] *Ibid.,* p. xii.

[30] *Ibid.,* p. xii. Caffaro quotes the term "moderate pay" as used by St. Thomas in contra-distinction to the "squandering away a whole estate upon players, or countenancing players who act scandalously" which was used by the reformers.

[31] *Ibid.,* p. xxiii.

In conclusion Father Caffaro emphasizes his opinion that for plays
to be lawful they should be free from immodest speeches and actions,
from blasphemy, from words and actions which are designed to raise
the passions; he insists they should be acted within the proper times, at
respectable places, and by decent persons. His parting words are these:

"I am conscious, Sir, that some People will blame me for having followed the most favourable Opinion concerning Plays;
for 'tis now the Fashion to teach an Austere Doctrine, and not
to practice it; but I assure you I have wholly been govern'd by
Truth, wishing still to observe that Father's Rule who directs
us to form our Actions by the most severe Opinions, and our
Doctrine by the most indulgent."[32]

Students of the Collier stage controversy are, generally speaking,
unmindful of the wide influence which Caffaro's letter had both on
those who attacked the English stage and on those who defended it.
The influence is discernible not only in the arguments advanced in
favor of plays or against them, but in attacks made openly upon Caffaro
or Bossuet. Among those works in which are evidences of this influence I mention *A Short View, A Vindication of the Stage, The Occasional Paper IX, The Stage Condemn'd, A Defence of the Short
View, The Usefulness of the Stage, The Stage-Beaux Tossed in a
Blanket, The Stage Acquitted, Reflections on the Stage and on Mr.
Collyer's Defence,* and *Some Remarks upon Mr. Collier's Defence of
his View.*

3

Collier had dared to attack Dryden; had dared to call in question
the morality of his plays; had dared to censure certain literary principles of the "Father of our Modern Drama."[33] He had dared to attack
him,—not once but many times throughout the *Short View,* and to
attack caustically. Those who were acquainted with Dryden, those who
remembered his controversies with Howard, with Shadwell, and with
Shaftesbury expected a sharp reply. More than once Dryden had used

---

[32] *Ibid.,* pp. xxiii-xxvi.
[33] This title is applied to Dryden by the author of *A Letter in Answer to some
Queries Relating to Irregularities charged upon the Stage,* p. 21.

his pen to paint an ignominious picture of him who had aroused his
ire; now, offended playwrights and humiliated play-goers, as well as
indifferent readers of the *Short View* had reason to anticipate an answer in the language of *The Medal,* of *MacFlecnoe,* or of *Absalom and
Achitophel.* Months passed; Charles Gildon, Peter Motteux, and
a host of anonymous writers were uniting in protest against Collier.
One or other of the combatants in attempted vindication questioned the
uprightness of his motives in attacking the stage; they charged him
with fallacy in criticism, with error in quotations, and with what is
worse—personal dishonor; but Dryden was silent. This silence chafed
the less gifted of the playwrights and angered those more capable of
satiric rejoinder; it mystified his friends and confused his enemies.
D'Urfey later asserted of it:

> "I could have wished one who is best able, and whose ad-
> mirable Genius and Skill in Poetry would have been remark-
> ably serviceable, had drawn his Pen to defend the Rights of
> the Stage, tho he had own'd the loosenesses of it, . . . but since
> we, the forlorn, are not so happy to have that aid, let my An-
> tagonist, the Reformer, . . . be pleas'd to take the length of my
> Weapon at that sport, . . . "[34]

One anonymous author declared:

> ". . . I shall say no more on this head [i.e., that Collier's ill
> nature was the basis of his censure]; nor shall I follow him in
> his Reflections on *Amphytrion, Don Quixote,* and the *Relapse,*
> but leave him to the handling of the Gentlemen who are more
> nearly concern'd."[35]

Another one said:

> "Where Mr. Collier made so vigorous an attack upon our
> Stages as shook the Foundation; what was the Reason, in so
> desperate a Juncture, . . . that only the *Minor* Poets appear'd?
> . . . Where was the great Master of the Muses, and Father of
> our Modern Drama,"[36]

But Dryden made no effort to disprove the charges of Collier either
against the immodesty or profanity of his plays, or against the licen-

---

[34] *The Campaigners,* Preface, p. 3.
[35] Anonymous, *A Vindication of the Stage,* p. 21.
[36] Anonymous, *A Letter,* p. 21.

tiousness of the times. His reason, says Dr. Johnson, was that "His conscience or his prudence withheld him from the conflict."[37]

Although Dryden did not formally enter the lists he is, because of his "Poetical Epistle to Motteux" in 1698, definitely entitled to a place among the 1698 disputants. In this Poetical Epistle he not only reveals his attitude toward Collier and stage-reform, but he makes himself the target for Ridpath in *The Stage Condemned*,[38] and also for the author of the Preface to the Translation of Bossuet's *Maximes et réflexions*.

In the opening lines of the "Poetical Epistle" Dryden refers to the recent attacks on the stage by Blackmore and Collier, and states that the Muse of poetry employed by Moses, David, and Solomon is to be silenced:

> " 'Tis hard, my Friend, to write in such an Age,
> As damns not only Poets, but the Stage.
> That sacred Art, by Heav'n it self infus'd,
> Which Moses, David, Solomon have us'd
> Is now to be no more."[39]

As he continues his lines to Motteux he hints at Collier's inconsistency in urging eradication of that which is admittedly of benefit in reforming the morals of the nation:

> "Were they content to prune the lavish Vine
> Of straggling Branches, and improve the Wine,
> Who but a mad Man wou'd his Faults defend?
> All wou'd submit; for all but Fools will mend;"[40]

he asserts that the stage-condemners have misinterpreted the glosses of the poets:

> "But, when to common sense they give the Lie,
> And turn distorted Words to Blasphemy, . . . "[41]

---

[37] S. Johnson, *Lives of the Poets*, ed. Chalmers, X, 260.
[38] Ridpath, *The Stage Condemned*, p. 155.
[39] P. Motteux, *Beauty in Distress*, p. xxvii. The above quotation is the one ridiculed in the Preface to the translation of Bossuet's *Maxims*, pp. vii-ix.
[40] *Ibid.*, p. xxvii.
[41] *Ibid.*, p. xxvii.

he expresses his contrition for the scurrility of his writings:

> "What I have loosly, or profanely writ,
> Let them to Fires (their due desert) commit,"[42]

and lastly, he voices his purpose of amendment:

> "But let us first reform: and then so live
> That we may teach our Teachers to forgive."[43]

Mr. Saintsbury considers this epistle a reply to Collier:

> "The preliminary and more important part of the verses
> regards Jeremy Collier's violent attack upon the dramatic
> authors of the stage for immorality and indecency. To this
> charge, our author [Dryden] on this as on other occasions,
> seems to plead guilty while he deprecates the virulence, and
> sometimes unfair severity of his adversary."[44]

He points out, besides, that both here and in the prose Dedication
to the *Fables* the reader will find the same grumbling though subdued
acquiescence under the chastisement of the moralist, the poet much re-
sembling an overmatched general who is unwilling to surrender though
he is conscious of his inability to make an effectual resistance.[44a]

4

A very interesting anonymous pamphlet published in the early
weeks of the controversy is *A Letter to A. H. Esq.; Concerning the
Stage.*[45] Judging from the tone of the letter we are safe in inferring
that the author was well versed in the progress of the controversy, was
thoroughly acquainted with all the arguments which Collier had advanced in the *Short View,* and was personally known to the wits. He
resents the attack on the stage:

> "But what can Mr. *Collier* mean by exposing the Stage so? He
> would not surely have it silenc'd: That would be a little too
> barbarous, and too much like Cant to be entertain'd by Men
> of Thought or Ingenuity."[46]

---

[42] *Ibid.,* p. xxvii.
[43] *Ibid.,* p. xxvii.
[44] J. Dryden, *Works,* ed. Scott and Saintsbury, XI, 65-66.
[44a] *Ibid.,* p. 66.
[45] 22 pages; printed for A. Baldwin. As was mentioned previously, the work
was probably published early in May. It is not mentioned by Halkett and
Laing, nor are the initials identified by Cushing.
[46] Anonymous: *A Letter to A. H.,* p. 1.

He argues in defence of a regulated stage and declares that the looseness of the times is not to be laid at the door of the play-house. He
takes up significant arguments of Collier and answers each, and in
numerous instances we note that he champions Dryden but questions
the literary ability of D'Urfey as well as the morality of his plays.[47]

In his reply to the argument that the clergy are abused by the poets
the author proves his reverence for such men as Stillingfleet, Tillotson,
and Burnet, and justifies Vanbrugh for showing the clergy in caricature
upon the stage:

> "Who can believe, that when Mr. Vanbroug disguises a Parson,
> that he thought of these Men, or any who lives soberly, and
> makes Religion their Business, and at the same time, don't make
> it inconsistent with good Manners?"[48]

He gives repeatedly his opinion of such critical principles as the nature
of comedy and tragedy and the purpose of plays and he volubly discusses the lawfulness of attending plays for the purpose of diversion.[49]
It is here that his arguments bespeak recent study of Caffaro's letter and
agreement with the Theatin.

5

The anonymous twenty-nine page letter replying to Mr. Collier's
View of the Profaneness and Immorality of the Stage has a threefold
challenge for the interest of every student of the Collier Controversy:
first of all the subject matter is interesting; secondly, the occasional
echo of the Caffaro letter to Boursault demands attention, and lastly—
and I might say in greatest measure—the question of its authorship is
important. I shall treat, first, of its subject matter especially in its relationship to the *Short View.*

A Vindication of the Stage, printed about May 17, 1698[1] was occasioned by the gift from some unidentified friend of "Mr. Collier's
Book against the Stage," while the author was visiting in Staffordshire.
In his opening paragraph the Vindicator gives his reasons for writing
his treatise concerning the usefulness of dramatic representations:
(1) to prove his gratitude for the gift of the *Short View;* and (2) to

---

[47] *Ibid.,* p. 1; p. 2; p. 9; p. 20.
[48] *Ibid.,* p. 8.
[49] *Ibid.,* p. 15; p. 16; p. 18.

[1] *The Post-Man,* May 17.

encourage his friend to remember him across the miles. Having acquitted himself thus of his personal obligations he proceeds to jot down "some Thoughts as they occurr'd on a slight perusal of it [the *Short View*]"[2] and at the same time he promises to send these thoughts better digested with, perhaps, some further remarks on Collier if his visit to Staffordshire is prolonged.

His first thrust is at Collier who, he says, has employed abundance of rhetoric in the cause and who has expended great pains to show his knowledge of the *Greek* and *Latin* poets. He hints that the reward— 50 pounds—was of greater influence in evoking the pamphlet than "the stab he suppos'd he shou'd give to Vice and Debauchery."[3] He believes that the flashy display of Collier's learning is likely to influence heedless and unobserving readers; he cannot agree, however, that there is much strength in his arguments and to prove it he states his determination to refute them despite the disadvantages under which he labors of having an indifferent memory and none of the plays which Collier so severely condemns.[4] He is undecided whether or not plays have any purpose but is inclined to the opinion that the end of comedies is "to divert the Audience, and relieve the Mind Fatiegu'd with the business of the foregoing part of the day." He states that when he goes to a play his only motive for so doing is to unbend his thoughts from all manner of business, so that he may raise again his wearied spirits and fit them for the affairs of the next day.[5] After enumerating Collier's four censures against modern play-wrights the Vindicator begins with the first charge, namely, immodesty. He quotes Sir Philip Sidney and Cicero to prove that "Comedy is an imitation of life" and that inasmuch as it is, we must expect to see the common errors of life depicted.[6] He points out that if Collier really believed what he states about women's modesty when he said that "it is wrought in the Mechanism of the Body . . . The Enemy no sooner approaches, but the Blood rises in Opposition . . ." then he should have considered it superfluous to point out to them the danger in plays as their native

---

[2] Anonymous, *A Vindication of the Stage*, p. 3.
[3] *Ibid.*, p. 4.
[4] *Ibid.*, p. 4.
[5] *Ibid.*, p. 4.
[6] *Ibid.*, p. 5.

modesty would have discovered it.[7] He likewise asserts that Collier
should have followed his own advice and refused to bring to light
that which was well hidden, especially since the divulging of it may—
to use Collier's own words—"probably raise those Passions, which can
neither be discharg'd without trouble, nor satisfi'd without a Crime."[8]

The Vindicator selects two examples, Euripides and Seneca, and
proves from them that modesty was less esteemed among the Ancients
than it is among the Moderns.[9] He calls attention to the fact that the
Romans permitted the scandalous *Ludi Florales,* and wittily asks that if
the Ancients were not guilty of immodesty why should Plato have banished from his Commonwealth those guilty of it.[10] Even Plato, he asserts,
was not exempt from the sin; and as for the Ancients having no lewd
songs in their plays, that argument, he affirms, is without foundation
for in all probability the ancient dramatic poets never meddled with
the musical entertainment, inasmuch as either the

> "Masters of Musick were so much Poets as to make their own
> Words, or some others of an Inferior Class were hired to the
> purpose."[11]

Under the charges of "Profaneness" the Vindicator advances two
arguments which he places under the caption of "Oaths and Abuse of
the Scriptures." That our stage-poets are guilty of oaths, he tells us,
need not to be proved inasmuch as Collier charges the offence but does
not substantiate the charge.[12] That our stage-poets abuse Scripture, the
Vindicator admits, but he declares that it is impossible for them to do
otherwise because the recent translations of the Bible have made certain expressions current literature and because Scripture contains such
varied matter, is so admirably adapted to all estates and conditions of
life, and contains all the different phrases that the English tongue meets
with, that if the poets are to avoid all phrases that savour of Scripture
a new alphabet and a new language will have to be contrived for
them.[13] The Vindicator next assembles the Ancients who had appeared
in Collier's coterie and shows how they used their Religion. From the

---

[7] *Ibid.,* p. 6.
[8] *Ibid.,* p. 7.
[9] *Ibid.,* p. 8.
[10] *Ibid.,* p. 9.
[11] *Ibid.,* p. 10.
[12] *Ibid.,* p. 12.
[13] *Ibid.,* p. 13.

Greeks, he selects Aristophanes, Aeschylus, Euripides, Sophocles, and Homer; from the Latins, Plautus, Terence, and Seneca, and he compels each of them to prove that the Moderns are not more guilty than their predecessors.[14]

In refutation of Collier's chapter on the modern stage-poets' abuse of the clergy, the author of *A Vindication* asserts that in no country will the deep respect for the clergy be found to have greater proportions than in England.[15] He cites instances from France, Holland, Italy, Spain, and Poland to prove that England has the best ministry in the world,[16] and he adopts the ungallant method of censuring Collier's conscientious objections to taking the oath of allegiance as evidence that

> "Mr. Collier himself, and all others of his Principles, are more bitter and sharp Invectives against his Order, by their refractory and Obstinate Separation from the Greatest and most Pious part of their Brethren, than any can be writ by the most Atheistical Pen."[17]

The fourth charge which the Vindicator takes up is that of "Immorality," and here he throws upon the clergy the blame for bad plays. He reasons thus:

> "If delight be the chief end of comedy, it becomes necessary for the stage-poet to study the tastes of his audience in order to contribute to his delight. Now, if the audience is delighted with immoral plays, it is evident that their tastes are vitiated. Inasmuch as it is the duty of the clergy to instruct the people in morality, it follows that the clergy must be to blame if the people's tastes are vicious, and if their manners are immoral;[18]

and in the conclusion of *A Vindication* the author discusses the excellences of the Moderns as contrasted with the Ancients, and gives a defence of plays.

That the author of *A Vindication of the Stage* has perused the arguments in the letter of Father Caffaro, is evident in several places.[19]

---

[14] *Ibid.*, p. 16.
[15] *Ibid.*, p. 17.
[16] *Ibid.*, pp. 17-18.
[17] *Ibid.*, pp. 18-19.
[18] *Ibid.*, p. 20.
[19] See pp. 64-67 for details of the Caffaro Controversy.

Caffaro, it will be observed, relying on his guide, St. Thomas, had asserted:

> "a man being fatigu'd by the serious actions of Life, has need of refreshments;" and again, "'tis the part of a Wise Man, sometimes to unbend his Mind which is too intent upon his Business."[20]

The Vindicator, using almost the same terms, states that he is not yet convinced that the business of plays is "to relieve the Mind Fatiegu'd with the business of the foregoing part of the day," and declares that his own purpose in going to the theatre is "to unbend his thoughts from all manner of business."[21]

To bring further emphasis to bear upon his statements, the Vindicator declares that not only does he hold these opinions but that they are entertained by "several very famous and Learned Persons."[22]

Let me point out, likewise, that the author of *The Vindication* in weighing the evidence of the Fathers adopts the view which is the vein of Caffaro's letter, that is, that the Fathers' invectives were pronounced against the excesses of the Ancients and that inasmuch as the ancient theatre is not on a par with the modern, their invectives are not applicable to modern drama.[23] In his attempt further to prove the case of the ancient and modern theatres not parallel, the Vindicator quotes in proof of the same point the identical passages which Caffaro had given.[24] Both the Vindicator and Caffaro state that St. Cyprian's invectives were hurled against "the idolatrous Heathen Shows," and they both refer to the Third Council of Cathage to prove their statement.

The third point of interest in the study of *A Vindication of the Stage* is the question of its authorship. Two authors have been suggested—Wycherley and Gildon. Mr. Gosse suggests Wycherley as the author. He says:

> "I have little hesitation in attributing it to Wycherley. It is the freshest and most vivacious of all the replies to Collier, although not the most weighty."[25]

---

[20] P. Motteux, *Beauty in Distress*, Preface, p. xi.
[21] Anonymous, *A Vindication of the Stage*, p. 4.
[22] *Ibid.*, p. 5.
[23] P. Motteux, *Beauty in Distress*, Preface, pp. xii ff; Anonymous, *A Vindication of the Stage*, pp. 21 ff.
[24] P. Motteux, *op. cit.*, p. x; p. xiii; Anonymous, *A Vindication of the Stage*, p. 23; p. 22.
[25] Edmund Gosse, *Life of Congreve*, p. 113.

Besides, he believes that Wycherley's living near to Staffordshire (a village mentioned in the *Vindication*) as well as his defending Congreve and no one else, gives the clue to Wycherley's authorship.

Mr. Taylor, however, in his bibliography to the stage controversy, refutes Sir Edmund Gosse's theory that Wycherley wrote the *Vindication* by calling attention to a question inserted in the second edition of Collier's *Dissuasive*. The question is:

> "Where was the mighty Wycherley? . . . A Wit certainly of the first Magnitude; and with so great a fund of sense, that besides his contributions to the Stage's Diversion, he could not want a stock for its Defence, even when the common Bank of Wit fail'd."[26]

He argues further for the authorship of Gildon:

> "The pamphlet is probably by Gildon, who had said he would write a vindication of the stage. His other writings show the same wit and vivacity which we find in this book, and there is no other record of his promised vindication."[27]

There is record also that Mr. Robert Stewart has noted the silence of Wycherley. He asks, "What did Wycherley publish on the Subject?"[28]

Before accepting or refusing to accept either William Wycherley or Charles Gildon as the author of *A Vindication of the Stage* it is necessary to recall several pertinent facts. It will be remembered that in the Preface to *Phaeton* Gildon gives his intentions regarding the Vindication he is to publish. In the first place, he emphatically states the time when the *Vindication* will be published: "The coming summer" will see the completed work.[29] Next, he repeatedly refers to his lack of time and space to enter into detail: "I have no room in this Place [the Preface to *Phaeton*] to shew all the abuses, and Absurdities this Author is guilty of."[30] And again, "I have not room here . . . but I do not doubt in my answer to prove . . . "[31] and "I have neither Room nor Leisure now to examine his Charge on the Stage, . . . But of this

---

[26] J. Collier, *Dissuasive from the Play House; . . . To which is added A Letter written by another Hand;* p. 22.
[27] D. Crane Taylor, *William Congreve,* pp. 123-4.
[28] *Notes and Queries,* 3rd. S., IV, 435.
[29] Charles Gildon, *Phaeton,* Preface, p. ix.
[30] *Ibid.,* p. ix.
[31] *Ibid.,* p. xi.

more hereafter."[32] Because of these statements the reader expects Gildon to write his treatise when under less pressure and to give due consideration to each item that he censured in the *Short View;* he expects him, moreover, to fulfill his promise of vindicating the stage against Mr. Prynne and "The Younger Histrio-Mastix."[33] But the *Vindication* in question does not mention Mr. Prynne, neither does it refer to Collier by the above title.

Now, let us glance at the *Vindication* to see how closely it conforms to the promises which Gildon had made in its behalf and to discover whether it coincides with the literary opinions which Gildon is known to have held. In the first place, the *Vindication* is anonymous. Why should Gildon conceal his identity when three weeks before he had made no secret of his intention to write against Collier? In the second place, the *Vindication* appeared not during the summer of 1698 as Gildon had repeatedly promised it would appear, but on May 17th.[34] Moreover, Gildon had given his reader occasion to expect a lengthy treatise refuting all of Mr. Collier's abuses and absurdities. The anonymous *Vindication* in reply to Collier's 288-page *Short View* is a "Letter" of a little over twenty-eight pages. Thirdly, Gildon had also given the reader to expect in the summer's publication the final pronouncement of his views on the *Short View*. However, the anonymous author of *A Vindication* rather evasively states:

> "If I stay longer here, I may send you these thoughts better digested, or some farther Remarks on the same Author."[35]

and later he emphasizes the tentativeness of his vindication by stating: "There are several other places may be produc'd, which he has either forgot or skip'd over; I shall instance in two only *at present*."[36] Later on we read much to the same purpose, "Thus have I done, what *my haste,* and the *disadvantages I labour under,* will permit on this Head, . . . *but more of this hereafter.*"[37] There is besides, in the *Vindication* a statement quite the reverse of that which we should expect from one

---

[32] *Ibid.,* p. xi.
[33] *Ibid.,* p. xi.
[34] *The Post-Man,* May 17, 1698.
[35] Anonymous, *A Vindication of the Stage,* p. 4.
[36] *Ibid.,* p. 7. (italics mine).
[37] *Ibid.,* p. 11. (italics mine).

who promised to attack *all* the abuses and absurdities of his opponent
and to defend the poets against his foul dealing:

> "But I shall say no more on this Head; nor shall I follow him
> [Collier] in his Reflections on *Amphytrion, Don Quixot,* and
> the *Relapse* but leave him to the handling of the Gentlemen
> who are more nearly concern'd,"[38]

—a proof that the author of *A Vindication* had no thought either of
refuting all of Collier's abuses or of defending the poets against his
attacks.

Further evidence that Gildon did not write *A Vindication* is found
in the fact that the author sends to his friend the thoughts on the
Short View as they occurred to him upon *a slight perusal* of the work.
The intentions which Gildon had mentioned in his Preface to *Phaeton*
are not referred to. Now, it seems inconsistent that Gildon who had
so pompously stated his determination to refute *all* of Collier's abuses
and absurdities should assert that he gave the *Short View* no more than
a slight perusal.

An argument which bears much weight on the subject lies in the
diversity of critical opinions held by Gildon and by the author of the
Vindication. If Gildon wrote the *Vindication of the Stage* why should
he in less than three weeks' time shift ground so evidently and so
emphatically on the opinions which he held? To illustrate: in the
Preface to *Phaeton* published about April 30, 1698, Gildon gives several opinions regarding the Ancients and Moderns, and in each he
emphatically prefers the Ancients whereas the author of *A Vindication* distinctly prefers the Moderns. Note the following:

> "The Moderns . . . generally spin out theirs [plays] to an un-
> reasonable extent, by adding *Under-plots* and several *Persons,*
> no way necessary to their Design which was admirably avoided
> by the Ancients."[39]

He says again:

> "The Ancients introduced no more *Characters* than were in-
> despensably necessary to *One compleat Design.* And in this I
> endeavour'd, here to imitate them;[40]

---

[38] *Ibid.,* p. 21.
[39] C. Gildon, *Phaeton,* Preface, p. vi.
[40] *Ibid.,* p. vi.

and in exculpating the great men of the English Nation for choosing "Tumult" to divert the audience he says:

> "I'm confident those who have so much excell'd others in this, wou'd have excell'd themselves in the more *Natural Way of the Ancients.*"[41]

His preference for the Ancients in the following passages is note-worthy:

> "The Antients differ'd from the *Moderns,* in the choice of their *Subject.* We are for making the scene of our Plays, the Field of Battle; . . . etc. The *Ancients* never, as I can remember, chose such noisy Opportunities of perverting the End they propos'd in their Tragedies, *viz.,* the moving *Terror* and Compassion, which can never be touch'd, where such tumultuary objects come in View,"[42]

and again

> "The *Ancients* differed from our Poets in their *Incidents.* We seek after various, and surprising Turns in the Fortune of the Persons introduc'd which seldom or never happen in Common Life (the just Object of a Poet) and so very often lose all *PROBABILITY,* in what we *falsely* esteen *ADMIRABLE.*"[43]

Now, a comparison of these opinions with those of the author of *A Vindication* published shortly after proves that on the same topics —plot, characters, subject, and incidents—the author emphatically prefers the Moderns. He says "Our Modern Poets, and especially the *English,* have excell'd all the Ancients in Theatrical Performances."[44] and again

> "The plots of the Ancients were for the most part single, without any turns or admirable surprises to delight or refresh the Audience.[45]

Concerning characters in the plays of the Ancients he remarks:

> "Their [The Ancients'] *Characters* had no Variety of Humour with which our English Stage so excellently abounds; when you

---

[41] *Ibid.,* p. vi.
[42] *Ibid.,* p. vi.
[43] *Ibid.,* p. vi. Gildon's critical opinions are also very well given in his scholarly work: "Essay on the Art, Rise and Progress of the Stage in Greece, Rome and England" prefixed to Vol. VII of *The Works of Mr. William Shakespeare* printed for E. Curll in 1710, pp. i-lxvii.
[44] Anonymous, *A Vindication of the Stage,* p. 23.
[45] *Ibid.,* p. 24.

see one or two of their Plays, you see all the different Humours of their Theatres,"[46]

and

"With us [the Moderns] you meet with Variety, you find something always New on our Theatres. *This one thing will carry us far beyond any of the Ancients.*"[47]

In the following passages his regard for the Moderns is unmistakable:

"When any of our Poets have chose the *Subjects* of the Ancients . . . they have far surpassed them; better Modell'd the Plot, and they have contrived the *Incidents* more surprising and admirable;[48]

and

"They [the Moderns] have worked their *thoughts* to a greater Elegancy, and made the Turns more Nice, Easie, and Sublime, and their Characters, which were often Irregular, more Just and Natural."[49]

Striking as is this evidence against Gildon's authorship of *A Vindication of the Stage* there is a more overwhelming evidence against it in the fact that in 1699 Gildon published his edition of Langbaine's *Lives and Characters of the English Dramatick Poets*,[50] with an account of their plays. Now, as Langbaine had died in 1692 the collecting of the material which was written between 1692-9 must have been either Gildon's work or that of one who worked under Gildon's direction, and an analysis of it shows that there is comprehensive and detailed treatment given to the plays of Congreve, D'Urfey, Dryden, Vanbrugh. Congreve's *The Old Batchelour* acted in 1693, *The Double Dealer* acted in 1694, *Love for Love*, 1695, and *The Mourning Bride*, 1697, are discussed fully.[51] D'Urfey's *Don Quixote* acted in 1694 is dis-

---

[46] *Ibid.*, p. 24.
[47] *Ibid.*, p. 24.
[48] *Ibid.*, p. 24.
[49] *Ibid.*, p. 24.
[50] *D.N.B.*, VII, 1226, (1908 Edition). The title as it appears on the title-page in Gildon's edition is, *The Lives and Characters of the English Dramatick Poets. Also An Exact Account of all the Plays that were ever yet Printed in the English Tongue; their Double Titles, the Places where Acted, the Dates when Printed,. and the Persons to whom Dedicated; with Remarks and Observations on most of the said Plays. First begun by Mr. Langbaine, improv'd and continued down to this time by a Careful Hand.*
[51] G. Langbaine, *The Lives and Characters of the English Dramatick Poets*, pp. 21-25.

cussed;[52] Captain Van Brug's (Vanbrugh's) *The Provoked Wife* acted in 1697 and *The Relapse* also acted in 1697, are considered.[53] Moreover, of the seventeen works of Dryden (nine plays and eight critical pieces) of which Collier makes mention, Gildon omits none in his review of that author's work.[54]

It might be objected that the works of Dryden discussed in the *Lives* and published before Langbaine's death were not Gildon's work; however, Gildon's own words identify him as the reviewer of Dryden's plays in the 1699 edition of the *Lives*:

> "I shall give some instances of his playing the Plagiary, omitting all those scurrilous and Digressory Reflections with which Mr. Langbain has bespatter'd him, and through which indeed runs all along a great evidence of private and ungenerous Malice, brought in, tho' nothing to the Business before him."[55]

Now, it seems highly improbable that Gildon to whom it was second nature not only to review the plays of the Moderns but to trace their plagiarisms, should remark

> "I cannot so much as procure those plays which he [Collier] so severely condemns,"[56]

when from his own statement in the Preface to *The Lives of the Poets* we learn that he did have the plays on hand and that he gave to them careful thought. Note, for example, the following:

> "I have lately read Mr. Congreve's *Love for Love* over, and am of Opinion, . . . "[57]

From Gildon himself, then, we learn that he had on hand and had lately read at least one of the works of Congreve, and that he had recently analyzed the works of the poets whom Collier had attacked. In accordance with this evidence it is hard to believe that Gildon deliberately deceived his reader and still harder to discover his motive for practicing such deception.

---

[52] *Ibid.*, p. 50.
[53] *Ibid.*, pp. 143-5.
[54] *Ibid.*, pp. 40-47.
[55] *Ibid.*, p. 40.
[56] Anonymous, *A Vindication*, p. 4.
[57] Langbaine, G., *op. cit.*, Preface, p. ii. Recall that this work was published in 1699, and *A Vindication of the Stage*, 1698.

6

Meriton's *Immorality, Debauchery, and Profaneness Exposed to the Reproof of Scripture,* is mentioned by Mr. Taylor in his *William Congreve,* page 240. He states that he found the announcement of it in the *Post-Man* for May 17-19. Although there is no record of it either in the *Term Catalogues* or in the *Catalogue of the British Museum,* there is a copy of it in the British Museum.

7

Taking his stand with Collier against the allies of the stage, the author of *The Occasional Paper IX* in a twenty-three page letter, not only defends the *Short View* but expresses his opinions on the dangers lurking in the play-house. The pamphlet challenges the interest of the student of the Collier Stage-Controversy both as regards authorship, its relationship to the Caffaro letter, and its connection with the stage-controversy.

First, regarding authorship. *The Occasional Paper*[58] (I-IX inclusive) has been ascribed to Richard Willis, Bishop of Winchester, both by Halkett and Laing, and by Stonehill, Block and Stonehill.[59] On the other hand, Allibone ascribes to Richard Willis only eight of the nine parts,[60] and the *D.N.B.* fails to list any issue of *The Occasional Paper* among Willis' works.[61]

Besides the above sources of information concerning the *Occasional Paper Number IX,* we have valuable biographical data concerning Willis from Thomas Hearne of whose literary works Bentley said "The very dust of his writings is gold." Hearne remarks that the Richard

---

[58] Anonymous, *The Occasional Paper: Number IX. Containing some Considerations about the Danger of going to Plays, In a Letter to a Friend,* was printed for M. Wotton, at the Three Daggers in Fleet-Street, 1698. Mr. D. C. Taylor lists this work as first appearing May 21, 1698. Besides, he lists for Feb. 17, 1704, a pamphlet entitled *Some Considerations about the Danger of going to Plays* stating that the date is on the MS. title page. I am of the opinion that this is the second edition of the original *Occasional Paper Number IX* inasmuch as there was a second edition of it published in 1704. Mr. Krutch also mentions the reprint in 1704 of *Some Considerations about the Danger of going to Plays* in *The Occasional Paper Number IX* published in 1698.

[59] *A Dictionary of Anonymous and Pseudonymous Literature IV,* 230; *Anonyma and Pseudonyma,* III, 2016.

[60] *Critical Dictionary of English Literature,* III, 2758.

[61] *D.N.B.,* XXI, 491-2.

Willis who died at Chelsea on August 9, 1734, was Lord Bishop of Winchester and one of the Commissioners for the building of fifty new churches; he states moreover

"The said Willis was (as I have heard) first of Wadham College. Thence he was elected fellow of *All Souls* College, as a member of which he took the Degree of M.A. by Diploma, March 15, 1694, he being then (I think) chaplain somewhere abroad to the Prince of Orange, commonly called King William III, and oftentimes Old Glorious. He never took the Degree of Dr. at Oxford, perhaps he might at Lambeth, being commonly called Dr. Willis. He was a man of little or no learning. Nor had he any other true merits, that I know of, worthy of the Lawn Sleeves. He hath published one or more Sermons."[62]

It is rather difficult to reconcile Hearne's statement concerning Willis' dearth of literary ability with that of Allibone unless we take into consideration the political creeds of Hearne and Willis, and even then it is hard to accuse the honest character of Hearne with depreciating Willis. Willis was a staunch adherent of William III having accompanied him in 1694 to Holland. Later as a loyal Whig in the reign of George I he was made bishop of Gloucester in 1714, and in consequence of a sermon "The Way to Stable and Quiet Times" preached before the King, was rewarded with the commission of which Hearne speaks.[63] Hearne, on the contrary, in 1731—three years before the death of Willis—had become a Non-Juror, and, in consequence, entertained opposite political opinions from Willis, but yet he was impartial in his comments on the non-juring movement, for according to Broxap we learn

"Hearne's comments on the progress of the movement as contained in his *Remarks,* etc., make curious reading. They are obviously written by one who was far removed from the activities of the London Non-Jurors and they are on that account more valuable as affording information from the point of view of one who was to a large extent a 'looker on'."[64]

In the light of this evidence the authorship of *The Occasional Paper* seems uncertain. In order to arrive at some definite conclusion

[62] Thomas Hearne, *Remarks and Collections,* IX, 367-8.
[63] *D.N.B.,* XXI, 491-2.
[64] Henry Broxap, *The Later Non-Jurors,* p. 317.

regarding it, it is necessary to examine minutely the contents of this
pamphlet. It is this minute examination which brings to light four
facts. First, there is a similarity of argument in *The Occasional Paper:
Number IX* with the arguments set forth in the *Short View* published
just a short time before; second, there is an occasional similarity of
style in it as compared with Collier's anti-stage works; third, there is
a similarity in allusions and epithets; and lastly, there is an awareness
of the author to criticisms that had been made of the *Short View* and
a definite attempt to answer them.

The similarity of argument in *The Occasional Paper* and in the
Short View is shown in the fact that both authors believe that the
theatre is a nursery of vice and that in consequence it should not be
frequented by Christians;[65] both regard frequenting the play-house as
opposed to the vows which a Christian has pronounced at Baptism;[66]
both consider the stage a factor in ridiculing devotion, in moving the
passions, and in vaunting lewdness over religion and virtue;[67] both
decry the disrespect of God and of earthly authority that it engen-
ders;[68] both quote to the same purpose St. Paul's proverb "Evil Communications corrupt good manners;[69] both refer to the influence of
plays on young people and bewail the poet's rewarding of vice in the
characters of the players;[70] both refer to the need which a nation has
for its priesthood,[71] and both speak with reverence of marriage, and
decry the loose morals which are tending to destroy the sanctity of
the marriage-bond.[72]

The second point of similarity between *The Occasional Paper* and
A Short View is that of style. First, there are found in *The Occasional
Paper* the typical Collier sentences introduced with "But": "But I
doubt we never began . . . " (p. 6) ; "But for those who are satisfied
of this . . . " (p. 11) ; "But tho' these shou'd be well enough armed

---

[65] Anonymous, *The Occasional Paper*, p. 5; *A Short View*, pp. 280-5.
[66] *The Occasional Paper*; p. 11. *A Short View*, p. 285.
[67] *The Occasional Paper*, pp. 12-13; *A Short View*, Chap. II; Chap. III.
[68] *The Occasional Paper*, pp. 9-10; p. 12. *A Short View*, Chap. II; p. 175; p.
273.
[69] *The Occasional Paper*, p. 19. *A Short View*, p. 181.
[70] *The Occasional Paper*, p. 10. *A Short View*, p. 5; p. 2. Collier's argument
in the *Short View* was that the poet made his characters libertines and rewarded them with a fortune at the end of the play.
[71] *The Occasional Paper*, p. 17; *A Short View*, Chapter III.
[72] *The Occasional Paper*, p. 10; *A Short View*, Chapter I; Chapter III, Chapter
V.

. . . " (p. 21). Compare these with similar examples found in the *Short View*: "But it may be said the Freedoms of Distraction go for nothing, . . ." (p. 10) ; "But then such People ought to be kept in dark Rooms, . . . " (p. 10) ; "But after all the Modern *Stage* seems to depend upon this Expedient; . . ." (p. 10) ; "But rather than not be Vitious, . . ." (P. 12) ; "but of this, more hereafter." (p. 12).

In the second place we note in *The Occasional Paper* the use of the consecutive staccato questions so typical of the Collier pamphlets:

> "For are then all Diversions alike? And can there be none without such follies, as no Man in his sense wou'd endure? Must all easie Conversation be lost, unless Men have leave to be loose and profane? And can there be no coming together of Strangers or Friends, but some naked Vice must dance and be praised, or some Virtue made a Sacrifice of, to fill up the Feast?[73]

Scores of similar examples could be cited from *A Short View* but I shall illustrate by giving six from the fourteen which occur on pages 138-139.

> "but the Clergy mismanage sometime, . . . What then? Are the *Poets* their *Ordinaries?* Is the Pulpit under the Discipline of the *Stage?* And are those fit to correct the Church, that are not fit to come into it? What makes them fly out upon the *Function;* and rail by wholesale? Is the Priesthood a crime . . . ?"

Besides, *The Occasional Paper* gives examples of a peculiar type of balanced sentence which Collier frequently used in his anti-stage works. Note the following:

"No *Greatness* like a Thorough *Revenge,* nor any *Spirit* so mean as that which forgives, . . . " (p. 10) ; and again, "Their *Faith* wavers upon many Surprises, their *Hopes* languish, and their Fervour decays, . . . " (p. 12) ; and "Their *Souls* one wou'd Think shou'd be vex'd at such daring *Impieties,* and their *Spirits* stirr'd in them to see such Vices Adored; to find *Lewdness* vaunting it over Religion and Virtue, . . . " (p. 12), and compare these with examples taken from the *Short View*: "They laugh at *Pedantry* and teach *Atheism,* cure a Pimple and gives the Plague," (p.287) ; and again, "Innocence is often owing to Fear, and Appetite is kept under by Shame," (p. 14).

---

[73] Anonymous, *The Occasional Paper IX,* pp. 21-2.

"To go to Heaven in jest is the way to go to Hell in earnest." (p. 62.)

A minute examination of the two works proves that both authors use similar epithets and both make identical allusions. First, both place emphasis on Congreve's quotation from *The Old Batchelour*, "Eternity was in that Moment." [74] Second, the comparisons and allusions made so frequently by Collier in his anti-stage works are found in this pamphlet. For example, the comparison of the play-house to a place of corruption; a contagious place; a seat of pestilence, a place of pollution, poison food;[75] the association of "burlesque" with religion; e.g., "Burlesquing the Old and New Testament;"[76] "burlesquing the attributes," "burlesquing the Scriptures," "burlesquing the four Gospels,"[77] "burlesquing an absurd religion."[78] Then there are the references to the blood "rising to defy an indecency," and to Nature "making the ferment of the Blood for such occasions"—both of which appear consistently throughout the stage-pamphlets *known* to be Collier's and in *The Occasional Paper*.[79] We find, too, that there is in *The Occasional Paper* a vocabulary similar to that in Collier's other attacks on "smut," "profaneness," "blasphemy," "lewdness" and "the Nursery of the play-house."

The fourth evidence as to authorship of *The Occasional Paper IX* is the awareness of the author to criticisms that had been passed upon the *Short View* and the spirited attempt to correct those defects in *The Occasional Paper*. One of the criticisms made of the *Short View* was Collier's frequent references to the Greeks and Latins.[80] The author designs to make up for this criticism by avoiding the fault in *The Occasional Paper*:

"But for as much as the thread of that serious Design [the Short View] may seem broken too often with Observations

---

[74] William Congreve, *The Old Batchelour*, p. 31. Collier's stinging reply occurs in the *Short View*, p. 63, and the author of *The Occasional Paper* refers to it in much the same vein, p. 12.

[75] Anonymous, *The Occasional Paper*, p. 14; p. 16; p. 18; p. 22; etc.; J. Collier, *Short View*, pp. 34-35; *Dissuasive from the Play-House*, p. 7; p. 8; pp. 10-11; *A Farther Vindication*, p. 26; p. 31, etc.

[76] J. Collier, *Dissuasive from the Play-House*, p. 6.

[77] J. Collier, *A Short View*, p. 182; p. 286; J. Collier, *A Farther Vindication*, p. 21.

[78] Anonymous, *The Occasional Paper*, p. 20.

[79] *The Occasional Paper*, p. 14; J. Collier, *Short View*, p. 11; *Defence*, pp. 38-39.

[80] Anonymous, *A Vindication of the Stage*, p. 4.

of Learning, and Reflections of Wit, to be closely follow'd by those who are either not used to the one, or too fond of the other; the same good End may perhaps be helped forward a little, by setting this matter in a less interrupted Light, and a Simpler View."[81]

Note that the author here desires to advance the *same good end* which prompted the writing of the *Short View* and that he desires to advance it by setting the *same matter* in a less interrupted light. Wherefore, we can infer that he designed to approach those people who either *could* not or *would* not understand the first discourse on the immorality and profaneness of the stage. Moreover, the remark concerning "Observations of Learning" to which the author of *The Occasional Paper* referred relates very likely to the following quotation in which the *Vindication of the Stage* gives its author's opinion of Collier's classical learning:

> "Mr. Collier has employ'd abundance of Rhetorick in his Cause, he has made use of all his Judgment in digesting his Matter, and shew'd his great Reading in his Quotations from the Greek and Latine Poets, and the Ancient Fathers; and has given them so bright and dazling a lustre . . . "[82]

One of the interesting features concerning *The Occasional Paper* is that in four statements the author proves himself well informed on certain phases of the Caffaro-Bossuet argument about the lawfulness of attending plays, and that he adopts the arguments of Bossuet as opposed to those of Caffaro. He says "I have always found you doubting the *Lawfulness* at least the Expedience of going to Plays, as they are now acted amongst us;[83] He refers to Tertullian's argument that the Scriptures do not expressly forbid assisting at plays, as well as to St. Cyprian's rule that reason is to be used where the Scriptures are silent:

> " . . . good Christians certainly cannot have the much easier thoughts of such freedoms as these, for not finding them in so

---

[81] Anonymous, *The Occasional Paper*, p. 4. That Collier was in earnest about attacking the stage has been previously mentioned; that a restatement of some of his censures against it might bear fruit must have suggested itself to his mind.

[82] Anonymous, *A Vindication of the Stage*, p. 4.

[83] *Ibid.*, p. 4. Caffaro had argued that plays as they were then acted in France were not, as a general thing, vicious. *Beauty in Distress*, Preface, xxii.

many words expressly forbid. Such as these will consider the
end and design of the Gospel, . . . "[84]

He agrees with the Fathers who had declaimed against the *excesses*
of the drama and who had forbidden the Christians' attending plays:

" . . . We have places enough to show them of what importance
it is, to withdraw from those that walk as very disorderly, as
wou'd not have been in the times of a livelier Faith, allowed
the outward Communion of Saints."[85]

The author disagrees with Caffaro in permitting Christians the
play-house and joins with Bossuet, a Casuist, who forbade even the
modester plays:

"And this instance is so far from being the worse for coming
from France, that it is a great deal the more fit to be urged
in the present debate. For if, in a Country disposed to a lighter
Temper and Air, where the Church has greater Corruption, and
the Theater fewer, there can yet be whole Bodies of Casuists
found, disallowing the sight of their *Modester* Plays; . . . "[86]

The Occasional Paper IX is one of the very early evidences that
the *Short View* had stirred up Collier advocates and had strengthened
popular doubts as to the lawfulness of going to plays:

"And a fresh sense of this [the fear that plays are not coinci-
dent with the faith of the Gospel] I perceive has been given
you by the late *lively Account of the Stage,* . . . "[87]

and it offers reasonable ground to believe that Collier had something
to do with the writing of it. We know that Collier's first attack on ·
the stage was in high favor with William III;[88] we know, too, that

---

[84] *Ibid.,* p. 19. Caffaro had remarked "Tertullian very well observes, "We no
where find that we are as expressly forbidden in Scripture to go to the *Circus*
and *Theatre,* . . . as we are forbid to worship Idols." *Beauty in Distress,* p. x.
He had said, besides, "Let. us . . . endeavour to make use of St. Cyprian's
Rule who says, *That Reason is to be heard where Holy Writ is silent." Ibid.,*
pp. x-xi.

[85] *Ibid.,* pp. 19-20. *Beauty in Distress,* pp. xii-xiii.

[86] *Ibid.,* p. 26. The reference to the Casuists in France who disallowed the seeing of even the more modest plays was no doubt meant for Bossuet whose
Maxims and Reflections, 1694, refuted Caffaro's arguments in favor of plays,
as well as for Leleval, de la Grange, Le Brun, and P. Coustel—all of whom
at this time, published opinions on the subject.

[87] *Ibid.,* p. 4.

[88] C. Cibber, *An Apology,* ed. by Lowe, 1889, I, 275.

Willis was in high favor with the same king, having been at one time his chaplain;[89] hence the supposition is plausible that Willis—either for personal motives or because he was asked to do it—undertook to write in similar vein against the stage. In view of his own not over-competent literary ability,[90] he may have turned to Collier for help. Collier would, no doubt, welcome the opportunity of emphasizing the principles set forth a short time before in the *Short View* and of repairing some of the blunders he had there committed. It is interesting to note after close study of the *Occasional Paper* that a twofold style is obvious. Examples of the style characteristic of Collier occur chiefly in sentences in the Introduction and Conclusion. Hence it is logical to suppose that Collier had something to do with the writing of these and that he offered, besides, frequent suggestions which Willis incorporated in the body of his pamphlet.

8

On May 26, 1698, there was printed for Elizabeth Whitlock and published anonymously a pamphlet of 118 pages, entitled *A Defence of Dramatick Poetry Being a Review of Mr. Collier's View of the Immorality and Profaneness of the Stage*.[91]

---

[89] T. Hearne, *Remarks and Collections*, IX, 367-8.

[90] *Ibid.*, IX, 367-8.

[91] The authorship of this work as well as of the anonymous *A Farther Defence of Dramatic Poetry* published about a month later, has been variously ascribed. The *C.H.E.L.*, VIII, 433, Beljame in *Le Public et Les Hommes*, p. 457, D. C. Taylor in *William Congreve*, p. 241, E. Gosse in *Life of Congreve*, pp. 115-119, W. Hunt in his "Life of Collier" (*D.N.B.*, IV, 802), and A. W. Ward in *A History of English Dramatic Literature*, III, 513, state that Filmer is the author. On the other hand, neither G. Goodwin in his "Life of Filmer" (*D.N.B.*, VI, 1304), Allibone in *A Critical Dictionary*, I, 596, Krutch in *Comedy and Conscience*, p. 269, nor the *Catalogue of the British Museum* gives to Filmer any participation in the Collier Controversy save in his *A Defence of Plays*, 1707. To this latter work Collier replied with *A Farther Vindication*. In the opening paragraph of this work Collier asserts: "Dr. Filmer has *at last* enter'd the Lists, and revived the Quarrel, . . . By taking Horace's Advice of—*Nonumq: prematur in annum*, He has had great leisure for bringing his Thoughts to Review and Recollection. . . . "Both the phrase *at last* and *Nonumq: . . . in annum* are significant, as is obvious. From the statement *at last* we infer that Filmer was not a former participant in the stage controversy, while from the *Nonumq: . . .* we understand that he allowed himself the proverbial nine years for moulding and polishing his thoughts before giving them to the world, and we infer that he wrote no previous *Defence*. Likewise, in the *History of the Works of the Learned* we find a review of *A Defence of Plays* as well as copious references to the stage controversy, but no reference to any of Filmer's previous vindi-

The author in the Preface lets a shaft fly at Collier for his non-jurancy:

> "But it had been an infinite higher Glory, both to the Book and the Author, had the Argument been taken up in his Pulpit Reign. Then he would have convinced the World that he put Pen to Paper in the spirit of Zeal and Piety, and not left himself open to that untoward Suspicion, viz. That all this Labour'd Pile of Stage-Reformation is only the Product of Idleness and Abdication. He takes up the whip for the Play-house, as Dionysius the Tyrant did the School-birch, when he had lost the Scepter."[92]

He admits the wit and learning of Collier but believes that the pulpit has been more satirized than the stage; and then, somewhat in the strain of Dennis' *The Usefulness of the Stage,* the author argues that the early pages of the *Short View* would seem to dictate a correction of the abuses of the stage, while the last chapter discloses his design —not "Reformation but Eradication."

> "For here he throws by the Pruning Hook, and takes up the Axe. In due prevention, therefore against so dangerous a Weapon, in so angry a Hand, we'll endeavor first to guard the Root; . . ."[93]

The defender of Dramatic Poetry begins with an examination of the last chapter of the *Short View;* that is, "The Opinion of Paganism, of the Church, and State, concerning the Stage," but declares that of these three authorities discussed by Collier, he will set out first "from home" and treat of the opinion of the English State concerning plays.[94] He gives a lengthy analysis of his views on this point, and follows it up by a discussion of the attitude of the Greeks and Romans concerning the stage. The statements of Tully, of Livy, and those found in the Theodosian Code which were cited by Collier are turned against him.[95]

---

cations. Besides, Collier himself usually pugnacious and always fearless does not once refer to Filmer's other work—a fact which renders Filmer's authorship in the above instance questionable. Collier does make mention of *"The Defence of Dramatic Poetry"* in his *A Defence of the Short View,* p. 132, but he refers to the author only as *"The Defender."*

[92] Anonymous, *A Defence of Dramatick Poetry,* Preface, p. i.
[93] *Ibid.,* pp. 1-2. Recall that Collier had said, "Tis my business rather to kill the *Root* than *Transplant* it." *Short View,* p. 3.
[94] *Ibid.,* p. 2.
[95] *Ibid.,* pp. 14-17.

He very carefully examines all the evidence both of the Councils and of the Fathers which Collier had brought against the stage, and thence he concludes:

> "the open and publick Stage continued unshaken, in defiance of all this Holy Breath against it; what can we in all Reason conclude, but that these Christian Princes lookt back to the foremention'd Fathers louder Thunder against the Stage, as only a temporary Blast; . . . "[96]

To Collier's charge that Mr. Dryden in *King Arthur* makes a "strange hodg-podg of Matters, Angels, Cupids, Syrens, and Devils, etc., . . . " *The Defence* answers:

> "Not at all, Learned Sir, but because his betters have done it before him, and Mr. Dryden thinks it no scorn to follow his elder Brother *Gamaliel,* Mr. Milton, in his *Paradise Lost.*"[97]

Dryden is upheld against Collier's censure of a "fairy" way of writing.

> "Good Heaven! How perversly does this angry Gentleman Scribble."[98]

The whole argument of the first part of *A Defence of Dramatick Poetry* is very abruptly concluded:

> "But this I must say, to come up to all the Heights of that Christian Champion, he professes himself, undoubtedly he must have a double Portion of Faith and Hope, to make up for his Diminutive Talent of Charity."[99]

The *Defence of Dramatick Poetry* is not only uninteresting, but it is a weak and verbose reply to Collier. It is considered—especially by those who believe Filmer the author—to be an attempted vindication of himself for his play *The Unnatural Brother.* D. C. Taylor, of the same opinion as Mr. Gosse concerning it, states:

> "Filmer felt the need to champion the stage because he was the author of a tiresome tragedy called *The Unnatural Brother,* which was a failure after being acted three times at Lincoln's Inn Fields in 1697. His *Defence* is worthless, for the thought is shallow, and the style flabby and absurdly ornate. His principal concern is to prove that contemporary drama is not more immoral than classic drama, from which he culls the most unsavoury passages to prove his point."[100]

---

[96] *Ibid.,* p. 65.
[97] *Ibid.,* p. 99.
[98] *Ibid.,* pp. 100-102.
[99] *Ibid.,* p. 118.
[100] D. C. Taylor, *William Congreve,* pp. 125-6.

CHAPTER IV

The June Replies to the Short View

1. J. Dennis: *The Usefulness of the Stage, to the Happiness of Mankind,* . . . June 6.

2. J. Vanbrugh: *A Short Vindication of the Relapse and the Provok'd Wife,* June 8.

3. Anonymous: *A Farther Defence,* June 23.

Each of the three June replies listed above shows their authors at white heat against Collier and the *Short View.* Each reply is a caustic vindication of the stage, of stage-poets, and of stage-plays. Besides, Vanbrugh has a personal axe to grind because of Collier's attack on his comedies; the anonymous author of *A Farther Defence* takes up the thread of his previous *Defence of Dramatick Poetry,* while Dennis argues that a regulated stage is an asset to religion, to government, and to the happiness of mankind. His pamphlet is the most logical in argument and the most convincing in tone of all the 1698 replies.

I.

The *Short View* was a challenge to John Dennis not only to vindicate the English stage and stage-poets from the attack of Collier but to come in a special manner to the rescue of Wycherley. Dennis had no objections to Collier's attacking the licentiousness of the English stage but he indignantly resented the charge that "his design was against the Stage itself."[1] Angry with Collier and desirous of proving a regulated stage an asset to England, Dennis determined to reply. Of this reply he says:

"This little Treatise was conceiv'd dispos'd transcrib'd and printed in a month; and tho on that very account it may not be wholly free from error, yet this I can assure the Reader, that I have industriously endeavour'd not to err, tho I verily believe

---

[1] J. Dennis, *The Usefulness of the Stage, To the Happiness of Mankind. To Government, and to Religion. Occasion'd by a late Book, written by Jeremy Collier, M.A.* Introduction, p. iii. The book was printed for Richard Parker at the Unicorn under the Piazza of the Royal Exchange, and was announced by the *Post-Man* for June 6, 1698.

that Mr. *Collier* industriously endeavour'd to err, as far as he thought it might be consistent with the deceiving of others."[2]

The design of Dennis—as is evident from the title of his book—is not to refute all of Collier's contentions, a thing which Gildon pompously boasted of doing;[3] it is not to survey each of the chapters; it is specifically to prove the "Usefulness of the Stage to the Happiness of Mankind." Consequently, in analyzing the work it will be impossible to parallel Dennis' arguments with those of Collier.

In the "Introduction" to his work Dennis calls attention to Collier's statement concerning the usefulness of the stage, and then shows how Collier later contradicts his own statement. Dennis points out that in the beginning of his book Collier states his reasons why stage reform ought to be encouraged, and that in the end of the same treatise he proves, by citing other men's opinions, how necessary it is for the stage to be abolished. Dennis makes a candid acknowledgment of the grandeur of virtue[4] and very pointedly remarks:

> "My business therefore is a vindication of the Stage and not of the Corruptions or the abuses of it. And therefore, I have no further meddled with Mr. *Collier's* Book, than as I have had occasion to shew, that he has endeavour'd to make some things pass for abuses, either of the Stage in general, or of the *English* Stage particularly, which are so far from being abuses, that they may be accounted excellences."[5]

His purpose stated, Dennis outlines his method, which is to show that the stage in general is useful to the happiness of mankind, to the advancement of religion, and to the welfare of government, that it does not encourage revenge and that it provides for the happiness of particular men as well as for the well-being of the public.[6] His parting

---

[2] *Ibid.,* p. iv. Mr. Gosse quotes the above, strange to say, as proof that *Collier* wrote the *Short View* in a month. Although he does not give the title or the page of his authority it is evident that he misinterpreted this statement of Dennis's. He says: "What event it was that excited Collier to the composition of the *Short View* does not seem to be known. . . . Dennis tells us that the volume was conceived, disposed, transcribed, and printed in a month," and though the preface is dated March 5, 1698, it was issued only a few days later." E. Gosse, *William Congreve,* 1924, p. 99.

[3] Charles Gildon, *Phaeton,* Preface, p. ix.

[4] John Dennis, *The Usefulness of the Stage.* Introduction, pp. i-iii.

[5] *Ibid.,* p. iv.

[6] *Ibid.,* pp. iv-v.

word to Collier in the Introduction is an accusation of not having shown in his book

> "either the meekness of a true Christian or the humility of an exemplary Pastor! . . . neither the reasoning of a man of sense, . . . nor the style of a polite man, nor the sincerity of an honest man, nor the humanity of a Gentleman, or a man of Letters."[7]

In proving that the stage is instrumental to the happiness of mankind in general, Dennis defines happiness as pleasure, and pleasure as the consequence of passion. He argues that "Nothing but passion can please us, which every one may know by experience;"[8] that for a man to be superlatively happy he must be superlatively pleased which state of mind comes from being very much moved; that the abundance of happiness promised in the next life proceeds from passion; and that being delivered from these mortal organs and reason being no more, we shall lead the glorious life of angels, a life exalted above all reason—a life consisting of ecstacy and intelligence.[9]

The second chapter is brief but in its narrow compass of three pages Dennis tells us that morose people are seldom happy because their passions are seldom raised, and he declares further:

> "Now there is no Nation in *Europe,* as has been observ'd above a thousand times, that is so generally addicted to the Spleen as the *English.* . . . Now the *English* being more splenatick than any other people, and consequently more thoughtful and more reflecting, . . . it follows that the *English* to be happy have more need than other people of something that will raise their passions in such a manner, as shall be agreeable to their reasons, and that by consequence they have more need of the Drama."[10]

Evidently wishing to emphasize the importance of dramatic entertainment for the English temperament he reiterates his opinion:

> "Drama may be said to be instrumental in a peculiar manner to the welfare of the English Government; because there is no

---

[7] *Ibid.,* p. vi.
[8] *Ibid.,* p. 7.
[9] *Ibid.,* pp. 7-8.
[10] *Ibid.,* pp. 12-13.

people on the face of the Earth so prone to rebellion as the *English,* or so apt to quarrel among themselves."[11]

Dennis' third chapter proposes to answer those objections which have in the past been raised against the stage or which may be advanced against it in the future. These objections are listed under three headings: objections from reason, objections from authority, and objections from religion.[12] Dennis refutes the claims of Collier and his abettors that plays not only indulge terror, pity, and the rest of the passions, but indulge love where it is, and create it where it is not.[13] He censures Collier's interpretation of the Greek and Latin authorities;[14] he vindicates Wycherley;[15] besides, he asserts that whether we refer to the Ancients or Moderns, whether to the Athenians, Romans, French, or English, we shall find that

" . . . Arts and Sciences have for the most part begun, but all of them at least begun to prosper with the Stage, and that as they have flourish'd, they have at last declin'd with it."[16]

Clear thinking, forceful reasoning, and coherent diction characterize Dennis' arguments in defence of the stage. Glancing over England's literary past, he notes the names of Spenser, Bacon, and Raleigh. He calls them

"three mighty geniuses so extraordinary in their different ways that not only England had never seen the like before, but they almost continue to this very day, in spight of all emulation, in

---

[11] *Ibid.,* p. 63. It is interesting to note that in September, 1698, *The Stage Condemned* called the attention of the "Right Honourable Lords and Commons of England in Parliament Assembled" to Mr. Dennis' book in behalf of the stage. *The Stage Condemned,* Ded. Epistle, p. i. It is even more interesting to note the action which was taken, in consequence, against Mr. Dennis. Narcissus Luttrell gives an account of it in his *Brief Historical Relation of State Affairs,* IV, 455; "Yesterday being the last day of the term [i.e. Monday, Nov. 28, 1698], the grand jury of Middlesex presented Mr. Dennis his book, called a Vindication of the Stage, in answer to Collier, as a libell against the government for asserting that the people of England are the most prone to rebellion of any in the world, and alwaies quarrelling among themselves, if not diverted by plays; upon which the court ordered an indictment against him, and the attorney generall to prosecute him."

[12] *The Usefulness of the Stage,* p. 15.

[13] *Ibid.,* pp. 15-16.

[14] *Ibid.,* pp. 29-30.

[15] *Ibid.,* pp. 30-2.

[16] *Ibid.,* p. 40.

spight of time, the greatest of our Poets, Philosophers and Historians."[17]

From eulogy of the past Dennis turns to complaint of the present and condemns the Puritan regime which so stifled the genius of the day that there were no greater stars in its literary firmament than Withers, Prynne, and Vickars, together with a "herd of Scribblers of obscurer infamy: Wretches who had not desert enough to merit even contempt."[18] And when the Civil Wars sounded their awful note in England, Dennis tells us that Denham, Davenant, Waller, and Cowley were writing, not in their mother-country, but mostly in a country (France) where the stage and learning flourished.[19] He enumerates the orators of the day—Calamy, Case, Hugh Peters, Manton, and Sibbs; he compares these names with the more illustrious ones of Tillotson and the Bishop of Rochester and with those of the philosophers Newton and Lock who flourished after the Restoration.[20]

The second part of Dennis' pamphlet begins with a discourse designed to prove that the stage is useful to Government in general, to the English government in particular, and to the present government especially.[21] He attempts to prove first that the stage is useful to rulers[22] and second that the stage is useful to the governed. Tragedy, he says, not only cements a union between the ruler and the ruled by checking ambitions, by diverting apprehension of grievances and by dispelling unreasonable jealousies, but it cements a union of one citizen with the other, and this in five ways: by diverting from unjust designs, by purging those passions whose excesses cause injustice, by instructing in duty, by setting them above injustice, and by terrifying with conclusions of violence and injustice.[23] His third point proves the stage useful to government in relation to the common enemy. Here Dennis shows from contemporary experience, as well as from the governments of Athens, Rome, France, and England that the stage is useful.[24]

---

[17] *Ibid.*, p. 40.
[18] *Ibid.*, pp. 39-40. Dennis' failure to mention Milton is noteworthy.
[19] *Ibid.*, p. 41.
[20] *Ibid.*, p. 42.
[21] *Ibid.*, p. 50.
[22] *Ibid.*, pp. 50-53.
[23] *Ibid.*, pp. 56-58.
[24] *Ibid.*, pp. 58-62.

Dennis' pamphlet is a more scholarly composition in defence of the stage than any that had previously appeared; it shows throughout the author's loyalty to the government and to the church of England; it gives evidence of his wide acquaintance with and serious study of the poets, philosophers, and scientists of his day .Throughout, the tone is hostile to Collier, and in the light of his subsequent defences of the stage we may assert that the *Short View* awakened in Dennis a personal aversion to the author and bitter resentment for the attack on the play-house and the poets. Whether or not Dennis attributed the failure of his plays to the public sentiment against the stage awakened by Collier can only be conjectured, but that his plays from 1697 to 1709 were not successful in a matter of record.[25]

2

Contemporaneously with Dennis, Vanbrugh appeared in the ranks of the vindicators of the stage. That he should reply to Collier is not surprising; one could scarcely imagine the jaunty captain's not taking up his pen in defence of his attacked plays. He gives as his reason for writing *A Short Vindication of the Relapse and the Provok'd Wife, from Immorality and Prophaneness:*

> "This Lampoon has got Credit enough in some Places to brand the Persons it mentions with almost as bad a Character, as the Author of it has fixt upon himself, by his Life and Conversation in the World. I think 'tis therefore now a thing no farther to be laught at. Should I wholly sit still, those people who are so much mistaken to think I have been busy to encourage Immorality, may double their Mistake, and fancy I profess it: I will therefore endeavour, in a very few Pages to convince the World, I have brought nothing upon the Stage that proves me more an Atheist than a Bigot."[26]

In military jargon, the captain refers to Collier as the "General" whose head was too hot for his conduct to be wise, that his shot was

---

25 *D.N.B.*, V, 820.

26 John Vanbrugh, *A Short Vindication of the Relapse And the Provok'd Wife From Immorality and Profaneness* . . . p. 3. The pamphlet of seventy-nine pages was printed in the early part of June, (cf. *The Flying Post*, June 8, 1698), for H. Walwyn, at the Three Legs in the Poultrey, against the Stocks-Market.

too much at random ever to make a breach in the wall; and that the
siege would be raised without his (Vanbrugh's) taking the field.[27]
From the language of the soldier Vanbrugh passes to that of the tennis-
player:

> "I must be content to take the Ball as it comes, and return it if
> I can; . . . His most threatening Strokes end in nothing at all;
> when he Cuts, he's under the Line; when he Forces, he's up in
> the Nets. But to leave Tennis, and come to the Matter."[28]

He comes first to the rescue of Miss Hoyden whom Collier had
accused of immodesty. He lamely responds that he knows of no
"Bawdy" she talks, and attributes to Collier's vicious imagination and
to the number of bawdy plays he has read any wrong interpretation
that has been extracted.[29]

He next defends *The Provoked Wife*. He complains that Collier
has given as evidence of immodesty only incomplete quotations, and
because such is the case, he will supply the omitted words. Consequently, he gives to the reader the whole of the conversation in question between Belinda and Lady Brute, and then makes this reflection:

> "Now which way this Gentleman will extract anything from
> hence, to the Discouragement of Modesty, is beyond my
> Chymistry: 'Tis plainly and directly the contrary. Here . . . two
> Women (not over Virtuous, as their whole Character shews),
> . . . are put in mind . . . That . . . if they quit their Modesty,
> they lose their Charms: Now I thought 'twas impossible to put
> the Ladies in mind of anything more likely to make 'em pre-
> serve it."[31]

He justifies himself for certain statements made by his characters concerning which Collier had rebuked him; he shows his chagrin at Collier's styling Berinthia's comment to Amanda "a Lewd and Prophane
Allegory:"

> "I confess it has at a glance, the appearance of somewhat which
> it has not, and that me thinks Mr. Collier might have been con-
> tent to have charg'd it with; but he always takes care to stretch

[27] *Ibid.*, p. 2.
[28] *Ibid.*, pp. 5-6.
[29] *Ibid.*, p. 7.
[31] *Ibid.*, p. 9.

that way that becomes him least, and so is sure to be in the wrong himself, whether I am or not."[32]

There are references throughout to the "Business of Plays" upon which Collier had discoursed in the Introduction to the *Short View*, and with the opinions of the clergyman upon this topic, Vanbrugh is in perfect accord.[33] He goes further, moreover, and insists that

"The Stage is a Glass for the World to view itself in; People ought therefore to see themselves as they are; if it makes their Faces too Fair, they won't know they are Dirty, and by Consequence will neglect to wash 'em."[34]

In answer to the charge of swearing as being contrary both to Religion and good manners, Vanbrugh replies:

"what he calls *Swearing* in the Play-House, (at least where I have to answer for it) is a Breach upon neither."[35]

In Vanbrugh's answers to the scathing charges of Profaneness against the *Provoked Wife* and *The Relapse*, the strength of the defense lies most frequently in accusing Collier either of foul play, of faulty criticism, or of finding profaneness where none was intended.[36] In behalf of Berinthia's "Now consider of what has been said, and Heaven give you grace to put it in practice," Vanbrugh agrees that it does sound much like the ending of a sermon, and that as such it sounds loose upon the stage. But he defends it:

" 'Tis only a loose Expression, suitable to the Character she represents, which throughout the Play, sufficiently shews, she's brought upon the Stage to Ridicule something that's off on't.[37]

Impatient with Collier's accusations of blasphemy, and appealing to the reader to disprove them in the statements of the last-mentioned characters, Vanbrugh proceeds to answer the accusation of "Abuse of the Clergy." As is to be expected, he gladly takes the opportunity

---

[32] *Ibid.*, pp. 25-26.
[33] *Ibid.*, pp. 42-43.
[34] *Ibid.*, p. 46.
[35] *Ibid.*, p. 10.
[36] *Ibid.*, pp. 23-27.
[37] *Ibid.*, p.28.

for clerical castigation as well as for venting his spleen upon Collier. He preludes his replies by stating:

> "And here we are come to the Spring of the Quarrel. I believe whoever reads Mr. Collier, needs take very little pains to find out, that in all probability, had the Poets never discover'd a Rent in the Gown, he had done by Religion, as I do by my Brethren, left it to shift for itself."[38]

With unfeigned sarcasm he ridicules Collier for his courage in starting his attack; he asserts that Collier is opening a large field for the adversary to rove in; that forgetting the weakness of the garrison, he is unbarring the gate of the town.[39] He tells us that he is abandoning his one-time determination to discourse at length upon the topic of "Abuse of the Clergy," and is giving instead only a few casual remarks upon the subject. Here he very pompously asserts that if ever he takes Orders, he will very likely entertain similar opinions on the creditableness of the function of the priesthood, but that his present preference is for remaining in his heresy to which he appends his three Articles. At a glance we perceive their sarcasm and their relevancy to Collier.

His vindications of the charges of abuse of the clergy are, for the most part, feeble parryings. To defend Sir John Brute for his disrespect to the sacred ministry, Vanbrugh repeats his excuse that,

> "no body but a Man of Mr. *Collier's* heat, could have mistaken so much, to quote it under the head, of the Clergy abus'd by the Stage."[40]

The vindication of "Bull," and "Fashion" in *The Relapse* are of much the same color as that of "Sir John Brute."[41] Vanbrugh ends his remarks on this score by an eulogy of the Church of England, by sarcastic reflections upon Collier, and by a diatribe against the Church of Rome of which he says he is reminded when he talks of the Viewer:

> "I must declare, my Thoughts are got to Rome while I am talking thus of the Clergy."[42]

Vanbrugh next takes up the vindication of his plays from the charges of immorality, but he defends them without strength of argu-

---

[38] *Ibid.*, pp. 28-29.
[39] *Ibid.*, p. 29.
[40] *Ibid.*, p. 33.
[41] *Ibid.*, pp. 34-36.
[42] *Ibid.*, pp. 36-42.

ment. First of all he champions "Constant," and then rebukes Collier for falling upon this character who is depicted as a fine gentleman but without fidelity to the exact rules of his religion. He asserts that if Collier's charge rings true, then:

> "he'll have a more general Quarrel to make up with the Gentle-men of *England* than I have with the Lords, tho' he tells 'em I have highly affronted 'em."[43]

In vindicating himself against Collier's censure of having rewarded with a wife and benefice the abused chaplain Bull he asserts that Collier is ignorant of the nature of comedy which is

> "to shew People what they shou'd do, by representing them upon the Stage, doing what they shou'd not."[44]

In defence of his lady characters he tells the reader to apply to them what has already been said regarding the gentlemen inasmuch as the case is "much the same."[45]

Collier's devoting a chapter of the *Short View* to castigating *The Relapse* draws from Vanbrugh sarcastic rejoinders. He ironically expresses his gratitude to the clergyman for that which he calls the last of his favours, but finds fault with his opponent for suggesting a new title to his book, for criticizing his plots, characters, words, dialogue, etc., and he attempts a further justification of himself:

> "I don't pretend however to have observ'd the nicety of Rule in this Play; I writ it in as much haste (though not in so much fury) as he has done his Remarks upon it; 'Tis therefore possible I may have made as many foolish Mistakes . . . And I can assure Mr. Collier if I wou'd have weakened the Diversion, I could have avoided all his Objections and have been at the expense of much less pains than I have: And this is all the answer I shall make to 'em, except what tumbles in my way, as I'm observing the foul play he shews me, in setting the *Relapse* in so wrong a Light as he does at his opening of the Fable on it."[46]

---

[43] *Ibid.*, p. 43.
[44] *Ibid.*, p. 45.
[45] *Ibid.*, p. 47.
[46] *Ibid.*, pp. 54-59.

With some grossly personal remarks upon Collier's life Vanbrugh refers to Collier's attack of *The Relapse,* and weakly concludes his *Short
Vindication* in the words:

> "The World may see by this what a Contempt the Doctor
> has for a Spark that can make no better use of his Mistress,
> than to admire her for her Virtue. This methinks is something
> so very extraordinary in a Clergyman, that I almost fancy when
> He and I are fast asleep in our Graves, those who shall read
> what we both have produc'd, will be apt to conclude there's a
> Mistake in the Tradition about the Authors; and that 'twas the
> Reforming Divine writ the Play, and the Scandalous Poet the
> Remarks upon't.[47]

3

In less than a month after the appearance of *A Defence of Dramatic Poetry* its garrulous author published *A Farther Defence of
Dramatick Poetry: Being the Second Part of the Review of Mr. Collier's View of the Immorality and Profaneness of the Stage.* He apolo-
gizes for the fragmentary form of the first *Defence* and places the
blame upon the bookseller's hasty publication of it.[48] In his first
Defence the author had failed to elaborate upon Collier's criticism of
Vanbrugh's *Relapse,* hence he begins his *Farther Defence* by making
up for this omission. He hotly resents Collier's association of *Don
Quixote* with *The Relapse* and acidly asserts:

> "I durst venture to say, the *Relapse* and the *Quixot* are no more
> of Kin, then the *Cavalier to the Church-man;* not so much as
> Mr. Collier's Modern Beau Wigg, Crevate and Sword, to his
> old cast Gown, Cassock and Scarf."[49]

He takes from the *Short View* all of Collier's critical passages on *The
Relapse* and declares:

> "I shall spend a few more Thoughts then ordinary upon this
> Play, and examine it briefly (*in Twelve Leaves of Paper*) in the
> *Fable,* the *Moral,* the *Characters,* etc."[50]

Beginning with the Fable he quotes Collier verbatim as far as "Now
when a Poet can't rig out a *Title-Page* 'tis but a bad sign of his holding

---

[47] *Ibid.,* pp. 78-79.
[48] Anonymous, *A Farther Defence of Dramatick Poetry,* Preface, p. 1. This 72-
    page book was printed for Elizabeth Whitlock and was announced in *The
    Post-Man* for June 23, 1698.
[49] *Ibid.,* p. 2.
[50] *Ibid.,* p. 3.

out to the *Epilogue*" to which he gives a half-page of criticism. He accuses Collier of having read only half the title-page of *The Relapse* even though he took such great pains to examine the whole play, and asserts

> "And did not all the Play-house Bills call it the *Second Part of the Fool in Fashion?* . . . Now if his Twelve Leaves of Remarks upon that Play, end no better then they begin, 'tis shrewdly to be suspected that the *Remarker* has more bad signs of not holding out than the *Relapser*."[51]

The author of *A Farther Defence* refutes Collier's criticisms of the moral in Vanbrugh's *The Relapse*[52] and to show his contempt of Collier's method he declares:

> "This dead-doing Critick thus flush'd with all his success against the *Relapser* is resolved to make Through Work with his slaughtering Hand, and consequently the *Characters* in the Play, shall be as Monstrous as the *Conduct*.[53]

He analyzes from his authorities of the Primitive Fathers the evidence which Collier had given as forbidding plays. His conclusion is:

> "But in all these Declamations . . . 'twas the General Opinion of the Christians that Plays were a *Lawful Diversion;* and therefore the whole business of those Declamations, is the opening the Christians Eyes, and refuting that too Epidemical Erroneous Opinion [concerning the Scriptural silence regarding plays]; . . ."[54]

He next inquires into the nature of history and romance, and argues that if Collier designs to close Drury Lane and little Lincolns-Inn-Fields, he will, if he is consistent, have a general conflagration among the book-sellers.[55]

A *Farther Defence* does not go into great detail in replying to Collier's charges of profaneness, immorality, and abuse of the clergy. When the author does retort he speaks acidly:

> "But if our *English* Stage has now and then a little exposed some of the Tatter'd and Daggl'd *Gowns, etc.,* Methinks the

---

[51] *Ibid.,* pp. 4-5.
[52] *Ibid.,* pp. 5-22.
[53] *Ibid.,* p. 22.
[54] *Ibid.,* pp. 38-39.
[55] *Ibid.,* pp. 52-56.

Author of the *Persuasive to Consideration* [Collier], that falls
himself so heavy, both upon the *Head* and *Body* of the *Church,*
should not be so severe upon the Stage, for only rallying some
part of the *Tail* of it. Nay, 'tis yet a little more strange, that
this Author should quarrel with the Stage for this Boldness
with the Clergy, when he himself has furnish'd it with one of
the most Divertive *Characters* for a *Comedy;* and one that
would bear as just and as honest a *Satyr, as* any that ever appear'd upon it: For his very *Remarks* upon the *Relapse,* . . .
would supply a Subject even for a whole Farce; and carry as
fair a Title, call'd *The Parson turn'd Critick,* as ever grac'd a
Playhouse-Bill."[56]

Throughout his work, the author of *A Farther Defence* attempts to
be witty; he makes a flashy display of learning; he would have his
reader believe him a literary critic as well as a student of the classics;
he addresses his opponent by the term "Remarker," "Characterizer,"
"Criticiser." However, despite his superficiality, he makes several valuable digressions, one of which is his opinion of the motive which
prompted Collier to write the *Short View:*

"For though Religion and Reformaton was the Pretence; instead of a Cole from the Altar to inspire Zeal, here was a
warmer *Dulcis Odor,* fifty Guinea's Copy-money that animated
the cause."[57]

Another digression reports the current opinion regarding the spirit in
which "Dryden, Congreve, and some other great authors" received
the *Short View:*

"For it goes for current Authority round the whole Town, that
Mr. *Dryden* himself had publickly declared it *Unanswerable;*
and thanked Mr. *Collier* for the just Correction he had given
him; and that Mr. *Congreve,* and some other great Authors
had made much the same Declaration; which is all so notorious-
ly False, so egregious a Lye, that Mr. *Dryden* particularly always
look'd upon it as a pile of *Malice, Ill-nature* and *Uncharitable-
ness,* and all drawn upon the utmost Rack of *Wit* and *Inven-*
tion[58]

---

[56] *Ibid.,* p. 62.
[57] *Ibid.,* p. 69.
[58] *Ibid.,* p. 70.

Every page in the *Farther Defence* shows the author's bitter hostility to Collier; every page shows his love for the Moderns and for the English stage. As a literary work the book is unimportant; as a contribution to the stage-controversy it is of little value. It is hard to read, undoubtedly, and this difficulty is not compensated for by interesting diction or by powerful arguments.

CHAPTER V

The July Replies

1. T D'Urfey: *The Campaigners,* July 9, Preface.
2. W. Congreve: *The Amendments,* July 12.

Both D'Urfey and Congreve had been attacked in the *Short View,* and early in the controversy they took up the cudgel in their own defence. Both champion the cause of the English stage and attempt to justify themselves in the eyes of critical London.

1

Thomas D'Urfey attacked by Collier for profaneness, immorality, abuse of the clergy, and want of modesty and regard for the audience defends himself in his Preface to *The Campaigners* and in his poem "A Satyrical Fable of the Dog and the Ottor." His wrath flames as he considers Collier's disparagement of his dramatic ability and condemnation of his comedy *Don Quixote.* Collier's reference to him as "Vox, et praeterea nihil"[1] he felt had branded him with ignominy in the eyes of his fellow-poets and he gives vent to his rage in heated invectives, descending at times to crude and vulgar epithets and to abusive personal retorts.

D'Urfey, both in his "Epistle Dedicatory to the Right Honourable Thomas Lord Wharton," in his "Prologue" and "Epilogue," is sarcastic at Collier's expense. To Lord Wharton he preludes his remarks by stating:

> "As I doubt not but your Lordship has been Entertained with the baiting of the Poets, by a late horrible severe and rigid Critick, so I also hope, that now, or very suddenly you will be diverted with the aforesaid Critick's being exercis'd by the Poets."[2]

---

[1] J. Collier, *A Short View,* p. 208.

[2] Thomas D'Urfey, *The Campaigners: Or, The Pleasant Adventures at Brussels.* p. i. *The Campaigners* is a five-act comedy and was printed for A. Baldwin near the Oxford Arms Inn in Warwick Lane. The date of its initial appearance has been variously assigned. Mr. Gosse in his *Life of Congreve,* p. 113, asserts that it was published shortly after *Phaeton;* this makes the date approximately the first week of May. D. C. Taylor in his *William Congreve,* p. 129, asserts on the authority of the *Post-Man* that the book did not appear until July 9. This date seems to me more probable inasmuch as D'Urfey in his *Campaigners,* p. 2, mentions not only "The late Ingenious Author" of *A Vindication of the Stage* but states besides: "Several ingenious authors

In the Prologue D'Urfey gives vent to his anger at Collier; he casts reflection upon his clerical and private life, and holds up to derision his scruples concerning taking the Oath of Allegiance.[3] In the Epilogue spoken by Cibber we learn that D'Urfey believed Collier's attack on comedy a failure.[4]

The Preface to *The Campaigners* is a 27-page vindication of the stage, of stage-poets, and of his own attacked reputation. It is a vindication scintillating neither with scholarship, elevated diction, nor logical argument. The opinions which the author entertains are buried in heaped-up verbiage; they are attempts to soothe his own offended feelings, and those of his brother poets Dryden, Congreve, and Vanbrugh. Occasionally he scores a point on Collier, but his victories are not important; they do not stultify Collier—the mission designed for them by D'Urfey. The preface, viewed as a whole, presents D'Urfey frequently either violently angry, or childishly peeved. And as parting proof of his angry resentment, he appends the Fable of *The Dog and the Ottor,* chanting in verse a litany of the clergyman's sins—his denial of James II's abdication, his refusal to take the oath of allegiance to William and Mary, his denial of the rights of the new monarch, his deserting of his clerical post, his slighting his patron, his roaming abroad as a malcontent, and his mad railing against the government.[5]

2

In the same month in which D'Urfey published his reply to Collier, Congreve produced his own vindication entitled, *Amendments of Mr. Collier's False and Imperfect Citations, etc. From the Old Batchelour,*

have already, I think, so well confuted his Assertions against the Stage, by proofs from the Antient Poets, the Primitive Fathers, and their Authorities, . . . " *Ibid.,* p. 3. D'Urfey is probably referring to four replies: *A Vindication of the Stage* announced for May 17; Dennis' *Usefulness of the Stage,* June 6; The Preface to Motteux's *Beauty in Distress,* early in May, and to the Anonymous *A Defence of Dramatic Poetry,* May 26. These four confutations answer to the description given by D'Urfey and, moreover, they had been in circulation prior to July 9. Had D'Urfey's comedy appeared the first week in May as Mr. Gosse unauthoritatively asserts, (Cf. *Life of William Congreve,* p. 113), it would have had no predecessor except *Phaeton,* and the Preface to *Phaeton* cites no "proofs from the Antient Poets, the Primitive Fathers, and their Authorities."

[3] *Ibid.,* p. v.
[4] *Ibid.,* p. vi.
[5] *Ibid.,* p. 28. The Fable is written in approximately 125 heroic couplets.

Double Dealer, Love for Love, Mourning Bride. By the Author of those Plays.[6]

The vindication is disappointing in that it betrays very little of the wit and genius one might expect from the lauded playwright. Although it proves Congreve's desire to preserve his moral reputation, its arguments are weak and unconvincing. The author tells us in his opening lines that, wavering between the fear of being considered idle and the stigma of being thought lazy, he has decided to answer the charges advanced by the author of the *Short View* against his four plays[7] He preludes his first thrust at Collier by climactically stating his intentions in writing the *Amendments*. He says:

> "I have no Intention to examine all the Absurdities and Falsehoods in Mr. Collier's Book:" (p. 2)

> "Least of all, would I undertake to defend the Corruptions of the Stage;" (p. 3)

> "I will not justifie any of my own Errors; I am sensible of many;" (p. 3) and,

> "My Intention, is to do little else, but to restore those Passages to their primitive Station, which have suffer'd so much in being transplanted by him: I will remove 'em from his Dunghil, and replant 'em in the field of Nature; and when I have wash'd 'em of that Filth which they have contracted in passing through his very dirty hands, let their own Innocence protect them." (pp. 3-4)[8]

Congreve informs the reader that Mr. Collier's method of criticism is to blacken characters with his own smut, to bring to nearer focus an expression which was remote in the original, frequently to vary and new-mold that expression and, finally, to stamp his own image upon it whereupon it becomes current deformity and is fit to be paid into the

---

[6] The reply is 119 pages in length and was printed for J. Tonson. According to *The Post Boy* it was announced July 12. The pagination 70-80 of the first edition of the *Amendments* is repeated, therefore the 109 page are really 119.

[7] W. Congreve, *Amendments*, pp. 1-2.

[8] *Ibid.*, pp. 2-4.

Devil's Exchequer.[9] The idea of the "Devil's Exchequer" gives Congreve a new idea:

> "I will therefore take the Liberty to exercise this evil Spirit, and whip him out of my Plays, wherever I can meet with him,"[10]

and in answer to Collier's application to his opponent of such names as "buffoons, foot-pads, and slaves," Congreve says:

> "I will onely call him Mr. *Collier,* and that I will call him as often as I think he shall deserve it."[11]

He further asserts that because he must "for method's sake" premise some few things to the reader, he will lay down his four postulata. In the first of these he asserts that his analysis of Collier's criticisms will be in accord with Aristotle's "Definition of Comedy." He says that in accordance with the basic principle of that definition, we are to understand the term "comedy" as being an imitation of the worst class of people,—worst, not as regards quality, but as regards manners.

> "For Men are to be laugh'd out of their Vices in Comedy; the Business of Comedy is to delight, as well as to instruct: And as vicious People are made asham'd of their Follies or Faults, by seeing them expos'd in a ridiculous manner, so are good People at once both warn'd and diverted at their Expence."[12]

As his second postulatum Congreve declares that inasmuch as writers of comedy are obliged to represent foolish and vicious characters, they are not, in consequence, to be condemned for having these vicious characters behave themselves foolishly or immorally in word or deed:

> "It were very hard that a Painter should be believ'd to resemble all the ugly Faces he draws."[13]

As the third postulatum Congreve desires the reader not to consider as accurate any expression or passage cited by Collier, nor to pass any sentence or censure upon it when it is out of its proper scene or alien-

---

[9] *Ibid.,* pp. 5-6.
[10] *Ibid.,* p. 6.
[11] *Ibid.,* pp. 6-7.
[12] *Ibid.,* p. 8.
[13] *Ibid.,* p. 9.

ated from its proper character. Collier's censure of immodesty or profaneness does not, according to Congreve, stigmatize his play; it may
be, he argues, that his adversary is presenting objects to be viewed
through a stained glass, and that things appear profane when in reality
they are seen only through a profane medium, or when the true color
is dissembled by the help of a sophistical varnish.[14]

His fourth postulatum is aimed at Collier's chapter on the profaneness of the English Stage. Not only does Congreve disagree with these
arguments of Collier but he states with emphasis that

> "when Words are apply'd to sacred things, and with a purpose
> to treat of sacred things; they ought to be understood accord-
> ingly: But when they are otherwise apply'd, the Diversity of
> the Subject gives a Diversity of Signification."[15]

To these four postulata Congreve tells us he will refer when occasion offers. He says, moreover, that his comedies give "instruction"
as well as "delight" and asserts that a very common expedient made
use of by the stage-poets to recommend the "instruction" of the play
is to sum up in the concluding lines of the poem the moral intended,—
and this for the purpose of preventing the audience's being so strongly
possessed with "delight" as to make them overlook the lesson to be
derived.

His prelude completed, Congreve analyzes the censure which his
four plays received in the *Short View* under the the charges of immodesty, profaneness, immorality, and abuse of the clergy. He is extremely careful to vindicate himself from the stigma of the first three
vices, but he does not appear greatly concerned to refute the charge of
abusing the clergy.[16] He ridicules Collier for misquoting "wasting"
for "wafting:"

> "He is very merry, and as he supposes with me; in laughing
> at *wasting* Air . . . But where does he meet with *wasting* Air?
> Not in the *Mourning-bride;* for in that Play it is printed
> *wafting Air;*"[17]

---

[14] *Ibid.,* pp. 9-10.
[15] *Ibid.,* p. 11.
[16] *Ibid.,* p. 14; p. 28; p. 16; pp. 37-42; pp. 42-48; pp. 48-57; pp. 57-71;
p. 78.
[17] W. Congreve, *Amendments,* p. 27.

for misusing the word "learning" in the phrase "Learning a Spaniel to set!"[18] as well as for his simile of "a litter of epithets:"

> "The Comparison is handsome, I must needs say; but I desire the Reader to consider that it is Mr. *Collier* the Critick, that talks at this odd rate; not Mr. *Collier* the Divine."[19]

Congreve refers to the authority of Aristotle's *Rhetoric* to justify himself for his use of epithets, and insists that even if Collier calls them stiff, nevertheless, they are not, and so their fate is to be determined by better judges. He emphasizes his contempt for Collier's metaphors by stating that pitiful and mean comparisons proceed from pitiful and mean ideas—ideas which have their beginning in a familiarity with pitiful and mean objects—and that, in consequence, from Collier's

> "poor and filthy Metaphors and Similitudes, we may learn the Filthiness of his Imagination; and from the Uncleanness of that, we may make a reasonable guess at his rate of Education, and those Objects with which he has been most conversant and familiar."[20]

In bidding farewell to Collier Congreve heartily thanks his adversary for the opportunity of reforming many errors in his plays—errors occasioned, as he affirms, by inadvertance or inexperience; he admits that he is as willing to acknowledge the benefits which he derived from Collier's book as he is to demonstrate its vices:

> "if I resent the later, it is because they were intended me; and if I do not thank him for the other, it is because they were not; He wou'd have poison'd me, but he overdosed it, and the Excess of his Malice has been my Security."[21]

He blames his antagonist, Collier, for writing more from prejudice than opinion, for railing rather than for reasoning, for scurrilous reproaches rather than for gentle reproofs, and for looking upon his adversaries as his enemies. He declares that Collier's passion does not only

---

[18] *Ibid.*, p. 28
[19] *Ibid.*, p. 29.
[20] *Ibid.*, pp. 85-86.
[21] *Ibid.*, pp. 93-94.

make him appear in many places to be in the wrong, but that it makes him appear to be conscious of being in the wrong.[22] He pleads for the theatre as a diversion necessary for the English people, and in that plea we hear the echo of Dennis' *Usefulness of the Stage* published about five weeks before:

> "Is there any where a People more unsteady, more apt to discontent, more saturnine, dark, and melancholick than our selves? Are we not of all People the most unfit to be alone, and most unsafe to be trusted with our selves? Are there not more Self-murderers, and melancholick Lunaticks in *England,* heard of in one Year, than in a great part of Europe besides? Whence our Plots, Conspiracies, and Seditions? . . . Not they who frequent the Theatres and Consorts of Musick."[23]

That Congreve's reply to Collier should be freighted with indignation is not surprising. The cause may be attributed to the contempt which Collier entertained for him and which he showed on every possible occasion in the *Short View*. It may also be ascribed to the fact that shortly after the *Short View* was published,

> "The justices of Middlesex did not only present the playhouses, but also Mr. Congreve, for writing the *Double-Dealer;* . . . and Tonson . . . for printing [it]."[24]

That he should receive public indictment was humiliating to Congreve and was likewise evidence that Collier was victorious in the argument. No wonder, then, that between May and July Congreve should have been busy composing his vindication which, he says, is intended

> "to do my self a necessary Right, which might be affected with so very little Pains."[25]

---

[22] *Ibid.,* pp. 94-95.
[23] *Ibid.,* pp. 108-109.
[24] N. Luttrell, *A Brief Historical Relation,* IV, 379. This entry is made for Thursday, May 12, 1698.
[25] W. Congreve, *Amendments,* p. 2.

CHAPTER VI

The September Replies

1. Anonymous, *A Letter to Mr. Congreve,* September 2.
2. Anonymous, *Animadversions on Mr. Congreve's Late Answer to Mr. Collier,* September 8.
3. Anonymous [George Ridpath]: *The Stage Condemned,* September 16.
4. Anonymous: *The Immorality of the English Pulpit.*

Three of the September replies are a vindication of Collier. Although the author of *The Stage Condemned* steps into the arena with new arguments against the stage and stage-poets, he, nevertheless, warmly commends Collier's castigation of the play-house. Both the *Letter to Mr. Congreve* and the *Animadversions* are not only vindications of Collier but they are attacks on Congreve; both make him the victim of raillery and abuse for his reply to Collier in the *Amendments;* both renew censure of him for writing the four plays which he had attempted to vindicate in the *Amendments. The Immorality of the English Pulpit,* an acid attack on Chapter III of the *Short View,* is a mixture of political, ecclesiastical, literary, and moral censure of Collier.

1

One of the most interesting replies evoked by the *Short View* is the anonymous *A Letter to Mr. Congreve on his Pretended Amendments, etc. of Mr. Collier's Short View of the Immorality and Prophaneness of the English Stage.*[1] It was written in vindication of Collier who had been caustically attacked by Congreve in the *Amendments,* and its every page indicates that the author felt a strong personal antagonism toward Congreve. The authorship of this work is a subject of particular interest inasmuch as a serious study of it gives many convincing proofs that Collier wrote it. Both the arguments and the diction show the author flippantly free with Congreve, and that he indulges in personal abuse and sarcastic reproofs. Treatment such as this might be expected from Collier, especially if he were writing anonymously. The arguments show, further, an intense desire to even up scores with Congreve in the eyes of the world, and this retaliation could be carried

---

[1] The *Letter to Mr. Congreve* is forty-one pages in length, was printed for Samuel Keble, and was announced in *The Post-Man* for September 2, 1698.

on to better advantage if the author concealed his identity. It is only by a careful reading of the entire pamphlet, however, together with a detailed comparison of it with Collier's other anti-stage works that the student will be able to see the resemblance of *A Letter to Mr. Congreve* to them.

Collier has an unmistakable style; his arguments and diction are so distinctly his own that one who reads his works for any length of time becomes Collier-conscious. Collier's use of a series of staccato questions,[1a] of frequent antithesis, of similes based on the same thought in different chapters of the same book, his frequent introducing of sentences with "But," his caustic arguments against profaneness, smut, burlesquing the Scriptures, abuse of the clergy, and "making the top characters libertines and rewarding them with a fortune,"—these are a few of the characteristic features of Collier's anti-stage works.

Inasmuch as Collier's *Defence of the Short View* was published just about two months after the *Letter to Mr. Congreve* appeared, and, further, since both works attacked Congreve's *Amendments,* an analysis of each of them together with a comparison of the two will also furnish interesting data in identifying the author. Undoubtedly the short space of time which had elapsed between the publication of *A Letter to Mr. Congreve* and *A Defence* would preclude any great change in the author's style, phraseology, views, grievances, etc., so that if Collier wrote *A Letter* he might be expected unconsciously to discover the fact in *A Defence*. Besides, the two pamphlets seek to vindicate Collier and *The Short View;* each seeks to emphasize the principles set forth in the *Short View*.

To the above reasons might be added that in both pamphlets emphasis is placed on the same line of thought. Of the many instances that might be cited, the following are significant: both the author of *A Letter to Mr. Congreve* and Mr. Collier in his *A Defence* play on the word "Latitude" used by Congreve in laying down his Postulata;[2] in both pamphlets there is cited the same quotation from the conclusion of Congreve's *Love for Love* and concerning it there is made the

---

[1a] Collier's contemporaries twitted him about this. Cf. Congreve's *Amendments,* p. 32: "see him [Collier] in Page 80. there he puffs and blows, and deals mightily in short periods:" Cf. also *Animadversions.* p. 35.

[2] Anonymous, *A Letter to Mr. Congreve,* p. 13; J. Collier, *A Defence of the Short View,* pp. 5-6.

same charge—that Congreve took a poor way to enforce a moral;[3] both comment to the same purpose on the ravings of Almeria and Osmin;[4] both lash Congreve for his rejoinder to Collier's attack on his use of the word "Jesu," which occurs in *The Double Dealer,* and both ridicule his reference to the "old woman" who had written to him to remonstrate concerning its use.[5] Besides, both justify with religious vehemence the sentence:

"Nature made the Firment and rising of the Blood for such Occasions;"[6]

both argue over Congreve's misuse of the word "Inspiration;"[7] both condemn Congreve's manner of accepting rebuke on the use of the Scriptural phrase, "I am truth;"[8] both exonerate Collier for his miscitation of Congreve's "wafting air;"[9] and both refer to Sir Roger L'Estrange, to Dennis, and to Tully.[10] Then, too, both justify Collier's censure of Congreve's use of the word "Martyr" and both ridicule Congreve's criticism of the censure;[11] both ridicule Congreve's attempted sarcasm of the words "Jeremy" and Collier;"[12] both ridicule Congreve for censuring Collier's phrase "Lewd but not little;"[13] both in similar vein eulogize the clergy and both refute similar arguments which Congreve had advanced against them;[14] both jest about Congreve's "enlarged spleen,"[15] and both express their preferences for the Ancients.[16] We note, too, that both refer sarcastically to Congreve's "The Corruption of a Rotten-Divine, is the Generation of a sowre Poet" but in each case the author does not quote the original. In *A Letter* we read

"You must not be angry, if I take this occasion, of turning the *but*-end of a quaint expression of your own against you; *The*

---

[3] *A Letter,* p. 13; *A Defence,* p. 20.

[4] *A Letter,* p. 16; *A Defence,* pp. 33-36.

[5] *A Letter,* p. 41; *A Defence,* pp. 46-7.

[6] *A Letter,* p. 21; *A Defence,* pp. 38-39.

[7] *A Letter,* pp. 24-25; *A Defence,* pp. 50-51.

[8] *A Letter,* p. 12; *A Defence,* p. 64.

[9] *A Letter,* p. 10; *A Defence,* pp. 36-37.

[10] *A Letter,* pp. 7, 37; *A Defence,* pp. 27, 114, 132.

[11] *A Letter,* p. 26; J. Collier, *A Defence,* pp. 54-55.

[12] *A Letter,* p. 9; *A Defence,* pp. 56-57.

[13] *A Letter,* pp. 30-31; *A Defence,* p. 79.

[14] *A Letter,* pp. 26-37; *A Defence,* pp. 66-80.

[15] *A Letter,* pp. 24-25; *A Defence.* p. 81. Mr. Taylor makes the reference to Congreve's gout an argument for Collier's authorship of *A Letter.* D. C. Taylor, *William Congreve,* pp. 136-137.

[16] *A Letter,* p. 19; *A Defence,* pp. 7, 12, 25, 51, 76, 85.

Corruption of a Rotten-Poet, is the Generation of a very sowre, and awkward Divine;"

while in *A Defence* Collier rather awkwardly refers to this statement of Congreve's:

"And then [Congreve] makes a miserable jest about *Corruption* and *Generation*."[17]

Both comment acidly upon Congreve's writing the *Old Batchelour* as an amusement when he was recovering from a fit of sickness.[18]

Another reason for believing that *A Letter to Mr. Congreve* is Collier's is its style. As has been pointed out above, Collier displays not only in the *Short View* and *A Defence* but also in *A Second Defence* and in *A Farther Vindication* a marked tendency to break off into a series of staccato questions. For instance, in *A Defence* we find the following all on the same page: "And pray what is there exceptionable . . . ?" "Vehemence against what . . . ?" "And where lies the Mistake . . . ?" "Are these then such harmless Practices . . . ?" "Is the Honor of God, the Interest of Religion . . . ?" "Are these things beneath our Passions . . . ?" "And won't they justify a little warmth . . . ?"[19]

To illustrate the familiar staccato interrogations note the following four questions which follow consecutively in *A Letter to Mr. Congreve*: "For, do we not know . . . ?" "That you have no other excuse for the 'present dulness' . . . ?" "That you have no other excuse for writing such a book . . . ?" "That 'tis impossible you should write . . . ?"[20] In Collier's *Second Defence* published about a year later we find the characteristic style: "Were not Comedies and Tragedies acted in the Theatres?" "Not in Pompey's Theatre . . . ?" "Were farces so much preferred . . . ?"[21]

In Collier's *A Farther Vindication,* printed in 1708, we find the questioning again: "And is not the Name of God abus'd in Common swearing?" "Does not the Act declare against . . . ?" "Not abus'd when the Divine Majesty . . . ?" "For what are plays but . . . ?"[22]

---

[17] *A Letter,* p. 22; *A Defence,* p. 33.
[18] *A Letter,* p. 25; *A Defence,* p. 42.
[19] J. Collier, *A Defence,* p. 39.
[20] Anonymous, *A Letter,* p. 24.
[21] J. Collier, *A Second Defence,* pp. 10-11.
[22] J. Collier, *A Farther Vindication,* p. 18.

Collier persistently introduces a sentence with "But." To illustrate from *A Defence*: "But I plainly perceive . . ." p. 1. "But since the Mischief works in English . . ." p. 2. "But since the reader . . ." p. 2. "But which way do I call them slaves?" p. 4. "But now he may be assured . . ." p.4.[23] Compare this with examples taken from *A Letter to Mr. Congreve*: "But if it will not by your own confession . . ." p. 4. "But yet you need not fall absolutely into despair . . ." p. 4. "But really you have so very foully . . ." p. 4. "But Mr. Collier was not an Idiot . . ." p. 7. "But be advised; whip the Devil gently . . ." p. 8.[24]

In *A Second Defence* the same style is used: "But I suppose he despairs . . ." p. 16. "But here he is much as untoward . . ." p. 16. "But after all, Plato . . ." p. 17. "But does not this commend the . . ." p. 17. "But that Aristotle did not . . ." p. 20.[25]

In *A Farther Vindication* Collier has lost nothing of the habit: "But if 'tis an ill thing . . . ?" p. 12. "But are there any affidavits . . . ?" p. 14. "But the Doctor is of another mind . . ." p. 14. "But I have reply'd to this Objection . . ." p.14 "But I believe everybody will . . ." p. 15. "But Stage-swearing is only . . ." p. 15. "But what's all this to the Doctor's Advantage?" p. 38.[26] Besides, Collier frequently makes use of ironic exclamations. He does it in *A Defence*,[27] in *A Second Defence*,[28] in *A Letter to Mr. Congreve*,[29] in *A Short View*.[30]

Then, too, there is a similar use and sometimes an identical method of using transitional and connective words and phrases in the works of Collier and in *A Letter to Mr. Congreve*,[31] while another characteristic of Collier's style and of that of the author of *A Letter to Mr. Congreve* is the use of antitheses and of balanced sentences.[32]

---

[23] J. Collier, *A Defence*, pp. 1-4.
[24] Anonymous, *A Letter*, pp. 4-8.
[25] J. Collier, *A Second Defence*, pp. 16-20.
[26] J. Collier, *A Farther Vindication*, pp. 12-38.
[27] J. Collier, *A Defence*, pp. 40, 67, 81, 94, 99.
[28] J. Collier, *A Second Defence*, pp. 10, 89.
[29] Anonymous, *A Letter to Mr. Congreve*, pp. 14, 28, 33, 41.
[30] J. Collier, *A Short View*, pp. 32, 33, 42, 45, 63, 64, 65, 66.
[31] J. Collier, *A Short View*, p. 17; p. 39; *A Defence*, p. 9; p. 13; *A Second Defence*, p. 44; *A Farther Vindication*, p. 28; p. 46; Anonymous, *A Letter to Mr. Congreve*, p. 16; p. 38.
[32] J. Collier, *A Defence*, pp. 17, 40; *A Second Defence*, p. 38; *A Farther Vindication*, p. 18; *A Short View*, pp. 8, 140, 273, 286; Anonymous, *A Letter to Mr. Congreve*, pp. 3, 36.

Mr. D. C. Taylor is also of the opinion that Collier wrote *A Letter to Mr. Congreve.* He gives as the reasons for his belief that the pamphlet was printed for Samuel Keble who also printed the *Short View;*[33] that the directness and rugged force of *A Letter* are also characteristic of the *Short View;* that no one but Collier would have taken the trouble to refute Congreve's personal attack;[34] and, lastly, that the references to, in reality a taunt of Congreve's gout, were not above the nature of Collier and other pamphleteers of the period.[35] Mr. Taylor's opinion that the pamphlet is by Collier because it was printed for Samuel Keble who also published the *Short View* becomes a more convincing reason when we remember that not only Collier's *Short View,* but also his *Defence of the Short View* was printed for S. Keble just two months after *A Letter to Mr. Congreve had appeared.* Likewise, Collier's *A Second Defence* was printed for Keble in 1700. Too, Mr. Taylor compared the *Letter to Mr. Congreve* with the *Short View* to discover Collier's authorship. I believe that a comparison with *A Defence* is more to the purpose for reasons that I mentioned above.

Another mark of Collier's authorship of *A Letter to Mr. Congreve* lies in the fact that the author of *A Letter* refers in two places to the trouble with the government in which Congreve's plays involved their author. In each reference there is the same sarcasm which Collier had displayed in the *Short View* when he referred to the penalties threatened by the government to

"All Bearwards, Common Players of Enterludes, and Counterfeit Egyptians,"

as well as to the keepers of Play-Houses and Dicing-Houses.[36]

---

[33] D. C. Taylor, *William Congreve,* p. 136.

[34] *Ibid.,* p. 136.

[35] *Ibid.,* p. 137.

[36] J. Collier, *Short View,* p. 242. The two references to the difficulties which Congreve faced for his plays occur in *A Letter to Mr. Congreve,* pp. 11, 36. In the first case the author writes: "If you demand the privilege of the *Habeas Corpus Act,* to remove your offensive Plays, from the *Quarter-Sessions of Middlesex, to the King's-Bench Bar* . . . " while in the second he states: "[at] the . . . *Quarter-Sessions,* the *Grand Jury of Middlesex* . . . presented Mr. *Congreve* and some others, for their obscene Plays." The references are clarified by an entry which Luttrell makes for Thursday, May 12, 1698. We read "The justices of Middlesex did not only present the playhouses, but also Mr. Congreve, for writing the Double-Dealer, . . . and Tonson . . . for printing." N. Luttrell, *A Brief Historical Relation,* IV, 379.

Besides these distinct resemblances between *A Letter to Mr. Congreve* and *A Defence,* it should be noted also that the author of *A Letter* upholds Collier's intellectuality and morality against Congreve's attack,[37] a defence not in the least surprising were Collier his own champion. Moreover, the author of *A Letter* speaks with special favor of Collier's *Essays,* and we know from previous references the esteem which Collier had of this work of his:

> "You [Congreve] fall Egregiously foul, both upon his Intellectuals, and his Morals; you have endeavoured to detect Mr. Collier, to be a man of great *absurdity,* and *ignorance.* Now, he that makes so very bold with another, ought, in prudence and good manners, to be some considerable degrees above him, both in Virtue and in Sense: but when I compare the several *Essay's* that Gentleman has given, of his Judgment, and penetration, with your *four poor Plays,* I cannot think the right lay on your side, to render him so contemptible for his Ignorance."[38]

Again we read,

> "But Mr. *Collier* was not an Idiot, when he set his name to his Book: . . . And I do not find, either that Mr. *Dennis,* who sate at the head of a Club, above a Month to impeach him, or Mr. *Congreve* who has staid longer upon the Inquisition, have laid any considerable instance of Immorality to his charge, except it be the writing of a very ingenious book against it."[39]

All of the above evidence, I feel sure, substantiates the opinion that Collier wrote *A Letter to Mr. Congreve.*

An analysis of *A Letter to Mr. Congreve* proves no less interesting than does the problem of its authorship. We note that the author has a fund of arguments to use in counter-attack. To Congreve's unwillingness to defend the corruption of the stage, the anonymous letter-writer replies:

> "not while you write Comedies for it; . . . and if Mr. *Collier* had laid the wickedness of a great many more Plays, besides your own, at your door, he had not much abus'd you;"[40]

---

[37] Anonymous, *A Letter,* p. 5.
[38] *Ibid.,* pp. 5-6.
[39] *Ibid.,* p. 7. Dennis states in his *Usefulness of the Stage,* p. iv, that he conceived, wrote, and published his book in a month.
[40] *A Letter,* p. 4.

and as to Congreve's intention of restoring those passages of plays to their primitive condition and of "replanting them from Collier's dunghill to the Field of Nature," he says

> "I had thoughts, to put all your dirty, *Billings-gate* language, against him, into one Paragraph, . . . but, when I had done, I found, I had in effect, copied your whole Book; there were only a few impertinent, and senseless lines left, scarce worth observation; and then, it made such a loathsome *Dunghill*, as you call it, that I was forced to hold my Nose; and away with it."[41]

Another vindication which is found in *A Letter*, and which might be expected of Collier, pertains to Congreve's tactlessness in remarking about Collier's pitiful and mean comparisons as evidence of the filth of his imagination.[42] This is answered with:

> "You represent him, . . . for a most notoriously lewd and immoral man, a person *in the high Vigour of obscenity;* and you have a pretty way with you to keep up his Character when you bestow so many damnable lewd allegories on him, in your Answer: He *commits a rape upon your words,* . . . I must step forward a little, to mind you here; that you say, *Metaphors do chiefly distinguish the manner of a man's Breeding and Conversation.*[43]

Eloquently, the author of *A Letter* asserts that Collier, in placing his name to his book did it because he was not conscious to himself of any considerable immorality; that neither Mr. Dennis nor Mr. Congreve laid any charge of immorality against him unless it be the writing "of a very ingenious book against it."[44]

If Congreve thought his liberty "of whipping the devil out of his plays" was to pass unheeded, he was mistaken. Note the retort:

> "You represent him for an *evil Spirit* ent'ring into your Plays: Now *evil Spirits* have shewn a very great alacrity and inclination, at ent'ring into anything that is *Swinish*: Therefore I cannot blame you for taking alarm at the word *Legion,* in relation to your own little Herd:"[45]

---

[41] *Ibid.,* p. 5.
[42] W. Congreve, *Amendments,* pp. 85-6.
[43] Anonymous, *A Letter to Mr. Congreve,* p. 6.
[44] *Ibid.,* p. 7.
[45] *Ibid.,* p. 8.

Then, too, there is a counter-charge on the score of Congreve's alleged ignorance of Collier's nomenclature:

> "You seem to be in pain and remorse, with your self, that you have not duly *return'd his Civilities in calling him Names*: But be out of pain: you have done pretty well, for a Gentleman: And, I believe, I have a Collection of yours, out of this short Essay, that will be a Match for Mr. Collier's *Nomenclature*, at any time. Beside, when it seemed to run low with you, his own Personal Names, *Jeremy* and *Collier*, proved great helps to you."[46]

The author chuckles over Congreve's postulata. The first he grants because it is Aristotle's. The second he refuses to accept because it is Congreve's and unreasonable.

> "You might as well argue, it would be of use to have idle Fellows Swear and Curse in the Streets, purely for the sake of giving sober Men, an opportunity to Chide them."[47]

With a cynical "Remember here again your Doctrine of Ideas," the writer replies to Congreve's statement that the painter should not be thought to resemble all the ugly faces he draws:

> "Can we think, his Thoughts were altogether so chastly taken up, and employ'd, when they were directing the Pencil?"[48]

The Third postulatum is granted even though it is Congreve's, for the writer of *A Letter to Mr. Congreve* sees very little difference whether a reader peruses the passages in the original or in the *Short View*.[49] The fourth postulatum, aimed as it is at profaneness, shares the same fate as its predecessors.[50]

To Congreve's protest against the charge of smut and profaneness in *The Mourning Bride*,[51] the author of *A Letter to Mr. Congreve* answers:

> "I am not now upon charging it with *Smut,* but when I have dropped this one remark more to the two former, I will leave

---

[46] *Ibid.,* p. 9.
[47] *Ibid.,* p. 9.
[48] *Ibid.,* p. 10.
[49] *Ibid.,* pp. 10-11.
[50] *Ibid.,* pp. 11-13.
[51] W. Congreve, *Amendments,* p. 23.

it to your self to judge, whether it is not now and then a little *Prophane.*"[52]

Upon Congreve's attempt to lord it over Collier in point of criticism, the writer of *A Letter* is silent inasmuch as Congreve, the playwright, should be a greater master in that art than is Collier, the clergyman. But for daring to reprimand Collier for his phrase "learning a Spaniel to Set," the anonymous author asserts:

> "You quarrel at Mr. Collier's Phrase of *learning a Spaniel to Set;* which shews, that you are yet to *learn* the compass of our English tongue, . . . For, is Mr. *Congreve* yet to be told, that *to learn,* is often used Actively, for *to teach?* Does he not remember it to be so used in the *Psalter?* O learn *me true Understanding!* I chuse to refer you to that Ejaculation, because it may be a proper one for you to use in your Devotions."[53]

To Congreve's references to St. Chrysostom he banteringly answers:

> "Over leaf we have you in another fit of *Divinity* again; I am glad to find it; 'tis a good sign: And though you are still very awkward at it, there's hopes you may improve; 'tis but young dayes with you in that profession: You should let alone St. *Chrysostom* yet; 'tis a vanity with all young Divines, to be nibling and retailing the Fathers, before they are well grounded in the Bible."[54]

A Letter to Mr. Congreve supports Collier in his charge of smut and prophaneness. It offers to produce a great many more instances than the ones cited, but it asserts that there is one great difficulty encountered when dealing with Congreve:

> "If Mr. *Collier* past any of it over, out of Modesty, with a Dash, as being too Baudy to be express'd; then you cry, *it lyes yet upon him to prove it; his bare Assertion without an Instance is not sufficient*: and if he disobliges his Paper with a little of it expressly, to prove *downright smut* upon you, then all your Thanks is *why e'en let him take it for his pains.*"[55]

---

[52] Anonymous, *A Letter to Mr. Congreve,* p. 16. The author calls attention to the fact that Congreve himself seemed conscious of the profanity because in his reply he vindicates his play only on the charge of immodesty. He says: "You silently let fall the word *Prophaneness* and cry out, 'if there be immodesty in that tragedy . . . '"

[53] *Ibid.,* p. 20.

[54] *Ibid.,* p. 22.

[55] *Ibid.,* p. 23.

Congreve's frequent references to Mr. Collier's "Absolutions" are placed under fire, and here we find—if not Collier himself breathing out his pent-up bitterness for the returns received from following the dictates of his conscience—then at least, one who suffered with him during the years which followed that act at the scene of execution:

> "You [Congreve] so often triumph at Mr. *Collier's Absolutions,* that I can't choose but take notice of it; you don't consider what a very mean, and contemptible man you appear your self while you strut and crow thus over anothers misfortunes; . . . But if that Gentleman has been so unfortunate in dispencing his *Absolution* once, he will be more wary for the future; and endure a great deal of *pounding,* . . . before he will yield to prostitute his Office so far, as to squander away an *Absolution* upon anyone belonging to the Stage."[56]

The author of *A Letter* becomes sarcastic when he vindicates Collier for his censure of Congreve's abuse of the clergy:

> "You mount in your defence hugely, concerning the Clergy; and having smelt at your Adversaries Arguments, you despise them; and march along in Triumph for many Pages and carry it with such a high hand, and lay about you so furiously; that it is hardly safe for a stander by to step in, and interrupt you."[57]

He comments upon Congreve's three "bouts" with the priests, and in his rejoinder to the third—Collier's statement "In short he is represented Lewd, but not Little"—he humourously expresses his contempt for Congreve:

> "*Lewd,* but not *little*: if that be all, I'll fetch but two Small Stitches, and it shall be as sound a Limb, as any Mr. *Congreve* has about him. Let me see—*Lewd,* as to his Person; but not *Little,* as to his Office. There, now 'tis done. This is plainly Mr. *Collier's* meaning, and all he contends for, in so many Pages before, where he is so strangely put to the banter."[58]

---

[56] *Ibid.,* pp. 27-28. Collier's absolution of Friend and Perkins just before their execution for treason in 1696 is to what Congreve refers when he tells Collier "I do not see why the Players should not lay hold of him [Collier], and pound him till he has given them Absolution." W. Congreve, *Amendments,* p. 77.

[57] *A Letter,* p. 28.

[58] *Ibid.,* p. 31.

Concerning Congreve's assertion "that no man living has a greater respect for a good Clergy Man, than myself," our author declares:

"Let all that are good of the Order, rise up and thank you for it! But what method do you take to manifest your respect to them? Why truly, by never bringing a Clergy-man on the Stage, but in a ridiculous Manner: and consequently, you never take occasion to put your audience in mind of one of that order; but to expose him to contempt."[59]

He refers to Mrs. Trotter's play, *Fatal Friendship,* as an example of entertaining an audience "with all the Judgment, Wit, and Beauty of Poetry; without *shocking our senses* with intollerable profaneness or obscenity."[60] In addition, he points out the defects of Congreve's prose. He says of it:

"I must speak freely, I never could yet meet with a Dramatick Poet that could write good Prose. Your Essays that way do commonly dwindle, and run off into Dialogism, Ramble, and Banter;"[61]

and asserts of it, besides, that it is filled with glaring inconsistencies, especially where Collier is concerned.[62] He terminates his citation of Congreve's inconsistencies and contradictions by stating:

"I have not leisure to compare you any farther with your self, but these few instances of varience between you, are sufficient to convince you, that the next time you write in angry Contro-versie, you should make use of more sincerity, or at least a better memory."[63]

The letter-writer's parting words are grossly personal remarks evoked by Congreve's promise to omit the profanity from the *Double-Dealer* when the next impression of that play is made:

"when the *Double Dealer* has another Edition, I believe you . . . may think of mending some other faults of yours, that more nearly concern your Person."[64]

---

[59] *Ibid.,* p. 32.
[60] *Ibid.,* pp. 36-37. Allibone in his *Critical Dictionary,* I, 400, identifies *Miss* Catherine Trotter or *Mrs. C. Cockburn* as the author of *Fatal Friendship.*
[61] *Ibid.,* p. 37. The author's attempt at literary criticism in the *Letter to Mr. Congreve* is another evidence that Collier is the author. Collier, as we know, never lost an opportunity in the *Short View* to voice his critical principles.
[62] *Ibid.,* pp. 37-41.
[63] *Ibid.,* p. 41.
[64] *Ibid.,* p. 42.

With this thrust at Congreve, the author of *A Letter to Mr. Congreve* concludes. Fast and furiously throughout his pamphlet he has attacked Congreve, sparing him neither on literary, intellectual, nor moral grounds. He is decidedly more partisan in this vindication of Collier than is Collier of himself in his *Defence,* perhaps because here he was writing anonymously. He does not answer all the charges which Congreve had taken up in his *Amendments* but saves several important topics to be vindicated in *A Defence.* He declines in *A Letter* to enter into detail concerning Lord Touchwood and Belmour, characters in Congreve's plays; but the supplement is found in *A Defence.* Congreve's jest of the Anagram is answered, too, in *A Defence,* while here the author elaborates only upon his preference for the Ancients.

2

Several days after *A Letter to Mr. Congreve* was published, there appeared the anonymous *Animadversions on Mr. Congreve's Late Answer to Mr. Collier. Collier in a Dialogue Between Mr. Smith and Mr. Johnson. With the Characters of the present Poets; and some Offers towards New-Modeling the Stage.*[65] The Dedicatory Epistle is addressed to the "Ingenious Mr. --------," and consists of approximately fifty heroic couplets painting ludicrous portraits of "the characters of the present poets." The author mentions no fellow-poet by name but gives, merely, two or three identifying letters. He criticizes his contemporaries Se--le (Settle), D----y (Durfey), Gil--n (Gildon), Hop---s (Hopkins), D----s (Dennis), the Beau-writer (Vanbrugh), and even includes

". . . the two Female things
With Muse Pen-feather'd, guiltless yet of Wings,
And yet, it strives to Fly, and thinks it Sings!"[66]

He satirizes in the concluding couplets both Motteux and Dryden; the former for his preface to *Beauty in Distress,* the latter for his change in

[65] This pamphlet is seventy-two pages in length and was published September 8, 1698, having been printed for John Nutt whose shop was near Stationers-Hall. It is appended to an interesting Dedicatory Epistle and a unique preface.

[66] Anonymous, *Animadversions,* pp. i-viii. Reference is very likely made to Catherine Trotter and to Mrs. Pix. Both had plays produced at the Theatre in Lincoln-Inn-Fields in 1698. Cf. Charles Gildon, *Lives,* p. 111, and Allibone, *A Critical Dictionary,* I, 400.

religion and for bestowing eulogies on Motteux in the *Poetical* Epistle. Of the play he says:

> "Poor ev'ry way, in Poetry and Pence,
> Keep your Advice, and write, to shew your Sense.
>
> .   .   .
>
> But be as conscious still, you want a prop,
> As when both Priest and Poet bore you up."[67]

The explanation of his censure is found, perhaps, in such of Dryden's eulogies as the following:

> "Thy Incidents, perhaps too thick are sown:
> But too much Plenty is thy fault alone:
> At least but two, can that good Crime commit,
> Thou in Design, and Wycherley in Wit.
>
> .   .   .
>
> Words, once my stock, are wanting to commend
> So Great a Poet, and so Good a Friend."[68]

With the conclusion of the couplets the author begins his Preface. It is an informal address to an unidentified friend of Congreve. The opening lines prepare the reader for the kind of raillery that is to follow:

> "Being very Idle, I made bold to seize the Reins of your Friend Will's Prose Pegasus,"[69]

As the raillery continues the reader is convinced that Congreve is the object of bitter personal animosity:

> "(and yet his most fiery Poetic Steed is no better) to make my Remarks a little how he foam'd and champ'd upon his Bit; and

---

[67] *Ibid.*, p. vii. Undoubtedly, the priest and poet referred to are Caffaro and Dryden. It is interesting to note that though the author of the *Animadversions* enters the stage controversy to vindicate Collier against Congreve, he introduces side issues. He attacks Dryden's Poetical Epistle as do Ridpath in *The Stage Condemned* and the author of the Preface to the Translation of Bossuet's *Maximes et réflexions,* but each of the three authors argue over different statements made by Dryden.

[68] P. Motteux, *Beauty in Distress,* Poetical Epistle by Dryden, p. xxviii.

[69] Note the play on the word "idle" and recall Congreve's opening lines in the *Amendments*: "I have been told by some, that they should think me very idle, . . . " To understand the reference of the "Prose Pegasus" it is necessary to recall that Congreve, in his *Amendments,* p. 83, had said of Collier: "He shall appear mounted upon a false Pegasus, like a Lancashire Witch upon an imaginary Horse, the Fantom shall be unbridled, and the Broomstick made visible.

tho' he was a Guift Horse to the World this bout (for I think no body bought him) I presum'd to look him in the Mouth. He had many faults, I found as I View'd him; very Headstrong; when Spurr'd, apt neither to run, nor Pace, but Kick and Fling, or at best, fall into a hard uncouth, unsufferable Trot. I observ'd him from Head to Tail, he was both Crop'd and Bob'd. He was so untoward, he had given his Rider (while he pretended to shew him) several Falls, and so I thought fit to take hold of him."[70]

To appreciate the manner in which the animadverter takes hold of Congreve it is necessary to read the entire pamphlet. He handles the playwright roughly,—at times brutally. Gibes are flung not only at his private life, but at his plays, and at his attempted vindication of them. When critics attempt to solve Congreve's subsequent lack of interest in comedy they naturally, and quite correctly, take into consideration the treatment accorded him by Collier and Collier's abettors of whom the author of the *Animadversions* was one.[71]

The remaining pages of the Preface are a castigation of Congreve's plays under the charges of immorality, profanity, irreligion,[72] while occasionally amid the lashings the author makes some biographical comments:

"If that be Mr. Congreve's Opinions, he need not covet to go to Heaven at all, but. to stay and Ogle his dear Bracilla [Mrs.

---

[70] Anonymous, *Animadversions,* pp. xii-xiii.
[71] A. Kippis, *Biographia Britannica,* IV, 72-73: "In all probability, this quarrel created in our author [Congreve] some distaste for the stage: he afterwards brought on another Comedy, the last, not the least valuable, of his performances. It was entitled *The Way of the World,* of which it was so just a picture, that the world could not bear it, which compleated the disgust of our author to the Theatre: upon which Mr. Dennis . . . said a very fine, and a very kind thing, 'That Mr. Congreve quitted the stage early, and that Comedy left it with him.' "
D. C. Taylor, *William Congreve,* p. 163, argues much to the same purpose: "When his [Congreve's] anger against Collier had overcome his better judgment he referred to the stage as a 'war with knaves and fools,' and even in a tranquil mood, a residue of this attitude doubtless remained."
It might be well to state here that four of the stage pamphlets, *A Short View, A Letter to Mr. Congreve, Animadversions,* and *A Defence of the Short View* published within the first seven months of the controversy singled out for castigation *all* the plays of Congreve; if we further consider that the last three pamphlets satirized the author not only of these plays but the *Amendments* as well, we can readily understand the subsequent aversion to a literary career which Congreve entertained.
[72] Anonymous, *Animadversions,* pp. xv-xx.

Bracegirdle], with sneaking looks under his Hat, in the little side Box."[73]

The Animadverter, in several instances, gives credit to the tradition that Congreve was born in Ireland:

> "However, this Gentleman's Countrymen are not much oblig'd to him; for he is pleas'd (where he confesses his Demerits) to say he hopes the Faults are to be Excused in a young Writer, and especially a Man of Ireland. None I think, but the Author of such a Play, would have writ such a Thing. I resent it, for perhaps I have the misfortune to have been born in Ireland, and to own it too. However, I think Mr. Congreve would have done well to have made the like Excuse (in spight of Stafford-shire) for his Poetry."[74]

He anticipates objections to the light, airy nature of his pamphlet and replies to the objectors by asserting that the title *Animadversions* sig-nifies only loose thoughts, and not a set and studied discourse, and that dialogue is the method of narration chosen because it affords a

---

[73] *Ibid.*, p. xviii.

[74] *Ibid.*, pp. xxi-xxii. It is important here to note that there is an apparent misquotation on the part of the author of the *Animadversions*. Why he should misquote this passage invites analysis. Congreve's statement as it appears in a first edition of the *Amendments* says nothing of having been born in Ire-land. It simply states "Indeed I cannot hold Laughing, when I compare his dreadful Comment with such poor silly words as are in the Text: especially when I reflect how *young a beginner*, and how very much a Boy I was when that Comedy [the *Old Batchelour*] was Written; which several know was some years before it was Acted: When I wrote it I had little Thoughts of the Stage; but did it to amuse myself in a slow Recovery from a Fit of Sick-ness." W. Congreve, *Amendments*, p. 39. *Concerning* the place of Congreve's birth, biographers are pretty much in agreement that it was Bardsey, or Bardsa. *D.N.B.*, IV, 931; D. C. Taylor, *William Congreve*, pp. 12-13; D. E. Baker, *Biographia Dramatica*, 1782 ed., I, 95; A. Kippis, *Biographia Britan-nica*, III, 1439; S. Johnson, *Life of Congreve*, ed. by Chalmers, X, 257. Johnson, however, states: "For the place [of his birth], it was said by him-self, that he owed his nativity to England, and by every body else, that he was born in Ireland." *Ibid.*, X, 257. A. Kippis, *Biographia Britannica*, III, 1439-40, goes into great detail concerning the place of Congreve's nativity. He says: "As to the place, and indeed as to the kingdom, in which he was born, authors differ, and not only so, but are positive on both sides; some are clear that he was a native of Ireland, but it . . . is morally certain, that he was a native of England." Kippis then states that the source of informa-tion which gives Congreve's birth-place as Ireland is *The Works* of Sir James Ware, III, 294, and he adds that "in a very large collection of the same kind with this [*General Dictionary*, IV, 427] we find the same fact asserted, from the information of the late ingenious Thomas Southerne, Esq." On the other hand, he bases his opinion that Congreve was born in England on the authority of Mr. Giles Jacob, *Lives of the English Poets*, I, p. 41.

free and easy way of writing. Moreover, to those "carpers" who believe *The Amendments* deserve a weighty or an elaborate reply he asserts that there is only this to be said, "I think it does not deserve it."[75] There is, besides, a statement made for the benefit of those who might condemn the animadverter's severity upon Congreve:

"I shall only desire these Gentlemen to take a slight View of his Book, and I dare engage they'll soon be of another Opinion. They'll find his Pages fuller of Malice than right Reasoning, and instead of being stor'd with Sense, blacken'd with Gall and Spleen. His way of Answering Mr. Collier, is with Satyr and Reflection; and since he has set the Copy, he can't take it ill if he is Imitated, especially when he sees we have observ'd our Distance, and not presum'd to cope with him in his Master-piece."[76]

The *Animadversions* begins with the two characters, Mr. Smith and Mr. Johnson, seated where "Wit and Wine may flow together;"[77] and makes clear from the very first that its purpose is condemnation of Congreve. Frequent quotations from the Amendments, at other times phrases torn from their context in Congreve's plays,—all are jumbled together to paint an idiotic picture of the dramatist.

JOHNSON: I have a great passion for Congreve . . . Ah! he's so fine, so extremely Fine, so everything in the world that I like.

SMITH: Cowley I believe you mean.

JOHNSON: No, no; our English Horace, I mean. . . .

SMITH: I make a doubt if there be so great a Poet breathing.

JOHNSON: O Lord! *Will Congreve's* alive, Man, he's my Countryman, he has been regenerated ever since he turn'd Poet, . . .

---

[75] *Ibid.,* pp. xxii-xxiv.

[76] *Ibid.,* p. xxv.

[77] *Ibid.,* p. 1. The names *Smith* and *Johnson* may be more than a coincidence. I call attention to a possible significance: Thomas Hearne, in *Collections,* II, 19, tells us that Collier occasionally assumed the name of Smith: "My friend . . . wishes he had known that the 'Mr. Smith' who was examining MSS. in Bodley was Collier; . . ." Moreover, John Johnson of Cranbrook, a later Non-Juror, was a friend of Collier's, who together with Collier entertained for a long time similar views on the "Oblatory Function of the Holy Eucharist." H. Broxap in his *The Later Non-Jurors,* p. 5 tells us: "J. Johnson of Cranbrook published in 1710 *The Propitiatory Oblation of the Holy Eucharist,*" and from the title we infer that this clergyman was one with Collier in his fourth of the *Four Usages* for which he later suffered so much.

SMITH: What Miracle has made him a *Staffordshire Man,* I know not, but I'm sure his *Muse,* for all his fine Flights, is but a Bog-Trotter still.

JOHNSON: Fie, fie, I don't like that 'Still'; 'tis no good word, *vide Congreve.*"[78]

Smith and Johnson continue their entertainment at Congreve's expense. They call him "all Love for Love" and "not one jot The Double Dealer."[79] With great solemnity they make ready to open Congreve's vindication of his four plays. Smith, meanwhile, asserts:

"By the Muses, tho' this Helicon of Wit will please you better than that of Wine, come, bless yourself, and I'll open the Book."[80]

They twit Congreve for always being about to say something but leaving off just before he says it;[81] they accuse him of plagiarism:

"Those pretty things Friend Congreve you rehearse,
Were once my Words, tho' they are now your Verse."[82]

They scorn the defence he makes of himself in the *Amendments:*

"if he were acquitted at all, it must have been before he offered his Defence; for he has made so mean and wretched a business of it, that he is now Cast in Opinion of the World: He has said nothing that can hinder Sentence from being past upon him, even in the Opinion of his bigotted Friends."[83]

They ridicule his "Postulata":

"JOHNSON: Well, what think you now of his four Postulata's?

SMITH: Ay . . . but *he sends his Wits for a Venture* and I fear they will be plaguily Weather-beaten before they come home: . . . But he's Affronted I suppose to be turn'd up by Mr. *Collier,* because taking him unawares, the dirty linnen appears in view."[84]

---

[78] *Ibid.,* p. 3. Congreve had objected in his *Amendments,* p. 47, to Collier's "filching" the word "still" from the context of *The Double Dealer.*
[79] *Ibid.,* p. 4.
[80] *Ibid.,* p. 5.
[81] *Ibid.,* p. 6.
[82] *Ibid.,* p. 7.
[83] *Ibid.,* p. 8.
[84] *Ibid.,* pp. 10-11.

They hold up to derision certain lines of his poetry:

> "SMITH: For Example, I'll repeat you one or two of his smooth lines. *For Love's Island: I for the Golden Coast.* Now if you can get a shore on that Island without being plaguily out of Breath, I'll be bound to find out the Golden Coast for Mr. *Congreve.*
>
> *Let's have a fair Trial, and a clear Sea.* There's a line for you that has sayl'd itself into a clear Sea of Prose.
>
> JOHNSON: No indeed, 'tis a Verse, I'm sure, for it Rhymes to three lines going before."[85]

Smith answers Congreve's defence against the charge of profaneness with the statement that Congreve,

> "To shew himself a Man of Letters, . . . talks of the Alphabet here in the fourth place, and says, that tho' he claps a Scripture Sentence into the Mouths of Persons in a Play (which by the by, may be Bawds or Whores) 'tis allowable, because the same Letters are requisite to the spelling of all Words whatever."[86]

The objection which Congreve had taken to Collier's short sentences receives this stinging rejoinder:

> "SMITH: . . . here he talks of *puffing, and blowing, and laying about in short Sentences,* sure he has been an Apprentice to a Blacksmith that he's always stirring the Coals thus, only to make himself more smutty; but the mischief on't is, he can never strike the Iron while 'tis hot:"[86]

A few pages further he comes to Congreve's promise to strike out in the next impression of the *Double Dealer* the profanity censured by Collier and ironically replies:

> "Who will ever be at the charge of another Impression of such a piece of heavy Stuff as *The Double Dealer?*"[87]

By hashing over the *Amendments* Smith contrives for the author the name *Jeremy Congreve;* then, stating that because he has fed so long

---

[85] *Ibid.,* pp. 12-13.
[86] *Ibid.,* p. 35.
[87] *Ibid.,* pp. 42-44.

upon the defence written by Congreve, he needs a change of diet, he says to Johnson:

> "I'm almost a-sleep, prithee drink to me, all this stuff is so plaguy dry and insipid, I want something to put my mouth in Taste."[88]

For a while longer the two speakers continue in jovial mood at Congreve's expense: a jest here, a pun there mingled with reflections on Congreve's profanity, on his scoffing at the clergy, and upon the instances of immorality pointed out by Collier. Finally their stock of wit and fun exhausted they have another round of the bottle and thence pass on to reading a short essay which Smith recommends to Johnson for consideration. The essay in question is fifteen pages in length and was written, Smith tells us, by a young lady friend of his. It begins by demonstrating the truth of the Latin quotation "Totus Mundus agit Histrionem,"[89] and thence passes on to a discussion of the purpose of the stage which is held to be both to "Instruct and to Delight," and to the ways and means of regulating plays.[90]

3

Shortly after the bantering conversation between Smith and Johnson had appeared under the title of *Animadversions*, there was published the *Stage Condemned, and The Encouragement given to the Immoralities and Profaneness of the Theatre, by the English Schools, Universities, and Pulpits, Censur'd. King Charles I. Sundays Mask and Declaration for Sports and Pastimes on the Sabbath, largely Related and Animadverted upon. The Arguments of All the Authors that have Writ in Defence of the Stage against Mr. Collier, Consider'd. And the Sense of the Fathers, Councils, Antient Philosophers and Poets, and of the Greek and Roman States, and of the First Christian Emperours concerning the Drama, Faithfully Deliver'd. Together with The Censure, of the English State and of several Antient and Modern Divines of the Church of England upon the Stage. And Remarks on diverse late Plays, as also on those presented by the two Universities to King Charles I.* This ponderous, breath-taking title-page to the anonymous two-hun-

---

[88] *Ibid.*, pp. 52-58.
[89] *Ibid.*, p. 73.
[90] *Ibid.*, pp. 76-87.

dred-sixteen-page book gives very little promise of interesting contents, and a perusal of the treatise confirms the anticipation. The author is generally reputed to be George Ridpath.[91] Ridpath in his Dedicatory Epistle adressed to "the Right Honourable the Lords and Commons of England, in Parliament Assembled," emphasizes the corruption of the stage by calling attention to the fact that many of the recently published stage-vindications and especially the Preface to *Beauty in Distress,* to the *Defence of Dramatick Poetry,* and to the *Usefulness of the Stage* admit the need of reformation. He advances a new argument, however, by stating that

> "The Corruption of the Stage is in a great measure owing to the method of Educating our Youth in Schools;"[92]

and that the honour of the English Nation as well as of Religion requires an examination of the Theatres. However, he leaves the time when and the method how this is to be done to be determined by the wisdom of the King and Parliament.[93]

Ridpath, after requesting that all English ladies and gentle-women be pleased to absent themselves from the play-house,[94] points to Collier and the *Short View*:

> "but, tho' that Author hath done excellently well, there may still be some gleanings left for another. Mr. Collier strikes directly at the Miscarriages of the Stage, because they were most obvious and nearest to View; but this ought not to supersede the Endeavours of others, nor to put a stop to their Inquiry into the Root of the Mischief."[95]

A perusal of *The Stage Condemned* reveals that Ridpath found abundant "gleanings" for censure; it reveals, too, that he laid much of the

---

[91] Various sources identify Ridpath as the author. Halkett and Laing, *Dictionary of Anonymous and Pseudonymous English Literature,* V, 354; *D.N.B.,* XVI, 1178-9; Tom Brown, *Stage-Beaux,* p. 30, while throughout the anonymous pamphlet, *The Stage Acquitted,* reference is made to the author of *The Stage Condemned* as Mr. R—th.

George Ridpath was a whig journalist. He went to Edinburgh University and in 1699 took his degree. He conducted for some years *The Flying Post,* or *Postman* established in 1695. Of this paper Tutchin said, "it is the honestest of all newspapers." *D.N.B.,* XVI, 1178-9. *The Stage Condemned* was printed for John Salusbury and its announcement appears in the *Flying Post* for September 16, 1698.

[92] Anonymous, *The Stage Condemned,* p. ii.

[93] *Ibid.,* pp. iii-iv.

[94] *Ibid.,* p. iv.

[95] *Ibid.,* p. 1.

blame for the immorality of the age upon the schools. It is his opinion that much fault is to be found with the education which is given the students; for, as no one can be fit to write for the stage who has not first been at school, so if the schools instruct in plays and romances,

> "it's but natural we should think ourselves good Proficients, and that we have in a great measure answered the End of our Education, when we can oblige the World with those of our own Composure."[96]

Ridpath focuses attention on Motteux's *Beauty in Distress* with its Poetical Epistle by Dryden, its Caffaro Letter, and its Epilogue spoken by Mrs. Bracegirdle and he renews his castigations of the persons concerned.[97] From Motteux to D'Urfey, Ridpath turns. He censures him for his Preface to *The Campaigners* in which he attempts to ward off the heavy charge which Collier had brought against his *Comical History of Don Quixote;*[98] he bluntly calls attention to Vanbrugh's *The Relapse* in which are found such opprobrious names for the clergy as "Saygrace," and "Cuff-cushion;"[99] and he devotes Chapter XIX to answering "Mr. Dennis' Usefulness of the Stage."[100] Ridpath recognizes both the cleverness of Dennis and his forceful reasoning for he asserts:

> "The Title is sufficient to discover, that I am to combate a Man of Assurance, who like another *Goliah* bids Defiance to the Armies of Fathers, Councils, Scriptures, etc. and all that have brandished their Swords against the Theatre."[101]

Ridpath's attempt to link issues with Collier, to censure those points which Collier had slighted and to give his own opinions on the unlawfulness of the stage-performance resulted in the expenditure of much time and ink. With the exception of the possible influence which his arguments exerted in having Dennis presented for his book *The Usefulness of the Stage,* his work is generally considered ineffectual. That it resulted in any reformation of manners or that it deflected any play-goers from the play-house is not recorded. His views on the lawfulness of diversion are more narrow than Collier's, his diction is at

---

96 *Ibid.,* p. 1.
97 *Ibid.,* p. 160.
98 *Ibid.,* pp. 162-169.
99 *Ibid.,* p. 163.
100 *Ibid.,* pp. 170-206.
101 *Ibid.,* p. 170.

times incoherent, and his arguments are generally unconvincing. When his work is referred to it is generally with contempt.

4

Among the venom-tipped pens that wrote in reply to Collier and in defence of the English stage we include that of the anonymous author of *The Immorality of the English Pulpit*.[102] The *Letter* is directed specifically to answering the third chapter of the *View*: "The Clergy abus'd by the Stage."

Into the very opening paragraph, the writer injects his disapproval of Collier's nonjurancy and he suggests the Stuart profligacy as the cause of the low ebb of morals:

"That the Licentiousness of the Stage should ask the Correction of your Pen, is a sad and manifold Confession of the Degeneracy of the Times, and withal shews the pressingness of the Occasion. What else could provoke a man to write against himself? For 'tis to your dear Times that we owe the vileness of the Theatre; Those very Loose Times, to the Protector whereof you are so constant a Devotee; so that in the Cause depending you are both Plaintiff and Defendant."[103]

He further censures the degeneracy of the theatre especially on the score of profanity and immorality, but he emphatically denies that the poets have abused the clergy:

"I frankly agree that most of his charge against them [the stage-poets] is just, undeniable, and well seconded with Proofs. But I must beg his pardon, if it be an Affront to tell him, that his Hat hung in his Light when he wrote that *Chapter*, wherein he accuses the Stage as *guilty of abusing the Clergy*;"[104]

and reminding Collier that a clergyman should employ his time otherwise than in reading plays he caustically adds:

"that such a one should snarl over his beloved Diet, is remarkably Currish; however not at all beside his Character."[105]

---

[102] *The Immorality of the English Pulpit as Justly Subjected to the Notice of the English Stage, as The Immorality of the Stage is to that of the Pulpit. In a Letter to Mr. Collier, Occasion'd by the Third Chapter of his Book, entitl'd, A Short View of the Immorality of the English Stage* is an 8-page pamphlet, and was printed in London in 1698. The title-page does not bear a printer's name.
[103] *Ibid.*, p. 3.
[104] *Ibid.*, p. 6.
[105] *Ibid.*, p. 4.

The author enters the lists of those who discuss the purpose of plays,[106] and very cleverly uses his argument to arrive at the proof which he had as his objective in addressing Mr. Collier:

> "It is the Office of the Stage to detect the *Roguery*, as well as the *Folly* of a *Knave*; and if such a one creeps into the Pulpit, 'tis Their Concern to cry *Ware shins* to the gaping Auditory, lest whilst he is drawing their Eyes towards the Pulpit-Roof, he should let them unawares through a Trap-door into Hell."[107]

---

[106] *Ibid.*, p. 7.
[107] *Ibid.*, p. 7

CHAPTER VII

The Publications from Nov. 10, 1698 to Nov. 26, 1699

1. J. Collier: *A Defence of the Short View,* Nov. 10, 1698.
2. Anonymous: *Some Remarks on Mr. Collier's Defence,* Dec. 6, 1698.
3. Anonymous: *The Stage Acquitted,* J n. 1, 1699.
4. Anonymous [J. Oldmixon]: *Reflections on the Stage and on Mr. Collyer's Defence.* March 4, 1699.
5. Anonymous [J. Drake]: *The Antient and Modern Stages survey'd,* March 7, 1699.
6. J. Wright: *Historia Histrionica: . . . A Dialogue of Plays and Players,* 1699.
7. Anonymous: A Translation of Bossuet's *Maximes et réflexions sur la comédie,* 1699. Preface.
8. Anonymous [J. Woodward]: *An Account of the Societies . . .* 1699.
9. Anonymous: *Feigned Friendship, or The Mad Reformer,* June 15, 1699.
10. J. Dryden: "Letter to Mrs. Eliz. Thomas," Nov., 1699.

The publications between November 10, 1698, and November 26, 1699, the respective dates of Collier's first and second defences of his *Short View,* prove that the stage attack was still a popular topic and that Collier was still making friends and foes to his cause. His *Defence* refuted the replies received in 1698, but especially those received from Congreve, Vanbrugh, Dennis, the author of *A Defence of Dramatick Poetry* and of *A Vindication of the Stage.* The next four pamphlets listed are attacks on Collier and vindications of the poets. In the sixth, *A Dialogue of Plays and Players,* Wright takes a neutral stand and attempts to give impartially his views on Collier and the stage. The seventh work cited, A Translation of Bossuet's *Maxims and Reflections,* has for its preface a vindication of Collier and an attack on the stage. The eighth, *An Account of the Societies,* presents Woodward on the side of reformation of manners and against the liberties of the stage-poets. The ninth, *Feigned Friendship, or, The Mad Reformer* is discussed by D. E. Baker, *Biographia Dramatica*, II, 123, and is included by Mr. Krutch in his Collier Bibliography, *Comedy and Conscience*, p. 269. He was unable to secure a copy of the play, and I, too, failed to do so. In the tenth of the pamphlets mentioned, Dryden in his letter to Mrs. Thomas gives evidence of contrition for the scurrility of his poetry.

1

In rapid succession the more aggressive of the stage-poets had discharged their shot against Collier and his abettors; one by one they had attempted to vindicate themselves and to defend the stage, and occasionally they had attempted to espouse the cause of an attacked brother-poet. Collier, however, was neither disabled nor disheartened by the onslaught. He had gathered his forces during the skirmish, and on November 10, 1698, he renewed the fray. He gloried in battle, and with courage inspired by belief in the justice of his cause, he never thought of deserting it until he should hoist the banner of victory. Squarely confronting Congreve and Vanbrugh as the "most eager of the Complainants" he asserts that he has endeavoured to satisfy them in the present *Defence;* and to prove that the *Volunteers*—as he terms the other vindicators—have not been overlooked, he addresses some remarks to them. He singles out for special notice three of these volunteers: Dennis, the Defender of Dramatic Poetry, and the Vindicator; as for the others he tells them,

> "they will find themselves affected with the Fortune of their Friends; and besides, I may probably have an opportunity of speaking farther with them hereafter."[1]

In the Preface we become aware that Collier takes notice of the criticism which he had received, that he is conscious of his unpopular-

---

[1] J. Collier, *A Defence of the Short View of the Profaneness and Immorality of the English Stage.* It is 139 pages in length, and was printed for Keble, Sare, and Hindmarsh. Mr. Taylor finds authority in *The Post-Man* that it appeared Nov. 10, 1698. The title page of the first edition curiously reads 1699. However, in view of the fact that advertisements of and answers to *A Defence* appeared in 1698, it seems likely that this pamphlet was published in 1698; hence, "1699" is either an error of the printer, or a deliberate post-dating by the printer of a work published near the end of the year 1698; or, it may be that the printer dated his title-pages N.S. only, rather than O.S./N.S. which latter dating sometimes appears.

ity, and that he characteristically pours oil on the flames by attacking *new* foes.

> "Since the publishing my late *View,* etc., I have been plentifully rail'd on in Print: . . . But being charged with miscitations and unfair Dealing, 'twas requisite to say something: For Honesty is a tender point, and ought not to be neglected. . . . The Reader . . . may please to take notice, that the *Plot and no Plot* swears at length, and is scandalously Smutty and Profane. The *Fool in Fashion* for the first four Acts is liable to the same Imputation: Something in Swearing abated, *Caesar Borgia,* and *Love in a Nunnery* are no better Complexion'd than the former. And lastly, *Limberham,* and the *Soldier's Fortune,* are meer prodigies of Lewdness and Irreligion."[2]

Collier had been repeatedly censured by stage-advocates for combining literary criticism with his attack on the morality of the play. He explains why he has done it. He believes that if he can darken a poet's literary reputation, he will be able to lessen his dramatic popularity:

> "I conceive it very defensible to disarm an Adversary, if it may be, and disable him from doing Mischief."[3]

He declares that inasmuch as the poets are the aggressors they must first lay down their arms; that the only fault of which he and his abettors are guilty is in having silently borne with them so long.[4]

a. Collier's Reply to the Amendments

Collier's initial address to Congreve is unceremonious and his treatment of him throughout 96 of the 139 pages is ruthless:

> "Mr. *Congreve* being a Person of no great Ceremony, I shan't salute him with any Introduction; but fall to the Business without more Ado."[5]

---

[2] *Ibid.,* Preface, pp. i-ii. The *Plot and No Plot* was written by J. *Dennis,* and acted at the *Theatre Royal,* 1697. Gildon's *Lives,* p. 38.
The *Fool in Fashion* was written by Cibber, and acted at the Theatre Royal, 1696; *Ibid.,* p. 20. *Caesar Borgia,* written by Nath. Lee, was first acted at Duke's Theatre, 1680; *Ibid.,* p. 85. *Love in a Nunnery* by John Dryden was first acted at the Theatre Royal, 1678; *Ibid.,* p. 41. *Limberham* by J. Dryden was first acted at the Duke's Theatre in 1680; *Ibid.,* p. 45. *Soldier's Fortune* was written by Otway and first acted by their Royal Highness' Servants at the Duke's Theatre, 1681; *Ibid.,* p. 108.
[3] *Ibid.,* Preface, p. ii.
[4] *Ibid.,* Preface, p. ii.
[5] *Ibid.,* p. 1.

He takes the *Amendments,* and, page by page, justifies his *Short View* against Congreve's recriminations. To the charge that he had "raked in obscene and profane passages" he replies,

" . . . since the Mischief works in *English,* 'tis time to think of an *English* Remedy."[6]

He consistently maintains throughout the *Defence* that he has tried not to quote any passages that contained *indecent* language; that where the objectionable part was guilty of it he made only a general reference to *play* and to *character*. However, he did not deem it necessary, he says, to be thus reserved with the profane part.

"The profane Part, tho' Bolder, and more Black, will bear the Light better, and therefore when 'twas clear of Obscenity, I have set it to the *Bar*. Upon the whole; I was willing to Guard the Virtue, and awaken the Caution of the *Reader*."[7]

He dissects Congreve's four postulata. First of all he declares that the term "postulatum" carries the force of an axiom. Then he takes Congreve's assertion that, "they seem at first Sight to comprehend a Latitude." To this he replies:

"Then they are not Self-evident; They are unqualified for the Post he has put them in; . . . if He intends to deal clearly, why does he make the Touchstone faulty, and the Standard uncertain?"[8]

Because Congreve by his own statement thus owns his propositions *not evidently true,* Collier determines to prove the greatest part of them *evidently false,* and for a space of fourteen pages he subjects the four axioms to such rigid scrutiny that they crumble.[9]

He icily declares that Congreve's statement "the Business of Comedy is to delight, as well as instruct" needs explanation, and he proceeds to dwell upon the meaning of the words "as well," making them the secret of the definition,

"If he means as much, by *as well,* he is mistaken. For Delight is but the secondary End of Comedy, as I have prov'd at large;"[10]

---

[6] *Ibid.,* p. 2.
[7] *Ibid.,* p. 2.
[8] *Ibid.,* pp. 5-6.
[9] *Ibid.,* pp. 6-20.
[10] *Ibid.,* p. 9.

and he quotes as substantiating evidence Dryden's Preface to *Fresnoy's Art of Painting*. He sarcastically refers to Congreve's statement that the stage

> "being careful to secure the instruction of the audience generally sums up in the concluding lines of the poem, the moral of the play and puts it into rhyme in order that it may be easy and engaging to the memory."

In Collier's answer we discover a triple ring:

> "1.   This expedient is not always made use of. Examples that lack it are *The Relapse* and *Love in a Nunnery;*
> 2.   Sometimes these comprehensive lines do more harm than good: Examples of this nature are *The Soldier's Fortune* and the *Old Batchelour.*
> 3.   When the play is lewd, a grave moral amounts to little. 'The Doctor comes too late for the Disease, and the Antidote is much too weak for the Poyson.' "[11]

He further illustrates this third statement by stating that other parts of a discourse besides the conclusion ought to be free from infection; that if a man is sound only at his fingers' ends, he will have little comfort in his constitution.[12]

Each of Congreve's counter-attacks is given detailed consideration. To Congreve's rejoinder "if four Women were shewn upon the stage, and three of them were Vitious, it is as much as to say that three parts in four of the whole Sex are stark naught," Collier retorts "the Case is not parallel."[13] He proves by two arguments that Congreve's precedents from Virgil are inapplicable;[14] and he refutes the testimony from Rapin cited by the stage-poets.[15] To Congreve's boastful assurance of the decency of the *Mourning Bride*—"If there be Immodesty in this Tragedy I must confess myself incapable of ever writing anything with Modesty"—Collier dryly replies: "It may be so: An ill Custom is very hard to Conquer, with some People."[16]

---

[11] *Ibid.*, pp. 19-20.
[12] *Ibid.*, p. 21.
[13] *Ibid.*, p. 22.
[14] *Ibid.*, pp. 23-24.
[15] *Ibid.*, pp. 27-29.
[16] *Ibid.*, p. 31.

The Viewer attacks Congreve's defence of the violent rants in the parting of Osmin and Almeria. He declares:

> " . . . I think the Play was not worth the Candle. 'Tis much as Wise as it would be for a Man to make a long Preparation to get out of his Wits, and qualifie himself for Bedlam."[17]

He admits his error in quoting wasting for wafting but with his usual assurance asserts:

> "Now to my Mind, the restoring of the Text is a very poor relief. For this later *Epithete* is perfectly expletive and foreign to the matter in hand; there's neither Antithesis nor Perspicuity in 't."[18]

He likewise replies to Congreve's censure of his figure of speech, "The litter of epithets," and he vindicates himself by stating:

> " . . . bad company is often a disadvantage; besides, I was illustrating his fine Sentences, and showing his *Buckram* to the Reader."[19]

The stage-reformer scathes Congreve's excuse that he was not only very young when he wrote the *Old Batchelour* but that he wrote it to entertain himself in a slow recovery from a fit of sickness.

> "What his Disease was I am not to enquire; but it must be a very ill one, to be worse than the Remedy. The writing of that Play is a very dangerous Amusement either for *Sickness* or Health, or I'm much mistaken."[20]

He justifies himself for his censure of lewdness and profanity in the *Old Batchelour* and adds new charges to its already long litany of sins. He professes to doubt the author's repentance for his profane use of the word "Jesu" in the *Double Dealer,* arguing that the author had a chance to prove his sincerity by striking it out of the new editions of the *Old Batchelour,* but that inasmuch as he didn't do it, we cannot take his word that it will be struck out of the next edition of the *Double Dealer.*[21]

---

[17] *Ibid.,* p. 32.
[18] *Ibid.,* p. 37.
[19] *Ibid.,* p. 37.
[20] *Ibid.,* p. 42.
[21] *Ibid.,* pp. 44-46.

Congreve had attempted a defence of the *Double Dealer* by asserting:

"Ben Jonson is much bolder in the first Scene of his Bartholomew Fair. . . . [He] makes Littlewit say, Man and Wife make one Fool. I have said nothing comparable to that."[22]

To this Collier witheringly replies:

"Nothing comparable! Truly in the usual sense of that Phrase, Mr. *Congreve,* tis possible, has said nothing comparable to *Ben. Johnson,* nor it may be never will: But in his new Propriety he has said something more than comparable, that is a great deal worse."[23]

Congreve had called Collier to task for his use of the word "Martyr." Collier explains its Greek significance and then to chastise the playwright for his poor understanding of English, he tantalizingly tells the story of a misfortune which had recently happened to a country apothecary. The doctor, it seems, had prescribed for a lady a certain medicine to be taken in something liquid, and the prescription according to custom called the liquid a vehicle. The apothecary, at a loss to understand the term vehicle, consulted Littleton's *Dictionary* and found there that the meaning was, "cart, wagon, or wheel-barrow," The apothecary, unwilling to give the lady too much trouble in finding a conveyance, decided on the wheel-barrow. The prescription was complied with and the footman drove the wheel-barrow about the lady's room.[24] After this digression Collier returns to Congreve's use of the word martyr and by further argument strengthens his position.[25]

He then carefully weighs the censure which Congreve had heaped upon his condemnation of each of the four plays. Indecency in language, irreligion, abuse of the clergy, and making the important characters vicious after which they are rewarded—all these charges Collier carefully re-evaluates. That he becomes somewhat wrathful in his second "defence of the clergy" is evident from his statement:

"In earnest, I'm almost tired with answering these things. To strike the Air, does but make a Man's Arm ake."[26]

---

[22] W. Congreve, *Amendments,* p. 47.
[23] J. Collier, *A Defence,* p. 53.
[24] *Ibid.,* pp. 54-56.
[25] *Ibid.,* p. 56.
[26] *Ibid.,* p. 66.

He re-emphasizes his triple vindication of the reputation of the ministers of the Gospel, and refutes each of Congreve's attacks upon them.[27] He does not apologize for having "assaulted the Town in the seat of their principal and most reasonable Pleasure;" on the contrary, he scathingly replies:

> "I am sorry to hear the encouraging of Vice, the Liberties of Smut, and Profaneness, the Exposing of Holy Things and Persons, are such lively satisfactions. The Palate must be strangely vitiated to relish such Entertainment as this."[28]

He dwells at length upon his pet topic of proving the Fathers and Critics averse to the dangers of the playhouse,[29] and comments upon Congreve's "Panegyrick upon his Country,"—a panegyrick that had included expressions such as "Are there not more Self-Murtherers, and Melancholick Lunaticks in England, heard of in one year, than in a great part of Europe besides":

> "Tho' I somewhat question the Truth, as well as the civility of this Reflection; but if 'tis true, 'tis probable the *Play-House* may in some measure account for the *Fact*. If there are more Self-Murthers and Lunacies in *England* than elsewhere, 'tis probably, because there are more bad Plays in *England than in a great part of* Europe *besides*: I believe I may say, than in all *Europe* besides."[30]

In the last pages of his reply to Congreve, Collier vindicates himself for those expressions to which the stage-poet had taken exception,[31] and in return for his civilities, he presents the reader with new improprieties in phraseology and sense.[32] He concludes by referring to Congreve's failure to vindicate himself for the censure which had been given to two of his scandalous songs:

> "This is somewhat unfortunate: One would have thought, if he had neither Modesty to make them, nor Reason to defend them, he might, at least, have had a little Conscience to have given them up."[33]

---

[27] *Ibid.*, pp. 67-81.
[28] *Ibid.*, p. 83.
[29] *Ibid.*, pp. 83-88.
[30] *Ibid.*, pp. 88-89.
[31] *Ibid.*, pp. 90-91.
[32] *Ibid.*, pp. 91-95.
[33] *Ibid.*, p. 96.

Every line of the ninety-six pages devoted to answering Congreve proves that Collier has dipped his pen in vitriol. Stinging rebukes are everywhere applied to the author as well as to the four plays he had attempted to vindicate in his *Amendments*.

b. A Reply to the Short Vindication

Caustically, Collier proceeds to reply to Vanbrugh who had asserted in his *Short Vindication* that the Reformer had little to accuse him of on the subject of immodesty, and that he came to no particulars except to mention Miss Hoyden with others as examples of that vice:

> "By his favour, I am particular in the matter objected, and since he calls for it, I shall direct the *Reader* to some more Decencies of this young Lady. To deny Matter of Fact in the beginning of a vindication is a little unlucky."[34]

He asserts that Vanbrugh's "being at a loss to know in what Miss Hoyden is indecent in speech" does not look promising.

> "Customary Swearing takes away the sense of doing it ,and I'm afraid it may be applicable to other matters;"[35]

he examines Vanbrugh's defence of a quotation from the *Provoked Wife* and justifies himself for having stated that modesty has been out of fashion with the stage since the time of Euripides;[36] he vindicates his assertion that the *Relapse* and *The Provoked Wife* were particularly rampant and scandalous in the matter of swearing;[37] and very curtly replies to the Vindicator's confession of making a very great distinction between his respects to God and the devil:

> "Then it seems he has some Regard for both of them, some Respects for the Devil."[38]

To his petulent attack on the Viewer for being "as angry with him for being *for* Religion as before for being *against* it" when the liberties given to Lord Foppington had been scourged, the Viewer replies:

> "Not altogether. However here's a frank confession that he was against *Religion* before. Now by his managing, one would guess he had not changed his side."[39]

---

[34] *Ibid.*, p. 97.
[35] *Ibid.*, pp. 97-98.
[36] *Ibid.*, pp. 98-100.
[37] *Ibid.*, pp. 100-102.
[38] *Ibid.*, p. 106.
[39] *Ibid.*, p. 106.

Vanbrugh had found fault with Collier not for complaining that young Fashion was a finished debauchee, but for calling him Vanbrugh's favorite. To this Collier replies:

> "And why so? Has he not provided him a *Plot,* a Fortune, and creditable Figure? And are not all these signs of good Will and Inclination? Well, but *his Wife is likely to make his Heart ake.* Indeed so says the *Vindicator.* But *young Fashion* tells another story. He is in no Fright about the matter. Upon observing some Signs of Extravagance in Hoyden, he says to himself . . . ' *'Tis no matter. She brings an Estate will afford me a separate Maintenance* . . . This soliloquy . . . teaches the Art of marrying the Estate without the Woman, and makes a noble Settlement upon Lewdness.' "[40]

Collier in his answer to Vanbrugh upholds his former statements on the vices of profaneness, blasphemy, irreligion, abuse of the clergy, and immorality,[41] and bids him farewell by a bantering allusion to a statement he had made in his *Short Vindication* that when both he and the Viewer are in their graves, posterity will be likely to mistake the authorship of the *Relapse* and the *Short View,* believing Collier wrote the one and Vanbrugh the other.

> "I am glad to hear him talk of *his Grave:* 'Twas a seasonable Thought, and I heartily wish it its due improvement; Such a Consequence wou'd be of great service, both to himself and the Publick. For then, I am well assured, he would neither Write *Plays,* nor Defend them, at the rate he has done."[42]

c. *Reply to the Defender of Dramatic Poetry and to the Author of The Usefulness of the Stage*

Collier's chief intentions in his answer to both the author of *A Defence* and to Dennis are to justify his previous statements on the silence of the Scriptures regarding the theater and to reply to the remarks made by these authors.[43] In order to emphasize his position, Collier translates a lengthy quotation from the treatise then lately pub-

---

[40] *Ibid.,* pp. 108-9.
[41] *Ibid.,* pp. 108-131.
[42] *Ibid.,* p. 132.
[43] *Ibid.,* p. 132-134.

lished by the Bishop of Meaux;[44] and he humiliates Dennis who had asserted of one of Collier's statements: "This Citation is absolutely false." To Dennis Collier angrily replies: "Right! 'Tis false in the Latin, but 'tis true in the Greek.[45] He refutes only one other remark from Dennis, but he assures the reader that present business compels him to await a future opportunity before he will be able to answer at length the critic's arguments.

In a brief section called *Reply to the Vindicator of the Stage* Collier justifies himself by a triple argument for his translation of *Saecularia Spectacula* as *Stage Plays*,[46] and with the advice to the author to consult the *Defence* if he would have further answers to his arguments, he concludes his pamphlet.[46a]

2

As the title indicates, *Some Remarks Upon Mr. Collier's Defence of his Short View of the English Stage, etc. In Vindication of Mr. Congreve, etc. In a Letter to a Friend,* was evoked by Collier's *Defence* which, less than a month before, had attempted to vindicate the *Short View* against Congreve, Vanbrugh, and the "Volunteers" who had replied to the attack on the stage-poets.[47] The pamphlet bears an eight-fold resemblance to *A Vindication of the Stage* published anonymously about seven months before and of which Collier took notice when in the concluding pages of the *Defence* he said:

"This Gentleman appear'd early in the Cause and has given

---

[44] *Ibid.,* pp. 134-137. The Bishop of Meaux is Bossuet who in his *Maxims and Reflections* had answered Caffaro's arguments on the lawfulness of the stage entertainment.

[45] *Ibid.,* p. 137.

[46] *Ibid.,* pp. 138-139.

[46a] I desire to call attention to an oversight on the part of Mr. H. G. Paul who in his *John Dennis His Life and Criticism,* pp. 30-31, notes Collier's response to Dennis as contained only in *A Defence of the Short View* pp. i-ii. He does not point out Collier's further replies on pp. 132-138 of the same work nor those in *A Second Defence* p. 19; p. 52; p. 53; p. 54, nor the reply in *A Farther Vindication,* p. 34.

[47] The *Letter* in question is eighteen pages in length, and was written to a person called "Frank" who admits that he has heard of but never seen Collier. Anonymous, *Some Remarks,* p. 7; p. 13. It was announced in the *Post-Man* for December 6, 1698, having been printed for A. Baldwin near the Oxford-Arms in Warwick Lane. It is not mentioned by Halkett and Laing in a *Dictionary of Anonymous and Pseudonymous Literature.*

me very little trouble, and therefore 'twould hardly be civil
not to dispatch him at the first Hearing."[48]

The features of resemblance between the two exist in the fact that both
pamphlets are in letter-form and both are anonymous; both are champions primarily of the cause of Congreve and his plays; both allege
the motive of writing the letter to be the gift of Collier's book,—in the
first instance of the *Short View*, and in the second, of the *Defence*.
Besides, both give an unmethodical criticism of the works in question.
The first writer says that he is sending "some thoughts as they occurred
on a slight perusal of it [*The Short View*]"; the second says

> "I hate taking the pains to put them [his Remarks on the
> *Defence*] in a Method fit for your Perusal; therefore if you
> must be obey'd, you shall have them just as they are, Rough,
> Indigested, and about as Mannerly as the Defence which lies
> before me;[49]

both take note of Collier's allusions to the Ancients and Moderns;[50]
both authors show, by reference, their acquaintance with *Don Quixote*;[51]
both authors, in order to make contrast effective, refer to the conditions
of the clergy in Spain and Italy; they compare the clergy in these
countries to the clergy in England,[52] and both authors refer contemptuously to Collier's non-juring tendencies[53]

The author of *Some Remarks* uses four pages of the eighteen in
criticizing Collier's two-page "Preface" to the *Defence;* in the remaining twelve he jots down his opinions as they occur upon a cursory reading of the *Defence* itself. The gist of the opinions is a vindication of
Congreve[54] and of Vanbrugh,[55] a caricature of Collier, both as to his
private and his ecclesiastical life,[56] and a fourfold allusion to Collier's
personal grievance against Congreve:

---

[48] J. Collier, *A Defence*, p. 138.
[49] Anonymous, *A Vindication*, p. 3. Anonymous, *Some Remarks*, p. 1.
[50] Anonymous, *A Vindication of the Stage*, p. 4; p. 16; Anonymous, *Some Remarks*, p. 5.
[51] Anonymous, *A Vindication of the Stage*, p. 7; Anonymous, *Some Remarks*, p. 9.
[52] Anonymous, *A Vindication*, pp. 17-18; Anonymous *Some Remarks*, pp. 11-12.
[53] Anonymous, *A Vindication*, p. 18; Anonymous, *Some Remarks*, p. 10.
[54] Anonymous, *Some Remarks*, pp. 6-9, 14, 17.
[55] Anonymous, *Some Remarks*, pp. 10, 12, 16.
[56] *Ibid.*, pp. 2-17.

1. "Mr. *Collier's* Reproofs to me seem inveterate; he writes with Animosity, as if he had an Aversion to the Man as well as his Faults, . . . Who, but Mr. *Collier* wou'd have ransack'd the *Mourning Bride,* to charge it with Smut and Prophaneness, when he might have sate down with so many Scenes wherein even his malicious Chymistry cou'd have extracted neither?"[57]

2. " . . . the fruitful Mr. *Collier* in every Page discovers Rancor, and a plain Desire not to amend, but destroy."[58]

3. "This I observe in all Mr. *Collier's* Remarks, there's an Air of Spite; for when he has pickt out any thing for his Caviling purpose, if there's a following Line that will in the least extenuate, that's surely left out."[59]

4. "All my Acquaintance that discourse this Matter, are convinced Mr. *Collier* has a particular Pique against Mr. *Congreve;* nay, some will go farther, and guess the Cause; perhaps there may be Lines of that Author's that vex the *Non-Juror* more than all the smutty Jests he has pickt up; Lines that Mourn the Royal Pastora; Heroick Lines, that sound the glory of our Monarch. From this sweet Poetry they judge his Gall is raised; which being gorged and full, overflows, nor spares the dead or living, Friends and Foes, the bitter Deluge reaches and bespatters all."[60]

The letter-writer tells us, besides, that the *Mourning-Bride* retained its popularity despite Collier and the *Short View;*[61] he censures Collier's ridicule of Congreve by the reference to the physician who prescribed medicine to be taken in a wheel-barrow,[62] and concludes his epistle by contemptuously referring to Collier's excess of spleen and by suavely referring to his correspondent's lack of it.

3

About four months after Ridpath had published his pro-Collier work, *The Stage Condemned,* there appeared an anonymous reply directed against Collier, Ridpath, and the author of the *Animadversions.* It bore the title: *The Stage Acquitted. Being a Full Answer to Mr.*

---

[57] *Ibid.,* pp. 6-7.
[58] *Ibid.,* p. 15.
[59] *Ibid.,* p. 15.
[60] *Ibid.,* p. 17.
[61] *Ibid.,* p. 3.
[62] *Ibid.,* p. 15.

Collier, and the other Enemies of the Drama. With a Vindication of King Charles the Martyr, and the Clergy of the Church of England, from the Abuses of a Scurrilous Book Called The Stage Condemned. To which is added, the Character of the Animadverter and the Animadversions on Mr. Congreve's Answer to Mr. Collier. London, 1699.[63] The Preface was written by the publisher who signs himself A. D.[64] and in the opening lines of it he informs the reader:

> "I Being the Publisher of this Book, I think because I may'nt be guilty of the vanity some men are, that 'tis a justice to myself to let you know, I do not pretend to be the Author of it."[65]

He likewise tells us that he drew into the controversy his friend, the author of *The Stage Acquitted,* and that he offered him some suggestions to be included in the work. His anger against Collier, against the authors of the *Animadversions* and of *The Stage Condemned* is evident; his design to reply caustically is framed in unvarnished language.

The Stage Acquitted is written in the form of a dialogue between Fairly and Lovetruth who attack first *The Stage Condemned* and then Collier and the *Short View.* They remark on the "dulness" both of Ridpath and of the Viewer; they criticize Ridpath for sanctioning Collier's reading of plays; they ridicule him for censuring in sermons the use of the "Rhetorick of a Play," as well as for refusing to praise a sermon because the preacher has read a great many play-books and for banning stage-expressions from the pulpit. They censure Collier's *Desertion Discuss'd* and commend "King *Charles'* Sunday Masks."

For ninety-five pages they ramble on; their arguments are often illogical, their diction is redundant, and their style boring. Then weary of their sport, they decide to make short work of the rest of the pamphlet by answering in a single final chapter the "Material part of the rest of this scurrilous Book." In this final chapter the speakers say nothing that is interesting; they score very few points

---

[63] *The Stage Acquitted* is 185 pages in length, was printed for John Barnes at the Crown in the Pall-mall. On page iv of the Preface is the date January 1, 1698. The title page, however, reads 1699.

[64] The initials are identified by Stonehill, Block, Stonehill: *Anonyma and Pseudonyma,* I, 4, as A. Dutton who died in 1734. Neither the *D.N.B.* nor the *C.H.E.L.* give any information concerning A. Dutton.

[65] Anonymous, *The Stage Acquitted,* p. i.

either over Collier or R----th, and they terminate their discourse by telling the reader:

> " 'Tis well remember'd—and therefore I will only add this, that 'tis a good cause we defend, when passion and lies are brought against it, and which, like other Truths, will prevail as soon as people are cool enough to consider truly of its real Merits."[66]

As a supplement to the dialogue there are five pages devoted to giving *A Character of the Animadverter and the Animadversions on Mr. Congreve's Answer to Collier.* The author calls the gentleman who wrote *The Animadversions* a person "much of Mr. R----th's size, both of Honesty and Sense;"[67] he says that even though the *Animadversions* is designed to reflect adversely on the poets, it is rather a satire on Collier who should consider it a scandal to be praised either by a fool or a rascal.[68] He further believes that the pamphlet is not only composed of foolish lies and heavy nonsense, but that it is written in the dialect of Billingsgate, with a dash of "Porter-like railing, scurrility, and lewdness.[69] He complains that because the Animadverter has not betrayed his identity he has shielded himself from an answer; however, he says, he has not concealed his nationality, for in the preface he has announced that he is an Irishman, to which statement we find the following reply:

> "I hope he means wild Irish, for nothing of this side of wild Irish could sure ever write such stuff."[70]

4

One is not surprised to find a bigoted defender of Whig principles and a foe to the Stuarts attacking the works of a man who had valiantly upheld James II. This was the case of John Oldmixon who, in 1699, published in reply to Collier's *Defence* his stinging rejoinder entitled

[66] *Ibid.,* p. 181.
[67] *Ibid.,* p. 181.
[68] *Ibid.,* p. 181.
[69] *Ibid.,* p. 182.
[70] *Ibid.,* pp. 181-3.

Reflections on the Stage, and Mr. Collyer's Defence of the Short View. In Four Dialogues. London, 1699.[71]

Although the title-page of the *Reflections on the Stage* bears no author's name, the authorship is, nevertheless, acknowledged by John Oldmixon who subscribes his name to his Dedicatory Epistle to the Right Honourable Charles Montague. In this four-page letter he asserts that Collier seems to be on the winning side in the stage-controversy and that those who vindicate the poets or their writings need powerful protection to defend them from the public who espouse the cause of reformation.[72] In addition to the letter there is a six-page preface of caustic attack on Collier and his *Defence,* and 194 pages of equally caustic dialogue between Savage and Bevill.

Oldmixon has, in his *Reflections,* given us not only a vindication of Congreve and Vanbrugh, but a eulogy of Dennis; he has pointed out that Collier's object in attacking the stage was not so much to stab vice as to gain money, popularity and fame; he has declared that Collier's desire to influence the ladies to his way of thinking has been accompanied by ruining their most enjoyable diversion. He has not denied the necessity of stage reformation but he emphatically declares that reform will not be accomplished by Collier and his associates as readily as by the audiences themselves when they will hiss from the stage all smut, ill manners, immorality, and irreligion. The author undoubtedly displays the same anti-Collier attitude as is echoed in Oldmixon's *The History of England During the Reigns of King William and Queen Mary, . . .* Vol. III.

5

Of all the replies evoked by Collier that of James Drake is the longest and one of the least interesting. It bears the title *The Antient and Modern Stages survey'd. Or, Mr. Collier's View of the Immorality and Profaneness of the English Stage Set in a True Light. Wherein Some of Mr. Collier's Mistakes are rectified, and the comparative*

---

[71] S. Austin Allibone in his *Critical Dictionary,* II, 1452-3, refers to Oldmixon's loyalty to the Whigs and to his abuse of the Stuarts. He quotes from those who share his views: Lord Macaulay, *Essays,* 1854, ed., I, 30; and Disraeli, *Calamities of Authors,* 1840, ed., I, p. 52, n.

[72] J. Oldmixon, *Reflections on the Stage,* Ep. Dedicatory, pp. i-ii. The book was printed for R. Parker at the Unicorn under the Piazza of the Royal Exchange, and P. Buck at the Sign of the Temple at the Temple-gate in Fleet Street.

Morality of the English Stage is asserted upon the Parallel. London, 1699.[73]

The work is dedicated to the Right Honourable Charles, Earl of Dorset and Middlesex, and contains not only a fifteen-page "Table of Contents" but a thirteen-page Epistle. In this Dedicatory Epistle we learn that Collier's *Short View* during its circulation of a year had lost nothing of its popularity:

> "The Tyde of Prejudice runs high for my Adversary, and the less discerning Part of the Town are so prepossess'd with the Specious Title, and the Plausible Pretence of Mr. Collier's Book, that they think the whole Interest of Virtue and Religion embark'd on that Bottom."[74]

We learn, besides, that the "Town is divided in its Judgment of the Piece [the *Short View*]," and that Drake is in the ranks of those who call into question the integrity of Collier's motives in attacking the stage. We find, too, that he is in the ranks of those who resent the heat and violence of Collier's arguments, and of those who censure his style:

> "His Style is adapted to his purpose, fierce and bold, full of vehement exaggerations, and haughty menaces, he racks Sentences, and tortures Expressions, to extort a Confession from 'em of things to which they are absolute Strangers."[75]

---

[73] The book is 367 pages in length, was printed for Abel Roper at the Black Boy over against St. Dunstan's Church in Fleetstreet, and was announced in *The Flying Post* for March 7, 1699. Again the problem of authorship comes up. In this regard it is interesting to note that the *D.N.B.*, V, 1352 remarks: "[James Drake] is said to have written *Ancient and Modern Stages survey'd;*" S. Allibone says nothing at all of the pamphlet in connection with Drake: *A Critical Dictionary of English Literature*, I, 518. D. C. Taylor asserts that Edward Filmer is the author: D. C. Taylor, *William Congreve*, p. 242. However, J. Collier, in his *A Farther Vindication*, 1708, published in reply to Filmer's *A Defence of Plays*, 1707, refutes Filmer's attacks made against the "Authorities" cited in Chapter IV of his *Short View*, and refers *by name* to Drake as the author of *The Antient and Modern Stages Survey'd*. He says: "And that nothing material might be omited my *Second Defence* has more than fifty pages upon this Argument. Now, tho' this last Book has undertaken almost all Dr. Filmer's exceptions, and was published in 1699, yet he [Filmer] takes no notice of it, . . . The best thing I can say for him is, that he never saw my Reply [*Second Defence*] to Dr. Drake." pp. 34-35. It is evident form this that Collier himself settles the question of authorship in favor of Drake.

[74] J. Drake, *The Antient and Modern Stages survey'd*, Ded. Epis. p. ii.

[75] *Ibid.*, p. vi.

He summarizes the progress of the stage-controversy on the continent, tracing the first of the stage-quarrels to Mariana, a Jesuit in Spain, about the close of the sixteenth century. It is this same Mariana, he asserts, who published as a first blast against the Stage his *Contra Spectacula,* and after that another with the special approbation of the Provincial of the Jesuits in the Province of Toledo.[76] From Spain, Drake tells us, the stage controversy traveled into Italy where it was fomented by "Francisco Maria" a Sicilian Monk, and by P. Ottonelli, a Jesuit. From Italy it was translated into England about 1640 by Dr. Reynolds and Mr. Prynne. From England it traveled to France in 1670 through the Prince of Conti, and the Sieur de Voisin, and though the flame of the controversy died down after some years and remained smothered, it nevertheless broke out again.[77] The Stage-surveyor asserts, without qualification, that it was this latter quarrel which primed the guns of Collier:

> "at which Mr. Collier took fire, and reviv'd the quarrel in England."[78]

Throughout the 367 pages Drake gives, in verbose but acid arguments, his censure of Collier's private life, of his critical principles, of his interpretation of the Fathers, of his preference for the Ancients, and of his condemnation of the Moderns. His discussions, however, add no new points to the controversy and they score no new victory over his opponent.

Before dismissing Drake it might be of importance to the reader to learn in what light his scholarship as well as his style was regarded. The reviewer of his *Anthropologia Nova* in the *History of The Works of the Learned* for July, 1707, tells us that Drake was by profession a Doctor and that just prior to his death in 1707 he completed a learned 843-page dissertation on a "New System of Anatomy." The reviewer eulogizes Drake's *general* talents;

> " . . . it appears that he was not only Learned in his own profession, but did truly deserve the Character of an Universal

---

[76] *Ibid.,* p. 5.
[77] "[it] remained smothered"—a reference, no doubt, to the years 1694-1698.
[78] *The Antient and Modern Stages survey'd,* p. 5.

Schollar: That he had made a considerable Progress in all the Liberal Sciences: That his stile, both Latin and English, was manly, yet easy; concise, yet clear and expressive: that he had arrived to that difficult Perfection of knowing how to make use of his Learning without Pedantry or Affection: That his Knowledge was not confined to Books, since he had read and studied Men with the same Care and Exactness: . . . That he was steady to his Principles and had an awful Sense of Religion."[79]

It was inevitable that a person of Drake's reputation should have influence on his readers. However, had he refuted Collier with some of the conciseness, ease, clarity, and expressiveness which he is said to have used in his *Anthropologia Nova* the student would not be bored in reading; had he shown less hostility to Collier the student might expect more impartial refutation of those points on which he differed from Collier; had he given a less flashy display of learning there would be more respect for his talent.

6

James Wright in 1694 had proved his interest in diversions and in the arts by publishing his *Country Conversations, etc. chiefly of Modern Comedies, of Drinking, of Translated Verse, of Painting and Painters, of Poets and Poetry.* It is not surprising, then, that he should follow up his 1694 edition with a discussion of the English stage and players. This he did in 1699 in his *Historia Histrionica. An Historical Account of the English Stage; Shewing the Ancient Use, Improvement, and Perfection of Dramatic Representations in this Nation. In a Dialogue, of Plays and Players.*

Although the *Historia Histrionica* is not included in the Collier Stage-Controversy bibliography either by Krutch or by Taylor, and although Wright himself asserts of his position "My affection inclines me not to engage on either side, but rather mediate,"[80] I have, nevertheless, decided to include it in my study of the Collier Controversy. My reasons for so doing are six in number: first, because many of the

---

[79] *History of the Works of the Learned,* IX, pp. 423-424.
[80] J. Wright, *"Historia Histrionica,"* published in Dodsley's *Old English Plays,* XV, 413. It is 28 pages in length and was printed by G. Croom for William Haws, at the Rose in Ludgate Street.

opinions which the author voices in the *Dialogue* explain statements made by Collier, whose reflections, he asserts

" . . . are pertinent, and true in the main; the book ingeniously wrote, and well intended; but he has overshot himself in some places, and his respondents perhaps in more;"[81]

second, because he calls attention to "two or three general notions," in which he thinks Collier may be mistaken;[82] third, because the *Historia Histrionica* is by Wright's own admission designed to amplify what has been written of late "pro and con about the stage." The author says that he has no doubt but that

" . . . the subject admits of more, and that which has not been hitherto touched upon; not only what that is, but what it was about which some people have made such a bustle;"[83]

fourth, because he wishes to prove to the reader that

"Religion and religious matters were once as much the mode in public entertainment as the contrary has been in some times since;"[84]

fifth, because the opinion of Wright agrees, in the main, with that of Dryden and other critics on the illogical conclusion drawn by Collier from his premises as laid down in the "Introduction" to the *Short View*,[85] and lastly, because the author adds his opinion to that of other stage-disputants "that the profession of players is not so totally scandalous, nor are all of them so reprobate," and he substantiates his opinion by stating

"there has been found under that name [of actor] a canonized saint in the primitive church, as may be seen in the 'Roman Martyrology' on the 29th March:"[85a]

---

[81] *Ibid.*, p. 413.

[82] *Ibid.*, p. 413.

[83] *Ibid.*, Preface, p. i.

[84] *Ibid.*, Preface, p. ii.

[85] It is interesting to compare Dryden's statement, prefixed to *The Fables* with Wright's statement in the *Historia*. Dryden says: "He has lost ground, at the latter end of the day, by pursuing his point too far, like the Prince of Conde, at the battle of Seneff: from immoral plays to no plays, *ab abusu ad usum, non valet consequentia.* J. Dryden, *Works,* S. & S. edition, XI, 244. Wright declares: "If there be abuses relating to the stage—which I think, is too apparent—let the abuse be reformed, and not the use, for that reason only, abolished. . . . *Absit abusit, non desit totaliter usus.*" J. Wright, *Historia Histrionica* p. 413.

[85a] J. Wright, *Historia Histrionica*, p. 413.

The *Historia Histrionica* is an agreeable contrast to Drake's *Antient and Modern Stages* both in its diction, its subject matter, and its fairness to both sides of the question. The author shows himself an antiquary not only by profession, but in his preference for the Ancients over the Moderns.[85b] He is an advocate of moderate diversions and he sanctions the play-house; he is well read in Bossuet and Caffaro and advances his arguments in behalf of players so convincingly that he asserts a player has been canonized. He refers, quaintly, to the occasional private publishing of plays as a means of making money, and regrets that in his own day the appreciation of the art of music has declined.

7

Even though the French version of Bossuet's *Maximes et réflexions sur la comédie,* wielding as it did so decided an influence upon the stage-controvertists in England, had been published a half-decade before, I have included in my bibliography its English translation which was published under the title *Maxims and Reflections Upon Plays. (In answer to a Discourse of the Lawfullness and Unlawfullness of Plays. Printed Before a late Book Entituled Beauty in Distress.) Written in French by the Bp. of Meaux, And now Made English. The Preface by Another Hand.* There are several reasons why it is entitled to a place in the bibliography. In the first place, E. Arber associates the work with J. Collier. He states in *The Term Catalogues* that in November, 1699, there was printed for Richard Sare at Gray's-Inn Gate in Holborn

> "Maxims and Reflections on Plays; in Answer to a Discourse of the Lawfulness and Unlawfulness of Plays, printed before a late Book entituled, Beauty in Distress. Written in French by the Bp. of Meaux [J. B. Bossuet], with an Advertisement concerning the Book and the Author. By Mr. Collier. Octavo, 18d."[86]

[85b] *Ibid.,* p. i. Wright's scholarship is evident in many of his other works, among which may be mentioned *The History and Antiquities of the County of Rutland,* 1684, and *Monasticon Anglicanum now Epitomized from Dugdale, in England,* 1693.

[86] E. Arber, *Term Catalogues,* III, 159. A comparison of the two titles discloses only one difference: Arber's title is: *With an Advertisement concerning the Book and the Author.* The title-page of the copy which I used—and it was a first edition—reads: *And now Made English. The Preface by another*

In the second place, the preface to the translation throws new light upon several phases of the Caffaro Letter as well as upon the Bossuet reply, hence it is entitled to a place in the bibliography.

The Prefacer takes note of the *Short View* and of the replies to it and observes that some of the accused stage-poets though well qualified to answer the charges brought against them and to vindicate themselves have, nevertheless, given ineffective replies.[87] He then introduces the matter in hand, namely, Bossuet's *Maxims,* and the Preface to *Beauty in Distress* containing a portion of the famous Caffaro letter:

> "But since other Succours are called in from abroad, 'tis fit the World should know, that this Reserve too hath been already defeated in it's own Countrey. And that we ought not to be imposed upon here in England, with an Adversary, whose Arguments have been not only confuted and scorned by others, but also retracted by Himself, at home."[88]

He curiously refers to

> "that moroseness of humour, which Some in great good manners have of late been pleased to fix upon the English as their peculiar Character,"[89]

and sarcastically replies that as this moroseness might possibly be thought to dispose the English to a blameable extreme of rigor in these matters, there was needed a foreign authority to reproach their pretended niceness and austerity.[90] The writer goes on to say that in order to give the discourse on the lawfulness of plays a better face, a Divine of the Church of England introduces it, and that he introduces it to satisfy scruples of the aspiring stage-poet. He emphatically states, however, that before accepting the discourse at its face value,

---

Hand. It is important to note that both books were printed by R. Sare. Now, the printer in Collier's case is an important factor. I have previously pointed out that R. Sare published—either alone or with Keble and Hindmarsh—all of Collier's anti-stage works. Whether Arber meant to imply that the Advertisement only was Collier's work, or that both the translation and the Preface were his, is not clear. I am of the opinion that the preface at least is his. Kippis, in *Biog. Brit.*. IV, 18, calls attention to Collier's connection with the advertisement and the translation of the *Maximes.*

[87] J. B. Bossuet, *Maxims and Reflections, Preface,* p. 1. The translation is 118 pages in length.

[88] *Ibid.,* p. ii.

[89] *Ibid.,* p. ii. It will be recalled that Dennis made this statement in his *Usefulness of the Stage,* pp. 11-14, as also did Congreve in his *Amendments,* pp. 108-9, and that Collier had caustically answered: *A Defence,* pp. 88-9.

[90] *Ibid.,* p. ii.

two things are important to know, 1. who translated Caffaro's letter
from the French and, 2. did the worthy Divine peruse that letter in
French or in English.[91] He gives two reasons why it is important to
know whether he perused the letter in French or in English. In the
first place, he says, the French discourse has passages not found in
English:

> "the following Reply produces and answers some Passages of
> the French Discourse, not to be found in the English. And
> these not only Expressions or single Sentences, but entire Argu-
> ments. Such is that of Plays being a Diversion suitable to the
> Design of instituting the Sabbath. Such again That which justi-
> fies the Acting them the whole Lent throughout,"[92]

and secondly, he suspects the Caffaro letter was perused in the French
because the French Discourse speaks favourably of acting plays on
Sundays.[93] He censures the publication of the letter as also the fact that
the discourse appears as a preface to Motteux's play. He calls the first
"incautious" in that it exposes a reply to a letter written to dispel
conscientious scruples, and the second a "misrepresentation of authorities."[94] He praises the translated reply inasmuch as it bespeaks care
on the part of the translator in comparing with their originals passages
out of St. Thomas, St. Jerome, and others; he expresses the wish that
this translated reply rather than Caffaro's letter had fallen into the
hands of the Divine who gave himself the trouble of a vindication
of plays.[95] He states that in the Preface to *Beauty in Distress* there is
a certain secrecy about the author of the original letter. Secrecy, he
asserts, was not necessary inasmuch as Father Caffaro had been obliged
to retract his statements, and that these statements had been exposed
by Bossuet to the shame of Caffaro; he then observes:

> "If Mons'r Caffaro had the Hardiness to assert a Tract so un-
> worthy his Character, his Answerer would not add perhaps to
> the Scandall, when that shame had been taken to himself, with
> a Remorse, becoming the Fact . . . I hope the Bp. of Meaux,
> and his manner of writing, are at least as creditable an Evidence
> of this, as the Booksellers can be allowed to be, of that Letter

---

[91] *Ibid.*, pp. ii-iii.
[92] *Ibid.*, p. iii.
[93] *Ibid.*, p. iii.
[94] *Ibid.*, p. iv.
[95] *Ibid.*, p. iv.

being genuine, which refers Mr. M's Conscience to the Discourse for Satisfaction."[96]

Before concluding the preface the writer censures Dryden's poetical Epistle to Motteux. Dryden had written:

> "That Sacred Art, by Heav'n it self infused,
> Which Moses, David, Solomon have us'd,
> Is now to be no more: The Muses Foes
> Wou'd sink their Maker's Praises into Prose.'[97]

The writer says of the verses

> "A Popular one perhaps it may be, but sure a wilder Suggestion, never was offered to men of Common sense, than, that if the Stage be damned, the Art used by Moses, and David, and Solomon, must be no more . . . If Matters once should come to that Extremity, better and much more becoming of the Two, no doubt it were, that our Maker's Praises should be sunk into Prose (as this Ingenioius Person phrases it) than that in the midst of the Christian City, that Maker should be six days in seven publickly insulted and blasphemed in Poetry."[98]

Inasmuch as I am of the opinion that Collier is the author of the Preface of the Translation of Bossuet's *Maxims and Reflections,* it is imperative that I substantiate that opinion. In the first place, the Preface shows the same intolerance of the theatre as a nursery of vice as Collier exhibits in his *Short View,* his *Defence,* his *Second Defence,* and his *Dissuasive;* secondly, the writer of the Preface begins by allowing that the purpose of poetry, even of dramatic poetry, is good; but he concludes by asserting that if the vices prevalent in the playhouse are impossible of reformation, then—down with the theatre:

> "No man I presume is for exterminating that noble Art, no not even the Dramatick part; provided it can be effectually re-

---

[96] *Ibid.,* pp. v-vi. The reference to the booksellers was evoked, no doubt, by the fact that the English Divine had referred Motteux to the *Histoire des Ouvrage des Scaven,* Roterdam: *et Oeuvres de Boursault.* Motteux, *Beauty in Distress,* p. xxvi.

[97] P. Motteux, *Beauty in Distress,* p. xxvii.

[98] J. B. Bossuet, *Maxims and Reflections,* pp. vii-ix. The above statement is characteristically Collierian. It is an attack upon Dryden and it has all the sarcasm which is found in Collier's previous attacks upon him. It is concluded with the familiar figure, antithesis, which Collier so customarily uses as a climax. It touches upon the pet topic of irreligion with which Collier so frequently attacked the poets but Dryden in particular.

formed. But if the Reformation of the Stage be no longer practicable, reason good that the incurable Evil should be cut off:
If it be practicable, let the Persons concerned give Evidence of
it to the World, by tempering their Wit so, as to render it
Serviceable to Virtuous purposes, without giving just offence to
wise, and Good men."[99]

In the third place, he harps upon the familiar chord of profaneness
when he attacks Dryden's Epistle to Motteux;.

"And their Sophistry bears hard, methinks, upon Profaneness,
which insinuates the Hymns dictated by the Holy Spirit, of
God, to be so nearly related to the Modern Composition for
the Stage, that both must of necessity stand and fall together."[100]

Fourthly, the very manner in which the writer attacks Dryden recalls
Collier's former attacks in the *Short View*. He proposes his objection
in the rhetorical questioning so characteristic of Collier,

"Are we fallen into an Age so incapable of distinguishing, that
there should be no visible difference left between the Excellen-
cies and the Abuses of any Art?"[101]

and he immediately answers his own question and proves his answer
by a substantiating reference to Dryden's own critical opinion of the
matter. Fifthly, he attacks Dryden's *Absalom and Achitophel* and the
Translation of Virgil, both of which were particularly objectionable to
Collier. He traces a quotation from the translation of Virgil to the
Fourth Book of Lucretius,[102] and the manner in which he does it
betrays the old flashy display of knowledge of the Ancients in which
Collier had so frequently indulged. Sixthly, the Preface shows the
writer a warm advocate of Bossuet, and his advocacy is akin to that
expressed for him by Collier in the *Defence*.[103] And seventhly, and
lastly, he comments on the style of Bossuet's writing, a characteristic
which is in perfect accord wih Collier's previous comments on style

---

[99] *Ibid.,* p. vii. Collier, in the *Short View* holds the identical opinion. He
begins by informing the reader of the noble business of plays. Introduction,
p. i. And after lamenting the impossibility of reform, he concludes by declaring: "Nothing can be more disserviceable to Probity and Religion than
the *Stage.*" *Short View,* p. 287.
[100] *Ibid.,* p. vii.
[101] J. B. Bossuet, *Maxims and Reflections Upon Plays,* Preface, pp. vii-viii.
[102] *Ibid.,* p. vii.
[103] J. Collier, *A Defence,* p. 134.

as he voiced them at repeated intervals throughout the *Short View*.[104]

All of these facts show that the mind of the author of the preface to Bossuet's *Maxims and Reflections* was strikingly similar in its ideas and knowledge to that of the author of the *Short View*. Furthermore, the style of writing is the same. It is safe, therefore, to assume that the same hand penned the preface and the *Short View*. If this conclusion is true, then the preface is one more item which must be added to the anti-stage works written by Jeremy Collier.

8

Josiah Woodward's *An Account of the Societies for Reformation of Manners, in London and Westminster, And other Parts of the Kingdom. With a Persuasive to Persons of all Ranks, to be Zealous and Diligent in Promoting the Execution of the Laws against Prophaneness and Debauchery, for the Effecting A National Reformation* takes its place in the Collier Stage-Controversy by reason of an introduction given it by J. Feild in his *An Humble Application to the Queen*. In this work, Feild calls attention to Woodward's *Account* as being a very important document both as affecting the suppression of profaneness and immorality, and as stigmatizing the scandalous play-houses.[105] Feild directs the reader to the following quotation in the *Account* concerning play-houses, and a comparison of his quotation with the original proves that he quotes accurately:

"And it is well-known, to our Shame, . . . as if we were resolved to out-do the Impieties of the very Heathens, [that] Prophaneness, and even Blasphemy, was too often the Wit and Entertainment of our Scandalous Play-Houses, and Sincere Religion became the Jest and Scorn of our Courts in the late Reigns."[106]

---

[104] J. B. Bossuet, *op. cit.*, pp. v-vi.

[105] J. Feild, *An Humble Application to the Queen*, p. 7.

[106] Anonymous, *An Account of the Societies*, p. 4. Josiah Woodward's name does not appear in the *D.N.B.* Nevertheless, there are ascribed to him various works on the Societies for Reformation of Manners. Not only is the *Account* mentioned above said to have been written by him, but also *An Account of the Societies for Reformation of Manners, in England and Ireland*, . . . Halkett and Laing, *A Dictionary of Anonymous and Pseudonymous Literature*, I, 20. The fifth edition of this last mentioned work was published in 1701. There is also extant an edition of *An Account of the Rise and Progress of the Religious Societies in the City of London, etc., and of the Endeavours for Reformation of Manners*, 1698, to which he

Woodward, in the *Account,* enters further into detail and in it we note an anti-stage argument that is frequently used by Collier:

"And thus Debauchery diffused itself throughout the whole Body of the Nation, till, at last, our Morals were so corrupted, that Virtue and Vice had with too many changed their Names; it was reckoned Breeding to Swear, Gallantry to be Lewd, good Humour to be Drunk, and Wit to despise Sacred things; and it was enough to have rendered one suspected of Phanaticism or an abjectness of Spirit, . . . not to glory in those fashionable Vices."[107]

The entire *Account* deals not only with the vices that are prevalent in the English nation, but with the means of combating the evil and with the work being effected by the various societies for the reformation of manners.

9

The play *Feigned Friendship, or, The Mad Reformer,* appeared anonymously and was undated, according to D. E. Baker, *Biographia Dramatica,* 1782, II, 123. *The Post-Man,* however, announces it in its issue of June 13-15, 1699, and states that it was acted at the Theatre in Little Lincolns-Inn-Fields and that it was printed for Daniel Brown . . . F. Coggan . . . E. Rumbald . . . and Rob. Gibson at the Crown in Middle Row in Holborn. The title-page bears the motto "Satius est sic otiari turpius occupari." The author is, as we may infer from the title page, a champion of the play-house and a foe to Collier. The play is in the British Museum.

---

signs his name. *An Account of the Societies for the Reformation of Manners* is a book of 163 pages to which is prefixed not only a six-page proclamation issued by King William in 1697 for preventing and punishing immorality and profaneness, but a four-page letter issued by Queen Mary on July 9, 1691 to the Justices of the Peace in the County of Middlesex for the same purpose. There is in it, likewise, a five-page "Humble Address of the House of Commons to the King, for the Suppressing of Prophaneness and Vice," and a four-page epistle to the author sanctioning the design and method of the *Account.* To this Epistle are subscribed the names of twenty-nine Lords Temporal, nine Lords spiritual, and seven Judges. The book has an appendix containing a 9-page abstract of the Penal-Laws against immorality and profaneness.

[107] *Ibid.,* p. 4.

10

Dryden, in his *Epistle to Motteux* in 1698, had shown himself submissive to the castigations of Collier. He followed this in 1699 by another act of submission. In "A Letter to Mrs. Elizabeth Thomas," November, 1699, he admits his former guilt of immorality and he voices his willingness to practice reparation if the chance be given him. The Mrs. Thomas in question had sent to him two poems for criticism. Dryden's reply, in part, follows:

"Madam,—The great desire which I observe in you to write well, and those good parts which God Almighty and Nature have bestow'd on you, make me not to doubt, that by application to study, and the reading of the best authors, you may be absolute mistress of poetry. 'Tis an unprofitable art, to those who profess it; but you, who write only for diversion, may pass your hours with pleasure in it, and without prejudice; always avoiding (as I know you will,) the licence which Mrs. Behn allow'd herself, of writing loosely, and giving, if I may have leave to say so, some scandall to the modesty of her sex. I confess, I am the last man who ought, in justice, to arraign her, who have been my self too much a libertine in most of my poems; which I should be well contented I had time either to purge, or to see them fairly burn'd. But this I need not say to you, who are too well born, and too well principled, to fall into that mire. . . . "[108]

Although Dryden did not write this letter as a reply to the attack made by Collier on the licentiousness of his plays, it shows, nevertheless, just as convincingly as does the excerpt quoted from the Preface to *The Fables* in proof of his repentance, that the poet regretted the sinful liberties he had taken in his writings.

---

[108] W. Baptist Scoones, *Four Centuries of English Letters*, p. 140. On a previous occasion Mrs. Thomas had asked Dryden for a poetic name. He gave her that of "Corinna, the same as that famous Theban poetess who overcame Pindar five times." J. Dryden, *Works,* ed. Scott and Saintsbury, XVIII, 165.

CHAPTER VIII

Publications from November 26, 1699 to 1701

1. J. Collier: *A Second Defence*, November 26, 1699.
2. G. Farquhar: *Love and a Bottle*, Epilogue, December 29, 1699.
3. D. Defoe: *The Pacificator*, February, 1700.
4. S. Centlivre: *The Perjured Husband*, Preface, 1700.
5. C. Cibber: *Love Makes a Man*, Preface, 1700.
6. J. Dryden: Preface to *The Fables*, 1700.
7. J. Dryden: Epilogue to *The Pilgrim*, 1700.

In November, 1698, Collier in his *Defence* had replied to the vindications of angry stage-champions among whom Congreve, Vanbrugh, Dennis, and the authors of *A Vindication of the Stage* and *A Defence of Dramatic Poetry* were given prominent mention. The ensuing year, 1699, several caustic replies to this *Defence* were published, but only one author directly attacked the *Short View*. This was Drake, and to his *Antient and Modern Stages survey'd* Collier published in November his *Second Defence*. For some reason best known to himself Collier does not formally reply to the attacks made on his *Defence*.

About a month later was published Farquhar's *Love and a Bottle;* its Epilogue written and spoken by Jo. Haines attests to the improvement of morals since the stage-attack was begun in 1698, but mourns that the stage has been robbed of its former liberties. Defoe takes his place among Collier's crusaders, to use Beljame's quaint expression, and contributes to the cause his *Pacificator*. Mrs. Centlivre proves that she, too, has something to say to Collier on the topic of stage-reformation and she says it in her Preface to *The Perjured Husband*. Colley Cibber in his Prologue and Dedicatory Epistle to *Love Makes a Man*, refers to the topic, also. John Dryden in his Preface to *The Fables* repeats his act of contrition for his licentious writings, and in his Epilogue to *The Pilgrim* shows a chafed though subdued spirit, ascribing many of the vices of his day to their nursery, the court.

1

About nine months had elapsed between Drake's reply to Collier's *Short View*, and Collier's reply to Drake's *The Antient and Modern Stages survey'd*. However, with his customary pugnacity, Collier again entered the ranks in defence of his principles and replied to Drake's lengthy counter-attack with his *A Second Defence of the Short View of the Prophaneness and Immorality of the English Stage, etc. Being a Reply to a Book, Entituled, The Ancient and Modern Stages surveyed, etc*. London, 1700.[1]

Collier explains in his Preface that his failure to reply to Drake before was due to a doubt he had as to whether he should vindicate himself, and also to certain business for the press which he could not very well dismiss;[2] However, the business for the press having been completed, and Drake's charges of false quotation being considered a sufficient cause for vindication, Collier publishes his *Second Defence*. He very emphatically resents both Drake's manner and his defence of the stage:

> "His Eagerness to Defend the Stage has sometimes transported him into plain Rudeness: To this I shall only observe, That Railing is a scandalous Talent, and an Argument of an ill Undertaking. When a Man throws Dirt, 'tis a sign he has no other Weapon;"[3]

and just as emphatically does he state his despair of reforming the stage-poets, for

> "They make no scruple of coming over again with their Ill Plays; As if Immodesty and Prophaneness were the more valuable for being discover'd."[4]

---

[1] The *Second Defence* was printed at the press of Keble, Sare, and Strahan; it is 142 pages long, and has a two-page prefare. Its title-page bears the year 1700 but its Preface is dated November 26, 1699.

[2] J. Collier, *A Second Defence*, Preface, p. 1. It is interesting to note that Collier, in his first *Defence of the Short View*, p. 138, states: "I should now go on with Mr. Dennis and show his attempt on my other authorities, . . . but having some business at present, I shall wave it till a farther Opportunity," Now, the remark here of "some business at present," added to the remark in the *Second Defence* of "being engaged in business for the press which could not be dismissed" gives us leave to conjecture upon what Collier was writing between Nov. 1698 and Nov. 1699. The *D. N. B.*, IV, 802, states that Collier published in 1701 the first volume of *The Great Historical, Geographical, Genealogical Dictionary*, as well as his translation of *The Emperor M. Aurelius Antoninus, his Conversations with himself, together with other Pieces*. An examination of both volumes shows that they must have cost Collier an immense amount of labor, and it convinces the student that it was doubtless upon these that Collier was working. There is evidence in these volumes of tireless research, of careful analysis, and of painstaking work. It is likewise interesting to note that Collier does, in the *Second Defence*, follow up his promise to refute Dennis, cf. p. 19; pp. 52-53; p. 54.

[3] *Ibid., p. i.*

[4] *Ibid., p. ii.*

His Preface concluded, Collier begins his *Second Defence* by attacking the scheme, the compass, and the method of Drake's *Antient
and Modern Stages*. He says:

> "his Scheme is defective and the Compass of his Defence much
> short of the Charge, . . . he does not apply his Answer to any
> Particulars, nor so much as vindicate one Passage accused of
> Indecency and Irreligion. So that were his whole Book true the
> Imputation of *Prophaneness* and *Immorality*, would still lie
> heavy upon the *Stage*. This Author, . . . seems to rely more
> upon Stratagem and Surprize, than plain Force, and open At-
> tack. His Business is all along to perplex the Cause and amuse
> the Reader, and to Reason, and Represent amiss."[5]

He vindicates his statements as they appear in the *Short View*, justifies himself for translating "Theatrum" as "play house," and denies
that he has either misrepresented Tertullian or mistranslated the
Fathers:

> "For notwithstanding all his Clamour about my *Corrupt Ver-
> sion, Managing of Evidence,* and what not; he has not been
> able to shew that I have either mistaken the Sence, or misap-
> plied the Meaning in the least Instance; so that if *my main
> Strength,* as he is pleased to say, *lay in these Worthies,* the
> Forces are still entire, there is not so much as a Vein scratched,
> or a drop of Blood lost in the Encounter. But I can't forget his
> character and commendations of the *Fathers*."[6]

He defends his quotations from St. Cyprian, St. Chrysostom, and St.
Augustine; from Plato, Xenophon, and Aristotle; from Tully, Livy,
Valerius Maximus, the Massilienses, Tacitus, Plutarch, Ovid, and
Wycherley;[7] and sarcastically attacks Drake for his poor critical ability:

> "And now the *Surveyor* thinks fit to make a Halt, and seems
> extreamly satisfied with his performance: *I have,* says he, *at
> length run through all his private Authorities against the Stage.*
> Run through them! Yes, like a Bowl that gets nothing; or if
> you please, like a Souldier that runs the Gauntlet. Indeed this
> Author's Method is so very peculiar, he does so often fall foul
> upon his own Book, quote away his Argument, and mortifie

---

[5] *Ibid.,* p. 1.
[6] *Ibid.,* p. 15.
[7] *Ibid.,* pp 15-35.

himself, that one would almost fancy he wrote for a Pennance."[8]

Collier keeps his promise made in *A Defence* of answering Dennis' attack on his authorities:[9]

"The Objections against the Pagan part of the Authorities, were most of them made by Mr. *Dennis* before the *Surveyor;* The Answer to the one therefore will hold against the other;"[10]

and he vindicates not only the quotations which he had used from St. Augustine, but himself from the charge of not citing the authors "at length and in their own language." Concerning faulty citations he asserts:

"That my Meaning was fair, I have made good already; and that my Method was defensible, is no less plain, for I always took care to cite *Book, Chapter,* or *Page,* and sometimes *Edition,* too. Now how could Imposition and foul Play lie hid under such a Punctuality? When this was done what need was there of stuffing the *Margin* with Greek and Latin?"[11]

He repeats his censure of English play-house music as well as his statement that the stage encourages revenge and a false notion of honour;[12] he reasserts his opinion of the moral in the plays of Sophocles and Euripides, and declares concerning his previous attack on Hamlet:

"My exceptions to *Hamlet* related only to his Indecencies of Language; and how handsomly the Surveyor justifies that, we shall see afterwards."[13]

He upholds the Ancients against Drake's censure of them, and attacks the principle of Poetic Justice advocated by the Moderns despite Drake's praise of it:

" . . . thus I have endeavour'd to detect his Calumnies upon the *Antients,* to vindicate their *Fable,* and to disappoint him in his Project upon the Comparison. And alas! if the *Moderns* could have carried this part of the Preference, it would have done them but little service. A formal Piece of Justice at the

---

[8] *Ibid.,* pp. 39-40.
[9] J. Collier, *A Defence,* p. 138.
[10] J. Collier, *A Second Defence,* p. 53.
[11] *Ibid.,* p. 55.
[12] *Ibid.,* pp. 57-59.
[13] *Ibid.,* p. 77.

end of a Lewd Play, is nothing but a Piece of Grimace, and a Politick Hypocrisy. 'Tis much such a strain of conduct, as it would be to let a Mad Dog loose among the Crowd, and then knock him on the Head when he has bitten a great part of them."[14]

Concerning the definition of comedy, Collier does not waste words; he merely refers his readers to the *Defence* for the statements which he has hitherto made on the subject, and then passes on to analyzing Drake's opinion of the design of comedy. He says:

"He [Drake] says the design of Comedy is *rather Civil Prudence than Morality,* and . . . as for the *Characters,* . . . they must be all *Men of Pleasure;* for if they are tainted *with too much Honesty,* they will disagree *with the company, and spoil the Projects of the Stage.* Well, I perceive the *Surveyor* is resolv'd, notwithstanding his Pretences to the contrary, to make the Modern Writers of *Comedy* more Licentious than the *Antient.*"[15]

In the *Antient and Modern Stages survey'd* Drake had asserted:

"A Gentleman of Wit and Honour may be judiciously introduced into it [Comedy], but he must be a man of wild unreclaim'd honour, whose Appetites are strong and irregular enough to hurry him beyond his discretion, and make him act against the Conviction of his Judgment on the return of his Reason;"[16]

and Collier did not hesitate to denounce the assertion:

"A Man of Wild Honour! Truly, I think no Man's Honour can be Wilder then his Notion: Honour without Probity is next to a Contradiction in Terms, and besides, 'tis good for very little. For, to speak plainly, 'tis nothing more than Pride and Fashion, and Civility to a Man's self."[17]

As we have pointed out, Collier frequently gave critical opinions on such topics as the purpose of comedy, moral and poetical manners, and poetic justice. In the *Second Defence* he re-states many of his principles, vindicates them against the censure of Drake, and uses as

---

[14] *Ibid.,* p. 84.
[15] *Ibid.,* pp. 84-85.
[16] *J. Drake, Antient and Modern Stages survey'd,* p. 236.
[17] J. Collier, *Second Defence,* p. 86.

authorities Ben Jonson, Dryden, and Dacier.[18] Throughout, he shows himself a firm defender of the Ancients:

> "The *Surveyor* in his *Parallel*, blackens the *Antients* most unmercifully, and swells their Charge beyond all Truth and Proportion. This is done to make them the better in Countenance. But a little Pains will serve to wipe off most of the Spots, and restore them to their Complexion."[19]

He curiously says of Drake's defence of Ophelia " . . . by his Description, one would think he was raising a Muskmelon," and in comparing Sophocles, Aeschylus, and Seneca with the Moderns he says scornfully:

> "The *Moderns* compar'd with the *Greek* Tragedians and *Seneca*, in Point of Decency, and Sobriety of Language! . . . The *Moderns*! who not only glance, but dwell upon an ill Subject, bandy it between the two Sexes, and keep it up to shew their Skill in the Exercise. Yes: They love to flourish upon Lewdness, to refresh it with Repetition; and beat it out into Length and Circumstances. Sometimes to distinguish a foul Thought, they deliver it in *Scripture Phrase,* and set it in Gold to make it sparkle the better, . . . To lay their Disorders before the *Reader,* were the Sight proper, would swell into a Book, and be a tedious Undertaking."[20]

In typical Collier fashion he defends the clergy against Drake's attack[21] and says of Drake:

> "And here his spleen against the Church disorders him extreemly, and indeed almost throws him into Fits. He would gladly say something to purpose against the Clergy, but the Subject fails him. This makes him rail most unmericfully; for Spight and Impotence together are generally very Clamorous and Impertinent."[22]

His parting words are these:

> "I have now done with the Surveyor and heartily wish him a better Subject. For a bad Cause, besides its own Evil, is apt to produce a resembling Defence: If often runs an Author upon

---

[18] *Ibid.,* pp. 86-108.
[19] *Ibid.,* pp. 100-108.
[20] *Ibid.,* pp. 108-119.
[21] *Ibid.,* pp. 126-142.
[22] *Ibid.,* p. 126.

Calumny, Coarse Expedients, and Little Management: Which, as they are no sure Methods to raise a Character; so, at one time or other, they'l certainly displease a Man's self."[23]

The *Second Defence* shows Collier at boiling point with Drake, caustic in his impatience at the continued resistance of the vindicators of the stage, and tenacious of each and every principle which he had set forth in the *Short View* and in *A Defence of the Short View*. Although it does not add new principles it gives one valuable biographical note which is important in determining the authorship of *A Letter to a Lady*, 1706. In this *Letter* which has frequently been ascribed to Collier the author states, "I never in my Life saw a Play;" in the *Second Defence*, 1700, Collier declares "I must tell him [Drake], I have been there [at the Play house], tho not always for Diversion." In the subsequent analysis of the *Letter*, this biographical evidence will be used.

2

Beljame, in his *Le Public et Les Hommes de Lettres En Angleterre au 18 Siècle* calls attention to a number of stage-advocates who defended themselves and their brother-poets in replies to Collier's *Short View*. Among these he lists the epilogue to the five-act comedy *Love and a Bottle, A Comedy, As it is Acted at the Theatre-Royal in Drury-Lane*.[24] This epilogue was written and spoken by Jo. Haines in mourning, not for the poet or his play, but for the *Theatre-Royal*. He laments in mock-dramatic vein the wave of stage-reformation set in motion by Collier and his abettors.[25]

---

23 *Ibid.*, p. 142

24 A. Beljame, *Le Public et Les Hommes*, p. 253. The play was acted in 1699 at Drury Lane. D. E. Baker, *Biographia Dramatica*, II, 195. Baker censures the looseness of the character, Roebuck, and says that because of this looseness and "some other strokes of licentiousness that run through the piece, it has not been acted for many years past."

25 George Farquhar, *Love and a Bottle*, Epilogue, p. 191. That Dryden censured Haines' scurrility is evident from a couplet which he wrote in his Epilogue to *The Pilgrim*:
   "But neither you, nor we, with all our pains,
   Can make clean work; there will be some remains,
   While you have still your Oates, and we our Haines."
J. Dryden, *Dramatic Works*, S. & S. Ed., VIII, 504.

He satirizes the French Strollers and the Italian musicians, and after mimicing the singers he says to his audience

"Lastly, to make our House more courtly shine,
As Travel does the Men of Mode refine,
So our Stage-Heroes did their Tour design.
To mend their Manners, and coarse English Feeding,
They went to Ireland, to improve their Breeding;
Yet, for all this, we still are at a loss,
Oh Collier! Collier! thou'st frighted away Miss C-s.

. . .

Well, if 'tis decreed, nor can thy Fate, O Stage!
Resist the Vows of this obdurate Age;
I'll then grow wiser, leave off playing the Fool,
And hire this Play-house for a Boarding-School."[26]

If Baker decried the looseness in Farquhar's *Love and a Bottle*, Mrs. C - - - - - - - - - - - l [Astraea][27] praises the morality of his *Trip to the Jubilee*. We learn this from a letter which she wrote to Farquhar:

"To Mr. Farquhar upon his Comedy call'd A Trip to the Jubilee [acted 1700]:

For since the learned *Collier first essay'd*
To teach Religion to the Rhiming Trade,
The *Comick* Muse in *Tragick* posture sat,
And seem'd to mourn the Downfall of her State;
Her eldest Sons she often did implore,
That they her ancient Credit would restore.
Strait they essay'd, but quickly to their cost
They found that all their industry was lost.
For since the *Double Entendre* was forbid,
They could not get a Clap for what they did.
At last *Thalia* call'd her youngest Son,
The graceful and the best beloved one:
My Son, said she, I have observed thee well,
Thou doest already all my Sons excell;

. . .

Go, something Write, my Son, that may atone
Thy Brethren's Faults, and make thy virtues known.
I'll teach Thee Language in a pleasant stile;
Which, without Smut, can make an Audience smile.
Let fall no word that may offend the Fair;

---

[26] *Ibid.*, p. 192.
[27] The name is not identified in Cushing's *Anonyma and Pseudonyma*.

Observe Decorums, dress thy Thoughts with Air;
Go—lay the Plot, which Vertue shall adorn;
Thus spoke the Muse; and thus didst Thou perform."[28]

3

There are many evidences of Daniel Defoe's interest in the reformation of manners. Beljame calls attention to it as being expressed in
1698 in *The Poor Man's Plea. In Relation to all the Proclamations,
Acts of Parliament, etc. which have been, or shall be made, or publish'd, for a Reformation of Manners and suppressing Immorality in
the Nation.*[29] Defoe, in 1700, further emphasized his position in the
cause by publishing *The Pacificator: A Poem,*[30] while in 1702 he published his *Reformation of Manners, a Satyr, Vae vobis hypocritae* into
which he injected all the pent-up bitterness in his heart against the
attempted reformation of the lower classes of society by the higher
who do not practice what they preach.[31]

It is with *The Pacificator* that we are to deal, however, for here
DeFoe takes up the cause of Blackmore and of Collier against an army
of wits. The poem is an allegory written in heroic couplets; Defoe
uniquely gives as the setting a literary battle in which

"The strong Contention's grown to such a hight,
The Pen's already drawn, and has begun the fight.
The Men of Sense against the Men of Wit,
Eternal fighting must determine it."[32]

---

[28] Anonymous, *Letters of Wit, Politicks and Morality,* 1701, pp. 363-4. Farquhar wrote a "Discourse Upon Comedy, in Reference to the English Stage,"
The Works, . . . pp. 69-92, which proves him a literary critic of ability. He
refers in it to the stage-reform of Collier. *Ibid.,* p. 74.

[29] A. Beljame, *Le Public et Les Hommes,* p. 255. Beljame refers to the cru-
sade undertaken against immorality, and to Defoe's place in it. He says:
Des adeptes ardents [Defoe, R——h, the author of the *Animadversions,* of
the *Representation, and* Woodward] s'engagèrent avec passion dans la croi-
sade dont Collier s'était fait le Pierre l'Hermite."

[30] *The Pacificator* was printed in London by J. Nutt. The 1700 edition (14
pages) is in folio. A chronological catalogue of the Works of Daniel
DeFoe occurs in *Works of DeFoe* by W. Hazlitt, I, 1-17, as well as in
Paul Dottin's *Daniel DeFoe et Ses Romans,* pp. 802-849. Dottin tells us
that the *Pacificator* was published in February, 1700.

[31] The theme both in *The Poor Man's Plea* as well as in *Reformation of Man-
ners* is:
"The Magistrates must Blasphemy forbear,
Be faultless first Themselves, and then severe."

[32] D. Defoe, *The Pacificator,* p. 2.

As captain of the "Men of Sense" Defoe places Sir Richard Blackmore under the title "Nokor." He says:

"Heroic Nokor made the first Attack
And threw Drammatick Wit upon its Back;

.   .   .

His Sence was good, but see how Fate Decrees!
His hasty Talent threw him on his Knees,
A Storm of Words the Hero overtook,
Disorder'd all his Lines, and all his Squadrons broke.
The Adverse Troops pour'd in their light Dragoons,
Charg'd him with Forty Thousand Arm'd Lampoons;"[33]

Defoe introduces Collier next:

"C - - - - - r came next in order to the Charge,
His Squadrons thin, altho' his Front was large,
A modest Soldier, resolute and stout
Arm'd with a Coat of Sense from head to foot;
No more than need, for he was hard put to't.
He Charg'd the strongest Troops of all the Foes,
And gave them signal Overthrows."[34]

In the succeeding couplets Defoe refers to the replies to the *Short View* and to the lapse of time between the *Defence* and the *Second Defence*. He makes a statement concerning the attitude of the wits

---

[33] *Ibid.*, p. 3. Defoe here refers to Blackmore's *Satyr against Wit* published early in 1700, which attacked the wits of his day on the score of irreligion and immorality and which evoked a storm of replies. Notable among these replies are *Commendatory Verses on the Author of the two Arthurs and the Satyr against Wit by some of his particular Friends.* To this Blackmore replied by *Discommendatory Verses.* Dryden attacked him in the Prologue to *The Pilgrim,* Garth in *The Dispensary,* while Sedley and Steele also showed their displeasure. *D.N.B.,* II, 592. It is to Blackmore's *Discommendatory Verses* that Defoe refers when he says:
"But Nokor, like a Prudent General,
Resum'd new Courage from a seeming Foil,
The same Campagne again in Arms appear'd,
And what the *Prince* had lost, the *King* repair'd."
The Pacificator, p. 3.
[34] The strongest troops referred to are, undoubtedly, Dryden, Wycherley, Congreve, and Vanbrugh. There were two others against whom the *Short View* was directed, Otway and D'Urfey, but Otway was dead and D'Urfey was considered by Collier only a "Vox, praeterea nihil." J. Collier, *Short View,* p 208.

toward Collier and this I have not met with elsewhere in my study of
the controversy:

> "The Wits wou'd fain ha' bought his fury off,
> And proffer'd him *Applause,* and Gold enough,
> But 'twou'd not do, he boldly Charged again,
> And by Ten thousand Wounds at last was slain.
> Some say he was by his own Men betray'd,
> And basely left alive among the Dead,
> But I cannot understand how that can be,
> For how can Treachery and Sense agree?
> In *Honours Truckle-Bed* the Hero lies,
> Till Sense again, *The Lord knows when,* shall rise."[35]

Defoe goes on with his narrative to tell of the progress of the battle.
D - - - - s [Dennis], he says, a "stiff, politick Critick" commanded the
forlorn of wit; C - - - - e [Crowne], D - - - - n [Dryden], H - -
- - - s [Hopkins], M - - - - - x [Motteux], D - - - - - y [D'Urfey]

> "Led up the Battel Fifty thousand strong,
> Arm'd with *Burlesque, Bombast,* and *Bawdy-Song;*
> Flesh'd with great C - - - - - ' s Slaughter they led on,
> Shouting *Victoria,* the Day's their own;
>
> . . .
>
> Never such Devastation sure was known,
> A Man of Sense cou'd not be seen in Town.
> T - - - - n [Tonson], even Hackney T - - - - n, would not Print,
> A Book without Wits Imprimatur in't."[36]

The story of the progress of the battle is continued in fascinating
manner. Nokor revives, reassumes the commander-ship; he charges upon
and overthrows whole wings of foot [soldiers]; Pun-Master-General-
D'Urfey led the grenadiers from Scotland where they had been making sonnets. The left flank, Defoe tells us, was formidable in its appearance for

> " . . . it was form'd of seven large Brigades,
> Of *Farces, Opera's,* and *Masquerades,*
> With several little Bands of *Dogrel* Wit,
> To Scowre the Ways, and Line the Hedges fit.
> Between these mighty Wings was rang'd in sight,
> A solid Phalanx of Compounded Wit;

---

[35] *The Pacificator,* p. 4.
[36] *Ibid.,* p. 6.

Ten thousand *Lyrick Foot,* all Gallant *Beaux,*
Arm'd with *soft Sighs,* with *Songs,* and *Billet-Doux.*
There was Eight thousand Elegiack Foot,
By *Briny Tears* and *Sullen Grief* made stout,
Five Pastoral Bands, lately bred up in Arms,
By Chanting *Gloriana's* Mighty Charms."[37]

It is upon this formidable line-up that Nokor and his troops make battle and come off victorious:

"The Troops of Wit, Disorder'd, and O'r-run,
Are slain, Disperc'd, Disgrac'd, and Overthrown,"[38]

Defoe's ensuing parallel between wit and sense is delightfully entertaining; he assigns each of the wits to his respective position in poetry, and his moral in the concluding verses is worth remembering:

"What Fools Indite, let none but Blockheads Read,
And may they write in vain, who write for Bread:
No Banters on the Sacred Text admit,
Nor *Bawdy Lines,* that *Blasphemy of Wit."*

4

One of the first instances of the women-dramatists entering into the stage-controversy occurs in the preface which Mrs. Susanna Centlivre wrote to her tragedy *The Perjur'd Husband: Or, The Adventures of Venice.*[39] The authoress, in the very first lines, hotly asserts:

"I should not trouble my Reader with a Preface if Mr. Collier had taught Manners to Masks, Sense to Beaux, and Good-nature to Criticks, as well as Morality to the Stage; the first are sure to envy what they can't equal, and condemn what they don't understand; the Beaux usually take a greater Liberty with our sex than they wou'd with their own, . . . "[40]

and just as hotly does she place the blame for the ill success of her

---

[37] *Ibid.,* pp. 8-9.
[38] *Ibid.,,* p. 10.
[39] The play was acted at the Theatre Royal on "some unascertained date in 1700," and it fell short of the success Mrs. Centlivre had hoped for. Walter and Claire Jerrold, *Five Queer Women,* p. 152.
[40] S. Centlivre, *The Perjured Husband,* Preface, p. i.

play upon the "snarling Sparks" who censured a few expressions used by her minor characters:

> "These Snarling Sparks were pleas'd to carp at one or two Expressions, which were spoken in an Aside by one of the Inferiour Characters in the Drama."[41]

Mrs. Centlivre here attests to the general trend of audiences to be on the alert for expressions which are either profane or indecent, and, of course, she blames Collier for the censure which they receive. Even though biographers say that *The Perjur'd Husband* fell short of Mrs. Centlivre's expectations, she herself tells us in the concluding line of the preface that

> "it only wanted the Addition of good Actors, and a full Town, to have brought me a sixth night, there having been worse Plays within this twelve-month approv'd of."[42]

In addition to the attack on Collier by Mrs. Centlivre in the Preface, we find reference, also, in the Prologue and Epilogue to the effects of the stage reformation. The Prologue, written by "a Gentleman," reads:

> "Such dreadful Laws of late 'gainst wit are made, It dares not in the City show its head."[43]

and the Epilogue, written by Mr. B - - - - - - - n [Betterton] and spoken by Jo. Haines tells us:

> "Too long the Poets brought before the Bar, Have with their bold Accuser wag'd the War; They now plead Guilty: And confess the Stage Has been immoral, and debauch'd the Age."[44]

Haines gives us, then, his ideas of the requisites of a real reformation, and curiously enough, some of these ideas coincide with those of Defoe who believed that manners should be mended first among the higher classes and those in authority. He says that when politicians, lawyers, heroes, Cheapside Doctors, Town-Ladies, and peevish critics—each in his own way, will mend his faults, then

> "When all this heavy Task is well perform'd, We dare ingage the Stage shall be reform'd."[45]

---

[41] *Ibid.*, p. i.
[42] *Ibid.*, p. i.
[43] *Ibid.*, p. iv.
[44] *Ibid.*, p. v.
[45] *Ibid.*, p. v.

5

Cibber, by a fulsome epistle, dedicates to Sir William Brownlowe his five-act comedy *Love Makes a Man, or, The Fop's Fortune*.[46] In this epistle he seeks protection not so much from the critics, he tells us, as from the "formidable Zeal of a Presenting Middlesex Jury." He says of the critics:

> "Avarice, Hypocrisie, and Ignorance have thrown off their short Cloaks, spit in their Paws, and are every one resolv'd to have a blow at the root of the Bay-Tree, and when it's down, like Brethren, they are to share it among 'em: . . . But this we are not to wonder at; For there are among us a sort of Gentlemen, that have been us'd to *Lopping,* that know how to handle an Axe, and I think the last time they pull'd down the *Stage* in the City, they set up a *Scaffold* at Court."[47]

Under the names of "Avarice, Hypocrisie and Ignorance" Cibber addresses the reformers; under the figure of using the axe and lopping the branches he distinctly replies to Collier's purpose expressed in the *Short View* of "killing the root, rather than transplanting it," and of "laying the axe to the root." Subsequent statements in the Epistle give, besides, valuable evidence that Cibber entertained personal antipathy to Collier,—antipathy that he showed in his play, *The Non-Juror,* 1718, which topic forms the subject of a later study.

6

In the Preface to the *Fables* Dryden answers more directly the attack of Collier than he did in his two letters previously mentioned. In the Preface we find another admission of guilt; we find an apparently sincere expression of regret for the sins of the past:

> "I shall say less of Mr. Collier, because in many things he has taxed me justly; and I have pleaded guilty to all thoughts and expressions of mine, which can be truly argued of obscenity, and profaneness, or immorality, and retract them. If he be my enemy, let him triumph; if he be my friend, as I have given him no personal occasion to be otherwise, he will be glad of

---

[46] According to D. E. Baker the play was first acted at Drury Lane in 1700, and was published the same year. *Biographia Dramatica,* 1782, I, 83; II, 200. However, Mr. Krutch gives as the date 1701. *Comedy and Conscience,* p. 268. Cibber attaches to his "Dedication" the date Jan 16, 1700.
[47] Cibber, Colley, *Love Makes a Man,* Ded. Epistle, p. i.

my repentance. It becomes me not to draw my pen in the defence of a bad cause, when I have so often drawn it for a good one."[48]

In the lines which follow there is a quiet statement of fact, a simple assertion that in many places Collier had misinterpreted his meanings:

"Yet it were not difficult to prove, that in many places he has perverted my meaning by his glosses, and interpreted my words into blasphemy and bawdry, of which they were not guilty."[49]

Then, with just a tinge of his old irascibility, just a shadow of his old irony, he continues:

Besides that, he is too much given to horseplay in his raillery, and comes to battle like a dictator from the plough. I will not say, *The Zeal of God's House has eaten him up;* but I am sure it has devoured some part of his good manners and civility.[50]

Dryden, like many of his fellow-poets adds a stroke or two to the portrait of Collier which contemporary critics were sketching:

"It might also be doubted, whether it were altogether zeal which prompted him to this rough manner of proceeding; perhaps, it became not one of his functions to rake into the rubbish of ancient and modern plays: a divine might have employed his pains to better purpose, than in the nastiness of Plautus and Aristophanes, whose examples, as they excuse not me, so it might be possibly supposed, that he read them not without some pleasure."[51]

7

In my analysis of the anonymous "Letter Written by another Hand"[52] in the second edition of Collier's *Dissuasive* I have called attention to the fact that even though critics are of the opinion that Dryden did not participate in the stage controversy, the writer of the "Letter," nevertheless, holds that he did and that it was in the Epilogue to Fletcher's *Pilgrim* that he acquitted himself of his controversial obli-

---

[48] W. P. Ker, *Essays of John Dryden*, II, 272.
[49] *Ibid.*, II, 272.
[50] *Ibid.*, II, p. 272.
[51] *Ibid.*, p. 273.
[52] pp. 216-217.

gations. It is in the Epilogue that we find Dryden's opinion of the age; in it he traces its infection not to the stage, but to

" . . . a banished court, [which] with lewdness fraught,
the seeds of open vice, returning brought."[52a]

Then follows an account of the spread of the infection:

"Thus lodged (as vice by great example thrives),
It first debauched the daughters and the wives.
London a fruitful soil, yet never bore
So plentiful a crop of horns before."[53]

Dryden tells us, perhaps from reproachful memories that surge upon him, the part which the poets played in propagating the seeds of vice:

"The poets, who must live by courts, or starve,
Were proud, so good a government to serve;
And, mixing with buffoons and pimps profane,
Tainted the stage for some small snips of gain:

.   .   .

Thus did the thriving malady prevail
The court its head, the poets but the tail."[54]

In the ensuing lines he paints a picture of the ravages which lewdness has wrought upon the city. Dryden was no longer in his prime; nearing three-score and ten, he was suffering in body and spirit and was writing facts as he saw them. He had been disappointed in the great; he had been lampooned for his change of religious belief, and he had little reason to care either for praise or censure.

It is interesting to note that Scott and Saintsbury in their edition of Dryden's Epilogue to Fletcher's *Pilgrim* append verses relevant to Dryden's controversy with Blackmore and Collier. These verses appeared, however, after Dryden's death:

"John Dryden enemies had three,
Sir Dick, Old Nick, and Jeremy:
The doughty knight was forced to yield,
The other two have kept the field.
But had his life been something holier,
He'd foiled the Devil and the Collier."[55]

[52a] J. Dryden, *Works,* ed. S. and S., VIII, 502.
[53] *Ibid.,* p. 502.
[54] *Ibid.,* p. 502.
[55] *Ibid., VIII,* p. 501.

1. George Granville: *The Jew of Venice,* Epilogue, 1701.
2. Richard Burridge: *Scourge for the Play-House,* 1702.
3. Thomas Brown, Capt. Ayloff, Mr. Henry Barker: *Letters from the Dead to the Living,* written in 1701, published in 1702.
4. J. Feild: *An Humble Application to the Queen,* Dec. 10, 1702.
5. Anonymous: *A Refutation of the Apology for Actors,* 1703.
6. J. Collier: *A Dissuasive from the Play-House,* December 10. 1703.

The subsiding interest in the stage-controversy after 1700 is evident by the dearth of controversial publications. During the years 1701, 1702, and 1703, there are but six works listed, and two of the six I have been unable to obtain. I feel certain that more pamphlets than the ones cited here were written during these years. For example, one is justified in believing that the *Refutation of the Apology for Actors* was an answer to an *Apology for Actors* published shortly before, but of this pamphlet I could get no information. Besides, there was a great forward movement made by the Societies for Reformation of Manners, and, in consequence, much literature was printed pro and con on the topic of immorality and profaneness. De Foe's *Reformation of Manners,* W. Bisset's *Plain English,* . . . *for Reformation of Manners,* and J. Swift's *A Letter of Advice to a Young Poet* are examples. Inasmuch as these works and others of a like nature are on the subject of reformation in general but are not direct attacks on Collier or on the play-house, I have omitted them in my bibliography. Then, too, there is internal evidence in the pamphlets published between 1698-1726 that in sermons preached and attacks made on immorality and profaneness in general, there were attacks made on the stage in particular. The bibliographical chart appended to the present work illustrates this. However, we find in this period an occasional writer who hoped to advance the cause of reformation by attacking the play-house, and where he attacked it I have included the work. Such is the case in J. Feild's *Humble Application.*

Concerning the four available works whose titles are listed above, it may be said that George Granville in his Epilogue to *The Jew of Venice* introduces a new opinion for the low ebb of morality in the nation and discards not only Collier's opinion as expressed in the

Short View, but Dryden's as given in the Epilogue to *The Pilgrim.* Among the *Letters from the Dead to the Living* are three which scoff at reformation and ridicule the attempted stage-reformation. In Collier's *Dissuasive from the Play-house* we have a letter written after the great storm of November 26, 1703, in which the author revives many of his old arguments against plays and the play-house.

1

The Jew of Venice may be studied from several interesting angles, but the one which concerns us is its connection with the stage-controversy. It is in the epilogue that the author analyzes the cause of the immorality of the age; it is here that he declares Collier to be in error when he attempts to mend the matter by silencing the poets, and Dryden to be just as much in error when he fixes the blame on the court.

> "Each in his turn, the Poet and the Priest,
> Have view'd the Stage, but like false Prophets guess'd:
> The Man of Zeal in his Religious Rage
> Would silence Poets, and reduce the Stage.
> The Poet rashly, to get clear, retorts
> On Kings the Scandal, and bespatters Courts.
> Both err; for without mincing, to be plain,
> The Guilt is yours of every Odious Scene.
> The present time still gives the Stage its Mode,
> The Vices which you practice, we explode;
> We hold the Glass, and but reflect your Shame,
> Like Spartans, by exposing, to reclaim.
> The scribbler, pinched with hunger, writes to dine,
> And to your genius must conform his line;
> Not lewd by choice, but merely to submit:
> Would you encourage sense, sense would be writ."[1]

---

[1] George Granville, Lord Lansdowne, *The Jew of Venice, A. Comedy. As it is Acted at the Theatre in Lincoln-Inn's-Fields by His Majesty's Servants.* Epilogue, p. 61. The play is altered from Shakespeare's *Merchant of Venice* and, according to Baker, altered with judgment; D. E. Baker, *Biog. Dram.,* 1812, II, 345. Baker calls attention to the last lines of the Prologue written by Bevill Higgons which refer to the fact that the profits of the play were given to Dryden's son. They are spoken by the ghost of Dryden:
"I long endeavour'd to support thy Stage, . . .
But toiled in vain for an ungenerous Age.
They starv'd me living; nay deny'd me fame,
And scarce now dead, do Justice to my Name.
Wou'd you repent? Be to my ashes kind,
Indulge the Pledges I have left behind.' '
The Jew of Venice, p. iii.

2

The *Letters From the Dead to the Living* were written by a group
of wits among whom are mentioned Thomas Brown, Captain Ayloff,
and Mr. Henry Barker. The volume is comprised not only of satirical
letters written from Pluto's kingdom by well-known characters to their
friends on earth, but of replies returned from earth to hell. Of the
collection, three letters concern us: 1. "Will Pierre's Answer [to
Julian]. Lincoln's-Inn-Fields. November 5, 1701. Behind the Scenes
. . ."[2] 2. "Letter of News from Mr. Joseph Haines, of Merry Memory,
to his Friends at Will's Coffee-House in Covent Garden," December
21, 1701;[3] and 3. "An Answer to Mr. Joseph Haines, High German
Astrologer, to his friends at Wills," signed: Sebastian Freeman, Regis-
trarius, Nomine Societatis. January 10, 1701.[4]

In order to understand "Will Pierre's Answer to Julian" it is necessary to recall that "Julian the Late Secretary of the Muses" wrote to
"Will Pierre of Lincolns-Inn-Fields Play-House" addressing his letter
from "Pandaemonium, the 8th of the Month of Beelzebub."[5]

Will Pierre's Answer to Julian is dated November 5, 1701, and
was written "Behind the Scenes at Lincolns-Inn-Fields." Will Pierre
addresses Julian as "Worthy Sir of Venerable Memory," and early
introduces the topic in mind:

"Poetry was the Vehicle that conveyed all your Scandal to the
Town, and I being conversant about the skirts of that Art, my
scandal must dwell chiefly thereabout;"[6]

---

[2] Thomas Brown, Captain Ayloff, Mr. Henry Barker, *Letters from the Dead
to the Living*, pp. 68-75. The Letters were printed in London, 1702. No
printer's name appears which fact may be due to the risk incurred by the
printer of publishing such satire as is contained in the *Letters*. "Will
Pierre's Answer" was written by Barker.

[3] *Ibid.*, pp. 1-35. Written by Thomas Brown.

[4] *Ibid.*, pp. 35-40. Written by Thomas Brown.

[5] Barker intended by the name of Will Pierre, doubtless, to satirize the stage-
reformer, Will Prynne. Several statements give this clue and among them we
note that Julian says to him: "you, Sir, if I mistake not, are one of the most
ancient of his Majesty's Servants, . . . your station qualifying you for a right
Information of the Scandal of the Town, I hope you will not fail to answer
my expectation; . . ." *Ibid.*, p. 65. *Ibid.*, p. 71.

[6] *Ibid.*, pp. 68-69.

He states that there is a scarcity of satire but not a scarcity of vices; that hypocrisy is prevalent and that railing is the utmost effort. Besides,

> "The Women grow greater Hypocrites than ever . . . they rail at the Vices they indulge, they forsake publick Diversions as Plays, etc., to gain the reputation of Vertue, to give a greater loose to the Domestick Diversions of a Bottle and Gallant, and Hypocrisie heightens their Pleasures."[7]

He states further:

> "There has a terrible Enemy arose to the Stage; an abdicated Divine, who when he had escaped the Pillory for Sedition and reforming the State, set up for the Reformation of the Stage; The Event was admirable, Fanaticks presented the Non-juror, and Misers and Extortioners gave him bountiful Rewards; one grave Citizen that had found his Character too often on the Stage, and famous for the ruine of some hundreds of poor, . . . laid out three score Pound in the Impression to distribute among the Saints that are zealous for God and Mammon at the same time; . . . "[8]

From satirizing Collier, Will Pierre attacks the greater mischief that has befallen the Stage:

> "Here are Societies that set up for *Reformation of Manners;* Troops of *Informers* who are maintain'd by Perjury, serve God for *Gain,* . . . This noble Society Consist of Divines of both Churches, Fanatick as well as Orthodox; Saints and Sinners; Knights of the Post and Knights of the Elbow, and they are not more unanimous against *Immorality* in Their *Informations* than for it in their *Practice.* They avoid no sins in themselves, and will suffer none in any one else."[9]

He says that for the interest of the Crown-Office they pick harmless words out of plays in order to indict the players, and pick twenty

---

[7] *Ibid.,* p. 70. It is important to note here that Barker and Dennis hold the same opinions—that suppressing plays gives birth to greater evils. Dennis gives his views on this topic in his "Essay on the Operas after the Italian Manner," 1706, as well as in his "Person of Quality's Answer to Mr. Collier," written in reply to Collier's *Dissuasive.*

[8] *Ibid.,* pp. 70-71. Collier here as elsewhere is called simply "The Non-Juror," a fact which becomes significant in our subsequent study of Cibber's *The Non-Juror.*

[9] *Ibid.,* pp. 71-72. Note the similarity of opinion here with Defoe as expressed in his *Poor Man's Plea,* and in his *Reformation of Manners.*

pounds a week out of them for exposing pride, vanity, and other darling vices of the Master of the Informers.[10] He sends a message to Ben Jonson that a new author "that has wrote a taking play is writing a *Treatise of Comedy,*" and, before concluding, he gives a curious description of the contents of this Treatise which attacks the very topics which Collier's *Short View* had so persistently upheld:

> "he shews what a Coxcomb Aristotle was and what a company of senceless pedants the Scaligers, Rapines, Vossii, etc. are; proves that no good Play can be regular, and that all rules are as ridiculous as useless, . . . and that common Sence and Nature was not the same in *Athens* as in *Drury Lane,* . . . and that irregularity and nonsence were the chief perfections of the Drama."[11]

For a correct understanding of the significance of the second letter of our study, viz., "A Letter of News from Mr. Joseph Haines," one needs to understand that Brown describes Haines as writing from Pluto's Kingdom where surroundings are such that a description of them will be interesting even though Homer, Virgil, Dante, Don Quevedo and others have described them before. Haines tells us that for a long time he has wished to communicate with his friends at Will's Coffee-House, but due to the difficulty of sending the letter to earth, he was obliged to wait for a considerable length of time before he could get the letter beyond the River Styx. However, he has recently learned that a fresh war is about to break out in England and that Pluto is dispatching a messenger to see how Parliament is going to behave. It is with this messenger that the letter is being sent to Will's.[12] The letter touches upon a variety of topics; in fact, upon all of those topics which form the subject of conversation at Will's. There is, how-

---

[10] *Ibid.,* p. 73.

[11] *Ibid.,* pp. 74-75, Barker is most likely referring here to George Farquhar whose *Constant Couple,* 1700, and its sequel, *Sir Harry Wildair,* gained their author great reputation. Farquhar, in 1702, published his *A Discourse upon Comedy in Reference to the English Stage.* The reference to the Scaligers, Rapines, and Vossii appears thus: "The Scholar will be very angry at me for making that the Subject of a Question, which is self-evident without any Dispute; for, says he, who can pretend to understand Poetry better than we, who have read *Homer. Virgil, Horace, Ovid,* etc. at the University? What Knowledge can out-strip ours that is founded upon the Criticisms of *Aristotle, Scaliger, Vossius* and the like?" George Farquhar, *The Works,* (1772), I, 71.

[12] *Ibid.,* pp. 1-2.

ever, one reference concerning the attempted stage-reformation which must not be overlooked! Mr. Haines meets with Mr. Nokes, the Comedian, who having greeted him cordially, says:

> "Mr. Haines, I am glad with all my heart to see you in Hell; . . . My dear Jo, . . . How go affairs in Covent Garden? . . . and the Play-house in Drury Lane, is it as much frequented as it us'd to be?"[13]

To these queries Haines returns a satisfactory answer, and in a short time the men find themselves in the suburbs of hell whereupon Haines in a care-free manner states that his friend Nokes

> "With that Gaiety and openness, which became him so well at the Play-House; . . . carry'd me to a little blind Coffee house in the middle of a dirty Ally,"[14]

and there, plucking him by the sleeve, pointed out several notorious characters of the infernal regions, among whom were Semiramus and Cyrus. On Bow Street where they shortly found themselves there were

> "No sawcy Tradesmen or Mechanick . . . but wholly inhabited by fine gaudy fluttering Sparks, and fine airy Ladies, who in no respect are inferiour to yours in *Covent Garden*."[15]

Haines' description of the abode of the rhimers and versifiers is humorous in the extreme:

> "But of all the various sorts of Mad-men that come hither, the Rhimers or Versifiers far exceed the rest in number. . . . The first Man I saw was *Sir John Peak,* formerly Lord Mayor of *London,* who bluntly came up to the door and asked me what was Rhime to Crambo;[16] "immediately Sir Thomas Pilkington popt over his Shoulder, and pray friend, says he, for I perceive you are newly come from the other world, how go the affairs of Parnassus? . . . What pretty conceits had Mr. Settle in his last *London* Triumphs? What Plays have taken of late? Mrs. Bracegirdle, does she still live unmarried, and pray, Sir, how do Mr. Betterton's Lungs hold out?"[17]

---

[13] *Ibid.,* p. 8.
[14] *Ibid.,* p. 8-9.
[15] *Ibid.,* pp. 8-13.
[16] "Dr. Crambo" it will be remembered, was the frequent title which Collier received from the stage-vindicators—Brown, D'Urfey, and Vanbrugh.
[17] Anonymous, *Letters,* pp. 25-26.

He closes his letter by stating that he intends to build himself a stage in one of the largest piazzas of the city, by apologizing for his prolixty, and by pleading for news from the upper world.[18]

Brown, in his letter, sounds a note of *quiet contempt* for things that are held sacred; he shows the same traits which two years later led him to satirize Collier and the stage-reformers by his *Stage-Beaux toss'd in a Blanket.*

"The Answer to Mr. Haines" is the subject of the third letter. The writer, Sebastian Freeman, registrar of the society at Will's, addressing his correspondent as "Worthy Sir" tells him that his letter had been read on January 9 in a full assembly at Will's;[19] he asserts that Will's Coffee-House is in much the same condition as when Haines left it and that there are four classes of persons who resort thither. He gives the requested information about the play-house:

> "The Play-House stands exactly where it did. Mr. Rich finds some trouble in managing his mutinous Subjects, . . . We have had an Inundation of Plays lately, and one of them by a great Miracle made a shift to hold out a full Fortnight. . . . A merry Virtuoso, who makes one of the Congregation *de propagando ingenio* designs to publish a weekly Bill for the use of the two Theatres, in imitation of that publish'd by the Parish Clerks, and faithfully to set down what Distemper every New Play dyes of."[20]

The wits at Will's send word to Jo that the wit of the town is debauch'd; they tell him 'tis well he died when he did, for Smithfield where he so often displayed his talent,

> has fallen under the City Magistrate's displeasure so that now *St. George and the Dragon, The Trojan Horse,* and *Bateman's Ghost,* the *Prodigal Son,* and *Jephtha's Daughter;* in short, all the Drolls of Glorious Memory, are routed, defeated, and sent to grass, without any hopes of a reprieve;"[21]

---

[18] *Ibid.,* pp. 33-34.
[19] *Ibid.,* p. 35.
[20] *Ibid.,* pp. 36-38.
[21] *Ibid.,* pp. 38-39. It is interesting to compare Brown's description of Haines in this letter with the remarks made about Haines in "A Letter, in Answer to some queries Relating to the Irregularities charged upon the Stage," in Collier's *Dissuasive,* 2nd edition. Besides, Collier, in his *Dissuasive,* p. 6, in

that the nation is being over-run with pamphlets, and that his life has
been written by a brother player who

> "pretends he received all his Memoirs from your own Mouth
> a little before you made a leap into the Dark."[22]

3

John Feild gives March 10, 1702, as the date on which he finished
writing *An Humble Application to the Queen, And Her Great Council,
The Parliament of England, To Suppress Play-Houses and Bear-Baitings, With all Prophaness and Immorality,* but the pamphlet was published in 1703. He minces no words in stating his request to the Queen
and her Great Council, the Parliament:

> "That they would, in the Fear and Wisdom of God, be pleased,
> for his Honour, the Good of the Nation, and Reputation of
> the Christian Religion, not to License or Countenance, with
> Authority, any Play-Houses, Revellings at the Temple, Dice-
> playing, Gaming, Stage-Players, Bull or Bear-baitings, but totally
> to suppress and put them down; for thereby Vice, Prophaness,
> Debauchery and Immorality, do greatly abound and are so Pro-
> vokingly Practiced, to the Scandal of Religion, and Ruine of
> many."[23]

He is particularly anxious that reformation be effected in the manners
of those in authority so that the Lord may "turn away his Wrath, and
the Blessings of God may be Enjoyed and Continued to this Nation;"[24]
he eulogizes Queen Anne and quotes the proclamation which she issued
on March 26, 1702, to encourage piety and virtue, and to prevent and
punish vice, profaneness and immorality.[25] It is on the basis of this
proclamation that he not only builds his invective against the play-
house, stage-players, revellings, gaming, bull-baiting and bear-baiting,
but it is on this that he enters his plea for their total suppression. He

---

condemning the profanity of the stage-poets states: "These infernal Sallys
put me in Mind of a late Instance of Resolution in one of their Fraternity;
I mean the Man that acted *Jephta's Rash Vow, or the Virgin Sacrifice* in
Smithfield.
[22] *Ibid.,* pp. 39-40.
[23] J. Feild, *An Humble Application to the Queen,* p. 3. The pamphlet is fifteen
pages long, and was printed and sold by T. Sowle in White-Hart-Court in
Gracious Street.
[24] *Ibid.,* p. 3.
[25] *Ibid.,* p. 3.

recalls a similar proclamation issued by King William on February 24, 1697, and by Queen Mary who, on July 9, 1691 in the absence of the king, wrote to the Justices of the Peace in the County of Middlesex for the suppressing of profaneness and debauchery.[26]

Feild quotes from "that noted Book, Intituled, *An Account of the Societies for Reformation of Manners, etc.,*" printed in 1699, published at the sanction of twenty-nine temporal lords, nine bishops, and seven judges, and the excerpt quoted proves that its author [J. Woodward] is antagonistic toward the "Wit and Entertainment of our Scandalous Play-Houses."[27] In triumphant summary, Feild asserts

"Thus we see, we have Three Crowned Heads, the Parliament of England, Twenty Nine Lords, Nine Bishops, and Seven Judges, Testifying against Vice and Immorality,"[28]

and on the strength of the illustrious abettors favoring the anti-stage movement, he repeats the request for total suppression of the playhouses.

The author quotes extensively from the *Histriomastix* in defence of his anti-stage views,[29] and concludes his pamphlet by a four-page "Brief Cautional Conclusion, more Generally respecting a Spiritual and Inward Reformation." The tone of the last pages is hortatory; Feild is solicitous for all persons in the nation who

" . . . expect God's Blessings, and that his severe Judgments should be Averted, [to] let not those things, that are neither Honest, Just, Pure, Lovely, or of good Report, that have no Vertue or Praise in them, be practiced, given way to, or frequented by any, as Stage-Plays, Bull and Bear-baitings, Drolleries, Drunkenness, or any Vice or Immoralities whatsoever; for they are contrary to the Law and Commands of God, the Mind of Christ, . . . "[30]

---

[26] *Ibid.,* pp. 5-6.
[27] *Ibid.,* p. 7.
[28] *Ibid.,* p. 7.
[29] *Ibid.,* pp. 8-11.
[30] *Ibid.,* p. 15.

4

The storm of November 26, 1703 was made the occasion of much exhortation both for a reformation of manners and for a reformation of plays. Collier seized the opportunity and published his *Dissuasive From the Play-House; in a Letter to a Person of Quality, Occasioned By the late Calamity of the TEMPEST.*[31] Collier refers to the storm as a "sad instance of God's judgments . . . Terrible beyond anything in that Kind in Memory, or Record,"[32] a calamity so awful that the world seemed in her last agony and ready to expire. Collier's means of conveying to his readers his concern at the immorality and profaneness of the play-house is, in the present case, an informal letter. By it he is able to express his horror at the liberties assumed by the stage-poets, his desire to safeguard the morals of those who resort to the play-house, and his belief that the late storm was provoked in large measure by the sins of the Nation.

Before beginning the body of the letter Collier tells the reader that he will be obliged to repeat some of the thoughts which he has embodied in the *Short View* because it is there that are contained in detail his opinions on the unbridled license of the English Stage. Whereupon Collier briefly discusses in the *Dissuasive* the various topics he had elaborated upon in the *Short View,* though not in the same order. The points made in the *Dissuasive* are the immorality of the stage,[32a] its profaneness,[32b] its indecency of language,[32c] its incorrigibleness,[32d] the instances from the church and state proving that the play-house has been looked upon as a public nuisance,[32e] the effect of scandalous diversions on the mind and heart,[32f] the inconsistency of the play-house with the duties and character of a Christian,[32g] and God's disapproval of present moral conditions as is proved by the late tempest.[32h] Collier very solemnly calls attention to the judgments of

---

[31] The first edition of this 16-page letter was printed for R. Sare, in 1703. The letter is dated Dec. 10, 1703. It was probably published some days later.
[32] J. Collier, *Dissuasive,* p. 14.
[32a] pp. 4-5.
[32b] pp. 5-7.
[32c] pp. 7-8.
[32d] pp. 7-8.
[32e] pp. 11-13.
[32f] p. 13.
[32g] pp. 13-14.
[32h] pp. 14-15.

God so manifestly meted out to the English people for their sins of defiance, and he predicts

> "if we go on still in such sins of Defyance, may we not be afraid of the Punishments of Sodom, and that God should destroy us with Fire and Brimstone?"[33]

His religious mind is horrified by the audacity of the English people who, on the same day and in the very face of the calamity, attended a representation of *Macbeth* with all its thunder and tempest:

> "Where at the mention of the *Chimnies being blown down,* the Audience were pleas'd to *Clap,* at an unusual Length of pleasure and Approbation.[34]

His reflections upon this are caustic:

> "Does it not look as if they had a Mind to out-brave the Judgment? And make us believe the Storm was nothing but an Eruption of *Epicurus's* Atoms, a Spring-Tide of Matter and Motion, and a blind Salley of Chance?"[35]

Collier believes that this "throwing Providence out of the Scheme" is an admirable Opiate for the conscience and he sarcastically concludes by asserting:

> " . . . when Recollection is laid asleep, the Stage will recover of Course, and go on with their Business effectively."[36]

The *Dissuasive* is a very valuable document in our present study of Collier for it gives a clear idea of what Collier himself thought of the *Short View,* of how he endeavoured to give a synopsis of the principal chapters of the *Short View* in the *Dissuasive,* and of how he borrowed from the *Short View* both in ideas and vocabulary. By means of the *Dissuasive* one is more easily able to form a definite opinion concerning Collier's authorship in the anonymous pamphlets which bear every mark of being his work.

---

[33] *Ibid.,* pp. 14-15.
[34] *Ibid.,* p. 15.
[35] *Ibid.,* p. 15.
[36] *Ibid.,* p. 15.

CHAPTER X

Publications of 1704

1. Anonymous [Josiah Woodward]: *Some Thoughts Concerning the Stage in a Letter to a Lady,* January 19, 1704.

2. Anonymous: *A Representation of the Impiety and Immorality of the English Stage,* January 19, 1704.

3. Anonymous: *Concio Laici, or The Lay-Man's Sermon,* February 1704.

4. John Dennis: *The Person of Quality's Answer to Mr. Collier's Letter,* February, 1704.

5. Anonymous: *Some Considerations About the Danger of Going to Plays,* February 17, 1704. Second edition of *Occasional Paper, Number IX,* . . . 1698.

6. T. Baker: *An Act at Oxford,* 1704. Dedicatory Epistle.

7. Anonymous: *Visits From the Shades, . . . Jo. Haines's Ghost, and the Reforming Mr. Collier,* Easter, 1704.

8. J. Collier: Second Edition of the *Dissuasive from the Play-House; . . . To which is added a Letter written by another Hand,* June 9, 1704.

9. T. Brown: *Stage-Beaux toss'd in a Blanket,* 1704.

It will be observed that seven of the nine publications listed for 1704 were printed before Easter and that five of them were anonymous. Moreover, five of the nine were evoked by the great storm of the preceding November and are exhortations to consider the vices of the nation a cause for God's vengeance. That the play-house was attacked especially at this time is told us by Bedford. He says:

> "When her Majesty was graciously pleas'd on that sad Occasion of the *Storm,* to appoint a Day of Publick *Fasting* and *Humiliation,* most of the *Bishops* and *Clergy* of the City of *London* did in their Sermons preach particularly against the *Notorious Profaneness* of the *Play-Houses.*"[1]

We note, on the other hand, that at this period the attacks on Collier and the *Short View* become more caustic, if such a thing is possible, and that T. Baker, J. Dennis, T. Brown, and the anonymous author of *Visits from the Shades* are among the foremost to dip their

---

[1] A. Bedford, *The Evil and Danger of Stage Plays,* p. 8.

pens in acid when vindicating the English stage and their brother stage-poets. Besides, they ridicule the idea of considering the great storm a chastisement for the sins of the theatre and rebuke the reformers in the familiar Scriptural phrase "Physician, heal thyself."

1

The anonymous *Some Thoughts Concerning the Stage In a Letter to a Lady*, is one of the pamphlets evoked by the Great Storm of November 26, 1703. In it the author blames the corruption of the play-house for the vengeance of the Almighty.[2] The writer laments the corruption of the age and, like Collier and Bedford, places the blame for it at the door of the theatres which he calls by the familiar title of

"The Nursery of all manner of *Wickedness,* where the Seeds of *Atheism* and *Irreligion* are sown, which weak and Tender Minds too readily cultivate, and from thence are easily led into a Contempt of all that's Serious."[3]

He is Collier-minded in his attack on the profaneness and immorality of modern plays; he argues in favour of Collier and the *Short View* and laments that the

"*Ladies* . . . should ever be seen at the last of these Places [the play-house] where they find themselves so scandalously treated."[4]

His enumeration of the vices emanating from the play-house omits none which Collier had ascribed to it;[5] he refers to the Sermon of Archbishop Tillotson on "The Evils of Corrupt Communication," and quotes against plays a page from this sermon.[6] The author shows him-

---

[2] The pamphlet is thirteen pages in length and was printed in London, 1704. Its title page bears neither author's nor printer's names. The author subscribes the date January 10, 1704, and, in consequence, it is given a place among the letters, sermons, and pamphlets published to inspire fervour and zeal before the Fast Day proclaimed by Queen Anne for January 19. The letter is ascribed to Josiah Woodward by Halkett and Laing; *Dictionary of Anonymous and Pseudonymous Literature,* V. 320.

[3] Anonymous, *Some Thoughts Concerning the Stage,* pp. 4-5.

[4] *Ibid.,* p. 4.

[5] *Ibid.,* p. 5.

[6] *Ibid.,* pp. 8-9. This same sermon was later referred to by the author of *The Conduct of the Stage Considered,* 1721, p. 29, and by William Law in his *Absolute Unlawfulness of the Stage Entertainment,* 1726, p. 38.

self akin to Collier both in argument and diction when he ascribes
to the play-house the vengeance of the Almighty as exhibited in the
late storm, when he refers to the proclamation of the queen as a call
to repentance, and when he censures the acting of *The Tempest* within
a few days after the storm.[7] He is like Collier, too, in that he argues
for a total suppression of the play-house; but in the event that total
suppression is impracticable, then he advocates such a strict regulation
of it both as to the plays that are acted and the audience that resorts
to it that

> "*Foreigners* may no longer *stand amaz'd* when brought into
> our *Theatres,* nor Good Men *tremble* at the Continuance of
> them: but that *Virtue* may appear there with all its Charms,
> and *Vice* be expos'd to the utmost *Contempt."*[8]

I remarked in my biography of Collier that there are many reasons
to believe that Collier was at the helm of the stage-controversy from
1698 to 1726, often-times supplying the ammunition for the attack
even when he did not make the attack himself. This is an instance of
of where most of the ammunition used is from the stocks of Collier.

2

Of all the pamphlets published after the Storm and in connection
with the Fast Day, the most discussed is the anonymous *A Represen-*
tation of the Impiety and Immorality of the English Stage, With Rea-
sons for putting a Stop thereto: and some Questions Addrest to Those
who frequent the Play-Houses.[9] It was written according to the author's
testimony, after the "Great Storm" and before the "Solemn Fast":

> "It is thought proper, under our present *Calamity,* and before
> the approaching *Fast* to collect some of the Prophane and

---

[7] *Ibid.,* pp. 10-12.
[8] *Ibid.,* p. 12.
[9] The pamphlet is 24 pages long and was printed by J. Nutt near Stationer's
Hall.

Immoral Expressions out of several late *Plays,* and to put them together in a little Compass, . . . [10]

The author tells us further that his purpose in writing it was to convince the nation

"Of the Impiety of the Stage, the Guilt of such as frequent it, and the Necessity of putting a Stop thereto, either by a total Suppression [of play-houses] for some considerable time, after the Example of other Nations. . . ."[11]

He refers to the "Ridiculous Representation of *Mackbeth* and the *Tempest,* as if they design'd to Mock the Almighty Power of God;"[12] he re-expresses his hope that her Majesty will suspend at least for some considerable time, all the players acting in the play-house,[13] and comments on the absence of the Queen from the play-house. He asserts that she has never once given any Countenance to the Play-House by Her Royal Presence, since Her happy Accession to the Throne.[14]

In outlining the scope of his treatise, the author asserts that he does not intend to include in it any of the abominable obcene expressions which so frequently occur in plays; he does intend, however, to give the reader a collection of profane expressions as they appear in the lately-acted plays.[15] He dwells upon the fact that the efforts of Blackmore, of Collier, and of others were unsuccessful in correcting

---

[10] Anonymous, *A Representation,* p. 3. J. Oldmixon, in his *History of England,* III, pp. 319-320, chronicles the two events. He narrates: "On . . . the 26th of November 1703, between eleven and twelve o clock at night, there was the greatest Tempest in the Western and Southern Parts of England, and in some parts of the Eastern, that was ever known or heard of." He enumerates the ships of war lost, tells of the destruction to property, describes various fatalities, and makes mention of the Fast prescribed by Queen Anne: "The Queen's Answer to an Address made for restoring the ships was very gracious, and two or three Days after was issu'd her Majesty's Proclamation for a general Fast, which was observed throughout England on the 19th of January ensuing, with more signs of Devotion and Sincerity than ever I saw any thing of that Kind . . ." Consequently, it is obvious that the author wrote the treatise between November 26, 1703, and January 19, 1704. It was published, according to the testimony of A. Bedford at the time of the Fast: "At the Time of the *Fast* above-mentioned, there was printed a small Treatise, intitul'd, *A Representation of the Impiety and and Immorality of the English Stage.*" A. Bedford, *The Evil and Danger of Stage Plays,* p. 9.

[11] Anonymous, *A Representation,* pp. 3-4.

[12] *Ibid.,* p. 5.

[13] *Ibid.,* p. 5.

[14] *Ibid.,* p. 6.

[15] *Ibid.,* pp. 6-16.

or in checking the abuses of the stage; that in 1699 several of the players were prosecuted in the Court of Common Pleas for profanely using the name of God upon the Stage; that in the Easter-Term of 1701, the players of one house were not only accused at the King's-Bench-Bar before the Right Honorable Lord Chief Justice Holt of using certain profane expressions, but that they were convicted of the offence.[16] In support of his statement he copies twenty-two of the censured expressions taken from *The Provoked Wife*. He pursues his point by asserting that the players of the other House, in the same Easter-Term of 1701, were accused of certain profane expressions; "but inasmuch as the indictment was wrong laid, they were acquitted: but they were Indicted the Term following, for the same, which Indictment is not yet tried."[17] He gives, besides, a collection of profane expressions from nine contemporary plays: from the *Humour of the Age*,[18] from *Sir Courtly Nice*,[19] from *The False Friend*,[20] from *The Inconstant*,[21] from *The Modish Husband*,[22] from *Vice Recalimed*,[23] from *Different Widows*,[24] from *The Fickle Shepherdess*,[25] and from *Marry or do Worse*.[26]

---

[16] *Ibid.*, pp. 6-7.

[17] *Ibid.*, p. 9.

[18] *Ibid.*, pp. 9-10. There are three quotations given. The play was written by Thomas Baker, and was first acted at Drury Lane in February, 1700. Allardyce Nicoll, *Eighteenth Century Drama*, 1700-1750, p. 296. Mr. Nicoll states that the *Post Man* is the only authority we have for the information as there are no records of the performance.

[19] *Ibid.*, p. 10. Nine expressions are quoted. The play was written by J. Crowne, and was acted at Drury Lane in 1703. A. Nicoll, op. cit., p. 128.

[20] *Ibid.*, pp. 11-12. Eight expressions are given. The author of *A Representation* states that this play as well as those plays mentioned in the following pages were acted and printed even after they were indicted for the objectionable passages. The *False Friend* was written by Mrs. Pix. It is a tragicomedy, and was acted at L-I-F, 1699. A. Nicoll, *op. cit.*, p. 96.

[21] *Ibid.*, pp. 12-13. Four expressions are quoted. The play was written by Farquhar, and was acted at D. L., 1702. A Nicoll, *op. cit.*, p. 40.

[22] *Ibid.*, p. 13. Four expressions are quoted. The play was written by Charles Burnaby, and acted at D. L., January, 1702. A. Nicoll, *op. cit.*, p. 301.

[23] *Ibid.*, pp. 13-14. Nine expressions are quoted. The play was written by Richard Wilkinson, and acted at D. L., 1703. A. Nicoll, *op. cit.*, 364.

[24] *Ibid.*, p. 14. Three expressions are cited. The play is by Mrs. Pix, and was acted at L-I-F (old Theatre), November, 1703. A Nicoll, *op cit.*, p. 350.

[25] *Ibid.*, pp. 14-15. Six expressions are given. The play is anonymous, and was acted at L-I-F, 1703. A. Nicoll, *op. cit.*, p. 224.

[26] *Ibid.*, pp. 15-16. Eighteen expressions are quoted. The play is by William Walker, and was acted at L-I-F (old Theatre), in November, 1703. A. Nicoll, *op. cit.*, p. 363.

The author concludes his treatise by proposing seventeen "plain questions" to those persons who, although they appear at times in Church, and at the Holy Sacrament, yet frequent the play-house.[27] They are designed to censure those who in the play-house hear God's name profaned and His Attributes ascribed to sinful creatures, as well as those who spend their time and money in seeing plays. They take note of the scandal given by those who assist "by their purses and their presence," all who act in plays;[28] they ask whether assisting at plays does not decrease the spirit of devotion which all should cultivate; whether there can be sincerity in saying "Lead us not into temptation" when the petitioner seeks it in the play-house; whether ladies can really dislike lewd discourse when they listen freely to it on the stage, and whether parents or guardians can, in conscience, permit their charges to go to plays where vices are taught openly.[29] The author asks whether or not the anathemas of General Councils and of the Primitive Fathers are entitled to regard; whether the guilt of those who attend plays is not increased inasmuch as they are fully conscious when they go of the fatal effects upon mind and heart.[30]

The authorship of *A Representation of the Impiety and Immorality of the English Stage* is, as was said above, anonymous, and neither Stonehill, Block, and Stonehill, nor Halkett and Laing mention the work. I believe, however, that Collier wrote it, and I base my conclusions upon the following facts: First, it re-states the opinions expressed by Collier in his anti-stage pamphlets, and restates them frequently in the same phraseology. To bring out this fact I have listed the views of the author of *A Representation* opposite the corresponding opinion of Collier as found in his anti-stage works.

---

[27] *A Representation*, p. 17.
[28] *Ibid.*, pp. 17-19.
[29] *Ibid.*, pp. 19-20.
[30] *Ibid.*, pp. 22-24.

A Representation of the
Impiety . . .

I. The author believes that no obscene expression should appear: "The abominable obscene Expressions which so frequently occur in our Plays, as if the principal Design of them was to gratifie the lewd and vicious part of the Audience, . . . are in this black Collection wholly omitted; lest thereby fresh Poison should be administered instead of an Antidote." p. 6.

II. The Author, acting upon his conviction that the *profane* part may be transcribed without menace to his readers, quotes the profane expressions from ten plays; pp. 7-16.

III. The author states his intention of collecting the objectionable expressions from several late plays, and of placing them "together in a little Compass;" he further tells us his reasons: "The various Methods that have been used for Preventing the outragious and insufferable Disorders of the STAGE, having been in a great measure defeated: . . . " pp. 3-4.

Collier's anti-stage Pamphlets

I. Collier was of the opinion that indecent expressions ought not be printed: "Besides as to the Smut, I have endeavour'd not to disoblige the Paper with any of it. . . . To have transcrib'd it at length, would not only have been an improper, but a tedious Employment." *A Defence,* p. 2.
"I would give the Reader some more of these fine Sentences, but that they are too much out of Order to appear . . . They [the stage-poets] are fortified in Smut, almost impregnable in Stench, so that where they deserve most, there's no coming at them." *A Short View,* p. 179.

II. "The profane Part, tho' Bolder and more Black, will bear the Light better, and therefore when 'twas clear of Obscenity, I have set it to the Bar. . . . And by the safest Method I could think of, give check to the Complicated Infection." *A Defence,* pp. 2-3.

III. Collier in the *Dissuasive* actually tries to present his views in "as narrow a Compass as possible": "You were pleased to desire me to draw up something by way of Preservation in as narrow a Compass as possible." *A Dissuasive,* p. 3.

IV. The author refers to the suppression of the play-houses in the reign of Queen Elizabeth; pp. 3-4.

IV. In the *Short View*, Collier quotes the petition made to Queen Elizabeth for suppressing play-houses; pp. 242-3. He calls attention to it, also, in the *Dissuasive*, p. 12, and in *A Farther Vindication*, p. 18; p. 36.

V. The author quotes twenty-two profane passages from Vanbrugh's *The Provok'd Wife*, pp. 7-9.

V. Collier, in his *Defence*, p. 102, calls Vanbrugh to task for his profanity and, to justify himself for his censure, refers by marginal notes to passages in *The Provok'd Wife*. A comparison of the passages indicated with those quoted in *A Representation* reveals the fact that some are *identical*.

VI. The author asks: "Can modest and prudent Christians think, that the opinion of the General Councils, Primitive Fathers, and so many wise and good Men in the several Ages of the Church, who have condemned the going to Plays as unlawful and as a renouncing the Baptismal Engagements, doth not deserve great regard?" p. 23.

VI. Collier says: "The Players stand condemned by several Councils of great Antiquity and Credit. And the most Celebrated and Primitive Fathers have declaimed loudly against the stage." *A Dissuasive*, p. 12.
"These Entertainments [Plays] are as it were Literally renounc'd in *Baptism*." *A Short View*, p. 285. "It argues they have strangely forgotten the engagements of Baptism." *Diss.* p. 8.

VII. He states further: ". . . these Instances of the prophane Language of Plays, . . . would not have been put together . . . had not the Incorrigibleness of The Players made it necessary." p. 16.

VII. Collier declares: "We must not forget Incorrigibleness of the *Stage*, . . . Their ill Plays have some of them been examin'd, their licentious Extravagance mark'd, and repeated Instances produced upon them. . . . The Players . . . are Proof against Fines and Arguments, and come over again with their old Smut and Profaneness." *Diss.*, p. 9.

VIII. "Can Ladies really dislike Lewd Discourse in Conversation, and yet like to see Lewdness represented in all the Dresses that can vitiate the Imagination . . . ?" p. 22.

VIII. "Can the Ladies be entertained with such Stuff as This? . . . Why do they venture upon a Place where they must expect to have their *Imagination* shocked, their Aversion put into a Fit, and their Blood call'd up into their Faces?" *A Dissuasive*, p. 8.

IX. "Can sincerely religious Persons hear of this most horrid, licentious Treatment of sacred things as is in our Plays, and this not among *Mahometans* and *Infidels*, not at *Rome* and *Venice* but in a Protestant Countrey, and upon the *English* Stage . . . ?" p. 23.

IX. "And here the English Poets and *Players* are still like themselves; they strain to a Singularity of Coarseness: The Modern *Theatres* of *Europe* are meer *Vestals* to them: They outdo the Liberties of *Greece* and *Rome*, etc." *A Dissuasive*, p. 7.

X. "Can such, tho' they could think themselves wholly secure from taking Infection in going to the Play-House, encourage others . . . by their Example?" p. 19.

X. "'Tis a sign they are strongly seized by the Infection, . . ." *Dissuasive*, p. 8.
"And how often has the best Blood been tainted, with this Infection?" *Short View*, p. 287.

XI. "Can sincere Christians encourage and *assist,* by their Presence and Purses, Men in committing such Practices, if they seriously reflect on the fatal Consequences of them?" p. 18.

XI. "Are we to *assist* such Places of Liberty and Profaneness with our Purse and Person?" *Dissuasive*, p. 14.

The parallel may be further drawn by citing similarities in vocabulary and diction:

A Representation of the Impiety . . .

Collier's Anti-stage Pamphlets

I, The author speaks of "The Holy Word Burlesqued," p. 17.

I. Collier mentions "Scripture burlesqued," *Short View*, p. 61. "The Old and New Testament burlesqued;" *A Dissuasive*, p. 6. "Burlesque the Discourse," *A Farther Vindication*, p. 33.

II. "Virtue Discountenanced and Vice Encouraged," p. 17.	II. Collier in *S.V.* p. 140, contrasts virtue and vice in much the same manner.
III. "Can such persons as go to the *Play-Houses* on week-days and appear in our *Churches* on the Lord's-day, . . . " p. 21.	III. "To spend the Week at the *Play-House,* and come to *Church* on the *Sunday,* looks little better than Fashion and Grimace." *A Dissuasive,* p. 13.
IV. The usual staccato questions to which I have often referred, occur with frequency in the *Representation.* In the concluding pages the author presents to the reader seventeen of them.	IV. Staccato questions are abundant in Collier's works. Cf. *Short View.* p. 95; p. 156; p. 164; p. 175; p. 218; p. 286; p. 287; *Dissuasive,* p. 14; p. 15; *A Farther Vindication,* p. 12; p. 28; p. 40; etc.

As has perhaps been noted, I have most frequently referred to the *Dissuasive* in comparing the stage-opinions of Collier with those of the author of *A Representation.* I do so for the same reasons that I gave when, in discussing the authorship of *A Letter to Mr. Congreve,* I compared it with *A Defence* rather than with *The Short View.* In the case of the *Representation,* however, only a few weeks had elapsed since the publication of *The Dissuasive;* in consequence, Collier would, if he wrote both pamphlets, unconsciously betray the fact by adhering to the same moral and literary principles, to the same prejudices, the same vocabulary, rhetorical devices, and allusions. This adherence *is* noted, hence it is reasonable to accept this as substantiating evidence in favor of Collier's authorship of the pamphlet in question. There is, however, in the Epistle Dedicatory of Baker's *Act at Oxford,* 1704, a more convincing proof that Collier wrote *A Representation.* Here Thomas Baker shows signs of being angry with Collier and his attack on the stage and the stage-poets, and his anger is easily explained. His comedy, *The Humour of the Age* had been attacked for profanity a short time before in the *Representation;*[31] not only are there listed profane expressions from it, but the galling truth is published that in

---

[31] Anonymous, *A Representation,* pp. 9-10. The *Representation* was published January 19. The *Act at Oxford* was published early in the spring of 1704. The sequence of the publication is determined by the fact that one of the dialogues in *Visits from the Shades* published in the Easter term of 1704 has for its subject "Ben Johnson and Mr. Baker, Author of the Oxford Act."

the "Easter-Term, 1701, the Players of one House were Indicted at the King's-Bench-Bar, before the Right Honourable the Lord Chief Justice Holt,"[32] for using profane expressions. Baker, consequently, surveying the late attack on the stage,—an attack "From the Pulpit and Bench, the Press and Conversation,"[33] seizes an opportunity for evening-up scores with Collier. He declares

> "that some of the Great Sticklers against the Theatre, hate to see any Act but themselves, and can't endure to be out-done in PERSONATING Men of Religion, Justice, and Loyalty, by those that tread the Stage."[34]

He says, too:

> "that Her Majesty's Regulations are not sufficient, and nothing but a total Suppression can remove it, is an assertion as Impudent as 'tis Mischievous, and only urged by those who have other Ends than publick Good in such a Wish."[35]

This denunciation is, apparently, directed against the author of *A Representation* who had said:

> "It is thought proper, under our present Calamity, and before the approaching *Fast,* to collect some of the Prophane and Immoral Expressions out of several late Plays, . . . that the Nation may thereby be more convinced of the Impiety of the Stage, the guilt of such as frequent it, and the Necessity of putting a Stop thereto, either by a total Suppression of the Play-Houses, or by a Suspension for some considerable time, after the Example of other Nations."[36]

Baker makes no secret of the fact that it is Collier he is attacking:

> "The Quarrel is chiefly manag'd by Enemies to the Establish'd Church, headed by the Author of the *Short View.*"[37]

He declares further:

> "The Viewer, (who wishes Her Majesty the same Place in the Throne She has in his Dictionary), thought the Proclamation against Irreligion, and Her Regulation of the Theatres as Im-

---

[32] *Ibid.,* p. 7.
[33] T. Baker, *An Act at Oxford,* p. iv.
[34] *Ibid.,* pp. vi-vii.
[35] *Ibid.,* p. vii.
[36] Anonymous, *A Representation,* pp. 3-4.
[37] Thomas Baker, *An Act at Oxford,* p. 8.

perfect as his Works; therefore on the Fast Day out comes his Supplemental Pamphlet to rectify the Government's Omissions with the same Modesty he formerly absolv'd it's Traytors."[38]

The authorship of this pamphlet is discussed by J. Ballein and by J. Krutch. Johannes Ballein gives a very interesting discussion in his *Jeremy Collier's Angriff auf die englische Bühne,* while Joseph Krutch, in his "Bibliography of the Collier Controversy" appended to his *Comedy and Conscience,* discusses Ballein's argument.[39] Ballein says:

"Aber bei dem *Supplemental Pamphlet* handelt es sich ganz augenscheinlich um eine am Fasttag neu herausgekommene Schrift, während Mr. Collier's *Dissuasive* schon drei Wochen Früher erschienen und in den berechtigten Kreisen jedenfalls schon vor dem Fasttage verbreitet and gelesen worden war. Auch weist die Bezeichnung *Supplemental Pamphlet* darauf hin, dass bereits eine andere Schrift Colliers vorangegangen war. Und endlich ist seine *Dissuasive* durchaus nicht gegen irgendwelche 'Omissions of the Government' gerichtet. Es wird zwar von dem Widerstand der Bühne gegen alle bisherigne Massregeln gesprochen, aber die Regierung wird mit keiner Silbe wegen irgendwelcher 'Omissions' getadelt. Auch von den andern genannten Schriften dürfte keine in Betracht kommen: denn erstlich ercheinen sie anonym, was bei der Frage stehen allem Anschein nach nicht der Fall war, und sodann stimmen auch sie inhaltlich nicht zu Backers Angaben. So dürfen wir wohl annehmen, dass wir es hier mit einer neuen, wahrscheinlich verlorenen Schrift Colliers zu tun haben."[40]

Here, as we observe, Ballein shrewdly infers from Baker's remarks, first, that the "Supplemental Pamphlet" in question is a treatise newly issued on the Fast Day and not the *Dissuasive* which had been in circulation for some three weeks; secondly, that the term "Supplemental Pamphlet" indicates that another treatise of Collier's had appeared; thirdly, that the *Dissuasive* is not at all directed towards certain "Omissions of the Government" and that although it contains a discussion of the opposition of the stage to all regulation of the government, it does not blame the government in even a single word for any

---

[38] *Ibid.,* p. 8. Baker is obviously referring to some pamphlet published by Collier on January 19. He calls it *Supplemental* because its design was to emphasize the Queen's pronouncements and to supply what she should have included.

[39] J. Krutch, *Comedy and Conscience,* pp. 265-6.

[40] J. Ballein, *Jeremy Collier's Angriff auf die englische Bühne,* pp. 170-1.

omissions, and lastly, that we may assume that we are dealing with a new and apparently lost writing of Collier's.

Ballein calls attention to the fact that the *Dissuasive* is not at all directed towards certain "Omissions of the Government" which Baker had asserted of the "Supplemental Pamphlet." This is true. Collier, in the *Dissuasive,* does not refer to omissions of the government. He merely laments under six captions the disorders of the stage; he regrets that the play-house has so much ascendancy in the town, and that it receives the "Countenance of Figure and Fortune." He assumes the "I told you so" attitude and says to his correspondent:

> "You seemed to presage that these Nurseries of Licence and Atheism would, if unrestrained, prove fatal to the Nation, make us ripe for Destruction, and pull down some terrible Vengence upon our Heads,"[41]

and now the terrible storm has verified your apprehensions. A little farther on Collier condemns the irreligious insolence of

> "mixing the most solemn, and the most ridiculous Things together, of prostituting the Inspired Writings in Places of Infamy, and of furnishing out a Droll from the Sacred History"

whereupon having given vent to his anger he calms down and says:

> "I am unwilling to say any more upon this Matter: To suppose the Outrage of such a Practice stands in need of Satyr and Aggravation, is a Reflection upon the Common Sense of a Nation, and looks as if we were blasted in our Understandings."[42]

He clearly asserts here that comment upon the irreligious insolence in question would be a "Reflection on the Common Sense of the Nation," but he makes no adverse reflection on Anne's government. On the contrary, he expresses his *satisfaction* that the law has given no quarter to the Players. He says:

> "The Laws have been let loose upon them; they have been disciplin'd at Westminster-Hall. . . . To come down to our own Constitution: The Players are forbidden to Act, and scatter their Infection through the Kingdom, under very severe and infamous Penalties,"[43]

but there is no word of censure for the government.

---

[41] J. Collier, *Dissuasive,* p. 3.
[42] *Ibid.,* pp. 6-7.
[43] *Ibid.,* p. 9.

Mr. Krutch, in discussion Ballein's hypothesis not only of one of Collier's pamphlet's being lost but of one that measures up to all the descriptions given of the "Supplemental Pamphlet" says:

"Here Ballein has, I think, quite unnecessarily hypothecated a lost pamphlet, where there   is no reason to suspect it ever existed. Baker (the author of 'An Act at Oxford') does not use the words 'Supplemental Pamphlet' as a title, but only means 'another pamphlet by Collier.' As Ballein himself points out earlier, the 'Daily Courrant' for the day following the storm advertises Collier's 'Dissuasive' for sale, and notes that on the fast day thousands of pamphlets were given away. No doubt Baker got one. If he received Collier's 'Dissuasive,' then, when it was being advertised in the newspapers, he did not observe whether it was published that day or three weeks before. There is little doubt that it was the 'Dissuasive' that he referred to as the Supplemental Pamphlet. Ballein objects that it is not directed against Anne, but this is not to the point. Baker in the preface calls attention to the fact that Collier is not loyal to his sovereign. What he means is 'Anne has just ordered a reform of the theater. Every good subject will have confidence that she will do all this, but if that non-juror Collier comes out with his Dissuasive he implies that the Queen does not know her business.' The German scholar has, apparently (to revive the old story), evolved the book instead of the camel out of his inner consciousness. Such subjective bibliography is not likely to please anyone but the compiler."[44]

Mr. Krutch asserts that Baker does not use the words "Supplemental Pamphlet" as a title, but that he means only "another pamphlet by Collier." I agree with Mr. Krutch in that opinion. Baker did not use the word "Supplemental" as part of the *title* of Collier's pamphlet but rather as an adjective to describe its nature; he used the word "Supplemental" to imply that Collier, considering his *Dissuasive* insufficient for the Fast Day, must needs amplify his original treatise by giving suggestions for closing the theatres. He will emphasize not only the Queen's decrees but will emphasize his own views against the playhouse and players. Besides, he will add

"some of the Prophane and Immoral Expressions out of several late Plays, . . . that the Nation may thereby be *more* convinced of the Impiety of the Stage, the Guilt of such as frequent

---

[44] J. Krutch, *Comedy and Conscience*. p. 266.

it, and the Necessity of putting a Stop thereto, either by a *total* Supression of the Play-Houses, . . . or by a Suspension for some considerable time after the Example of other Nations."[45]

Mr. Krutch further points out that thousands of pamphlets were given away on the Fast Day and that in all probability Baker got a copy of the *Dissuasive*. Again the statement is correct, and although he refers only to Ballein's authority of the *Daily Courrant* to substantiate his opinion, he might have referred to the advertisement found in John Dennis' "The Person of Quality's Answer to Mr. Collier's Letter" published in 1721, for a further corroboration of his views. This "advertisement" acquaints the reader with some very pertinent information:

> "The following Letter was writ by me about sixteen years ago. About four or five years after that [the publication of the *Short View*], as near as I can remember, Mr. Collier took occasion from the great Storm, which happen'd about that Time to renew his Attack upon the Stage, in a little Pamphlet call'd *A Dissuasive from the Play-House, written by way of Letter to a Person of Quality*. Which Pamphlet, upon the Fast Day that was order'd to be kept by publick Authority immediately after that Tempest, was given to People *gratis* as they came out of the Churches. The Design of it was to make the great Storm a Judgment upon the Nation for the Enormities of our Theatres."[46]

Mr. Krutch's inference that Baker took no note of the date of its publication is an argument which I believe we may dismiss as inconsequential. His conclusion that "there is little doubt that it was the *Dissuasive* that he referred to as the Supplemental Pamphlet" is not self-evident to me. On the contrary, I agree with Mr. Ballein that the *Dissuasive* is not directed against certain "Omissions of the Government" and that another pamphlet answering to Baker's description was published.

Let us cast a final glance at *A Representation of the Impiety and Immorality of the English Stage* to see if we can reconcile it with the statement of its being directed against certain "Omissions of the Gov-

---

[45] Anonymous, *A Representation*, pp. 3-4.
[46] J. Dennis, *Original Letters, Familiar, Moral and Critical*, II, 225-6.

ernment." The author states in substance: "The various methods—
pamphlets written against the stage, the disciplining of the stage-poets
at Westminster Hall,—have been used ineffectually for preventing the
outrageous and insufferable disorders of the stage. Therefore, I shall
try to help the cause along, especially at this time when the English
people will be more favorably disposed to receive my arguments inasmuch as they are preparing for the approaching fast; hence I shall collect some of the profane expressions out of several late plays and shall
put them into a little compass in order to convince the nation of the
impiety of the stage, the guilt of those who frequent it, and the necessity of putting a stop to it.[47] Besides, if I can convice the nation of these
facts they will agree that the best way will be either 'by a total suppression of the Play-Houses, as was done in the reign of Queen Elizabeth,
or by a Suspension for some considerable time after the Example of
other Nations.'[48] And, too, inasmuch as the Queen has appointed a day
of solemn fasting and humiliation throughout the kingdom for depre-
cating God's wrath, I shall use the occasion to suggest that the players
be dealt with severely:

> 'No surely, it cannot but be hoped, that a Suspension at least
> of the Players acting for some considerable time will follow,
> when the *Prophaneness and Immorality of the Stage* comes to
> her Majesty's Knowledge, who, 'tis to be remembered, has never
> once given any Countenance to the Play-House by Her Royal
> Presence, since Her happy Accession to the Throne.'[49]

"Lastly, I believe that it will not be amiss to help along the cause of
religion in the Kingdom, hence I shall propose certain questions to the

---

[47] One argument that Collier published a new pamphlet on January 19 lies
in the fact that most of the bishops and clergy, according to Bedford *(Evil
and Danger,* p. 13), took occasion of the fast to preach against the play-
houses. Of all the clergy in London likely to welcome the chance Collier
was the man. His *Dissuasive* had discussed the Storm, not the Fast. He
might logically make use of the *Dissuasive* to acquit himself of his clerical
obligations for January 19, but it would be in perfect accord with Collier's
anti-stage attitude to add another pamphlet to elaborate upon the Solemn
Fast to be observed in the whole of London by the Queen's command.

[48] Anonymous, *A Representation of the Impiety and Immorality of the English
Stage,* p. 4. The author obviously wishes more drastic measures taken than
have hitherto been used. Note also that he is suggesting what had been cited
in the *Short View,* p. 242. Moreover, to suggest to the authorities to use
an expedient in vogue during Elizabeth's reign, or one in vogue at present
in other nations was audacious, and it justifies Baker in censuring the effrontery of Collier.

[49] *Ibid.,* pp. 5-6.

English people: 'And now may not these plain Questions be proposed, without offence, to the Persons who frequent our Play-Houses; . . .' "[50]

All of the above arguments were very likely the factors which influenced Baker to call "A Supplemental Pamphlet" that pamphlet entitled *"A Representation of the Impiety and Immorality of the English Stage"* which the Viewer brought out on the Fast Day; these were, very likely, the arguments which made him assert petulantly:

> "The Viewer, (who wishes Her Majesty the same Place in the Throne She has in his Dictionary,) thought the Proclamation against Irreligion, and her Regulation of the Theatres as Imperfect as his Works; therefore on the Fast Day out comes his Supplemental Pamphlet to rectify the Government's Omissions with the same Modesty he formerly absolv'd it's Traytors."[51]

Since writing the above I have discovered in Bedford's *Evil and Danger of Stage Plays* a conviction of my opinions concerning the authorship of the "Supplemental Pamphlet." In the *Evil and Danger* Bedford censures play-house diversions and the incorrigibleness of the poets and actors; he mentions the fact that the actors care little for the laws of man and less for those of God. He refers to the plays *The Tempest* and *Macbeth* acted soon after the Storm and declares that here indeed was the brazen audacity of the players proved. Moreover, God would not be affronted, Bedford insists, and he then mentions two pamphlets—*A Dissuasive,* and the *Representation of the Impiety and Immorality of the English Stage*—published at this time concerning the incorrigibleness of the players, and he refers to the Dedicatory Epistle of Baker's *Act at Oxford* in connection with the pamphlets.[52] He states:

> "At the Time of the Fast abovementioned, there was printed a small Treatise entitul'd, *A Representation of the Impiety and Immorality of the English Stage;*"[53]

and after summarizing the contents of the pamphlet he declares that the author's purpose in writing it was to dissuade those religious-

---

[50] *Ibid.,* pp. 17-24.
[51] T. Baker, *An Act at Oxford,* Ep. Ded. p. viii. It might be of interest to note that Collier does not mention Anne in his *Dictionary*—an omission to which Baker was, doubtless. referring.
[52] A. Bedford, *The Evil and Danger of Stage Plays,* pp. 5-6.
[53] *Ibid.,* p. 9.

minded persons from frequenting such "Nurseries of Atheism and Licentiousness" as the play-house. In the same breath he asserts

"Mr. Collier also printed *A Dissuasive from the Play-House* at the same Time."[54]

This significant remark is followed by one equally as significant:

"These Methods made the Poets angry, but could not reform them. . . . One Quotation out of the Play call'd *An Act at Oxford,* in the Epistle Dedicatory may serve at present to show their Spleen;"[55]

whereupon he quotes at length from the Epistle Dedicatory concerning Collier's disloyalty to Anne. Inasmuch as I have already referred to the excerpt I shall omit it here. It is sufficient for our purpose to note that Bedford associated the two pamphlets *A Representation* and *A Dissuasive* as the cause of Baker's anger; he makes no mention of Baker's ire being aroused by any other pamphleteer except Collier whose efforts at reformation resulted in the two important anti-stage treatises published.

That Collier wrote *A Representation,* that this pamphlet is the "Supplemental Pamphlet" mentioned by Baker, and that it is also the lost pamphlet mentioned by Ballein is evident, I think, from the above arguments.

3

Bedford in his *Evil and Danger of Stage Plays* states that

"When the *Clergy* upon the *Fast Day* preach'd against the *Stage,* there was also a Book printed, intitul'd, *Concio Laici,* or the *Lay Man's Sermon;* endeavouring to prove That *Hypocrisy, more than open Lewdness, is the crying Sin of this Nation, and brought that dreadful Storm upon* us."[56]

---

[54] *Ibid.,* p. 10. Note the position of the word "also." Inasmuch as it is not punctuated it evidently should be understood as "Mr. Collier printed in addition to the above [*A Representation*] his *Dissuasive.* Bedford in his *Serious Reflections,* 1705, refers in similar vein to *The Dissuasive* and the *Representation,* (pp. iii-iv); he likewise associates the *"Short View"* by Collier and . . . the *Representation." Ibid.,* pp. 2-3.

[55] *Ibid.,* p. 10.

[56] Pp. 13-14. Mr. Krutch, *Comedy and Conscience,* p. 268, as well as Mr. Ballein in his *Jeremy Collier's Angriff,* p. 172, lists the *Concio* on the authority of Bedford. I, too, list it on Bedford's authority as I have not been successful in securing a copy of the pamphlet. E. Arber, lists the *Concio* in *The Term Catalogues,* (III, 387), for February, 1704, and gives

From Bedford's description I infer that the *Concio* was written to attack not the stage but hypocrisy as the cloak which the stage-reform was assuming; that Bedford castigated the author of the *Concio* for asserting that the clergy do not preach against hypocrisy and for daring to state that deceit is a vice friendly to the church.[57] Bedford adds a few caustic reflections of his own on the author's statements:

> "It is easy to prove, That in the *Language* of the *Play-House, Hypocrisy* now consists either in writing against the *Stage,* or putting the Laws in Execution against *Immorality* and *Profaneness.* It seems therefore (according to this *Author's Opinion*) that there was a Design of Reformation carry'd on, and this made God angry; but had we been profane, he had been better pleas'd. We had a Shew of *Religion,* and abhorr'd the *Abominations of the Play-House,* and this occasion'd such dreadful Judgments. This was *horrid Language* as a Preparation for a *Fast,* and not to be parallel'd by Jezebel her self."[58]

4

Although Dennis in 1704 wrote his answer to Collier's *Dissuasive* and published it shortly after,[59] the original letter is preserved by reason of its second publication in 1721 in a two-volume edition of *Original Letters, Familiar, Moral and Critical.* Dennis calls his answer *The Person of Quality's Answer to Mr. Collier's Letter: Containing a Defence of a Regulated Stage,* and he tells us why he does so:

> "tho' in the Title Page I call the Letter the *Person of Quality's Answer,* [I] have yet taken care in the Body of the Letter to acquaint the Reader, that I am only a private Gentleman. But

---

its title thus: *Concio Laici, or the Lay-Man's Sermon In order to an inward as well as an outward and formal Keeping of the Solemn Fast, appointed to be kept on January 19, 1703/4. Shewing that Hypocrisy more than open Lewdness is the crying Sin of this Nation; and that it brought us into danger of the Calamity now impending over us, and that it keeps us from getting out of it.* 1704.

[57] A. Bedford, *Evil and Danger,* p. 14.

[58] *Ibid.,* pp. 12-13.

[59] E. Arber, in his *Term Catalogues,* III, p. 390, states that in February there was sold in quarto by the Booksellers of London and Westminster a book bearing the title "The Person of Quality's Answer to Mr. Collier's Letter, being a Diswasive from the Play-House. In which are inserted the Apologies of a young Lady and young Gentleman in behalf of the Ladies and Gentlemen who frequent the Play-House;" he suggests that J. Dennis is the author. A comparison of the contents of the Letter published in 1721 with the title listed by Arber for 1704 proves the two letters to be identical.

I make no doubt but that I am a much more considerable Person than he to whom Mr. Collier's Letter was writ, who perhaps was no Body."[60]

Dennis, in the Advertisement to *The Person of Quality's Answer* published in 1721, tells the reader that

"The following Letter was writ by me about sixteen years ago. . . . As this Letter has been so long out of Print, that it is as scarce as any Manuscript of which there is but one Copy, I Thought it might be as new and as entertaining to most of its Readers as if it had been never publish'd."[61]

He gives a brief survey of his opinion of Collier's *Short View* which he calls a book true in a few particulars, yet

"The Author was manifestly so unfair an Aversary in general, that the latter End of the Book very grossly contradicted the beginning of it, and endeavour'd to decry even a Regulated Stage, which the Author at the beginning of the Book had acknowledg'd useful."[62]

From the *Short View* and Collier he turns to the *Dissuasive* and the Great Storm:

"About four or five Years after that [the publication of *A Short View*] as near as I can remember, Mr. Collier took occasion from the great Storm, which happen'd about that Time, to renew his Attack upon the Stage, in a little Pamphlet call'd *A Dissuasive from the Play-House, written by way of a Letter to a Person of Quality*."[63]

Irritated by the attitude of the Nation toward the stage, and resolving to expose the "hypocrisy, extravagance and sophistry of his [Collier's] *Dissuasive*," Dennis wrote "The Person of Quality's Answer to Mr. Collier's Letter"—an answer intended to consist of a mixture of reason and raillery. The writer, wresting expressions from the *Dis-*

---

[60] J. Dennis, *The Person of Quality's Answer*, p. 227. The 1721 edition of Dennis' *Letters* was printed for W. Mears. The *Letter* in question is 50 pages in length, has a 3-page advertisement, and addresses Collier as "Dear Doctor."

[61] *Ibid.*, pp. 225-7. The re-publishing in 1721 of this letter with its caustic advertisement against Collier and stage-censure indicates that the controversy was still smouldering, and it may point to the fact that Dennis considered Collier still active in it.

[62] *Ibid.*, p. 225.

[63] *Ibid.*, p. 226.

suasive and the *Short View,* applies them to nonsensical ideas—closely imitating the example of Johnson and Smith whose raillery in the *Animadversions* has previously been commented upon. He asserts that upon the reception of the "Edifying, Evangelical Dissuasive" which gave its readers the impression that the "Nurseries of Licence and Atheism" would pull down some terrible vengeance upon the heads of the English people, he determined to begin "Reformation" and the "Year" together.[64] In consequence of this resolution he summoned the members of his family immediately after dinner, intending to read long and solemn lectures from the *Short View;* but that

> "a strange Fatality had happen'd; for some audacious Rats had so prophanely gnawn it, that it was no longer legible; a Detachment, in my Conscience, of Play-House Vermin, whom the Devil had enter'd into for that purpose, at his Congregation in the Neighbourhood."[65]

Thus deprived of his homily, Dennis takes the "short, the divine Dissuasive"; he tells us that he read it over in a breath while all his audience stood gaping at him; that when he came to the last paragraphs he pronounced them with greater emphasis, laying before them with all the energy of his lungs: "the sad Instance of God's Judgment in the terrible Tempest, when we were almost swept into Chaos, when Nature seem'd to be in her last agony, and the World seem'd ready to expire," and that he ejaculated to his awe-struck listeners:

> "And what occasion, . . . to have Recourse to Tragedies, when those Rants, that Fustian and that Bombast, with which deluded Mortals are now-a-days so tickled, are engagingly inserted into our very *Dissuasives.*"[66]

With mock-gravity Dennis turns from addressing his audience to cite to the Doctor two remarks which he made to them:

> "And here, Doctor, I made two Remarks to them, . . . first, said I, the Outcries of the Play-House Practices are so aggravating, so horrible, that the Divine Vengeance which they brought down upon us, has involv'd the very Innocent. Not only the poor Inhabitants of Cologn, but the very *Hamburgers* and *Dantzick-*

---

[64] *Ibid.*, pp. 228-9.
[65] *Ibid.*, p. 229.
[66] *Ibid.*, pp. 229-230.

ers, and all the People of the *Baltick,* have suffered for the Enormities of our *English Theatres,* . . . The second Observation that I made was this, that we have reason to be thankful to Heaven, for forbearing us so long."[67]

His sarcasm mounts as he continues his attack. He refers to the popularity of the play-house diversion in the time of Elizabeth and of James; he points to Collier's censure of Shakespeare in the *Short View;*

"You would have open'd the Eyes of those Fools, who believ'd *Shakespear* to be Instructive as well as Innocent. You would have extracted more *Smutt* from his Comedies, than a Chimney does from Seacoal. And what Prophaness and Blasphemy had you not found in his Tragedies? You would have satisfy'd both Queen and Council, and Clergy too, that their Business was to suppress the Play-Houses, and to let *Spain* and *Rome* alone. That the Danger that they were in was not from *Philip* II, and Sixtus the Fifth, but from Tyrants who had been many a year defunct."[68]

He attacks Collier's non-jurancy by insinuating that Collier would have esteemed himself happy if by suppressing the stage he might see it restored with the restoration of the banished king,[69] and he insultingly reminds Collier that he did not fulminate against the play-house in the palmy days of James II:

"You yourself, I remember, Doctor, were then at Years of Discretion; and yet with passive Ears and Tongue, endur'd the Filth of Epsom Wells, the Bawdy of the *Soldier's Fortune and* the Beastliness of *Limber-Ham.* But the time of your Prophetic Mission it seems was not yet come, or perhaps you thought it improper to fall out with the Play-Houses, before you had fallen out with the Government. But you have at last, to the wonder of the world, declar'd yourself."[70]

---

[67] *Ibid.,* pp. 230-1.

[68] *Ibid.,* p. 234. Dennis here refers to Collier's statement in the *Dissuasive,* p. 12: "And in the Reign of the Famous Queen *Elizabeth,* there was an Order of Queen and Council, to drive the *Players* out of the city and Liberties of London, and to pull down the *Theatres,* which was executed accordingly." The meaning of Dennis' statement is, obviously: "You [Collier] desired to convince the people that Elizabeth should have suppressed the play-houses and not heeded the dangers impending from Philip II [1527-1598] and from Sixtus V [reigned from 1585-1590]. This censure is *not* of Anne or of her reign, which fact emphasizes Ballein's arguments for the existence of a new Collier pamphlet. Cf. p. 205 above.

[69] *Ibid.,* p. 238.   [70] *Ibid.,* p. 238.

With biting candor, Dennis describes the effect which the reading of the *Dissuasive* had upon his four children who were assembled after dinner on this New Year's Day. Jack, he says, satisfied that plays were abominable took his hat, sword, and cloak, and went to St. James; Susan went to take a walk in the Garden and to meditate there in the dark. On the other hand, Charles having promised his lady to escort her to the play made ready to fulfill the engagement, and Harriet to go with them.

In the conclusion of the *Letter,* Dennis with mock gravity, tells the effect of the evening on his four children:

> "Ah, dear Doctor, let me see you Tomorrow, to receive some Consolation from you. For here have happen'd two of the most unfortunate things in the World. For News is brought me from *Piccadilly* that *Jack* has lost a thousand *Pound* at Picket; and *Susan,* tho' she went out as black as a Raven, being in Mourning for her Great Aunt, . . . is return'd as white and powder'd as if she had been hard at work in a Bolting-House. So that I could wish that for this one Night they had both been with *Harriet* and *Charles* at the Tabernacle of the Wicked."[71]

Dennis here, as in the *Usefulness of the Stage,* defends a regulated stage as a means of lawful diversion, and he emphasizes its usefulness for English temperaments. He gives no quarter to Collier and the reformers for attempting to suppress the play-house, and insists that if the theatres are suppressed the people will commit greater crimes by participating in the three other reigning forms of diversion: "Gaming, Musick-Meetings, Balls and Meetings for Dancing."

5

Thomas Baker's *An Act at Oxford* was referred to when I discussed the authorship of *A Representation of the Impiety and Immorality of the English Stage,* hence I shall not here repeat the data given concerning the "Supplemental Pamphlet."[72] The play is dedicated by

---

[71] *Ibid.,* p. 278.

[72] Cf. pp. 201-209. *An Act at Oxford* is a five-act comedy, was printed for Bernard Lintott and must have appeared before the Easter term of 1704 inasmuch as the sixth dialogue in *Visits from the Shades,* Easter, 1704, is entitled "Ben Johnson and Mr. Baker, Author of the Oxford Act." That the play was forbidden the footlights is evident from the Prologue which Baker wrote to his next play *Hampstead Heath*:
"One Dispensation he [the Author] does humbly pray,

an eleven page epistle to the Right Honourable Edward Lord Dudley and Ward and in it the author refers to the *Short View*, to Collier, and to the Stage-Controversy; and like Collier's other foes he fights an anti-stage battle with jurancy ammunition.[73] Baker further declares that Collier's activities are seconded by *the Observator*,[74] and that the two walk hand in hand like the two Kings of Brentford, resolving to venture their Lives and Fortunes "in the Good Old Cause of Reformation and Ruin."[75]

6

In tone very similar to *Letters from the Dead to the Living*, 1702, are *Visits from the Shades*. There are nine dialogues to the pamphlet, but the one pertinent to the Collier Controversy is the "Dialogue Between Jo Haines's Ghost and the Reforming Mr. Col-

---

To borrow from his late forbidden Play;
The Ladies on his Side he dares ingage,
Since Patchwork is the Fashion of this Age.
If you find Humour, and the Scenes compact,
Let *Hampstead Heath* excuse the *Oxford Act*." p. i.

[73] T. Baker, *An Act at Oxford*, Ded. Epistle, p. viii. Neither the *D. N. B.*, I, 937-8, nor D. E. Baker's *Biographia Dramatica*, I. 9-10, give any clue to the place or time of T. Baker's birth. That he flourished from 1700-1709 both attest, and that he attended Oxford for a time, D. E. Baker asserts. D. E. Baker says, besides, that his language was easy and agreeable, his wit pure and genuine, and his satire just and poignant. *Biog. Dram.* p. 9. However, eulogy of style is about the only eulogy T. Baker is accorded, for both the *D. N. B.*, p. 938, Thomas Whincop in his *List of Dramatic Authors*, and Thomas D'Urfey in his Preface to the *Modern Prophets* speak caustically of Baker's plays. D'Urfey refers to the "barbarous, assassinating attempts of the two bloody Male-Criticks I have met with," and he says that "one stiles himself the Author of Tunbridge-walkes, [Baker] who dully forgetting the Plotless and trifling Quality of that, the worse Management of another Piece of his, where he has conjuring brought *Oxford* upon *Hampstead-Heath*, . . . has thought fit to shake his Dirt upon me; but I have contempt enough to answer his Injustice . . . ." Preface to the *Modern Prophets*, p. ii. The other critic, D'Urfey tells us, is "a profound Coffeehouse Wit whom I shall pretend to undeceive, at some hour of Leisure."

[74] The *Observator* was the product of Captain John Tutchin. It was a folio half-sheet appearing Wednesday and Saturday in 1702, and was concerned mostly with politics. In 1703 and 1704 it became a series of dialogues between a Countryman and the Observator. Up to the time of his death in 1708 Tutchin gave a reforming tone to the paper. If we accept what has been said of him, "that he was always croaking for piety," one may easily understand the reason that Baker associates Collier with Tutchin in the effort to reform the age. In Numbers 40, 57, 59, 78, 90, and 91 of the *Observator* Tutchin records ill-natured observations of plays and players. Cf. W. Graham, *The Beginnings of English Literary Periodicals*, p. 56.

[75] *Ibid.*, p. viii.

lier."[76] It was written in reply to Collier's *Dissuasive,* for in the opening lines the author states:

> "But since your little Three-penny Pop-Gun, has made as large
> a Report as any you have yet discharged against the Theatres, I
> have got leave to take this Trip back to Earth, to view the
> Wonders it has produced."[77]

The remarks made by Haines concerning plays are designed to
draw from Collier all his former anathemas against indecency in
language, profanity, abuse of the clergy, and immorality. They give
curious information concerning Collier's attitude on music,[78] and
banteringly allude to his non-jurancy, to his *Dictionary,* to his
Desertion Discuss'd, and to his "Absolutions." The author answers
Collier in the familiar phrasings of the *Short View,* and the accuracy
with which certain well-known expressions are quoted proves that Collier's censure of plays and play-wrights had branded itself upon the
stage-poets.

7

Collier's second edition of the *Dissuasive,* printed for R. Sare and
published June 9, 1704, contains an additional fifteen-page anonymous letter written as an answer to a request for an opinion on the
Dissuasive. Its title as it appears on the title-page is: *A Letter written by another Hand; in Answer to some Queries sent by a Person of
Quality, Relating to the Irregularities charged upon the Stage.* The
writer is evidently a person who has studied the stage-question thoroughly, perhaps under Collier's tutelage; he agrees with Collier on
every question proposed, argues in Collier's phraseology, and arrives
at Collier's conclusions. He couches his sarcasm at Dryden's audacity
in the familiar staccato questions and climactic replies which have
more than once been noted as peculiar to Collier. He defends the
Dissuasive, laments the moral lethargy of the English Nation, calls the
audacity of a people who could applaud *Macbeth* on the very day of

---

[76] *Visits From the Shades* is anonymous, bears no printer's name, and was—
according to E. Arber (*Term Catalogues,* III, 402)—published for Easter,
1704. The dialogue in question is eleven pages. In the Preface we read:
"It may, indeed, be thought that I took the hint of these Dialogues from
the *Letters from the Dead:* But I can assure the World, . . . I designed
something of this Nature a Year or two before those Gentlemen [Brown,
Ayloff, Barker] came out with their Letters."
[77] Anonymous, *Visits from the Shades,* p. 1.
[78] *Ibid.,* p. 8.

the tempest, " . . . another Prodigy of Horrour, to be chronicled with the Storm,"[79] and besides acquiescing with the statements of Collier's *Dissuasive,* adds a few significant but caustic touches to the contemporaneous English Stage. It is in this "Letter" that we are informed that when the Queen commanded to be read before the audience

> "her strict and solemn Order, prohibiting not only what was offensive on the Stage, but all other Disorders and ill Customs, . . . both Order and Actor who read it were hiss'd off the Stage;"[80]

here it is we read that when Collier had leveled his "Attack upon the Stage" and made so vigorous a charge as to shake its very foundations only the "Minor Poets" appeared in vindication even though the whole Posse of Parnassus was expected to be up in arms. He asks:

> "Where was the mighty W——— [Wycherley]?
> Where was the great Master of the Muses, and Father of our Modern Drama [Dryden]?[81]

The writer concludes his epistle by asserting that until Church and State pluck up courage for a common cause they both will suffer by the stage:

> "that Mr. *Haynes's* Primitive will be the Prevailing Church, the *Play-House* too hard for the Pulpit, and Play-Bills for Proclamations."[82]

8

Collier has been caricatured many times by the stage-poets but perhaps no poet has portrayed him with more venom than has Tom Brown. This is especially true of the portrait which he intended as a fac-simile of Collier in Sir Jerry Witwoud, the principal character of *Stage Beaux toss'd in a Blanket: Or, Hypocrisie Alamode; Expos'd in a True Picture of Jerry, . . . A Pretending Scourge to the English*

---

[79] J. Collier, *Dissuasive,* 2nd ed., pp. 17-19.
[80] *Ibid.,* pp. 20-21.
[81] *Ibid.,* p. 21.
[82] *Ibid.,* pp. 31-2.

Stage.[83] Both the Prologue, the play, and the Epilogue prove that Brown's biographer was correct when he stated: "Brown's satirical writings are more remarkable for coarseness than for wit."[84]

Brown evidently intended by his composition to satirize not only Collier but Mackworth and the Non-Conforming Divines as well, for in the Prologue which is spoken by a man dressed one-half as a non-conforming parson, and the other as an Orthodox Divine, there is frequent allusion to the pamphlet "Peace at Home and War Abroad" and caustic reference to the Non-Conforming Divines:

"A Pox upon their Zeal to save our Souls,
They'd make us Honest, that is, they'd make us Fools.

. . .

A Florid Friend [the author of the pamphlet Peace at Home]
of ours has prov'd of late,
That Pow'r wou'd make us dreaded by the State."[85]

In the Epilogue there is biting allusion to the effects which were consequent upon Collier's Stage-Attack:

"With Zeal and Sin at once we're strangely warm'd
And grow more Wicked as we grow Reform'd.
Oh! 'tis a blessed Age, and blessed Nation,
When Vice walks cheek by jowl with Reformation."[86]

In the play there are seven characters. Sir Jerry Witwoud, Collier's counter-part, is described as a pert, talkative, half-witted coxcomb. The questions addressed to him throughout the play are answered, for the most part, in sentences taken from both the *Short*

---

[83] This is a three-act comedy, was printed by J. Nutt, and was published in June, 1704. According to a statement in the *D. N. B.,* III, p. 31, the comedy was never acted even though it was dedicated to Christopher Rich, Patentee of the Theatre-Royal. However, the Prologue on "Occasional Conformity," and the Epilogue on the "Reformers" were spoken at the Theatre-Royal.

[84] *D. N. B.,* III, p. 30.

[85] T. Brown, *Stage-Beaux,* Prologue, p. ii. *Peace at Home* is a 12-page pamphlet with a two-page preface. It was written by Sir Humphrey Mackworth and is dedicated to the Queen. The title-page of the pamphlet reads *Peace at Home: Or. A Vindication of the Proceedings of the Honourable the House of Commons, On the Bill for Preventing Danger from Occasional Conformity. . . .* In the Dedicatory Epistle, p. 3, Mackworth urges the Queen to concur with Parliament in passing such a law as they conceive to be "Reasonable, and even Necessary to preserve *Peace at Home,* and to promote an Unanimous Zeal *for carrying on a Vigorous War Abroad." Political Tracts, 1660-1758.*

[86] T. Brown, *Stage-Beaux,* Epilogue, iii.

View and the *Defence;* they pertain to the abuse of the clergy, to the immodesty, profaneness, and immorality of which he had accused the English Stage and which, when torn from their context, are ridiculous as well as humiliating for Sir Jerry. Clemene, an admirer of Sir Jerry, is an

> "affected Hypocrite, Coquet, and Jilt, . . . pretends to be a profess'd Enemy to the Stage since the Publishing Mr. Collier's Book."[87]

Lord Vaunt-Title is vain of his quality and hostile to the stage because his plays have been refused. Urania, Eliza, Dorimant, and Hotspur, the remaining characters, direct the conversation throughout the play, and in most of their remarks they satirize Collier.

Besides the picture that Brown gives of Collier, there are, in *Stage Beaux,* interesting references to vindications that had appeared. Dorimant declares that Collier ought to define his terms:

> "For in all disputes the Terms ought to be clear and adequate, to avoid Cavils and endless Squabbles about Words, and *inextricable Obscurity.* This was told Mr. Collier at the first appearance of his First Book."[88]

He refers to Vanbrugh's *A Short Vindication:*

> "When the Ingenious Author of the *Relapse* had confuted him [Collier] in this Particular [that there are oaths in his plays] . . . he is resolv'd to yield nothing, tho' never so evident, and answers very rationally—*"There is no arguing from the Practice to the lawfulness of it."*[89]

He refers, besides, to Dennis' *Usefulness of the Stage:*

> "He [Collier] catches at a trifling Mistake of Mr. *Dennis's* about *Plutarch,* but at the same time takes no notice of the very material Contradiction Charg'd on him by the same Author in his Introduction to the same Book [*The Usefulness of the Stage*]."[90]

---

[87] *Ibid.,* p. viii.
[88] *Ibid.,* p. 34. Recall that Gildon in his Preface to *Phaeton,*—the first extant Vindication of the Stage against Mr. Collier—had stated: "Mr. Collier . . . shou'd therefore, to make himself understood, have given us the definitions of his Terms in the front of his book." p. xi.
[89] *Ibid.,* p. 22.
[90] *Ibid.,* p. 33.

In the attempt to justify Vanbrugh and Congreve, Hotspur asserts in regard to the *Vindication of the Relapse* and the *Amendments:*

> "If the Author be Easie, Genteel and Witty, like the *Vindicators of the Relapse, etc.*, then its Banter. If it be mixt with just Repartees, admirable Reflections, like the *Amendments,* then 'tis Scurrilous. If like others the Matter be seriously and plainly handl'd with sound Reasoning, then 'tis Dull."[91]

Brown concludes the first and second acts with two summarizing couplets; the third act he concludes with four. He proves by the remarks which he puts into the mouth of Dorimant and Hotspur that he has formed his own opinions of literary principles; through Clemene, Lord Vaunt-Title, and Sir Jerry he tells of his aversion for Collier and of his hatred for the stage-reform movement; through the Epilogue we get a picture of contemporary London and of the vices which are flourishing there despite the efforts of reformers to suppress the play-house.

---

[91] *Ibid.,* p. 25.

CHAPTER XI

Publications of 1705, 1706, 1707, 1708

1. A. Bedford: *Serious Reflections . . . A Sermon Preach'd . . . in the City of Bristol,* January 7, 1705.
2. A. Bedford: *A Second Advertisement concerning the Profaneness of the Play-House,* 1705.
3. T. Brown, E. Ward: *A Legacy for the Ladies. . . . With A Comical View of London and Westminster,* 1705.
4. Anonymous: *A Letter to a Lady Concerning the New Play-House,* written September 29, 1705; published, 1706.
5. Anonymous. *Esther, A Sacred Tragedy from Racine,* 1705.
6. A. Bedford: *The Evil and Danger of Stage-Plays:* . . . 1706.
7. J. Dennis: *An Essay on the Operas after the Italian Manner,* 1706.
8. Anonymous: "The Stage Vindicated, A Satyr, by I. H. Esq." (In *The Muses Mercury* for July, 1707).
9. E. Filmer: *A Defence of Plays,* 1707.
10. J. Collier: *A Farther Vindication of the Short View . . .* 1708.

A prominent Collier-advocate appeared in the person of the clergyman, Arthur Bedford, who preached and wrote against the stage and in behalf of reformation of manners. Strange to say, he appeared at the helm of the controversy oftener during the years 1705-8 than did Collier. He is not to be confused, however, with Collier's famous nonjuring contemporary, Hilkiah Bedford, who took part in the "Usages Controversy." Arthur Bedford introduces himself into the stage-reform movement with his *Serious Reflections . . . A Sermon* preached from his pulpit in Bristol the first Sunday of January, 1705. He kept himself in prominence as an enemy to the stage during 1705 by publishing this Sermon as well as his *A Second Advertisement concerning the Profaneness of the Playhouse,* and during 1706 by publishing his *Evil and Danger of Stage Plays.* Another Collier advocate appeared in 1706 in the anonymous author of a *Letter to a Lady,* who published his work as a solemn exhortation to shun the dangers of the playhouse. Collier ends the line with his *Farther Vindication,* a reply to Filmer.

The stage-advocates who came forward during these three years either to attack the reformers or to satirize the reform movement were Brown, E. Ward, Dennis, and Filmer. Brown and Ward in *A*

Comical View of London and Westminster refer satirically to the stage-reform movement in their remarks on the poets and on the vices prevalent in the theatres. Dennis, in behalf of English drama and against the "Operas after the Italian Manner," argues with much the same acuteness and vigor which he had displayed in his *Usefulness of the Stage*. Filmer pleads volubly but weakly in defence of plays.

Two pamphlets—*A Second Advertisement*, and *Esther, A Sacred Tragedy from Racine*—are not available. I have entered them in my bibliography merely for record.

1

Arthur Bedford was a prolific champion not only of Collier and of the stage-reformation, but of music.[1] His first attack on the stage was from his pulpit in the City of Bristol the first Sunday of January, 1705, and, shortly after, he published his Sermon under the caption *Serious Reflections On the Scandalous Abuse and Effects of the Stage; in a Sermon Preach'd at the Parish-Church of St. Nicolas in The City of Bristol, on Sunday the 7th Day of January, 1704/5.*[2]

Bedford states in the Preface that the Sermon was occasioned

"By the Acting of Comedies and Tragedies in St. James's Parish during the time of the Fair in the Year 1704, by the actual building of a Play-house in the City of Bath, and the great Apprehensions that such a Design was carried on in this City;"[3]

as well as by his desire both to perform his duty of dissuading his hearers from frequenting such places of amusements as the theatre and to awaken their consciences to a sense of God's judgments. However, due to misrepresentations both by those who heard the sermon as well as by those who heard of it, he was obliged to publish the discourse so that these persons might

---

[1] S. Allibone, *A Critical Dictionary*, I, 157; *D. N. B.*, II, 109-110.
[2] The Sermon is 38 pages in length, and has a 23-page Preface. As a conclusion to the work there is a six-page "Copy of the Presentment of the Grand Jury for the City of Bristol, which was mentioned in the Third Section of the former Sermon." The book was printed and sold by W. Bonny in Corn-street in 1705.
[3] A. Bedford, *Serious Reflections*, Preface, p. i.

"upon a serious Perusal be better Judges of those particular Expressions which have fallen under the Censure of some Men, whether they deserve that heavy Load which hath been cast upon them."[4]

Bedford bases the Sermon itself on the Epistle of St. Paul to Timothy: "But shun profane and vain bablings; for they will increase into more Ungodliness," and he begins by applying this admonition to the

"public Actings of the Stage, in Comedies and Tragedies, and other Diversions of the same Nature.[5]

He refers "to the *Short View* by Mr. J. Collier and to the *Representation*" as proof sufficient that play-house diversions are vain babblings;[6] he discourses on the evident displeasure of God for sins, a displeasure that has been manifested in the late storms; he speaks of the increase of ungodliness which has been effected by particular vices produced by the present stage; he traces to the stage murders, adulteries, idleness, and contempt of all religions.[7] In the conclusion of his sermon he requests two things:

"1. That such Books may be disperst through this City which give us a true and lively *Representation of the Impiety and Immorality of the English Stage*, . . . and 2. That such persons who after all that can be said will take no Warning, may be particularly taken notice of, as Persons who fear not God, and regard not Man."[8]

2

Tom Brown showed in his *Letters from the Dead to the Living* as well as in his *Stage Beaux toss'd in a Blanket* bitter hostility to the stage-reformers and contempt for reformation of manners. It was inevitable that this deep-seated bitterness should inject itself into his other writings, even those not primarily directed against the stage. That this is the case is obvious in various passages found in *A Legacy*

---

[4] *Ibid.*, pp. i-ii. Bedford enumerates seven objections made against his sermon and by their tone one infers that the congregation must have caviled over trifles.
[5] *Ibid.*, p. 1.
[6] *Ibid.*, pp. 2-3.
[7] *Ibid.*, pp. 15-31.
[8] *Ibid.*, pp. 36-37.

for the Ladies. . . . With a *Comical VIEW of London and West-minster: . . . In Two Parts. The First Part by Mr. Tho. Brown: The Second Part by Mr. Edward Ward, Author of the London Spy, etc. To which is prefixt the Character of Mr. Tho. Brown . . . by Dr. Drake.*[9]

The papers are written in diary-form, entries being made for each day. All of them are satirical, many are ludicrous, and most of them are opprobrious. For instance, Brown satirizes the theatre in his entry for Sunday, October 27 by stating "Great ogling at *Covent-Garden* Church . . ." while for Sunday, November 3 he writes: "Beggars take up their respective Posts in *Lincoln's-Inn-fields,* and other places, by Seven, that they may be able to Praise God in Capon and *March*-beer at Night.[10] The entry for November 5 portrays Brown venting his wrath on the Reformers and the Grand Jury of Middlesex both of which conjointly had been instrumental in presenting the poets for their plays.[11]

Ward, too, refers satirically to the work done by the societies for reformation of manners, and his comments agree in the main with those of Defoe expressed in the *Poor Man's Plea,* 1698, and in his Satyr, *Reformation of Manners,* 1703.[12] He satirizes Collier's comments on Shakespeare and the playhouse as we find in the entry for the week of January 20-27:

> "*Shakespeare* and *Ben. Johnson's* Ghosts, will in a little time pay a Visit to both Play-houses; and if their Fury be not appeased by a fair Promise of a new Regulation of their Stages, with Scorpion Rods, borrowed from the Furies, they will whip the *Barnet* Mimick and the *French* Tumblers out of both Houses, and convince the Spectators, a good old Play is a better Entertainment for a sensible Audience, than a modern Farce with *Bartholomew-fair* Sauce to it; and that a good Moral Speech, is far more Edifying than the Braying of an Human Ass; and

---

[9] The *Comical View* was printed for Sam Briscoe in 1705. It is in the same volume with T. Brown's *A Legacy for the Ladies.* Parts I and II of the *Comical View* are each 41 pages in length, and consist of papers published weekly from October 16 to March 3.

[10] T. Brown, *A Comical View,* pp. 120-122.

[11] This presentment is referred to by Luttrell, *A Brief Historical Relation,* IV, pp. 379, 455, 571, in connection with Congreve, D'Urfey, Dennis, and Vanbrugh respectively. It is referred to by Bedford, *Evil and Danger,* p. 19.

[12] T. Brown, *op. cit.,* p. 191.

the neat Contexture of a good Plot, far more delightful than the Flip-flap."[13]

3

There was published in 1706 *A Letter to a Lady Concerning the New Play House;*[14] it was apparently evoked by the uneasiness which the writer professed to feel for a wealthy young lady in whose neighborhood a "Topping Play-house" had been built:

> "I forgot then to ask your Ladiship at whose Charge that Topping Playhouse was Built; but I can't but think that the Money contributed towards it, would have been much better bestow'd in Building of Churches; of which at your End of the Town, there is, I'm sure, much greater want than of Playhouses; . . . I can't help but suspect, Madam, (tho' I hope I am mistaken in it) that your Ladiship has lent an helping Hand to this Work; . . ."[15]

The substance of the letter is the advice given concerning the lawfulness of attending the theatre. The writer would have his correspondent understand that even though it is not absolutely unlawful ever to see a play, nevertheless to frequent the play-house is a matter of no *good* report, and is ample proof that she has not so great an abhorrence for sin as she should have.[16]

There is a problem of authorship connected with *A Letter to a Lady* which relieves somewhat the dullness of its contents. Mr. Krutch suggests Josiah Woodward as the author,[17] while, on the other hand,

---

[13] *Ibid.,* p. 162. Unless the above quotation is viewed in the light of Collier's stage attacks, much of its meaning is lost. In the first place Collier in the *Short View*, pp. 50- 51, in speaking of the Immodesty of the English Theatre had said "To come Home, and near our own Times: The English Theatre from Queen *Elizabeth to* King *Charles* II will afford us something not inconsiderable to our purpose. As for Shakespear, he is too guilty to make an Evidence: . . . where there is most Smut, there is least Sense. *Ben Johnson* is much more reserv'd in his *Plays,* and declares plainly for Modesty in his *Discoveries,* some of his words are these . . . a *True Artificer* [will avoid] *Obscene* and *Effeminate Phrase."* The reference to "Bartholomew-fair Sauce" is an echo of references made by Collier to the same topic. *Short View,* p. 109; *Dissuasive,* p. 6.

[14] This *Letter* is sixteen pages in length and its title-page reads "Printed and Sold by Joseph Downing . . . 1706." On its concluding page is subscribed "Michaelmas day, Sept. 29th, 1705."

[15] *Ibid.,* pp. 3-4.

[16] *Ibid.,* pp. 4-9.

[17] J. Krutch, *Comedy and Conscience,* p. 269.

the *Anonyma and Pseudonyma*,[18] the *D. N. B.*[18a] and the *Dictionary of Anonymous and Pseudonymous English Literature*[19] state that Collier is the author. However, there is in the *Letter* internal evidence which, if compared with the evidence found in Collier's anti-stage works, points to the fact that Collier is not the author. The writer of *A Letter to a Lady* asserts:

> "I never in my Life saw a Play and have not read very many; a few of them were sufficient to give me a Surfeit, and I never car'd for them since."[20]

Now, in *A Second Defence* Collier stated definitely to Drake that he *did* see plays:

> "The Surveyor Complains of my Censuring the *Musick and Gestures of the Playhouse only upon Report, having never heard of one, nor seen t'other.* As to the Playhouse Musick, he has given me no occasion to resume that Argument, neither did I meddle with their Dancing. But here he runs too fast. I only told him, I was no Frequenter of the *Playhouse.* I must tell him, I have been there, tho not always for Diversion. I am not so much a Stranger to that place, as not to have seen the Behaviour of their Women bold, and the Gestures lewd sometimes, witness the *Hostess in Bartholomew Fair!*"[21]

The *Second Defence* was published in 1700, and the *Letter to a Lady* in 1706. I can see no reason why the author (if it were Collier) should mis-state facts in the *Letter,* especially when he had publicly admitted six years before that he attended the theatre.

With regard to the statement in *A Letter to a Lady* "I have not read very many [plays]" there is evidence in Collier's works that his dramatic bibliography was a rather extensive one. While we do not know what number the author intended by the phrase "very many," we may assert, nevertheless, that Collier's stage pamphlets give evidence that their author was well acquainted with ancient and modern play-lore. From the *Short View* we are convinced that he had read at least ten of Dryden's plays, four of Congreve's, two of Vanbrugh's, two of Wycherley's, one of Otway's, and Parts I and II of D'Urfey's *Don*

---

[18] II, 1292.
[18a] IV, 802.
[19] III, 280.
[20] Anonymous, *A Letter to a Lady,* p. 10.
[21] J. Collier, *A Second Defence,* p. 56

Quixote. We are convinced, besides, that he was well acquainted with the plays of Shakespeare, of Ben Jonson, of Beaumont, and of Fletcher. We know, too, that he must have read *all* the plays of Moliere and *all* of Corneille, otherwise he would not assert in his chapter on the "Clergy Abused by the Stage"

> "The famous Corneille and Moliere bring no Priests of any kind upon the Stage."[22]

We are convinced, besides, that he must have been acquainted with the plays of the Ancients, otherwise he would not draw such frequent comparisons between them and the Moderns, and to these comparisons we have pointed in our analysis of the *Short View.*

Add to the above enumerations the direct evidence that he gives us of those plays which he has read but which are too "out of place" to quote:

> "An Inventory of their Ware-House would have been a large Work: But being afraid of over charging the Reader, I thought a Pattern might do."[23]

Inasmuch as an inventory of their ware-house would have been a large work we may infer that Collier omitted many plays which he deemed too suggestive to include. Then, too, Collier gives us in his *Defence* his censure of six additional plays not listed in the *Short View,* and— assuming that he wrote *A Representation of the Impiety and Immorality of the English Stage*—we have as additional evidence his charges of profaneness against the stage-poets in his quotations from nine plays not hitherto mentioned by him. Again, there seems to be no reason on the part of Collier for falsifying. Hence, since Collier has admitted that he attended the theatre, and, since he has acquainted us to some extent with his repertoire, there is every reason to believe that he did not write *A Letter to a Lady concerning the New Play House.*

4

In 1706 Bedford appeared again in the ranks of Collier's crusaders by the publication of his *The Evil and Danger of Stage-Plays: Shewing their Natural Tendency to Destroy RELIGION, And introduce a*

---

[22] *A Short View,* p. 123.
[23] *Ibid.,* Preface, pp. iii-iv.

General Corruption of Manners; In almost Two Thousand Instances,
taken from the Plays of the two last Years, against all the Methods
lately used for their Reformation.[24]

The author states in the preface his intention of supplementing the
labours of Collier by giving a short account of the profaneness and
immorality of the English stage during the years 1704-6. In the vein
of his Sermon *Serious Reflections* preached at Bristol the year before,
he tells us that he is writing against the stage because of a three-fold
obligation on his part: first, because the vows of baptism bind him to
oppose those places where the devil is honoured, where the heathen
gods are adored, where religion is undermined, where vice is encouraged, and where adultery is pleaded for with all possible industry;
secondly, because the obligations of the Ministry bind him to oppose
everything which is contrary to God's honour, and, lastly, because the
actual building of a play-house in the city of Bristol, the frequent acting of plays near the city, and his own presence amid these very
surroundings demand action in the matter.[25] He is aware, he says,
that he is attacking the poets who are reputed to be men of the "greatest Parts, Wit, and Ingenuity," and that his attack exposes him to
their reproaches and ridicule.[26]

Bedford proves his acquaintance with all of the literature published pro and con within the decade on the topic of stage reform.
He acidly gives his opinion of Brown's *Stage-Beaux* designed to expose
Mr. Collier "in a plot filled with scurrility and profaneness,"[27] and he
refers to the Epistle Dedicatory of the *Act at Oxford,* and to the *Concio Laici.*[28] He praises Dryden for refusing to enter the controversy
and he censures Dennis and Congreve who were willing "to wash the
Black-Moor white," by writing vindications of themselves and the
Play-House.[29] In words that differ only slightly from the original
found in the *Short View* Bedford voices Collier's censure of the poets

---

[24] The book is 227 pages long, and has a nine-page preface. It was printed
and sold by W. Bonny and Henry Mortlock in London. At the time he
wrote the book Bedford was chaplain to the Duke of Bedford and Vicar of
Temple in the City of Bristol.
[25] Arthur Bedford, *The Evil and Danger of Stage Plays,* Preface, pp. i.-iii.
[26] *Ibid.,* pp. i.-iv.
[27] *Ibid.,* pp. 17-19; p. 7.
[28] *Ibid.,* pp. 10-14.
[29] *Ibid.,* pp. 2-3.

who make their principal characters libertines and reward them at the end of the play:

> "they represent their principal Persons, as most scandalously *vicious,* and reward them with good Wives and Fortunes at the End of the *Play,* at best they are not punished as they deserve."[30]

Bedford was well-intentioned in his attack on the stage, but his method was dull and heavy. He gives, however, a few touches of biographical and historical interest but they are buried beneath heaps of words which challenge the patience even of the most persistent reader.

5

Dennis reasserted his interest in the usefulness of the stage by publishing in 1706 *An Essay on the Operas After the Italian Manner, which are about to be establish'd on the English Stage: With some Reflections on the Damage which they may bring to the Publick.*[31] This work has not previously been included in a Collier Bibliography but it deserves a place there not only because it attacks the English Operas which threaten to overthrow the English Stage and to establish a diversion of far more pernicious consequences than the most licentious play that ever yet appeared on the English Stage, but also because it condemns the stage-reformers—"the two or three formal affected Bigots" —who have laid the axe to the play-house,[32] and because it censures the folly of destroying plays and the theatre.[33]

Dennis, from the very first lines of his preface, is careful to point out that he is writing in no way against the drama but only "against those Operas which are entirely Musical;[34] he proves, too, that he is bitterly hostile to the reformers who

> "have endeavour'd to contradict all these [the monarchs, ministers, philosophers who have encouraged plays] and the com-

---

[30] *Ibid.,* p. 124.
[31] This *Essay,* first printed in 1706, is eighteen pages in length and has an eight-page preface. It is no longer available in the 1706 edition but has been preserved in the 2-volume set of *The Select Works of Mr. John Dennis,* printed by John Darby in Bartholomew-Close, 1718.
[32] J. Dennis, *An Essay on the Operas,* pp. 444-447.
[33] *Ibid.,* pp. 445-447.
[34] *Ibid.,* p. 444.

mon Sense of Men, and upon a pretence of making all Men good Christians."[35]

He states the consequences of this attack on the stage:

"The Consequence of their [Collier's, R - - - - th's, Bedford's] Writings has been, that Plays have been for some Years discourag'd, and Diversions establish'd in the room of them, that have really been, and are like to be ten times more prejudicial to the Publick than ever Plays were pretended to be."[36]

He gives detailed attention to the evils which have followed in the wake of the stage-reformation and discourses both on the nature of pleasure as well as on the part that reason plays in pleasure, and on the importance to the English nation of the pleasures derived from the stage.[37] Of those diversions which have supplanted the play-house, Dennis decries gaming as having done unspeakable harm to both sexes in every part of the town[38] and he paints a picture of the pernicious results of the Italian Opera which has been established in place of plays and which has proved more baneful to morals than the "most licentious play that ever appear'd upon the stage."[39]

Dennis here, as in his other defences of the stage, argues in scholarly manner. He pleads for the drama, declaring that in his attack on a popular and prevailing caprice—the opera—he is presuming

"to defend the *English* Stage, which together with our *English* Liberties has descended to us from our Ancestors; to defend it against that Deluge of mortal Foes, which have come pouring in from the Continent, to drive out the Muses, its old Inhabitants, and seat themselves in their stead."[40]

He laments the degeneracy of the noble art of music; he declares his awareness of the fact that in whatever countries operas have been established after the manner of Italy they have driven out poetry from

---

[35] *Ibid.*, p. 446.
[36] *Ibid.*, p. 446. It is interesting to observe that Dennis retains all his opinions about the consequences of suppressing the play-house. He had expressed them in his *Usefulness of the Stage*, 1698, and in his *Person of Quality's Answer to Mr. Collier's Letter* published in 1705, and he repeats them here.
[37] *Ibid.*, pp. 444-45. Dennis' discourse here is very much the same as that he gave in the *Usefulness of the Stage*, pp. 1-10.
[38] *Ibid.*, pp. 446-7.
[39] *Ibid.*, p. 447.
[40] *Ibid.*, p. 453.

among that people; he boasts that at the beginning of the war the English were perhaps the only people in Europe who could justly glory in freedom or in poetry.[41] He concludes his Essay by eulogizing a young lady of the first quality who had given very strict order that the *Julius Caesar* of Shakespeare should be acted without singing or dancing:

> "Which order has shewn, that she is as much distinguish'd by the Beauty of her Mind, as by that of her Person."[42]

6

"The Stage Vindicated: A Satyr. By I. H. Esq." occurs in *The Muses Mercury* for July, 1707.[43] Before introducing the satyr the editor states briefly that the stage needs reformation but that popular feeling is hostile towards the reformers who would silence the stage-poets. He asks two pertinent questions of those who censure theatrical entertainments: 1. "Is it not necessary for those who have leisure time that they spend it in some useful recreation?" and 2, "Is there any more instructive form of entertainment than that which a regulated stage offers?"[44]

The poem itself is a caustic attack on Collier, Bedford, and on all those who second "Reformation of Manners." Of Collier, I. H. says:

> "Are Coll - - r and his Crew in such Esteem,
> That we must raze our Theatres for them?
>
> . . .
>
> I laugh to hear a common Cheat declare
> Against the Lewdness of a Play or Play'r:
> To see a proud *Absolving Priest* pretend,
> That *Haynes* was not so good a Saint as *Friend*."[45]

He refers to Bedford and his profuse marginal notes concerning suggestive plays:

> "Or a dull Vicar, to improve his Hint,
> Two thousand bawdy Texts produce in Print;

---

[41] *Ibid.*, pp. 453-5.
[42] *Ibid.*, p. 470.
[43] The "Satyr" is a poem of approximately 150 heroic couplets. The letters "I. H." are not identified by Cushing or by Stonehill, nor is the author suggested by Halkett and Laing.
[44] *The Muses Mercury*, p. 151.
[45] *Ibid.*, p. 153.

As if 'twas something that deserv'd our Praise,
For Priests, instead of *Pool,* to study *Bayes.*"[46]

The author gives some oblique political thrusts at Collier reminding him among other things, that he should have been more cautious than to begin a stage war inasmuch as the seeds of the mischief were planted in the reign of the Stuarts:

"But Collier should of all have taken care
The Crime which was his Monarch's Crime to spare;
Those Characters of which his Friends complain,
Are the true Pictures of that glorious Reign."[47]

He reproaches The Viewer for daring to censure those scenes which pleased Mary and which were allowed by Anne; he asserts that if farce and fustian were banished from the stage

"The Theatres would thrive, and Art succeed,
And Poets e're they write would learn to read."[48]

He enumerates the Greeks and Latins cited by Collier, and he devises a couplet to prove faulty the censure Collier had given to many of the Moderns. He intersperses his own acid reflections in condemnation of Chapter III of the *Short View.*[49]

7

Edward Filmer broke the comparatively long silence between the vindications published by the stage poets in reply to the *Short View* of 1698. After Collier's *Second Defence* of it in 1699 against Drake's *Antient and Modern Stages survey'd,* the poets had refrained from formal attack. True, there were many covert thrusts made at it and at its author but there was no open charge until 1707 when Filmer published his *A Defence of Plays: Or the Stage vindicated, From several Passages in Mr. Collier's Short View, . . .*[50]

---

[46] *Ibid.,* p. 153.
[47] *Ibid.,* p. 156.
[48] *Ibid.,* p. 160.
[49] *Ibid.,* pp. 152-160.
[50] The *Defence* is 167 pages long and has a 12-page preface. It was printed for Jacob Tonson. The work is interesting in that it is the last of the direct answers to Collier's *Short View* as well as in its being the work of the author to whom are ascribed two 1698 replies to Collier: *A Defence of Dramatick Poetry,* and *A Farther Defence.*

Quotations from the preface and from certain portions of the *Defence* itself show that the author is an admirer of Collier's learning and a respecter of his ability:

> "This [just Censure of those many and great Abuses of the modern stage] is indeed a very plausible Pretense, and not to be oppos'd without manifest Danger to the Opponent; especially when manag'd by a Man of Mr. Collier's Abilities. who is certainly a Person of great Parts, and good Learning;"[51]

but it shows him, too, a severe critic who differs from Collier on many points concerning plays and the characters in plays. In the opening lines Filmer stands shoulder-to-shoulder with Collier in admitting the many and great abuses which of late years have taken possession of the stage;[51a] he asserts, too, that when Collier's pamphlet first appeared, many of the poets took the alarm but only to defend themselves and their dramatic laurels:

> "For whilst every one flew to the Defence of his own particular Concern, the Stage was left naked, exposed to all the most furious Assaults of a violent and implacable Enemy: Or if by chance any one appear'd early in the Breach, 'twas only to defend the Stage with all its Abuses, without any Regard to such a convenient and due Regulation of it, as has been expected, and for a considerable time earnestly desir'd by the most sober and prejudic'd Part of the Nation."[52]

He refers to the lapse of time, between his determination to write his *Defence* and the completion of his work. However, he makes no reference—not even a remote one—to any earlier work in defence of the Stage.

> "In the mean time, above two Years slipt away, whilst they [the poets writing to defend the Stage with all its abuses] were still washing the Blackmore, and I still wavering, still in hopes that somebody of greater Abilities than myself, would *at last* attempt something in order to the *Reformation,* as well as the *Defence of the Stage.* But after so long an Expectation, noth-

---

[51] E. Filmer, *A Defence of Plays,* p. 2.
[51a] Edward Filmer, *A Defence of Plays,* Preface, p. i.
[52] *Ibid.,* pp. iii-iv. Here the author overlooks the 1698 *Usefulness of the Stage* —Dennis' plea for a regulated stage. He has excellent opportunity, too, to refer to *A Defence of Dramatick Poetry,* and were he the author of it, undoubtedly would have done so.

ing of that nature appearing, *I thought it high time, if at all, to set my Hand, how feeble soever, to the Work.* And this is the Reason why this Piece appears so late in the World."[53]

Following the example of most of the other vindicators of the stage, Filmer attacks Collier's non-jurancy, but unlike them he acknowledges his wit:

> "In a word he has attack'd us with the only Weapon they [those enemies of the Church who attack the Stage] never yet knew the Use of, I mean, Wit. Take away that, and you will see nothing in that celebrated Piece of his, but what has been before urg'd above a hundred times, and as often answer'd."[54]

Filmer bases the main discussions of his *Defence* upon the chapters of the *Short View.* He refutes Collier's arguments, one by one, and flippantly declares that a poet is permitted to give his characters some bold touches, i. e., touches of lewdness, atheism, and religious rants, but just enough to set those characters in a true light, and to give the spectators a right notion of the persons represened. He declares, too, that these touches should be carefully, nicely, and artificially managed.[55]

In his refutations of Collier's opinions on indecency, profaneness, and abuse of the clergy, Filmer gives little specific evidence of being the author of *A Defence of Dramatick Poetry,* or of a *Farther Defence.* However, in his discussion of Collier's "Opinion of the Pagans, of the Church, and State concerning the Stage" he brings in arguments that are almost identical with those advanced in *A Defence of Dramatick Poetry,* and he lists them in practically the same sequence and phraseology.[56]

Filmer's attack upon the stage is verbose, uninteresting, and devoid of any real merit. It adds but little to the arguments previously advanced either against Collier or in behalf of the stage.

---

[53] *Ibid.,* p. iv. Italics mine. The above quotation gives further ground for doubt as to Filmer's authorship of the two 1698 pamphlets ascribed to him. Why should he wish to come to the *Defence* of the stage if he already had written two voluble Defences?

[54] *Ibid.,* Preface, p. vi.

[55] *Ibid.,* p. 69.

[56] *Ibid.,* pp. 104-112; Anonymous, *A Defence of Dramatick Poetry,* pp. 18-33.

However, because Filmer is ordinarily associated with the 1698 *A Defence of Dramatick Poetry* and *A Farther Defence* the problem of the authorship of these pamphlets assumes new proportions here. Although there is a decided similarity between *A Defence of Dramatick Poetry* and *A Defence of Plays* in the chapters on "The Opinions of the Pagans, of the Church, and State Concerning the Stage" there are, nevertheless, three reasons that may be alleged against his authorship of the 1698 pamphlets; first, Collier in his *Farther Vindication,* 1708, does not hint that Filmer is the author of the previous *Defence of Dramatick Poetry* or of the *Farther Defence,* neither does he mention him in *A Defence of the Short View* or in *A Second Defence;* second, contemporaries who discuss Filmer's *A Defence of Plays* fail to list the 1698 works as his.[57] The third—and perhaps the weightiest —argument against Filmer's authorship is the fact that Filmer in his 1707 work takes no notice of the eighty pages of censure directed by Ridpath in *The Stage Condemned* against *A Defence of Dramatick Poetry* and *A Farther Defence.* If these attacked works were his he had splendid chance to vindicate himself in this *A Defence of Plays,* but he overlooks the attack and consumes 179 pages in attacking Collier's *Short View* and in defending the stage. It seems improbable that his silence under the censure would be due to an oversight.[57a]

The criticisms made upon Filmer by Professor Gosse and by D. C. Taylor are justifiable. The former calls him "a foolish and voluble creature, . . .[58] while the latter says of his *Defence* "[it] is worthless, for the thought is shallow, and the style flabby and absurdly ornate."

---

[57] Among the contemporaries whose opinion would bear weight would be the reviewer of Filmer's *A Defence of Plays.* In the *History of the Works of the Learned,* IX, 48-55, he gives a synopsis of this work and comments upon the length of time between the *Short View* (1698) and *A Defence of Plays* (1707). He makes no mention whatever of Filmer's having written either *A Defence of Dramatick Poetry* or *A Farther Defence,* nor does he intimate that he had previously come—in any way at all—to the defence of the stage. He *does* refer to replies evoked by the *Short View:* "It is needless to remind the World, that several Years ago, Mr. Collier publish'd [*A Short View of the Immorality and Profaneness of the English Stage*] which was received by the World with a general Applause, and was Answered by several Good Pens: To several of whom Mr. Collier made Counter Replys. . . ." p. 48.

[57a] Mr. Ballein, I believe, refers to this silence of Filmer.

[58] E. Gosse, *William Congreve,* 1924, p. 102.

8

Edward Filmer's *Defence of Plays*, published in 1707, did not pass unchallenged. The pugnacious stage-reformer had no intentions, even for a moment, of owning himself vanquished by the arguments of the learned Dr. Filmer. Summoning in behalf of the *Short View* his controversial weapons which had last been used in 1703-4, Collier wrote *A Farther Vindication of the Short View of the Profaneness and Immorality of the English Stage. In which the Objections Of a late Book, Entituled, A Defence of Plays, Are Consider'd.*[59]

Collier, with the customary heat which he had displayed in his vindications, begins:

> "Having receiv'd no Answer to my *Second Defence* of my *Short View*, etc. in seven years, I concluded the Stage-Controversie was over. But there's no reckoning upon the Intermissions of a Contest. Dr. Filmer has at last enter'd the Lists, and reviv'd the Quarrel,"[60]

and sarcastically refers by his quotation "Nonumq; prematur in annum" to the nine years leisure which Filmer had allowed himself to bring his thoughts to review and recollection.[61]

A Farther Vindication shows Collier at white heat against Filmer. It presents him dissecting, phrase by phrase, the Defender's vindications of those poets who take the liberty to present their characters under the disorders of profaneness and immorality; it presents him, too, justifying himself for citing in the *Short View* instances of scandal and profaneness. When the occasion arises he politely informs the Doctor that smut—regardless of its dress or veneer—may not be used; he asserts that the passions of men are in no need of suggestion or incitement inasmuch as they are prone to run too fast of themselves, and that fasting and mortification have formerly been deemed necessary for the security of virtue.[62]

---

[59] The pamphlet in question is forty-six pages in length, and was printed for R. Sare at Gray's-Inn-Gate in Holborn, and G. Strahan at the Golden Ball in Cornhill in 1708. Throughout his pamphlet Collier addresses Filmer by the title "Doctor," a title explained by Filmer's having taken his degree of D.C.L. at All Souls College, Oxford, in 1681. D. E. Baker, *Biographia Dramatica*, 1782, I, 164.

[60] J. Collier, *A Farther Vindication*, p. 3.

[61] *Ibid.*, pp. 3-4.

[62] *Ibid.*, pp. 27-28.

He bluntly tells his antagonist that he falls short of "Pagan Virtue" because his arguments when placed side by side with Livy's are off color: He says:

> "He [Filmer] lays it down for a Maxim that if *Smut and Profaneness* can't be allow'd, the *Poets must have few, or no Characters to practice on.* These things it seems are necessary Ingredients of Diversion, and Fundamental to the satisfaction of Mankind. But then to varnish over the Matter, he tells us, *Smut must not be out of Character, or too gross in Terms or Sense: But when 'tis wrap'd up in clean Linen, and lies in double Entendres, 'tis easie and natural, and he sees no great danger in it.* It may be so. However, Livy was not at all of the Doctor's mind,"[63]

He refers him to *A Defence of the Short View* and to *A Second Defence* if he would have a reply to his attack upon the authorities cited in Chapter VI of the *Short View.* Collier tells Filmer that inasmuch as his arguments are simply transcriptions of those formerly used by Dennis and Drake, he may apply to himself the answers there given to the same questions. [64]

In concluding, Collier states that a "Defence of the Play-House" is an impracticable undertaking; that ribaldry and profaneness will never pass undiscovered in a Christian country, and that all attempts to varnish over them with sophistry and distinction are bound to result in miscarriage and disappointment.[65]

Although Collier's *A Farther Vindication* is a repetition of most of his former arguments against plays it is important in the fact that it is the last of the direct answers which Collier published against the stage and to which he signed his name. It concludes a series of five acknowledged attacks: *A Short View,* 1698; *A Defence of the Short View,* Nov. 1698; *A Second Defence,* 1700; *A Dissuasive from the Play-House,* 1703; *A Farther Vindication,* 1708. In addition to these five, there were published during this decade two anonymous works of which I believe Collier to be the author: *A Letter to Mr. Congreve,* 1698, and *A Representation of the Impiety and Immorality of the English Stage,* 1704. Besides, I am of the opinion that Collier col-

---

[63] *Ibid.,* pp. 25-26.
[64] *Ibid.,* p. 35.
[65] *Ibid.* p. 46.

laborated with Willis in the writing of the *Occasional Paper Number IX, Containing some Considerations About the Danger of Going to Plays,* 1698, and that he published, in 1699, the Preface to the English translation of Bossuet's *Maximes et réflexions.* So that, in all, during the decade 1698-1708, Collier attacked the stage by a publication of eight pamphlets, and, in one instance, by collaborating with Willis.

CHAPTER XII

Publications from 1709 to 1719

1. T. D'Urfey: *The Old Mode and the New,* 1709.
2. Anonymous [J. Swift]: *A Project for the Advancement of Religion, and the Reformation of Manners,* Easter, 1709.
3. ———: *The Tatling Harlot,* {Part 1, Aug. 22, 1709 / Part 2, Aug. 26, 1709
4. Bourbon, Armand de: *The Works . . .* 1711. Translated from the French, To which are added some other Pieces, . . . never before published.
5. Anonymous [E. Settle]: *The City Ramble, or, A Play-House Wedding,* 1711.
6. A. Bedford: *The Great Abuse of Musick, . . .* 1711.
7. C. Cibber: *The Non-Juror,* acted in December, 1717.
8. Anonymous: *The Theatre-Royal . . .* By a Non-Juror, 1718.
9. W. Bulstrode: *The Charge . . . to the Grand Jury of Middlesex,* April 25, 1718.

The ten years which followed Collier's *Farther Vindication* were relatively calm ones in the stage controversy. There were but three attacks on the stage-reformers. Of these, two—*The City Ramble* and *The Non-Juror* show Settle and Cibber in hostile mood. The *Non-Juror* was aimed not so much at the stage as at the non-juring clergy in general and at Collier and Hickes in particular. It takes its place in the controversy, however, inasmuch as a counter-charge was returned to it with ammunition taken from the *Short View* by Collier. And Settle, in *The City-Ramble,* definitely intended to satirize Collier and the stage-reform movement.

D'Urfey's attacks on Collier in the Prologue and Epilogue of *The Old Mode and the New* were simply ill-humored grumblings of a hurt soldier against the opposing general, while two of the three extant numbers of the *Tatling Harlot* revived arguments concerning plays and players, and the purpose of plays found in the 1698 pro-Collier *Animadversions.* The remaining five works appearing in this chapter represent the labors of the reformers against profaneness, immorality, and abuse of the clergy.

I.

Collier's attack on D'Urfey in 1698 rankled deep. The vindication which the poet offered a few months later in his Preface to *The Campaigners* did not exhaust his ire, and, in consequence, we have echoes of it in his works throughout the first two decades of the eighteenth century. In the Prologue of his *The Old Mode and the New: Or, Country Miss with her Furbeloe, A Comedy, As it is Acted at the Theatre Royal By her Majesty's Servants*,[1] there is evidence that he resented the efforts of the reformers to cause deletion of portions of plays, that he placed at Collier's door the blame for starting stage-reformation, and that he realized the necessity of catering to an audience whose consciences had become sensitive on the subjects of immorality and profaneness.[2]

From censure of the Reformers in general the Prologue pays its caustic respects to Collier in particular:

"Our late absolving Saint new broach'd this Trade,
He that late, huge, false Dictionary made,
And left Reforming to be better paid."[3]

In the Epilogue there is another reference to Collier. It is freighted with the sarcasm which D'Urfey could so well employ when he remembered Collier's summary of his dramatic ability: *Vox, et praeterea nihil*.[4] The words are spoken by Miss Gatty who declares that in her audience is an incognito parson—a non-juror who is an enemy to plays:

"Yonder's a Non-Con Parson,—vads 'tis he
That catechized me so at Coventry.

---

[1] Printed for Bernard Lintott in 1709. Dedicated to Prince Charles, Duke of Richmond.

[2] Thomas D'Urfey, *The Old Mode and the New*, Prologue, pp. i-ii.

[3] *Ibid.*, p. ii. The three lines contain a four-fold criticism: first, a criticism of Collier's absolution in 1696 of Friend and Perkins; second, a criticism of his *Great Historical, Geographical, Genealogical, and Poetical Dictionary* of which two folio volumes were published in 1701, and because of complaints for inaccuracy and incompleteness, a *Supplement* had to be published in 1705; third, a criticism of Collier's apparent indifference to the progress of the stage reformation which he had begun in 1698, and during the last six years of which he had openly published only two attacks—The *Dissuasive*, and *A Farther Vindication*, and lastly, a criticism of Collier's mercenary motives in attacking the stage.

[4] J. Collier, *A Short View*, p. 208.

Nay,—you can't know him, for he's chang'd to Day,
And like true Shepherd clothed in Grey.
You,—Player Folks, take heed, he means ye harm,
Don't swear, nor say, a Pox, for he'll inform.
He hates all Oaths, and such rude blustering Folly;
But cants and lies like any Side-box Molly."[5]

2

There were many periodicals which saw the light in the first two decades of the eighteenth century. Some professed to be modeled upon the *Tatler* and the *Spectator;* others designed to caricature them. Some were advertised as giving spiritual advice to the doubting, some as admonishing the love-lorn, and some as retailing the gossip of the town. During the summer of 1709 there appeared *The Tatling Harlot, or, a Dialogue Between Bess O'Bedlam and her Brother Tom. By Mother Bawdycoat.* Its obvious purpose was, we are told, to parody the reforming aim of certain essayists, and in order to engage readers to subscribe, it selected such themes as "Drunkenness," "Marriage a Jest, Nowadays," etc.[6]

There are various topics—including actors and the stage—which Bess and Tom discuss. Their dialogue is a curious collection of excerpts taken promiscuously from the pro-Collier *Animadversions,* a 1698 pamphlet hostile to Congreve's *Amendments.* However, the chief claim which *The Tatling Harlot* has to a place in the Collier bibliography is by reason of the "Letter" of plays and players quoted as being Mrs. Bawdycoat's, but which is really a copy of the "Short Essay on the Stage" which concludes the *Animadversions* of 1698.[7]

Once again is proposed the topic of the purpose of plays—a topic on which Collier had, in the *Short View,* so caustically refuted Dryden:

"The use of the stage is to Instruct and delight, and where the Representation fails in either of these Points, it fails of the End;

---

[5] T. D'Urfey, *The Old Mode and the New,* p. vii.
[6] W. Graham, *The Beginnings of English Literary Periodicals,* p. 76. Mr. Graham tells us that *The Tatling Harlot* was a small four-page sheet, and that there are extant only three issues—that of August 22, of Aug. 26, and of Aug. 29, 1909. The periodical was printed and sold by J. Baker, at the Black-Boy in Pater-Noster Row.
[7] Anonymous, *The Animadversions,* pp. 73-87. The first five parts of the "Letter" are in the August 22 issue; the next seven parts appear in the August 26 issue.

for instruction (in a Theatre particularly) without Pleasure, is as Heavy, as Pleasure without Instruction is Light."[8]

Once again are cited the topics disputed in 1698 whereby the abuses committed in the theatre may be avoided: a player should not be a sharer; actors should never be characterized with more sense than they really have; actresses upon forfeiture of their virtue should be subjected to fine or, preferably, expelled from the theatre; a moderate share of the gains of the theatre should, by public orders, be set apart for some good use; players should be obliged to contribute toward charity a certain portion of every pound gained; the men should be seated separately from the women in the theatre, and strict censorship of plays should be enforced by the "Master of the Revels."

The very fact that a periodical such as the *Tatling Harlot* should quote from the pro-Collier *Animadversions* published eleven years before, and should, moreover, produce arguments which had been discussed during the heat of the controversy toward the close of the century shows that the embers of the stage-dispute were still smouldering.[8a]

3

Beljame calls attention to the interest displayed by Jonathan Swift both in the cause of reformation of manners and in the attack on the stage as is contained in his *A Project for the Advancement of Religion, and the Reformation of Manners. By a Person of Quality.*[9] Swift's discussion of the stage and of the reformation necessary if the English are to enjoy the diversion without jeopardy to their morals is given much in the manner of the *Short View* and the *Representation of the Impiety and Immorality of the English Stage.*[10]

The author calls attention to the indecency in language found in modern comedy, to its profanity, to the ridicule of the function of the priesthood, and to various other topics which were the distinct themes

---

[8] *The Tatling Harlot, August* 22, p. 4.

[8a] Cf. *The Muses Mercury,* 1707: ". . . the Occasion [the Clamour against the Stage] being still as crying as ever, . . . p. 151.

[9] A Beljame, *Le Public et Les Hommes,* p. 257. The *Project* is a 24-page pamphlet published anonymously in 1709 and "printed by H. Hills . . . For the Benefit of the Poor." E. Arber, in *Term Catalogues,* III, 637, tells us that it was printed at the Easter term of 1709. Both Beljame and Arber say that Swift is the author. However, the *Dictionary of Anonymous and Pseudonymous Literature,* IV, 441, ascribes it to J. Swift *or* to Thomas Lewis. The *Project* is addressed to the Countess Berkeley.

[10] J. Swift, *A Project,* p. 16.

of Collier and Bedford in their attacks on modern comedy;[11] he makes, besides, pertinent critical reflections on the character of a hero in tragedy and in comedy,[12] and remarks that the English poets prior to the reign of Charles II never suffered a criminal amour to succeed upon the stage,[13] but that since then many vices prevail in the theatre and will continue to thrive as long as the court is content to connive at or neglect them.[14] Strict censorship, he suggests, is the only remedy for existing play-house evils.

4

We are told that the Prince of Conti was born in 1629 and died in 1666, that he became exceedingly devout toward the end of his life, and that his works breathe his austerity of spirit. One of the works which concern us was published in Paris the year after his death under the title *Traité de la comédie et des spectacles, selon la tradition de l'Eglise*.[15] This work together with his other writings was translated from the French, and in 1711 the collection was published in London under the title: *The Works of the Most Illustrious and Pious Armand de Bourbon, Prince of Conti. With a Short Account of his Life, Collected and Translated from the French. To which are added some other pieces, and a Discourse of Christian Perfection, by the Archbishop of Cambray. Never before Published.*

Inasmuch as the censure of the play-house and of plays by the Prince of Conti as contained in *The Works* above mentioned antedates the Collier Controversy by more than thirty years, it does not deserve a place in my bibliography. However, because in the volume there are "Other Pieces and a Discourse of Christian Perfection" which were not published until 1711, and because several of these pieces are relevant to our present discussion, I include the volume. The book is a collection of pieces each paged separately, hence is impossible to give the reader intelligible pagination.

One of the interesting pieces included in the volume is a five-page narrative of "The Decrees of the Councils Concerning Plays and Publick Shews." In the article we find listed the six Councils to

---

[11] *Ibid.*, p. 16.
[12] *Ibid.*, p. 17.
[13] *Ibid.*, p. 17.
[14] *Ibid.*, p. 17.
[15] *Biographie Universelle, Ancienne et Moderne;* IX, 511.

which Collier makes reference in Chapter VI of the *Short View*. The volume contains, also, "The Sentiments of the Fathers Relating to Plays and Publick Shews" to which there is a 15-page Advertisement. Exclusive of the Advertisement there are seven pages of excerpts taken from the writings of St. Augustine, St. Cyprian, Tertullian, and St. Chrysostom, all of which give the anti-stage arguments found frequently in the writings of Collier, of Bedford, and of Bossuet. It is not amazing that Bossuet and his French abettors should, in the controversy of 1694, have been conversant with the Prince of Conti's *Traité de la comédie;* it is worth noting, however, that Collier was apparently acquainted with it and the "Other Pieces" before they were published in 1711.

5

Although Elkanah Settle was late in entering the stage-controversy, his entrance was, nevertheless, certain, and possessed of all the assurance which might be expected in one who was confident that an attack upon Collier would be popular among the wits he strove to please. He was unpopular and he realized it. Despite the literary handicaps he labored under he comes into the ranks against Collier and stage-reform by the publication of his five-act comedy *The City-Ramble: or, A Play-House Wedding, A Comedy, As it is Acted at the Theatre Royal; by Her Majesty's Company of Comedians*.[16]

The play is anonymous and undated. Mr. Krutch calls attention to this fact and suggests as a reason for its anonymity the unpopularity of the author.[17] The date of publication, however, has been the topic of much interested discussion on the part of scholars. Mr. F. C.

---

[16] The plot is based upon two plays of Beaumont and Fletcher: *The Knight of the Burning Pestle,* and *The Coxcomb.* Settle's indebtedness to Beaumont and Fletcher and his indignation at the lack of appreciation previously accorded his dramatic endeavours are confessed in his preface: "I must first acknowledge that I set Pen to Paper upon the Recommendation of my good friend Mr. Booth had given me two of the Plays of Beaumont and Fletcher, viz. *The Knight of the Burning Pestle* and *The Coxcomb;* from whence he thought I might borrow some small Foundation, and perhaps some little Fabrick-work toward a Comedy. . . . Having now by me some finished Pieces that have lain long dead upon my Hands, through my Exclusion from the Stage, I resolved to write this with that Silence and Secrecy, as to be able to surmount all Opposition, by bringing it into Sight by an adopted Father's Hand." E. Settle, *The City Ramble,* Preface, pp. i-ii.

[17] J. Krutch, *Comedy and Conscience,* p. 266.

Brown who published in 1910 his study, *Elkanah Settle, His Life and Works,* says:

> "Hazlitt gives the date as 1704; Ward, *History of English Dramatic Literature,* II, 681, as 1710; but the commonly accepted date of presentation and publication is 1711, (cf. Genest, *Some Account of the English Stage,* II, 482;. The *Biographia Dramatica,* II, 106; *Notitia Dramatica,* I, 58). There can be little doubt that 1711 is the correct date."[18]

Mr. Krutch, also, is of the opinion that 1711 is the date. He disagrees with Ballein who asserts that the play must have appeared earlier than August 17, 1711, which is the date Genest gives it.[19]

The prologue as well as the play itself is intensely hostile both to Collier and to the stage-reform movement. Statements made by one or other of the characters refute the chapters of the *Short View* and reiterate the arguments used by previous stage vindicators, adding at the same time, several distinctive touches to the caricature which had been drawn of Collier. The acid with which Settle writes resembles that which Brown had injected into his play, *Stage Beaux,* in 1704.

A glance at the nine works which are listed in the bibliography from 1709-1719 shows that Settle's comedy is the most direct refutation of the *Short View* published in ten years, and that it is rather unevenly balanced by the publications of the reformers. If *The City Ramble* was *published* in 1711 as is the opinion of the greater number of scholars, its plot may have been conceived and parts of it written in the early years of the stage-controversy, especially since Settle himself says in his preface:

> "Having now by me some finished Pieces that have lain long dead upon my Hands, through my Exclusion from the Stage,

---

[18] F. C. Brown, *Elkanah Settle,* pp. 105-106
[19] Mr. Krutch says: "Ballein finds support for his belief in Baker's 'Companion to the Play-House' which in one place gives the date as 1699, and then in another place leaves the play undated. The unsupported statement of an eighteenth century bibliography is not worth much, and a glance at contemporary newspapers will reveal several statements like the following: 'Never acted before. At the Theatre-Royal and Drury Lane, this present Friday, being the 17th of August, (1711), will be presented a new comedy call'd The City Ramble; or A Play-House Wedding.' " J. K. *Comedy and Conscience,* p. 266.

I resolved to write this with that Silence and Secrecy, as to be able to surmount all Opposition, by bringing it into Sight by an adopted Father's Hand."[20]

6

To include in the Collier Controversy Bedford's treatise on music may seem at first sight to be straining a point. However, it deserves a distinct place among the anti-stage pamphlets, and this for several reasons. First, Collier in his *Short View* had discoursed at length upon "Play-House Music" and upon the "Airy and Galliardizing Nature of Tunes" in modern comedy;[21] secondly, he had been asked by the "Society for Promoting Christian Knowledge" to write upon the subject. We have this information recorded in the minutes of the Society:

> "Sept. 25, 1712. That he [Robert Nelson], had according to the desire of the Society endeavored to engage Mr. Collier to prepare a Treatise on the Abuse of Music; but that he was at present so taken up in finishing his *Ecclesiastical History,* that he was obliged by his booksellers not to undertake any other work till that was finished."[22]

A further perusal of the minutes of this Society reveals that the actual request made to Collier by Nelson for a discourse on the "Abuse of Music" was the result of a well-formulated plan sponsored by Dr. Higden and Mr. Nelson. The entry for July 31, 1712 reads:

> "Agreed, that Dr. Higden and Mr. Nelson be desired to engage the Rev. Mr. Collier to write a small Treatise, proper to be put into the hands of organists, and other Musick-Masters, to dissuade them from teaching lewd songs, and composing tunes to obscene ballads or songs."[23]

Bedford's treatise on the same topic, "The Abuse of Music" appeared in 1711 under a title that would repel all but the most ardent readers: *The Great Abuse of Musick. In Two Parts. Containing An Account of the Use and Design of Musick among the Antient Jews, Greeks, Romans, and others; with their Concern for, and Care to*

---

[20] E. Settle, *The City Ramble,* pp. i-ii.
[21] J. Collier, *A Short View,* pp. 277-280.
[22] C. E. Secretan, *Memoirs of the Life and Times of the Pious Robert Nelson,* p. 69.
[23] *Ibid.,* p. 117.

prevent the Abuse thereof. And Also An Account of the Immorality and Profaneness which is occasioned by the Corruption of that most Noble Science in the Present Age.[24] It is dedicated to the "Much Esteemed Society for Promoting Christian Knowledge." Now, the fact that Collier had been asked by this same Society to write on the same topic but had refused to do so naturally leads one to question whether or not Bedford was asked as a substitute for Collier. The discrepancy in dates can hardly give "yes" as an answer. The minutes of the Society recording the request to Collier are dated July and September of 1712; Bedford's work was published in 1711. However, there is something significant in the title of Bedford's work, and a comparison of it with Collier's *A Short View of the Immorality, and Profaneness of the English Stage, Together With the Sense of Antiquity upon this Argument* indicates that it is not unlikely that Collier's work was the model by which Bedford planned his.

This was not Bedford's first discourse on music. In addition to spending much time and ink in advancing the cause of Collier and in fulminating against modern plays he studied extensively, and, during his life, wrote thrice on the subject of church music. We read that

> "His aim was to promote a purer and simpler style of religious music. He published *The Temple Musick,* Bristol, 1706, *The Great Abuse of Music,* 1711, and *The Excellency of Divine Music,* 1733."[25]

Bedford divides his book into two parts[26] and both divisions are replete with evidence that the author is not only attacking modern playhouse music—and attacking it from Collier's vantage-points of immodesty, profaneness, immorality, and antiquity,—but that he is giving,

---

[24] The book is 276 pages long and was printed by J. H. for John Wyatt in 1711. The authorship is claimed by "Arthur Bedford, M. A. *Chaplain to His Grace* Wriothesly *Duke* of Bedford, and *Vicar* of Temple *in the City of Bristol.*" Bedford held for twenty-four years this chaplaincy.

[25] *D.N.B.,* II, p. 109. It is worthy of note that there are extant records of an increasing interest in the early eighteenth century on the question of "The Lawfulness of Music." One such record occurs in the *History of the Works of the Learned,* II, 299 (April,1700) and it concerns Henry Dodwell's *The Lawfulness of Instrumental Musick in Holy Offices.*

[26] A. Bedford, *The Great Abuse of Musick,* Part I, pp. 1-61; Part II, pp. 62-235. The conclusion—pp. 235-268 contains 13 proposals for regulating the abuses of music and for promoting the ancient design "of this most noble Science." Besides, the author appends to his treatise seven pages of music which are a "Canon of Four Parts in One according to Mr. Purcell's Rule of Fuging."

likewise, a history of the art of music and a display of his own knowledge and proficiency in it. They prove, too, that the author bemoans
the degeneracy of the art which at one and the same time is capable of
producing a concord of sweet sounds, of delighting the angels and of
inspiring martyrs; they show that. he laments that the organ which
may be used as a tool to promote the interests of the harpsichord and
spinet should be made an instrument for teaching only the play-house
tunes, and for making church-music an introduction "to the other
place."[27]

7

In order to understand the Collierite attack on Cibber in 1718 as
contained in the pamphlet *The Theatre Royal*, it is necessary to know
a few facts about *The Non-Juror* which evoked it. *The Non-Juror, A
Comedy. As it is Acted at the Theatre-Royal, By His Majesty's Servants*,[28] was intended by Cibber not only to satirize the body of nonjurors in London[29] and to bring into disrepute *The Case of Schism*,[30]
but also, according to his own confession, to depict in the character of
Doctor Wolfe,

> "an English popish priest lurking under the doctine of our own
> Church to raise his own fortune upon the ruin of a worthy
> gentleman, whom his dissembled sanctity had seduced into the
> treasonable cause of a Roman Catholic outlaw."[31]

In order to understand the malignity in an attack of this kind and
the results accruing from it, one should recall three facts about the

---

[27] *Ibid.*, p. 209.
[28] Printed for B. Lintott at the Cross-Keys in Fleet-Street, 1718. It was acted at
at D. L. in Dec. 1717. A. Nicoll, *XVIII Century Drama*, p. 312.
[29] Their archbishop at the time was Jeremy Collier. *D.N.B.*, IV, 801.
[30] The author, according to evidence found in the *Theatre Royal*, was Bishop
Hickes. Cf. also, *D.N.B.*, (1891) XXVI, 354.
[31] C. Cibber, *An Apology*, ed by R. W. Lowe, II, 186. The parallel between
Cibber's character and Collier is too striking to be overlooked. Collier was
in 1718 living the life of an outlaw; he had been accused of being an Anglican priest with "Romish" tendencies; he was at that very time engaged in
a controversy concerning the *Four Usages* which was further emphasizing his
Romish views and his "Separation tendencies." Besides, he had been consecrated in 1713 by Hicks, an eminent non-juror whom Cibber was openly
attacking in the play, *The Non-Juror*, p. 3; p. 25. That Hickes, too, was
accused of leaning toward Catholicism we learn from Canon Overton. *The
Non-jurors, Their Lives, Principles and Writings*, p. 93. The acidity of
Cibber's attitude here corresponds with that which he had displayed toward
Collier in his Dedicatory Epistle to *Love Makes a Man*, 1700.

nonjurors in 1717: first their number as well as their moral and intellectual calibre; secondly, the hostile political feeling against them, and lastly, the penalties to which the law subjected them. Information concerning the first fact, the number and qualifications of the nonjurors, may be obtained from Overton and Relton:

"The two Universities, in which all the clergy had been trained, Oxford especially, and Cambridge to a greater extent than is commonly supposed, were honey-combed with Jacobitism, and the result was a growing alienation between the higher and the lower clergy. . . . These [Jacobites] were of two classes. . . . The Non-Jurors, who were churchmen to the backbone in the spiritual sense of the term, but who were temporarily alienated from the national establishment. Their alienation was intensified greatly by the accession of the House of Hanover. . . . They contained within their ranks some of the very ablest and some of the saintliest churchmen in the kingdom. Such men as Robert Nelson, Jeremy Collier, Nathaniel Spinckes, William Law, Charles Leslie, Thomas Baker, Thomas Brett, etc. And the worst of it was that they carried with them that element of the recognition of the principle of continuity, which was so grievously and glaringly lacking, that element which linked the church of the Georgian era with the church of the Primitive Fathers of the first three centuries."[32]

Concerning the second fact, the hostile political feeling against the nonjurors, Lathbury tells us:

"Many severe reflections were cast upon the Nonjurors, as if they were determined to overturn the government. The great majority, however, had no such desire,"[33]

and again, we read that the Rebellion of 1715 served but to intensify political feeling against them.[34]

Concerning the penalties to which the nonjurors were liable by law, we learn from a Broadside printed in 1710, entitled *A Proclamation by the Queen,* and signed "Given at our Court at St. James's this

---

[32] Overton and Relton, *The English Church,* p. 59.
[33] T. Lathbury, *History of the Nonjurors,* p. 198. Note 1.
[34] *Ibid.,* pp. 250-252. Further information concerning the Rebellion is found in Lowe's edition of *An Apology for the Life of Mr. Colley Cibber.*

second Day of March. In the Eighth Year of Our Reign," that a reward was offered to such as shall discover and seize

"Papists, Nonjurors, and other Enemies to our Title and Government . . . as have been the Occasion of the said late Tumults and Disorders."[35]

And from a sermon preached by Benjamin Hoadley we read that any of the

"Non-juring Clergy who neglect or refuse to take the Oaths, . . . are hereby adjudged deprived of His and Their Offices, Benefices, Dignities, and Promotions Ecclesiastical."[36]

Such being the state of affairs it is easy to see that Cibber realized the personal advantages to be derived from an attack on the nonjurors: first, he would secure the favor of the king and probably a reward; secondly, his comedy would be certain to arouse the interest of London play-goers, and, in consequence, there would be a crowded house, an ambition which all playwrights cherished. His calculations were verified, for he himself tells us that the play was acted for eighteen days running,[37] and that the king to whom he dedicated it was present at the performance.[38] We learn, besides, that the king rewarded his work with a gift of two hundred pounds and later with the poet-laureateship.[39]

The Dedicatory Epistle breathes throughout a tone of fulsome flattery; the Prologue, spoken by N. Rowe is caustic in its reference to papists and nonjurors; it is conciliatory in regard to Whigs and Tories:

"ToNight, ye Whigs and Tories both be safe,
Nor hope, at one another's Cost, to laugh:
We mean to souse old Satan and the Pope;
They've no Relations here, nor Friends, we hope,
A Tool of theirs supplies the Comic Stage
With just Materials for Satyrick Rage:
Nor think our Colours may too strongly paint
The stiff *Non-juring Separation-Saint*."[40]

---

[35] *Proclamation by the Queen, Broadside*, 1710.
[36] Benjamin Hoadley, *A Preservative against the Principles and Practices of the Non-Jurors Both in Church and State*, p. 25.
[37] C. Cibber, *An Apology*, ed. by Lowe, II, p. 186.
[38] C. Cibber, *The Non-Juror*, Ded. Epistle, p. v.
[39] W. H. Adams, *Good Queen Anne*, II, 18.
[40] C. Cibber, *The Non-Juror*, p. viii. Italics mine.

In the play itself, Cibber invidiously portrays a nonjuror in the character of Doctor Wolf; through Doctor Wolf Cibber attacks that body of men whose conscience had bidden them refuse the oath of allegiance; through him he brings a clergyman on the stage to abuse him. Although the play proved a stepping-stone to remuneration and promotion, it nevertheless aroused violent antagonism, and Cibber was aware of it. He himself tells us that Mr. Mist, editor of the *Weekly Journal*, an anti-Hanoverian sheet, scarce ever failed for fifteen years following the publication of the *Non-Juror* to pass some of his party compliments upon him.[41] We learn, besides, from Mr. Lowe:

"There can be little doubt that the Non-Juror was one of the causes of Pope's enmity to Cibber. Pope's father was a Non-juror."[42]

Dennis, too, criticized caustically both Cibber and *The Non-Juror*.[43]

Last but not least C. Cibber and his play were subjected to a scathing rebuke from *A Nonjuror* who published his work under the title *The Theatre-Royal*. Although the pamphlet is anonymous I am firmly convinced that its author is Jeremy Collier. However, this pamphlet and the proof for my statement will form the topic of the following study.

8

Cibber's play, *The Non-Juror*, could not but arouse the vindictive ire of Jeremy Collier whose pen from 1698 to 1708 had been used in open castigation of those stage-poets whose comedies abuse the clergy and of those who "play upon the *character*, and endeavour to expose not only the *Men*, but the Business."[44] Not long after it was acted there appeared *The Theatre-Royal Turn'd into a Mountebank's Stage. In some Remarks upon Mr. Cibber's Quack-Dramatical Performance, called the Non-Juror. By a Non Juror.* It was not only a

---

[41] C. Cibber, *An Apology*, ed. by R. W. Lowe, II, p. 187. Curious it is to read that Mr. Mist inserted in his *Journal* a death-notice of Mr. Colley Cibber at the time he was acting the part of Dr. Wolf: "Yesterday died Mr. Colley Cibber, late Comedian of the Theatre-Royal, notorious for writing the *Non-Juror*." *Ibid.*, p. 188.

[42] C. Cibber, *An Apology*, II, 189, Note 1.

[43] John Dennis, *Letters, Familiar, Moral and Critical*, I, 141.

[44] J. Collier, *Short View*, p. 97.

scathing reply to Cibber but it was an eloquent appeal to the principles of justice which had been violated in regard to the nonjurors who

> "made not an exchange of the Good Things of this Life, such as Opulent Preferments, and the Favour of Courts, out of meer Caprice and Sourness of Temper;"[45]

it was a spirited defence of the character and function of the clergy in general, and of Hickes in particular. The author does not identify himself other than as a "Non-Juror," but even though he gives no open acknowledgment of his work there are in the pamphlet convincing marks of Collier's authorship.

Before enumerating these points, recall Cibber's intention to depict an "English popish priest lurking under the doctrine of our own Church," and to assail *The Case of Schism* with its author, Hickes. Recall, also, Cibber's actual degradation in the play of the function of the clergy and of all the ideals for which Collier had openly fought from 1698-1708. It takes no flight of fancy, then, to suppose that Collier would expose Cibber's offence and scourge the offender, nor that he would step from the ranks to vindicate himself, his brethren, and the late Bishop Hickes whose life was unblemished and whose *Case of Schism* was a tribute to a man's honest convictions. That he did reply by the pamphlet *The Theatre-Royal* is a matter of conviction with me. The reasons I allege for Collier's authorship are the following: first, its anonymity. Because of the dangers in which Jacobites and priests lived constantly, and, moreover, because the liberty of the press had been denied to Jacobites after the Rebellion of 1715, Collier in concealing his identity would be acting in accordance with the demands both of reason and prudence. To emphasize the need of prudence Collier had the example of the severe treatment meted out to the nonjuror, Lawrence Howell.[46] Again, Collier would

---

[45] Anonymous, *The Theatre Royal,* p. 4. The pamphlet is 38 pages in length. It was published in 1718.

[46] Information concerning this severity toward Howell may be had from Lathbury. He tells us that just at the time of the denial of the press to nonjurors, some crown messengers, searching for a paper called *The Shift Shifted,* found in a printing office a book entitled *The Case of Schism in the Church of England truly Stated.* The authorship was traced to Lawrence Howell, not only a nonjuror but a learned controversialist who wrote in support of his party. He was committed to Newgate for the offence, tried and convicted at Old Bailey, and sentenced to a fine of five hundred pounds, to three years imprisonment, to be whipped, degraded, and stripped of his gown by the

write anonymously because he would be unwilling to become involved in a dispute with the wits of the day when he was at the time fighting "The Four Usages" controversy.

Secondly, we should expect Collier to reply to an attack which struck at the very root of his principles of honor and justice; to an attack which assailed Bishop Hickes who in 1713 had consecrated him; to an attack which degraded the clergy both in their person and in the function of the priesthood. Now, a man like Collier who had in 1698 expressed so pointedly:

> "To wipe off Aspersions, and rescue things from Mistake, is but bare Justice: Besides, where the Honour of God, and the Publick Interest are concern'd, a man is bound to speak,[47]

was not to be imagined letting a play like *The Non-Juror* pass unrebuked. Then, too, not only Collier's moral principles but his literary and dramatic principles expressed frequently in the *Short View* had been violated in the *Non-Juror;* in consequence, one is not surprised to find scathing censure given to Cibber for the violation. The censure in *The Theatre-Royal* is Collierian both in content and in tone, and it is in exact accord with the censure found in Collier's previous antistage pamphlets. Note the following:

1. In *The Theatre-Royal* the author refers sarcastically to Cibber's rant contained in his Dedicatory Epistle to the King. p. 17.	1. In the *Short View*, p. 207, Collier refers caustically to D'Urfey's Dedication of *Don Quixote* to the Duchess of Ormond, and p. 194, to Dryden's rants in that of *Don Sebastian* and of *King Arthur*.

---

hands of the public executioner. When he asked "Who will whip a clergyman?" the court replied: "We pay no deference to your cloth, because you are a disgrace to it, and have no right to wear it: besides, we do not look upon you as a clergyman, in that you have produced no proof of your ordination, but from Dr. Hickes, under the denomination of the Bishop of Thetford: which is illegal, and not according to the constitution of this kingdom, which has no such Bishop." T. Lathbury, *A History of the Nonjurors*, pp. 252-3.

[47] J. Collier, *A Short View*, p. 137.

2. He mocks Cibber for the Prologue spoken by Mr. Rowe who professes to "souze Old Satan and the Pope." p. 18.

2. He mocks Dryden, Wycherley, and Congreve, for their Prologues and Epilogues "scandalous in the last degree," and he scathes D'Urfey for his Epilogue to *Don Quixote*. *A Short View*, p. 13; p. 199.

3. He reviews the original *Tartuffe* and then, act by act, compares the *Non-Juror* with it in order to prove that Cibber had no precedent in the original, and that in many instances he had desecrated Moliere's masterpiece. pp. 12-37.

3. He traces Dryden's *Amphytrion* to its original, Plautus; he analyzes Vanbrugh's *The Relapse*, act by act; he analyzes the Greek and Roman poets to prove that the Moderns have no precedent for their scurrility. *A Short View*, p. 179; p. 211; ff., pp. 119-122; p. 107; p. 111; p. 149; p. 159.

4. Even though the author's purpose is an attack on Cibber's *Non-Juror* as a comedy contrary to morality and respect for the clergy, the author frequently chides Cibber for poor dramatic principles. Among these we note his censure of Cibber's violation of

4. Even though his purpose in the *Short View* is moral reformation, Collier, nevertheless, attacks dramatic principles. Although I have previously mentioned these criticisms, I shall complete the present parallel by recalling his censure of the stage-poets' violation of

a. Propriety of manners; p. 15.

a. Propriety of manners; p. 35; p. 138; p. 165; p. 185.

b. Unity; p. 17
c. Probability; pp. 31-32.

b. The Unities; pp. 228-230.
c. Probability; pp. 212-216; p. 225.

d. The Laws of the Drama; p. 32.
e. Nature, and the rules of the stage; pp. 26-27; p. 32.

d. The Laws of the Drama; pp. 210-218.
e. Nature, and the rules of the stage; pp. 181-185; pp. 204-219; p. 225.

f. Incident; p. 35.
g. Treating disrespectfully persons of quality; pp. 31-32.

f. Incident; p. 215
g. Treating disrespectfully persons of quality; p. 16; p. 47; p. 141; pp. 143-144; p. 173; p. 175; p. 205.

5. He censures Cibber for bringing a clergyman upon the stage and there abusing him. pp. 19-20.

5. Throughout the *Short View* but especially in Chapter III, Collier upholds the dignity of the priesthood and censures the stage-poets for bringing clergymen upon the stage and there abusing them. pp. 97-139.

6. He praises Moliere for using "no smut from first to last, no oaths, execrations, or Double Entendres." p. 14.

6. Throughout the *Short View,* Collier lashes the English poets for using smut—Oaths, and double entendres. Chapters I, II. III, IV, V.

7. The author calls the playhouse a "Nursery of Vice and Debauchery." p. 1.

7. Collier in his *Short View* gives the play-house the same appellation. p. 221; p. 281.

8. The author praises Moliere for his regard for the priesthood and he borrows his compliment from the *Short View:*
"*Moliere* . . . who with his Countryman *Corneille,* n e v e r brings Priests of any kind upon the Stage." p. 37.
Besides, we have another glimpse of the author's high regard for Moliere:
"The *Non-Juror* looks faint and languid in comparison of *Tartuffe.*" p. 27.

8. Collier praises Moliere and Corneille for the same quality:
"The famous Corneille and Moliere bring no Priests of any kind upon the Stage." *A Short View,* p. 123.
Besides, in his other pamphlets, Collier gives the French poets similar tribute: *A Defence,* pp. 27-29; *A Farther Vindication,* p. 33.

We note, also, in the *Theatre-Royal* and in Collier's pamphlets the use of a similar vocabulary, of similar figures of speech, of balanced sentences, of the familiar staccato questions, and of the frequent introduction of sentences with "But." There are, besides, many interesting Collierian highlights to be observed in the pamphlet. Among them note: first, the author's attack of "the lewd Censures of a Set of profane *Comedians"* abusing the practices of holy men in Sacred

Orders;[48] secondly, observe his censure of Cibber's lack of charity, of his compassion for the sufferings of others, and of his regard for justice:

> "A man of any tolerable Compassion for the Sufferings of his Fellow-Creatures, would have reflected within himself, upon the Infirmities of Humane Nature, and the Scruples that put tender Consciences upon the Rack, before he enter'd upon so uncharitable an Undertaking. . . . Had this Tormentor of Moliere's Ghost been tolerably civil to the Remains of that excellent Poet, he would . . . have expos'd the Hypocrite, rather than have fallen foul upon the Divine, and have brought a *Real Imposter* upon the Stage, instead of fixing that Character upon a Person who has lost all the Conveniences of Life for not being one, for not prevaricating with his Conscience, and breaking thro' the Ties of the most sacred Engagements."[49]

Note in the third place his attack not only on the publisher of a contemporary periodical for an article praising the *Non-Juror,* but upon the article itself. The author accuses Cibber of having written this article a part of which is transcribed in the following excerpt:

> "tho there may have been many Comedies, wherein Nature has been as well represented, . . . there never has appear'd, since the Stage of *Athens,* . . . any Work of Wit so immediately and justly calculated for the Service of the Publick, [as the *Non-Juror*] . . . Mr. Cibber has that same Merit [the merit of Collier in writing the *Short View*] as he more than corrects the Stage by writing well for it, and has shewn himself unreservedly a Friend to the Government, in provoking a Crowd of its Enemies to exert their Malice against him, . . . Add to this, that he himself plays the Part of the *Nonjuror;* . . . Shakespeare [is] a greater Poet, tho' not so good a Player as Cibber, according to *Play-house Tradition,* . . . Let the Town then consider what they owe to the Merit of him who has wrote so usefully in this *Drama,* and acted so skillfully in all other Comedies, *that is to say,* has performed so well as a *Writer,* and so eminently as a *Player,* that in the latter he excelld' such a Genius as SHAKESPEAR, tho' the Art was also his Profession."[50]

---

[48] Anonymous, *The Theatre-Royal,* p. 1.
[49] *Ibid.,* pp. 4-5.
[50] *Ibid.,* pp. 8-10.

The reply is not only sarcastic but is in exact accord with previous replies made by Collier to Congreve, Vanbrugh, Dennis, Drake and Filmer. The author of *The Theatre-Royal* asserts:

"Tho' the Name of the Writer of the foregoing Letter is not hereunto subscribed, it may with Justice enough be suppos'd to be written by Mr. *Cibber* himself, whose vanity is too well known in many Instances of the like Nature, not to have prompted him to very large Eulogies of himself."[51]

Of course, a reference to the stage of Athens would evoke from Collier a special mention, and the author here makes it:

"no one but he, or the Person to whom it is directed to, could have the Presumption to aver, that no one Performance on the Stage, since that of *Athens,* (whose Poets were under the greatest Restrictions from ridiculing the Priesthood) came up to the Perfection of Wit, and was so immediately calculated for the Service of the Publick as this, which he has most audaciouly adopted for the Issue of his own Brain, at the same time he has scarce any Right or Title to any one Thought or Incident that offends not chast Ears, nor violates the Laws of Decency and Morality."[52]

Note fourthly, the author's alteration of some "invectives written by Thomas Brown upon D'Urfey." They bespeak the ready sarcasm of Collier for his previous victims:

"Thou Cur, half Dane, *half* English *Breed,*
Thou Mongrel of Parnassus,
To think leud Lines grown up to Seed,
Can ever tamely pass us.

Thou write Nonjurors, *and be damn'd!*
Write Anagrams for Cutlers;
None with thy Frippery will be shamm'd
But Chamber-maids and Butlers.

In t'other World expect dry Blows,
No tears can wash thy Stains out,
Moliere *will pull thee by the Nose,*
And Shakespeare *dash thy Brains out."*[53]

---

[51] *Ibid.,* p. 10.
[52] *Ibid.,* pp. 10-11.
[53] *Ibid.,* p. 12.

Fifthly, Cibber's quotation of Greek words put into the mouth of Maria, would offer tempting opportunity to Collier both for comment and for a display of learning in tracing these words to their source. The author here grasps the opportunity to remark upon the words and upon Cibber's lewdness in making a lady of quality use them. Besides, he traces them to Juvenal.[54] Note, sixthly, that the author in referring to a "Key to Mr. Cibber's *Nonjuror*" sarcastically adds: "which has no such thing as a lock to it."[55]

The last and possibly the weightiest reason I allege in favor of Collier's being the author of *The Theatre Royal* is that in the conclusion of this pamphlet the greater part of two pages is taken verbatim from Collier's *A Short View*.[56]

The argument may be advanced that the Non-Juror who wrote the *Theatre-Royal* need not necessarily have been Collier; that the author plagiarized from the *Short View*. I am not of that opinion because throughout *The Theatre-Royal*, the author censures the plagiarism of Cibber. Note the following six quotations substantiating this statement:

1. "if a piece of *Plagiarism* may be so called that is as abhorrent of Reason and right Application, as of Truth and Humanity. . . ."[57]

2. "he, neither in *Prologue, Epilogue,* or *Dedication,* acknowledges the least Obligation to the deceas'd Author from whom he took all his best Hints, and most beautiful Turns; . . ."[58]

3. "the pilfering *Maroder,* that purloins all his Incidents from him [Moliere] even from the Beginning to the End."[59]

4. "the *Rib* of a play, called the *Nonjuror,* surreptitiously taken out of *Moliere's Side,* and converted into an Image for the Enemies of Religion to gaze at."[60]

---

[54] *Ibid.,* p. 21.
[55] *Ibid.,* p. 33. From Van Laun we learn something of interest concerning this "Key." He tells us: "It is said that Pope wrote a *Compleate Key to the Nonjuror* under the name of Joseph Guy, in which a comparison is drawn—and not in the choicest language— . . . between Moliere's *Tartuffe* and Cibber's *Nonjuror,* greatly to the disadvantage of the latter." J. B. Moliere, *The Dramatic Works,* translated and edited by Henri Van Laun, IV, p. 123.
[56] *The Theatre Royal,* pp. 37-38; *A Short View,* p. 123; pp. 138-9.
[57] Anonymous, *The Theatre-Royal,* p. 3.
[58] *Ibid.,* p. 11.
[59] *Ibid.,* p. 17.
[60] *Ibid.,* p. 17.

5. "Not but the *French* Author and *English Plagiary* tally very fitly together, and come up to each other almost Verbatim as to the Expression and way of Dialogue in most Places, . . ."[61]

6. "if the Reader, will take the Pains to examine the Comedy, from which Mr. *Cibber* has topp'd the Town, by filching his chief Characters, . . . "[62]

Considering Collier's pugnacity and his vindictiveness, considering his loyalty to his principles and to Bishop Hickes, one expects from him a reply to Cibber. *The Theatre-Royal* is this reply; it is a caustic attack on Cibber for breaches of modesty, morality, and respect for the clergy; it is an attack on incorrect literary principles and on plagiarism, and in the attack we note the same echoes which had sounded in the *Short View*. Add to this the fact that there are transcribed from the *Short View* several pages which Collier had written in 1698 as the climax of his attack on the poets who abused the clergy and we have reasonable grounds for believing that the Non-Juror who wrote the pamphlet *The Theatre-Royal* was the Archbishop of the Nonjurors, Jeremy Collier.

9

The author of the anonymous pamphlet *Of Plays and Masquerades,* 1719, quotes from Bulstrode's *Charge . . . to the Grand Jury of Middlesex,* "One Play-House ruins more Souls than fifty Churches are able to save." Two years later, the author of the *Conduct of the Stage Consider'd* places the same quotation on the title-page of his book. Inasmuch as contemporary evidence points to Bulstrode's *Charge* as an anti-stage pamphlet it is necessary to see what claim it has to a place in the Collier controversy.

Whitelocke Bulstrode was Chairman of the 1718 Sessions at Middlesex and was petitioned on April 25, 1718, by the Grand Jury to print the charge which he had delivered in his address to the jurors and constables a few days before. The petition is signed by twenty-three names. Bulstrode agreed and the publication appeared under the title "*The Charge of Whitelocke Bulstrode, Esq., to the Grand-Jury, and other Juries, of the County of Middlesex. At the General Quarter-*

---

[61] *Ibid.,* p. 25.
[62] *Ibid.,* p. 6.

Sessions of the Peace, Held April 21st, 1718, at Westminster Hall."
He inserted in the Introduction a copy of the petition and the twenty-
three signatures, and it is from this source that we derive the above
information.[63]

Bulstrode's *Charge* is divided into three parts each of which is
minutely subdivided. The first part outlines the duty of the jurors in
what relates to the Divine Majesty; the second in what relates to his
Vicegerent, the King, and the third in what relates to their fellow-
subjects.[64] Bulstrode reminds the jury of its obligations to suppress
immorality and vice, and to act at all times in the interests of religion;[65] he likewise cautions the jurors to legislate against bawdy-houses,
ale-houses, night walkers, and play-houses[66] telling them: "One Play-
House ruins more Souls, than fifty Churches are able to save,"[67]
and we recognize at once the source of the quotation referred to in the
opening paragraph of the present discussion.

From the tone of the whole *Charge,* from the author's insistence
on the preventing of vice, impiety, immorality, profanity, and blasphemy—especially in the play-house—we can understand why the
pamphlet gained great popularity with the reformers who cherished
the like opinions and who attacked the like vices.

---

[63] The *Charge* is a 39-page pamphlet, and is dedicated by an 8-page epistle to
the Right Honourable James Montague, Knight. It was printed for J. Brown
at the Black Swan without Temple-Bar.

W. Bulstrode was a controversialist and a mystical writer. His father,
Richard, was a Jacobite and followed King James to St. Germains. Whitelocke
was not sympathetic with his father's Jacobitical views, however. *D.N.B.,* III,
p. 260.

[64] *Ibid.,* pp. 4-9.
[65] *Ibid.,* pp. 10-15.
[66] *Ibid.,* pp. 34-35.
[67] *Ibid.,* p. 35.

CHAPTER XIII

Publications from 1719 to 1726

1. Anonymous [C. Gildon]: *The Post-Man Robb'd of his Mail*: . . . 1719; IV, 212-219.
2. A. Bedford: *A Serious Remonstrance* . . . 1719.
3. Anonymous: *Occasional Paper, Vol. III, Number IX. Of Plays and Masquerades*, 1719.
4. Anonymous: *Stage Plays Justly Condemned*, 1720.
5. Dennis and Gildon: *A New Project for Regulating the Stage. A Satire.* 1720.
6. Anonymous: *The Conduct of the Stage Consider'd*, . . . 1721.
7. Heydegger: *Letter to the Bishop of London*, 1724.
8. Anonymous: *A Seasonable Apology for Mr. H - g - r*, . . . 1724.
9. W. Law: *The Absolute Unlawfulness of the Stage-Entertainment*, . . . 1726.
10. Anonymous: *Law Outlaw'd:* . . . *Written at the Request of the Orange-Women*, 1726.
11. J. Dennis: *The Stage Defended*, . . . 1726.

In the Collier Controversy pamphlets published during the years 1719-1726 we observe a pretty even balance between the efforts of the reformers and those of the stage-defenders. Gildon and Dennis are the outstanding stage-champions of this period while Bedford and Law appear openly on the side of reform. There are several anonymous defenders of the stage but their defences are counterbalanced by the attacks of several anonymous reformers. Two of these attacks on the stage, *Of Plays and Masquerades* and *The Conduct of the Stage Consider'd*, are of special importance in that they bear conclusive evidence of being the work of Collier, and prove that he was working, though clandestinely, for the cause. We note, too, in this period the growing popularity of "masquerades" on the part of diversion-seekers, and a growing concern of the reformers to combat the evils attributed to them.

1

In 1719 there was published anonymously *The Post-Man Robb'd of his Mail: or, The Packet broke open. Being a Collection of Miscellaneous Letters, Serious and Comical, Amorous and Gallant. . . . In*

Five Books. By the best Wits of the present Age.[1] The letter in *The Post-Man Robb'd of his Mail* which directly concerns the Collier Controversy is that "to Mr. Galliard, at his House near Feversham in Kent, by George Goodtaste." It occurs as Letter IV in Book IV and is written to the fictitious Mr. Galliard to induce him to permit his nephew the diversion of the stage. The writer, upon concluding the customary epistolary introduction, proceeds to the topic at heart: "Why all this Indignation at Plays? Have you lately been reading *Prynn,* and his Copyist of a contrary Kidney?"[2] Here he begins a diatribe first against that mad Enthusiast who built his *Histriomastix* upon the evidence of those Fathers whose authority he not only misunderstood but misapplied and, secondly, against "The other great Enemy of the Drama, . . . a most violent *Jacobite* [Collier]."[3] The writer asserts that the cause of Collier's rage against the theatre as expressed in the *Short View* was chiefly political;[4] that the book had a great many advocates and that Collier was munificently rewarded for it.[5]

He speaks, too, of the illogical conclusion which Collier deduced from his very assuring premises set down in the beginning of the *Short View*:

> "He begins by assuring us that the Wit of Man cannot find out any Means more conducive to the promoting of Virtue, and the banishing of Vice, than the *Drama;* and yet at the End, he gives you a whole Crowd of the Fathers to prove that there should be no such thing at all in a Christian Country; that is, according to himself, that the Thing that is the *most conducive*

---

[1] Halkett and Laing ascribe the authorship of this work to Charles Gildon: *Dict. of An. & Pseud. English Lit.,* IV, 401. They base their opinions on a note in the handwriting of Isaac Reed: "This is I believe one of the publications of Charles Gildon which procured him a place in the Dunciad." Gildon, we remember, had published in 1691 a book with a similar title, *The Post-Boy Robb'd of his Mail, D.N.B.,* VII, 1226.
Each of the five books of *The Post-Man* is comprised of Letters which are signed by such names as Roger de Whimsey, Gabriel Gripus, William Trusty, Phillip Anecdot, etc.
[2] Anonymous, *The Postman Robb'd of his Mail,* p. 212. Gildon in his Preface to *Phaeton* 1698 had called Collier "this Younger *Histrio-Mastix,*" p. ix.
[3] *Ibid.,* p. 212.
[4] *Ibid.,* p. 213.
[5] *Ibid.,* p. 213.

to Virtue, which The Wit of Man could invent, shou'd not be made use of to that End."[6]

The writer touches upon other topics of a controversial nature: the necessity of diversion for a nature oppressed by care; the possibility that Collier wrote—not against the vices of the stage but against diversion itself; and the imprudence of spending the night in gaming and drinking when the harmless pleasure of the stage may be enjoyed instead. In concluding his letter the writer advises his correspondent to permit his nephew the diversion of plays, a diversion incomparably less harmful than the reigning vices of the town. Viewed in its entirety, the letter merely re-expresses Gildon's anti-stage opinions and links issues with Dennis whose views had been similarly given in *The Usefulness of the Stage,* in *The Person of Quality's Answer,* and in *The Essay on the Operas.*

2

Bedford's 1719 attack on the stage is the most lengthy of those which he published in the cause. It appeared under the title *A Serious Remonstrance In Behalf of The Christian Religion, Against The Horrid Blasphemies and Impieties which are still used in The English Play-Houses, to the great Dishonour of Almighty God, and in Contempt of the Statutes of this Realm. Shewing their plain Tendency to overthrow all Piety, and advance the Interest and Honour of the Devil in the World; from almost Seven Thousand Instances, taken out of the Plays of the present Century, and especially of the five last Years, in defiance of all Methods hitherto used for their Reformation.*[7] The author in this work gives us few new considerations, nor does he clothe in new language his previous fulminations against the play-house. He concludes his book by a postscript of sixteen questions proposing to Christians considerations on the viciousness of plays, the guilt of players, the vices prevalent in the play-house together with the punishments to

---

[6] *Ibid.,* p 213. (Italics mine.) In *Phaeton* Gildon had used some of the same arguments and even some of the same expressions. He tells us that the Vindication which he will publish in the coming summer "shall make evident that the *Wit of Man can invent no way as efficacious, as Drammatick Poetry to advance Virtue."* p. xi.

[7] 383 pages in length, and was printed by John Darby, for Henry Hammond, Richard Gravett, and Anth. Piesley.

be meted out to those convicted of crime committed there.[8] His preface, however, is unique in that it lists

"A Catalogue of above Fourteen Hundred Texts of Scripture, which are mentioned in this Treatise, either as ridicul'd and expos'd by the Stage, or as opposite to their present Practices."[9]

Besides, we should take note that in the *Serious Remonstrance* Bedford quotes as authorities against the play-house Archbishop Tillotson's Sermon, *Corrupt Communication,* Collier's *Short View,* and Sir Richard Blackmore's *Essays;*[10] second, that he displays his learning wherever the opportunity presents itself, and, third, that he proves his inexhaustible patience and zeal by pointing out almost seven thousand instances of impiety and immorality found in plays of the past five years. The marginal notes alone are so copious and so detailed that the author must have wearied himself in the compilation.[10a]

3

Besides the *Serious Remonstrance,* there is extant for the year 1719 the anonymous pamphlet *Of Plays and Masquerades* in *The Occasional Paper, Vol. III, Number IX.*[11] Although it advances no new arguments against plays and censures no feature of the play-house not previously censured, yet it is interesting for two reasons: first, the author definitely points out the dangers of masquerades and associates masquerades with plays; second, the content of the pamphlet, the style, the diction, the arguments, the references, and the literary eccentricities of the author—all suggest Jeremy Collier. Inasmuch as the author begins with a discourse on plays and concludes with a discussion of masquerades, we shall analyze the work in the same sequence, pointing out the alliance of this attack with Collier's other stage attacks.

---

[8] A. Bedford, *A Serious Remonstrance,* pp. 379-383.

[9] *Ibid.,* pp. v-xx.

[10] *Ibid.,* pp. 347-359.

[10a] *Ibid.,* pp. 359-366. Among the plays from which he quotes we note *The City Ramble, The Masquerade, The Man of Mode, The Basset-Table,* and *The Humours of Purgatory.* Concerning these plays D. E. Baker in *Biographia Dramatica* gives the following information: *The City Ramble* by E. Settle, acted at T. R. in 1712; (II, 56); The *Masquerade,* by Charles Johnson, acted at T. R. in 1719; (II, 225); *The Man of Mode* by George Etherege, acted at D. L. T. in 1676; (II, 217); *The Basset Table* by Mrs. Centlivre, published in 1706; (II,28); *The Humours of Purgatory* by Benj. Griffin, acted at L-I-F in 1716; (II, 158).

[11] 28 pages; printed for Em. Matthews, J. Roberts, J. Harrison, and A. Dodd, London.

1. The author begins:

"Plays and Publick Actings have been very *antient,* and may be innocent and useful under the Conduct of Wisdom and Virtue; and where there is a strict Regard to Truth and Decency, without anything shocking or offensive to Modesty and Religion. . . . They are proper to represent the Vices and Follies of Men to a Disadvantage, and put them out of Countenance; To rally the Follies of the Great, and to make fashionable Customs appear ridiculous; . . . " p. 3.

1. Collier, it will be remembered, gloried in tracing plays and public actings to their fountainhead—the *Ancients.* He believed, too, in the noble purpose of plays:

"The business of *Plays* is to recommend Virtue, and discountenance Vice; To shew the Uncertainty of Humane Greatness, the suddain Turns of Fate, and the Unhappy Conclusions of Violence and Injustice: 'Tis to expose the Singularities of Pride and Fancy, to make Folly and Falsehood contemptible, and to bring every Thing that is Ill Under Infamy and Neglect." *Short View,* p. 1.

2. He tells us that the reason plays do not fulfill the noble purpose of their institution is because of the

"vicious Disposition of the *Poet,* or the false Taste of the Audience, not from the Nature and Reason of the Thing." p. 3.

2. Collier had similar censure for the poets, and for the audience.. *Short View.,* p. 1; pp. 162-3. pp. 281-5. *Dissuasive,* p. 7.

3. In this pamphlet the author laments the perverse use to which the poets have subjected the stage:

"The modern Stage is calculated and design'd to fill the Mind with false Notions of Honour, and wrong Sentiments of Things; to *corrupt the Imagination,* to fire the Passions of unexperienc'd Youth, *to wear out Impressions of Virtue,* and to dispose, by Degrees, to every Evil;" pp. 5-6. (Italics mine.)

3. Collier had argued in the same vein:

"Such licentious Discourse [as occurs in modern comedy] tends to no Point but to *stain the Imagination,* to awaken Folly, and *to weaken The Defences of Virtue.*" *Short View,* p. 5. (Italics mine.)

4. He continues

"There are . . . Instances . . . where the lively *Images.* and beautiful *Descriptions,* mightily

4. Collier says:

"Sometimes you have it in *Image* and *Description* . . . to engage the Fancy, fasten upon the

engage and delight the mind."
p. 4.

Memory, and keep up the Charm from Languishing." *Short View*, p. 5. Cf. also p. 144; p. 233.

5. The author then sarcastically describes the hero's "romantick infatuation for his mistress:"
"the Courage of a romantick Hero is inspir'd by a Mistress; it is meer Effect of Love; . . . " pp. 282-3.

5. Collier says:
"The Hero's Mistress is no less than his Deity. She disposes his Reason, prescribes his Motions, and Commands his Interest." *Short View*, pp. 282-3.

6. He blames plays for a
"great amount of Undutifulness in children, disorders in the family, and contempt of commands of Parents; and, he asserts that plays are responsible for much unhappiness and unfaithfulness after marriage; that the institution of marriage is the common jest of the play-house." pp. 13-14.

6. Collier in the *Short View* says that the stage is the cause of disappointment of parents, confusion in families, and beggary in estates. P. 287. He censures the poets D'Urfey, Dryden, Vanbrugh and Congreve for dilating so much on the subject of love, and for contempt of the marriage bond. Chapter IV; Chapter V.

7. He protests against the profaneness of the stage:
"The Names of GOD and CHRIST are most trivially us'd, and sometimes most shockingly blasphem'd. . . . The Scriptures are burlesqu'd, and all Religion is undermin'd, p. 14,

7. In the *Short View* Collier devotes Chapter II (pp. 56-97) to censuring the profaneness of the play-house. And in the *Dissuasive*, p. 6., he blames the poets for
"making bold with the Name of God on the most trivial and scandalous Occasions; . . . they have blasphem'd the Attributes of God, ridicul'd his Providence, and burlesq'd the Old and New Testament."

8. and against the abuse of the clergy by the stage-poets:
"The *Priesthood* is scandalously abused and all manner of Superiors are insulted. The worst Vices are encourag'd and the brightest Virtues are sullied and disgrac'd. The *Church*, I say the *Church* is most scurrilously treated." p. 14.

8. Collier devotes pp. 97-139 of the *Short View* to condemning the same abuse. He condemns it too, in the *Dissuasive*, p. 5. And in his essay "Upon the Office of a Chaplain," *Essays*, I, pp. 167-215, he speaks of the reverence due to the clergy.

9. He continues concerning the abuse of the clergy:

"Tis a small Matter, . . . the exposing the *Character and Habit of a Clergyman* on these Occasions, as is often done. The Mischief lies in the Consequence of seeing such a one *play the Fool*, or lead off the Masque." p. 25.

9. Collier in the *Short View* asserts of the poet:

"They must ridicule the *Habit, as well as the Function, of the Clergy.* 'Tis not enough for them to *play the Fool*, unless they do it in Pontificalibus." p. 111.

The author refers to the incorrigibleness of the stage, and to substantiate his argument he indicates by a marginal note that he is quoting p. 9 of the *Dissuasive* to the effect that the poets continued acting even after their correction at Westminster Hall;[12] he likewise attacks those musicians and players who have lately come to England from foreign parts. Here for his purpose he quotes from page 10 of the *Dissuasive*;[13] and he follows this by giving Collier's favorite example of the Roman Republic which before the time of Julius Caesar stopped the building of a theatre lest foreign vice be brought in. The writer quotes from three of Collier's works, *A Defence*, p. 85, *A Dissuasive*, p. 12, and *A Short View*, pp. 242-3, to strengthen its arguments.[14] The author says in a very pro-Collier strain:

"And since Mr. *Collier* writ against the Stage, we have a Statute made in the Twelfth Year of the Reign of her late Majesty Queen Anne, intitled, *An Act for reducing the Laws relating to Rogues, Vagabonds, sturdy Beggars and Vagrants, into one Act of Parliament;*"[15]

and refers to the oft-quoted statutes of the English Constitution enacted in the reigns of Eliz. and of James I whereby players are forbidden "to act and scatter their Infection through the Kingdom."[16]

In order to make emphatic his invective against the stage, the author appeals to "the sense of religion of those whose Baptismal vows bind them to renounce the world the flesh and the devil,"[17] and in

---

[12] *Ibid.*, p. 15.

[13] *Ibid.*, pp. 15-16.

[14] *Ibid.*, pp. 16-17.

[15] *Ibid.*, p. 17. Cf. *A Farther Vindication*, p. 14; p. 20; p. 22; p. 24; p. 25; p. 28; p. 31; *Dissuasive*, p. 11; p. 4; p. 12.

[16] *Ibid.*, p. 16. *Short View*, p. 58; p. 73; pp. 242-3; *Dissuasive*, p. 12; *A Farther Vindication*, p. 17; p. 18; p. 36.

[17] *Ibid.*, p. 25. Cf., also, *Dissuasive*, p. 8; *Short View*, p. 285; *Representation*, p. 23.

true Collierian manner gives consideration to the quotation from St. Paul: "Evil communications corrupt good Manners"[18] as well as to the source of infection which the play-house is to the youth of the city. Besides, he likens the diversion of the stage to the plague which is endangering the people of the nation.[19]

He mentions in the vein of Collier, evidence contained in the *Freethinker Extraordinary*, Nos. 4, 63, and 68 against the morality of plays and masquerades,[20] as well as that contained in the *Honest Gentleman*, No. 4; and in the same tone and diction he refers to W. Bulstrode's *Charge to the Grand Jury of Middlesex.*[21]

Of Plays and Masquerades concludes with an excerpt taken almost verbatim from the conclusion of the *Short View*. It is taken, in this instance, without marginal reference, and without acknowledgement or apology to Collier:

> "They [plays] cherish those very Passions which 'tis the very Business of Religion to discountenance and conquer; they strike at the Root of all Principle, and draw off the Inclination from Virtue, and spoil all good Education. 'Tis the most effectual Method to baffle the Force of Discipline, to emasculate the Spirits, and debauch the Manners. And yet these *Syrens* go on to devour the Unwary: And Men continue to say, the best Blood of the Nation is tainted with the Infection."[22]

It is, undoubtedly, a baffling undertaking to attempt to prove Collier the author of this pamphlet, inasmuch as it is well-nigh impossible to transcribe the necessary references, phrases, quotations, peculiarities of diction, eccentricities of style, and pet figures of speech without transcribing all of the pamphlet and all of the pertinent part of the originals. However, I believe that sufficient data has been given above to substantiate the statement that Collier is the author of *Of Plays and Masquerades*.

4

There was published anonymously in 1721 an interesting addition to the Collier controversy. The title of the work is *The Conduct of the Stage Consider'd, Being a Short Historical Account of its Original,*

---

[18] *Ibid.,* p. 26. Cf. *Short View*, p. 18; *Farther Vindication*, p. 26.
[19] *Ibid.,* p. 24. *Dissuasive*, p. 11; *Short View*, p. 287.
[20] *Ibid.,* p. 21; p. 22; p. 27; p. 24.
[21] *Ibid.,* p. 28.
[22] *Ibid.,* p. 28. Cf. *Short View*, p. 287.

Progress, various Aspects, and Treatment in the Pagan, Jewish and Christian World. Together with the Arguments urg'd against it, by Learned Heathens, and by Christians, both Antient and Modern. With Short Remarks upon the Original and Pernicious Consequences of Masquerades. Humbly recommended to the Consideration of those who frequent the PLAY-HOUSES.[23] That it is a continuation of the Collier Controversy is proved from the first sentence:

"The ensuing Treatise does not only account for the Original, Progress, Conduct, and Treatment of the Stage in the several Ages of the World, but also does, *en passant,* show, that as it is now usually manag'd, it ought not to be permitted among Christians; being generally calculated for the Meridian of Vice, and to give a Relish to the frothy Pleasures of the vain part of Mankind, as Mr. *Collier* has abundantly prov'd. To give greater Force to this Charge of Impiety against the Stage, I shall, in the most concise and conspicuous manner, shew, . . . "[24]

The pamphlet assumes importance in our present study in view of the fact that it bears evidence of being Collier's work, and, as far as can be determined, of being his final contribution to the controversy which he began in 1698. This conclusion I base upon the following facts. First, the considerations submitted to the reader in *The Conduct of the Stage Considered* are identical with those submitted in the *Short View,* the *Defence,* the *Dissuasive, A Representation of the Impiety and Immorality of the English Stage, A Second Defence,* and *A Farther Vindication;* second, the considerations are submitted frequently in the identical sequence and phraseology. This statement I shall substantiate by giving, in several instances, a parallel study of the works in question. Third, the same eccentricities of style and diction, the same references and figures of speech are apparent in *The Conduct of the Stage Consider'd* as appear in Collier's anti-stage treatises.

---

[23] 43 pages in length, and was printed for Eman. Matthews in 1721, the same who printed *Of Plays and Masquerades,* 1719. The work is not listed by Halkett and Laing.

[24] Anonymous, *The Conduct of the Stage Consider'd,* p. 3.

The considerations submitted by the author of *The Conduct of the Stage Consider'd* are seven in number, and from the very first we perceive that we are on familiar ground:

"The Stage, with all its pompous Train, is of a Pagan Original, invented for the Honour and Worship of Daemons."[25]

Having stated his first proposition the author proceeds to prove it by references to Dionysius and to Valerius Maximus. He gives the familiar

"The Stage indeed may still pass for a Temple since 'tis often more crowded than the Church, and its Performances too often entertain'd with greater Gust than those of the Pulpit;"[26]

he asserts that comedy and tragedy were strangers at Rome while Roman virtue retained its pristine vigour,[27] and here we discover the counterpart of the assertion in Collier's *Dissuasive from the Play-House*:

"The Republick of Rome, before Julius Caesar, stopt the building of a Theatre, . . . being fully convinc'd that this Diversion would bring in foreign Vice, that the Old Roman Virtue would be lost."[28]

He tells of the origin of tragedy and comedy, and the consequences of dishonorable love. Occasionally we find whole sentences lifted from the *Short View,* and placed in an appropriate setting in *The Conduct of the Stage Consider'd.* The author gives no acknowledgment of his indebtedness to Collier, nor does he indicate the source whence he draws his inspiration; however, the identity is too evident to be overlooked. Note, as examples, the following:

---

[25] *Ibid.*, p. 4. Note the similarity of this statement to that which Collier quoted from Tertullian, *Short View,* pp. 253-60; cf. also p. 250; p. 14.
[26] *Ibid.*, p. 4; *Short View,* p. 235.
[27] *Ibid.*, p. 5.
[28] J. Collier, *Dissuasive,* p. 11.

The Conduct of the Stage Consider'd	*A Short View*
1. The author in speaking of the consequences of dishonourable love quotes Minutinus Felix: "Sometimes a luscious Actor shall whine you into Love, and give the Disease he Counterfeits." p. 5.	1. Collier in the *Short View* asserts: "Minutius Felix delivers his Sense in these Words: . . . Sometimes a Luscious Actor shall whine you into Love, and give the Disease he Counterfeits." p. 261.
2. The author refers to the 3rd Council of Carthage to substantiate his anathemas against the stage and players: "The Third Council of *Carthage* forbids Christians to attend the Stage, because the Actors are Blasphemers." p. 8.	2. Collier referred to the same Council for the same purpose and he concluded his anathema by the following: "Such sort of Pagan Entertainments being forbidden all the Laity. It beings always unlawful for all Christians to come amongst Blasphemers." p. 250.

The conclusion of Part I is couched in the familiar rhetorical questions so habitual to Collier, and to which attention has hitherto been called.

In developing his second consideration the author proposes the Greeks and the Romans as exemplars in handling the play-house situation, and he enumerates philosophers and poets in almost the same order that we find them in the *Short View;* moreover, he substantiates his arguments by references to the same sources:

The Conduct of the Stage Consider'd	*A Short View*
1. The author says: "I'll begin, 1. With Plato, . . . who would suffer no Stage-Plays in his Commonwealth, because those Diversions were dangerous to Morality, and consequently to Government." p. 9; *De Rep.*	1. Collier says: "To begin with Plato. This Philosopher tells us that *Plays* raise the Passions, and pervert the use of them, and by consequence are dangerous to Morality. For this reason he banishes these Diversions his *Commonwealth.*" p. 234; *De Rep.*
2. "*Aristotle* . . . forbids the seeing of *Comedies* to young People, because it would poison their Minds; . . . " p. 9.	2. "*Aristotle* lays it down for a Rule that the Law ought to forbid Young People the seeing of comedies." p. 234.

3. "*Xenophon*, . . . commends the *Persians* for not suffering their Youth to hear Comedies." p. 9.

3. "*Xenophon* . . . commends the *Persians* for the Discipline of their Education. They won't (says he) so much as suffer their Youth to hear any thing that's Amorous or Tawdry." p. 234.

4. "*Tully*, . . . declaims against Plays and licentious Poems as the Plague of Society; and in particular against *Comedies, that subsisted only by Lewdness.*" p. 9.

4. "*Tully* crys out upon Licentious *Plays* and *Poems,* as the bane of Sobriety, and wise Thinking: That *Comedy* subsists upon Lewdness, and that Pleasure is the Root of all Evil." p. 235.

5. "Livy, . . . says, That Plays were brought in upon the score of Religion, to appease the Gods in time of a Plague; but the Remedy prov'd worse than the Disease, and the Atonement more infectious than the Plague." p. 10.

5. "*Livy,* . . . tells us they [plays] were brought in upon the score of Religion, to pacifie the Gods, and remove a *Mortality.* But then He adds . . . That the Remedy in this case was worse than the Disease, and the Atonement more Infectious than the Plague." p. 235.

6. "Valerius Maximus, . . . having describ'd the Theatre in its Rise, Progress, and Decorations, tells how . . . the *Romans,* as they grew rich, added Pomp and Magnificence to the Plays, the Toleration of which he look'd upon as a Blemish to the *Roman* States." p. 10.

6. "*Valerius Maximus,* . . . gives much the same Account of the rise of the *Theatres at Rome.* 'Twas Devotion which built them. And as for the Performances of those Places, which Mr. *Dryden* calls the *Ornaments,* this Author censures as the Blemishes of *Peace.*" p. 235.

7. "Seneca, . . . complains how the *Roman* Youth were generally corrupted by the Countenance which *Nero* gave to the Stage, . . ." p. 10.

7. "*Seneca* complains heartily of the Extravagance and Debauchery of the Age: . . . " p. 236.

8. "Tacitus . . . inveighs against *Nero,* for introducing all kinds of Vice by Stage-Plays." pp. 10-11.

8. "*Tacitus* relating how *Nero* hired decay'd Gentlemen for the Stage, complains of the Mismanagement." p. 236.

9. "Plutarch, . . . does not only condemn Plays as lascivious Vanities, and contagious Evils, but *Poetry* itself as full of Lyes, . . ." p. 11.

9. "*Plays,* in the Opinion of the Judicious *Plutarch* are dangerous to corrupt Young People. And therefore *Stage* Poetry when it grows too hardy, and Licentious, ought to be checkt." p. 237.

10. "Ovid, . . . in his Poem, *de Arte Amandi,* . . . tells his leacherous Associates, That the Playhouses were the best Fairs for unchaste Bargains, the most commodious Haunts for amorous Fellows, and only Places for Panders and Whores. *Sed tu praecipue,* etc." p. 11.

10. "*Ovid,* . . . in his Book *De Arte Amandi,* gives his Reader to understand that the *Play-House* was the most likely Place for him to Forage in, . . . Nothing being more common than to see Beauty surpriz'd, Women debauch'd and Wenches Pick'd up at these Diversions. *Sed tu praecipue,* etc.," and here Collier quotes the *same two* lines which the author in 1721 quotes. p. 237.

11. The author, further, quotes the same two lines from the *de Tristibus,* I, 2, as appear in the *Short View*:
Ut Tamen hoc fateor, etc. p. 11. and from the *De Remed. Am., lib. 2.*
At tanti tibi sit non . . . p. 12.

11. Here Collier quotes from the *de Tristibus*:
Ut Tamen hoc Fateor, etc., p. 239, and calls attention to some lines from *The Remedy of Love:*

At tanti tibi sit non . . . p. 239.

The third consideration which the author of the *Conduct of the Stage Consider'd* calls to the attention of the reader is that the Primitive Church was inimical to the play-house. Here, too, we detect not only the familiar arguments of the *Short View,* but the very phraseology found in it.

The Conduct of the Stage Consider'd

A Short View

1. The anonymous author begins his proof with Minutius Felix and gives similar arguments to those found in the *Short View.* p. 13.

1. Collier in the *Short View* had proved the unlawfulness of the stage by arguments from Minutius Felix. p. 261.

2. His second argument, taken from Lactantius, is concerned with the baneful effects of tragedy and comedy, and it states of the actors:

"the more artful the Actors are in their Representations, the more Michief they do— . . . *vitanda ergo spectacula omnia,*" p. 13.

3. He tells us also:

"Tertullian . . . gives an Account of a Christian Woman, who, going to the Play-house, was there possess'd by the Devil, and when, at his casting out, was ask'd by the Exorcists, How he durst enter into a Christian? he answer'd, I found her upon my Ground." pp. 13-14; *De Spect.* c. 26.

4. "*Theophilus* of *Antioch,* . . . looks upon Plays as dangerous Sports, therefore forbids Men to frequent them, that their Eyes and Ears be not polluted." p. 14.

5. "Cyprian, . . . adds That those Christians, who attended the Stage, did not only approve the Folly and Madness of the Heathens, but renounc'd their Baptism." p. 14.

6. "Clemens Alexandrinus, . . . calls the Theatre the *Chair of Pestilence.*" p. 14.

7. "Chrysostom, . . . reproves the People of *Antioch* for their resorting to *Play-houses* which he

2. Collier in the *Short View,* besides treating of the effects of comedy, had given from Lactantius the English of the Latin quotation which the author of the *Conduct of the Stage* used:

"Let us avoid therefore, these diversions, etc." p. 265.

3. Collier had narrated:

"*Tertullian* [says] A Certain Woman went to the *Play-House,* and brought the Devil Home with Her. And when the Unclean Spirit was press'd in the *Excorcism* and ask'd how he durst attack a Christian. I have done nothing, says he, but what I can justify. For I seiz'd her upon my own Ground." p. 257; *De Spect.,* cap. 26.

4. "*Theophilus* Bishop of *Antioch:* Neither dare we presume upon the Liberty of your other *Shews,* least our Senses be tinctur'd and disoblig'd with Indecency, and Profaneness." p. 252.

5. "St. Cyprian [argues] . . . What business has a Christian at such Places as these? A Christian who has not the liberty so much as to think of an ill Thing." pp. 261-3.

6. "Clemens Alexandrinus affirms that the *Circus* and *Theatre* may not improperly be call'd the *Chair* of *Pestilence.*" p. 260.

7. "St. Chrysostom's . . . 15 *Homily ad Populum Antiochenum* runs thus: . . . Frequenting the

stiles the *Devil's Conventicles;"* p. 14.

Play-House has brought Whoring and Ribaldry into Vogue, and finish'd all the parts of Debauchery." p. 267.

8. In *The Conduct of the Stage* . . . , the author collects other evidence—some of it from the succeeding centuries — and he quotes from Isidore, 412 A.D.: Athenagoras, 177 A.D.; Cyril of Jerusalem, 350 A.D.; Greg. of Nazienzen, 370 A.D.; Epiphanius, and Salvian, pp: 15-16.

8. Collier, upon conclusion of the evidence collected from the Fathers against plays, remarks: "I could likewise run through the succeeding centuries, and collect Evidence all along." p. 275.

9. From the Councils of the Church we have a reference to the 3rd Council of *Carthage* which forbade laymen and the sons of clergymen to be actors or spectators at public shows because " 'tis unworthy of Christians to be present in a place where Blasphemies are spoken." p. 16.

9. Collier refers to the 3rd Council of *Carthage* which forbids the sons of Bishops or other clergymen to be present at public shows, because it is "always unlawful for all Christians to come amongst *Blasphemers.*" p. 250.

10. "The first Council of *Arles,* . . . ordains that those Christians who acted upon the Theatre should be excommunicated while they followed those Employments." p. 17.

10. "The first Council of *Arles* runs thus, Concerning *Players* we have thought fit to Excommunicate them as long as they continue to *Act."* p. 250.

11. "By the *African Code* it appears, that Stage-Players were ranked among Apostates." p. 17.

11. "By the 35th *Canon* of this *Council* [The 3rd Council of Carthage] 'tis decreed . . . that *Players* as long as they kept to their Employment were bar'd *Communion."* p. 251.

12. The author quotes from certain decrees of the *Eliberine* Council concerning Excommunication of Christian women who abet the players, p. 17.

12. Collier quotes from the *Eliberine* Council concerning the Excommunication of Women who entertain Comedians or Actors, . . . p. 250.

13. The author proceeds to give a brief account of the attitude of the Church toward plays and players as expressed by the decrees of her Councils. pp. 17-19.	13. Collier, in the *Short View* professed to give the sense of the Primitive Church only as it was expressed in her Councils. p. 250.

The anonymous author concludes the chapter by a series of rhetorical questions concerning Fathers, General Councils, and the whole "Current of Antiquity." The questions bespeak Jeremy Collier:

> "How long will ye suffer The Lambs of your Flock to be worry'd by those Wolves in Sheep's Clothing? Why don't you thunder out the Anathema's of the Church against the Theatre, from whence Virtue is banished for its Seriousness, and where Lewdness is Factor for Hell?"[29]

In the Fourth Consideration proposed by the author of *The Conduct of the Stage Consider'd* we again recognize the familiar arguments of the author of the *Short View*:

> "*The Diversions of the Stage have been discountenanced by the wisest States and Kingdoms, and even by those who upon their first Appearance were fond of them, as the* Greeks *and* Romans."[30]

The Conduct of the Stage Consider'd	*A Short View*
1. "We'll begin, With The *Athenians,* who were none of the worst Enemies to the Stage; these made a Law, that no Judge of the *Areopagus* should write a Comedy." p. 20.	1. To begin with the *Athenians,* This People tho' none of the worst Friends to the *Play-House* thought a *Comedy* so unreputable a Performance that they made a Law that no Judge of the *Areopagus* should make one." p. 240.
2. "The *Lacedemonians* would not allow of the Stage in *Sparta* upon any Condition whatever." p 21.	2. "The *Lacedemonians,* . . . would not endure the *Stage* in any Form, nor under any Regulation." p. 240.
3. "Plutarch [foresaw] the Luxury of the Drama would debauch their Youth as it did those of *Athens.*" p. 21.	3. "*Plays* in the opinion of the Judicious *Plutarch* are dangerous to corrupt Young People." p. 237.

[29] Anonymous, *The Conduct of the Stage Consider'd*, p. 20.
[30] Anonymous, *The Conduct of the Stage Consider'd*, p. 20.

4. "The Massilians, . . . would not allow or tolerate any Stage-Plays in their Country." p. 21.

4. "The Massilienses did well in Clearing the Country of them [plays]." p. 236.

5. The Romans, . . . before *Julius Caesar's* time, . . . stopt the building of a Theatre, as apprehending that the Entertainments of the Play-house would bring in foreign Vice, and that the old *Roman* Virtue would be lost, and the Spirit of The People emasculated and softened; therefore that wise Nation made the Function of Players scandalous, seized their Freedoms, and threw them out of their Privileges." p. 21.

5. We note a familiar echo in *The Conduct of the Stage* not from the *Short View* but from the *Dissuasive*: "The Republick of Rome before *Julius Caesar* stopt the building of a Theatre, being fully convinc'd that the Old Roman Virtue would be lost, and the Spirits of the People emasculated. This wise Nation made The Function of Players scandalous, seiz'd their Freedom, and threw them out of Privilege and Reputation." p. 11.

6. The author refers to the familiar proscription of the stage as contained in "39 Eliz: and in 1. Jac. ch. vii." p. 24.

6. The references by Collier to 39 Eliz. and 1 Jac. ch. vii have been previously referred to. *Dissuasive*, p. 12; *Short View*, pp. 241-2.

7. The author states: "In the Year 1697, by order of the *French* King, the *Italian* Players were expelled from the Kingdom; and I very well remember, that in 1703, the *French* Stage lay under Excommunication." p. 24.

7. In the *Dissuasive* we read: "In France some few years since the *Italian* Players were expell'd the Kingdom and now the French Stage lyes under Excommunication. The Theatres have lately been shut up in *Italy* by the Pope, and in the territories of *Brandenburgh* by the King of *Prussia.' Dissuasive*, p. 12.

The author's fifth consideration appears as follows:

"*Stage-Plays are no where authoriz'd or allow'd by the Church of England as such, but every where condemned by the Purity of her Doctrine, and by some of her most eminent Lights;*"[31]

and he substantiates his arguments by frequent references to St. Cyril, Tertullian, St. Cyprian, St. Austin, and to the Fathers who lived near the Apostolical times.[32] He gives information, too, of anti-stage pamph-

---

[31] Anonymous, *The Conduct of the Stage Consider'd*, p. 25.
[32] *Ibid.*, pp. 25-6.

lets written toward the end of the seventeenth century and in the early part of the eighteenth. Inasmuch as these pamphlets are not listed in existing Collier bibliographies I call attention to them:

The author condemns stage-plays, first, on the testimony of Archbishop Usher who, in his *Body of Divinity,* 1702, says that interludes and stage-plays offend against the seventh Commandment;[33] secondly, he quotes Dr. Bray who, in his *Discourse on the Baptismal Covenant,* p. 118, condemns modern plays;[34] third, he lists Dr. Horneck who, in his "Letter Agaist Plays" in his *Book on Judgment,* says:

> "Actor and Spectator go away from the Theatre worse than they came; and tho both come away laughing, yet both prepare for bitter Mourning and Lamentation. The Plays, . . . are suited to the loose Humour of the Age, which seems to hate all things Serious, and delights in nothing so much as in Jests and Fooleries, and seeing the most venerable things turned into Ridicule."[35]

fourth, he cites Dr. Tillotson who in his *Sermon 3, Education of Children,* censures parents who bring their children to the play-house;[36] fifth, he adds Dr. J. Edwards who, in his *Preacher,* I, 100, 101, cautions those who preach at Court to dissuade their hearers from frequenting play-houses;[37] sixth, he quotes Dr. Fogg who, in his *Two Treatises,* printed at Chester, 1712, says

> "if the Stage be not purged from that Filthiness both of Speech and Gesture, which is usually represented there, we must join with the antient Fathers, and civilized Heathens, in condemning it;"[38]

and he gives as his last authority Dr. Kennett who condemns plays and operas.

In his sixth consideration, the author calls attention to the fact that even

> "among the Papists, who have almost converted all Religion into Plays, are found Enemies to the Stage, upon the score of its Profaneness."[39]

---

[33] *Ibid.,* p. 28.
[34] *Ibid.,* p. 28.
[35] *Ibid.,* p. 28.
[36] *Ibid.,* pp. 28-9.
[37] *Ibid.,* p. 29.
[38] *Ibid.,* p. 29.
[39] *Ibid.,* p. 30.

Among the Roman Catholic enemies to stage-plays he lists Mariana, the Jesuit, Cardinal Baronius, Cardinal Bellarmine, Bulingerus, Spondanus, and Veronensis.[40] We may note in the concluding paragraph of this section the customary series of rhetorical questions, so chacacteristic of Collier's literary style.

In the seventh consideration the author asserts:

> *"Tho there may be an innocent Representation of Persons and Actions in a Dramatick Way; yet Play-Houses, as they have been, and now generally are managed, ought not to be frequented by Christians;"*[41]

and he appends four considerations which he calls "A Short View of Masquerades" wherein he proposes to

> "inquire briefly into their Original, and the Sentiments of the Heathens about them, and then shew how they and their Concomitants stand condemned not only by the Laws of the Land, but by the Voice of God and Nature."[42]

Throughout the considerations we find many familiar quotations and parallels from Collier's works.[43]

This analysis of the pamphlet does not exhaust, by any means, the various relationships which it bears to Collier's pamphlets, but it indicates clearly that Collier has very good claim to the authorship of *The Conduct of the Stage Consider'd.*

5

Although Mr. Heydegger's *Letter to the Bishop of London,* 1724, is not available, we may judge of its contents by the sharp reply which it evoked. This reply is entitled *A Seasonable Apology for Mr. H—g—r [Heydegger]. Proving The Usefulness and Antiquity of Masquerading from Scripture, and prophane History. With Observations on the several Species of Masks now in Use: And Likewise The Report from the Committee appointed to state and examine the Advantages arising from our present Masquerades.*[44]

---

[40] *Ibid.,* pp. 30-1.
[41] *Ibid.,* p. 31.
[42] *Ibid.,* p. 35.
[43] *Ibid.,* pp. 37-42; *Short View,* p. 14; p. 18; p. iv; p. 247; *Dissuasive,* p. 8; *Representation,* p. 22.
[44] A 26-page pamphlet satirizing the evils arising from masquerades. It was printed in 1724 for A Moor, near St. Pauls. Not listed by Halkett & Laing.

The Dedicatory Epistle is addressed to "that most Celebrated Matron,
disguis'd and distinguish'd by the Name and Title of Mother N———m
[Needham]' and is signed "P.W."[45]

A careful reading of *A Seasonable Apology* suggests that the writer
has modeled upon Dennis' *Usefulness of the Stage* that portion of his
satire in which he attempts to prove both from reason and experience
that masquerades are useful to the happiness and well-being of mankind. There is venom in every line of the Epistle, and we note it when
the writer hints at the vices consequent upon masquerades, attributing
much of the scandal to the gracious patronage of Mother Needham
in her house of ill fame:

> "For one Thing I am sure of, that scarce a Masquerade has been,
> but in Consequence of it, you have had the Entertainment of
> near one hundred Couples of Masqueraders; . . .[46]

we note it, too, in various arguments of *The Seasonable Apology* itself
where the writer attempts, satirically, to prove from Scripture, from
history, and from common sense the usefulness of masquerades. He
tells us that the first instance of the use of a mask was the devil's
counterfeiting the form of a serpent whereby to seduce Eve and to
despoil her and her posterity of innocence;[47] then he points out that
the mask of drunkenness sapped Lot's virtue, and that a mask de-
frauded Esau of the paternal blessing.[48] He analyzes what he calls
historical and social masks: The Spanish Armada, the gunpowder
plot, medicine, poetry, war, trade, sport, free-masonry,—each is a mask,
he tells us, and each performs in its way its duty in masquerade.[49]

Triumphantly, the writer interjects an apostrophe:

> "O Mask! Great has been at all Times thy Usefulness, and
> greatly art thou still in Use: By thee fell our first Parents, and
> by thee Sin and Death enter'd into the World: . . . By thee
> Great Ladies . . . envy our Oyster-Women no longer;"[50]

Caustically he interposes his reflections on the immense benefits to be
derived from masquerades, and in conclusion he promises to hang up

---

[45] The initials P. W. are not identified by Cushing.
[46] Anonymous, *A Seasonable Apology,* Dedicatory Epistle, p. iii.
[47] *Ibid.,* p. 3.
[48] *Ibid.,* pp. 4-6.
[49] *Ibid.,* pp. 12-18.
[50] *Ibid.,* p. 10.

his pen in the Theatre in the Hay-Market as a trophy of his complete victory in the cause of masquerades.

6

William Law was one of the later nonjurors. Several biographies have been written of him, among which may be mentioned that of H. Broxap and that of J. H. Overton. From Broxap we learn that Law was ordained by Henry Gandy in January, 1728, but that it is extremely doubtful when he entered the non-juring communion.[51] From Overton we learn that he was unpopular with all parties of the nonjurors in their various controversies, and that he developed thoughts in the direction of mysticism which further alienated him from his brethren. Whether or not he was unpopular with Collier is not stated, but it is most certain that he enlisted under Collier's banner of stage reform by the publication of his work *The Absolute Unlawfulness of the Stage-Entertainment Fully Demonstrated.*[52]

The pamphlet is important only for two reasons: first it is the last stage attack published in Collier's life time; second, it evoked several replies: one from John Dennis in 1726 entitled *The Stage Defended, From Scripture, Reason, Experience, and the Common Sense of Mankind for Two Thousand Years, . . .* and another, an anonymous pamphlet with the punning title *Law Outlaw'd,* published, also, in 1726.

Law advances arguments against the stage which proclaim him a more rigid reformer than any who had preceded him. He condemns the stage,

> "[not] as some other Diversions, because they are dangerous, and likely to be Occasions of Sin; but it is condemn'd as Drunkenness and Lewdness, as Lying and Prophaneness are

---

[51] Henry Broxap, *The Later Non-Jurors,* p. 313. *William Law* (1686-1761) has been the subject of an exhaustive study by J. H. Overton. He wrote *William Law, Non-juror and Mystic,* 1881, which is a sketch of Law's life, character, and opinions. In 1898 he edited Law's *A Serious Call to a Devout and Holy Life.* Overton says that Law's *Absolute Unlawfulness of the Stage-Entertainment* is decidedly the weakest of all his writings and that most of his admirers will regret that he ever published it. He further asserts: "Unlike himself, he gives away to passion and seems quite to lose all self-control; unlike himself, he indulges in the most violent abuse; and unlike himself he lays himself open to the most crushing retorts." Overton, J. H., *William Law,* p. 37.

[52] Fifty pages long and was printed for W. and J. Innys in 1726, the year of Collier's death.

to be condemn'd; not as Things that may only be the Occasions
of Sin, but as such as are in their own Nature grossly sinful."[53]

He attempts to impress his reader with the parallel with which his
mind is obsessed, that the stage-performance is as sinful as is the worship of images:

> Had a person, some Years ago, in the Times of *Popery*, wrote
> against the *Worship* of *Images*, as Worship absolutely unlaw-
> ful; our Ancestors would have look'd upon him as a Man of a
> very *irregular* Spirit, Now it is possible for the present Age to
> be as much mistaken in their *Pleasures*, as the former were in
> their *Devotions*, and that the allow'd Diversions of these Times
> may be as great a Contradiction to the most Essential Doctrines
> of Christianity, as the *Superstitions* and *Corruptions* of the for-
> mer Ages."[53a].

He makes a statement against the "Lawfulness and Usefulness of the
Stage" which is undoubtedly aimed at Dennis' *The Usefulness of the
Stage*. He says:

> "For to talk of the *Lawfulness* and *Usefulness* of the *Stage* is
> full·as absurd, as contrary to the plain Nature of things, as to
> talk of the Unlawfulness and Mischief of the Service of the
> Church;"[54]

he gives, besides, pages of tiresome reflections on an entertainment,
Apollo and Daphne, of which he sarcastically asserts:

> "[It] is so much to the Taste of this Christian Country, that it
> has been acted almost every Night this whole Season."[55]

In concluding, he answers those who, perchance, may criticise his
book as the result of a rigid or uncharitable temper:

> "he that is not reasonable enough to read impartially a Treatise
> against the *Stage*, has no Reason to think, that his Mind is in

---

[53] W. Law, *The Absolute Unlawfulness . . .* pp. 3-4.

[53a] W. Law, *The Absolute Unlawfulness of the Stage-Entertainment*, pp. 1-2.
It is with this reflection that he begins his treatise; to it he reverts frequently
in the course of his arguments, and with it he concludes. *Ibid.*, p. 2; p. 3;
p. 7; p. 10; p. 49.

[54] *Ibid.*, p. 12. Dennis answered this statement in his 1726 pamphlet, *The
Stage Defended*.

[55] *Ibid.*, pp. 23-47. *Apollo and Daphne, or The Burgo-Master trick'd*, by Lewis
Theobald, 1726, is nothing more than the vocal parts of a Pantomime Entertainment, performed two years before at L-I-F Theatre. "It was for many
years served up as an after-dish at the Theatre-Royal in Covent Garden."
Baker, D. E., *Biographia Dramatica*, II, p. 18.

better Order than theirs is, who cannot freely consider a Book that is wrote against the *Worship* of *Images,* and *Prayers* to Saints.''[56]

7

Law's attack on the stage in his *The Absolute Unlawfulness of the Stage Entertainment* evoked a reply from Dennis and from one who signed herself Mrs. S——O——. The title of her pamphlet is *Law Outlaw'd: or, A Short Reply to Mr. Law's Long Declamation against the Stage. Wherein The Wild Rant, Blind Passion, and False Reasoning of that Piping-hot Pharisee are made apparent to the meanest Capacity. Together with An Humble Petition to The Governours of the Incurable Ward of Bethlehem to take pity on the poor distracted Authors of the Town, and not suffer 'em to terrify Mankind at this rate. Written at the Request of the Orange-Women, and for the Publick Good, by the impartial Pen of Mrs. S—— O——, a Lover of both Houses.*[57]

The writer of the *Short Reply to Mr. Law* is merciless in her dealings. She asserts that the well-bred part of mankind is indulgent in its endurance of the addresses of madmen and children but that when these grow troublesome they must be snubbed and controlled;[58] she declares that because Law appeared in print against the stage he is in the number of those who deserve chastisement:

"When he presumes thus publickly to libel and defame my favourite Diversion, he is insupportable; nor shall I suffer the *Wall-Eyed* Hypocrite to pass unchastised.''[59]

She replies to Law's censure of the immorality of players by declaring:

"Why are not the Players hang'd as well as Thieves and Murderers? And why are they conniv'd at in the most abominable of Crimes? . . . I deny his every Assertion, and affirm to his

---

[56] *Ibid.,* pp. 49-50.

[57] *Law Outlaw'd* is an 8-page invective together with a 5-page "Humble Petition." It was printed according to an advertisement on page 15 for A. Moore near St. Pauls. The title-page, however, gives no clue to the printer but bears instead this curious notice: "Printed for the Benefit of the Candle-Snuffers, and sold by the Booksellers of London and Westminster. 1726. (Price Four Pence)." The letters S——O—— are not identified by Cushing in *Initials and Pseudonyms.*

[58] Anonymous, *Law Outlaw'd,* pp. 3-4.

[59] *Ibid.,* p. 4.

teeth: I. The Business of a Player is so far from being the most abominable of Crimes, it is repugnant neither to divine or human Law. II. Persons may go to hear Plays, and not be guilty of Crimes equivalent to Murder, Theft, etc. III. Mr. Law is more guilty than Players or their Audience."[60]

In the second part of her pamphlet Mrs. S. O. calls to the attention of the authorities "six objects of compassion" among whom is

"A poor lunatick Master of Arts, who raves like a Madman, preaching D——n to all Mankind, especially such who go to Plays, Operas, or other theatrical entertainments. This Man writes without Fear or Wit, and what is worse, finds out Persons as mad as himself to print what he writes; so that if he is not immediately taken care of, we shall certainly be over-run with Pamphlets, especially if he should follow the Example of some late Writers, and answer his own Works."[61]

After this direct thrust at Law, the writer concludes her Petition. She asserts that there are many more persons who should be cared for but their number is so great that all the hospitals in London would be inadequate to contain them.[62]

8

At the last mile-stone of the 1698-1726 stage controversy we find John Dennis with his scholarly reply to William Law: *The Stage Defended, From Scripture, Reason, Experience, and the Common Sense of Mankind, for Two Thousand Years . . . .*[63]

The Dedicatory Epistle contains several important statements not only concerning diversions in England but concerning Dennis himself, and concerning the controversy:

1. Concerning diversions in England in 1726 Dennis asserts that the established diversions of the town are combats of modern gladiators, Italian operas, masquerades, and tragedies and comedies. It is of the last-mentioned that he says: "they are the only genuine legitimate Entertainments of the Stage,"[64] and he refutes with all the anger

---

[60] *Ibid.,* pp. 6-7.
[61] *Ibid.,* p. 14.
[62] *Ibid.-* p. 14.
[63] Printed for N. Blandford, at the London Gazette, . . . 1726. xii, 34 pages. The Dedicatory Epistle is addressed to "The Right Honourable George Dodington, Esq.
[64] J. Dennis, *The Stage Defended,* p. iv.

that he had formerly showed toward Collier, this attempt of Law to suppress comedy and tragedy. Too, he censures caustically the entertainments which are being substituted in their stead.

2.   Dennis gives interesting autobiographical data:

> "This is the fourth time that I have appear'd in Defence of the Stage, and in this fourth Defence I have no manner of Interest, but that it has been purely extorted from me by the Force of Truth and by the Love of my Country. . . . But I have, since the publishing them, been used with such extreme Ingratitude by the present Managers of the Playhouse, that I have this Ten Years been oblig'd, by the most barbarous Treatment, to take Leave of the Play house for ever.[65]

3.   Concerning the controversy itself Dennis declares:

> ". . . Mr. Law's Pamphlet is obliquely designed [against the Established Government]; as were the writings of his two Predecessors, Collier and Bedford publish'd against the Stage.[66]

The Stage Defended is Dennis' avowed determination to give his "Sentiments concerning Mr. Law's late Pamphlet against the Stage,"[67] and, as may be inferred, these sentiments are attacks upon the various statements contained in The Absolute Unlawfulness of the Stage-Entertainment. These attacks reduce themselves to refutations of Law's erroneous assertions on topics of Scripture, morality, criticism, politics and literature, and often we find that Dennis uses as authority St. Paul, Archbishop Tillotson, Aristotle, Terence, Virgil, Moliere, Milton, and Cowley.[67a]. He emphasizes his former statements that stage-plays have not encouraged cursing, swearing, or any other form of profaneness, but that the suppression of plays has encouraged gaming:

> ". . . Gaming has increased ten-fold since Collier's Books against the Stage were published."[68]

---

[65] Ibid., pp. xi-xii. Dennis very likely refers here to his three former defences: The Usefulness of the Stage, 1698. The Person of Quality's Answer, 1704, and An Essay on the Opera after the Italian Manner, 1706. Dennis obviously, makes no reference to any defence made within "This Ten Years." This causes a question as to whether or not Dennis wrote with Gildon in 1720 the satire ascribed to them.

[66] Ibid., p. vi.

[67] Ibid., pp. 2-17.

[67a] Ibid., pp. 2-17.

[68] Ibid., p. 14.

He repeatedly refers to the *Three Nonjuring Priests* who have attacked the stage. Note the following:

> "For what is Mr. *Law?* And what are his Predecessors, *Collier* and *Bedford,* who attacked the Stage before him? Why *Jacobite* Nonjuring Parsons, all three of them, who have disown'd our Established Church, and disown'd our Government;"[69]

and he further asserts that each attack on the Stage was made at the time when the government was undergoing crucial trials and that, consequently, the only plausible explanation is the treasonable intentions of the writers.[70]

In this defence of poetry Dennis proves that he has retained all his mental acuteness, that he has not failed in the slightest degree in his devotion to the Muses, and that he has used every argument to prove that the stage is useful to the happiness of mankind and to the well-being of the government.

---

[69] *Ibid.,* pp. 32-33. I can secure no verification of Dennis' statement that Arthur Bedford was a nonjuror. The *D.N.B.,* II, 109-110, makes no mention of the fact though it *does* point out that Collier, *Hilkiah* Bedford, and Law were. The *C.H.E.L.* does not mention A. Bedford's nonjuring tendencies, neither does Broxap, Overton, or Lathbury.

[70] *Ibid.,* pp. 33-34.

CHAPTER XIV

Bibliography Based Upon Evidence Found in Pamphlets
Published 1698-1726

It is not surprising to find that the literature of the stage contro-
versy 1698-1726 contains references to such works as Stephen Gosson's
Schoole of Abuse,[1] Rainold's *Overthrow of Stage Plays*,[2] and William
Prynne's *Histrio-Mastix*.[3] Neither is it surprising to find that Collier is
more frequently compared with Prynne than with Gosson or Rainolds,
and that his *Short View* is more often censured in terms of the *Histrio-
Mastix* than in that of the *Schoole of Abuse* or of the *Overthrow of
Stage Plays*. There are several reasons which explain the fact. One is
that Gosson and Rainolds lived a century before Collier while Prynne
preceded him by only fifty years; another is that both were divines,
both were pugnacious and intrepid reformers of the stage, and both, on
occasion, played boldly with the government to advance stage reform.
A third reason is the general dependence upon the *Histrio-Mastix* which
Collier is said to have manifested. The author of *The Stage Condemned* in refuting the author of *A Defence of Dramatick Poetry*
speaks of it thus:

"But seeing the Author of the *Defence* says without any Limi-
tation, that Mr. *Collier* is the first who appear'd from the Pulpit
or Press upon this Subject [of Plays], I must put him in mind
of others that have Writ and Preached against the Stage long
before those I have already mentioned [Bray, Horneck, Wesley,
Collier and Blackmore]: And I think Mr. *Prin*, Author of the
Histriomastix, deserves the Honour of being nam'd with the
first. His Treatise being perhaps the Largest, Learnedst, and

---

[1] Stephen Gosson, (1555-1624): *The Schoole of Abuse, Containing a Pleasant Invective Against Poets, Pipers, Players, Jesters*, . . . [August] 1579.
Gosson is mentioned by [R------th] *The Stage Condemned*, p. 103; p. 108.
[2] John Rainolds, (1549-1607): *Th' Overthrow of Stage-Plays, by the Way of
Controversie betwixt D. Gager and D. Rainoldes*, . . . Referred to by [Rid-
path] in *The Stage Condemned*.
[3] William Prynne, (1600-1669), *Histrio-Mastix: the Players Scourge or Actors
Tragedy*, . . . 1663. Prynne is referred to in the 1698-1726 controversy in
connection with Collier by such writers as the author of *The Stage Condemned*, p. 94; p. 110; J. Dennis, *Letters*, 1721, p. 234; p. 236; C. Gildon,
Preface to *Phaeton*, p. ix; p. xi; C. Gildon, *Post-Man Robb'd*, pp. 212-214.

most Elaborate of any that ever was writ upon the Subject, and
to which Mr. *Collier* has been very much oblig'd for many
Things in his ingenious Book."[4]

J. Dennis satirically emphasizes, from another angle, what he considers the relationship between Prynne and Collier. He addresses the
"Doctor [Collier]" thus:

> "you would have *presaged* the Storm that the latter [Macbeth]
> would have pull'd down upon the Nation, a hundred Years
> after 'twas writ. You had then been *Histrio-Mastix* the first,
> whereas you are now but the second of that glorious Name;
> and then had old bungling *Pryn* been cropt for presuming to
> copy you;"[5]

and again

> "But then about that time [the time of Shakespeare and Jon-
> son], Doctor, there arose a Reformer indeed, Brother *Pryn* of
> Illustrious Memory; a Person indeed of an *amazing* Boldness.
> For to the Fervency of his furious Spirit, Ruine and Reforma-
> tion were all one. With these Zealot's Thoughts he set about
> reforming the Church as well as the Stage; and by preparing
> the Downfall of one made way for the Ruine of the other."[6]

Besides the references to Gosson, Rainolds, and Prynne there
is internal evidence found in the stage pamphlets published between
1698-1726 of additional controversial material. This material is
referred to as having been published either before 1698, between
1698-1726, or before 1698 but re-edited between 1698-1726. Inasmuch as these references have never been collected by Collier bibliographers I shall list them alphabetically according to author, and give
also the title of the work quoted, when it was published, and the source
of the reference together with the year of its publication.

In addition to the above bibliographical data concerning writers
and works anathematizing the poets and the play-house we have evidence concerning publications pertaining to plays and masquerades.
The question naturally rises "What connection have plays with masquerades?" To answer this query exhaustively would involve a more
extensive study than can at present be given to the subject. Suffice it

---

[4] Anonymous: *The Stage Condemned*, p. 94.
[5] J. Dennis, *Letters*, 1721, p. 234.
[6] *Ibid.*, p. 236.

AUTHOR	NAME OF WORK QUOTED	PUBLISHED	SOURCE OF REFERENCE	PUBL.
1. Sir Richard Blackmore (d. 1729)	1. *Essays* {Volume I / Volume II	1716 1717	1. Law: *Absolute Unlawfulness of the Stage Entertainment*, p. 32.	1726
2. Sir Richard Blackmore (d. 1729)	2. Preface to *Prince Arthur*	1695	2. Anonymous: *The Stage Condemned*, pp. 91-95.	1698
3. Doctor Thomas Bray (1656-1730)	3. *A Discourse on the Baptismal Covenant*, p. 118.	Nov. 1697	3. a. Anonymous: *Conduct of the Stage Considered*, p. 28. b. Anonymous: *Stage Condemned*, p. 89. c. Anonymous: *Stage Acquitted*, p. 135.	1721 1698 1699
4. Doctor Thomas Bray (1656-1730)	4. *Church Catechism*, Lect. 19.	1702	4. A. Bedford: *Serious Reflections*, p. 11	1705
5. Doctor William Cave (1637-1713)	5. *Primitive Christianity* Book II, Ch. 2, p. 32.	1672	5. A. Bedford: *Serious Reflections*, p. 8.	1705
6. Doctor John Edwards (1637-1716)	6. *Preacher*, Part I, p. 100; p. 101. Part III, p. 188; p. 189.	1705 1707	6. Anonymous: *Conduct of Stage Cons.*, p. 29.	1721
7. Doctor Laurence Fogg (1623-1718)	7. *Two Treatises*, p. 153.	1712	7. Anonymous: *Conduct of Stage Cons.*, p. 29.	1721
8. Doctor Anthony Horneck (1641-1697)	8. a. Letter against Plays in *Book on Judgment* b. Letter against Plays in *Book on Judgment* c. Letter against Plays in *Book on Judgment*	3rd. ed. corrected, 1705 2nd. ed. 1690	8. a. Anonymous: *Conduct of Stage Cons.*, p. 28. b. Anonymous: *Stage Condemned*, pp. 79-89. c. Anonymous: *Stage Acquitted*, p. 105; 133; 137.	1721 1698 1699
9. Doctor White Kennett (1660-1728)			9. Anonymous: *Conduct of Stage Cons.*, p. 29.	1721
10. Archb. John Tillotson (1630-1694)	10. a. Sermon 3. *Education of Children* p. 153; 154.	2nd ed. 1694	10. a. Anonymous: *Conduct of Stage Cons.*, pp. 28-9	1721
11. Archb. John Tillotson (1630-1694)	11. Sermon upon *Corrupt Communication*	Sermons ed. by Ralph Barker. 1695-1704. 14 Vols.	11. b. Law: in *Absolute Unlawfulness*, p. 38 c. [J. Woodward]: *Some Thoughts Concerning the Stage*, pp. 8-9.	1726 1704
12. Archb. John Tillotson (1630-1694)	12. *Sermons*—Volume 11	*Ibid.*	12. J. Dennis: *Letters*, p. 240.	1721
13. Archb. James Usher Not Listed in *D.N.B.* 1908 ed.	13. *Body of Divinity*	Author of *Conduct of Stage* says Ed. 1. in 4to, 1702 (Arber says 8th ed. in 1702)	13. Anonymous: *Conduct of Stage Cons.*, p. 28.	1721
14. Doctor Samuel Wesley (1662-1735)	14. *Life of Christ*, an Epic Poem	Revised 1697	14. a. Anonymous: *Stage Condemned*, pp. 76-79. b. Anonymous: *Stage Acquitted*, p. 105; 133; 137.	1698 1699

to say here that the term, masquerade—in the first quarter of the eighteenth century—was applied to "assemblies of persons wearing masks
and amusing themselves with dancing, conversation or other diversions."[7] That the term was also applied to forms of dramatic entertainments is ascertained from statements found in such pamphlets as *Of
Plays and Masquerades* and *The Conduct of the Stage Considered.*
Note the following:

> "Now to frequent these Plays [Masquerades] what is it but to
> *compliment Vice,* which, in Mr. *Collier's* Opinion, *is but one
> Remove from Worshipping the Devil.*[8]

We may infer likewise from a statement made by Dennis in *The Stage
Defended* that the term "masquerade" might be applied to a "stage
entertainment." Dennis declares:

> "The Publick Diversions which are at present establish'd in
> *Great Britain,* are either the combats of our modern Gladiators,
> or the *Italian Opera's,* or the Masquerades, or Tragedies and
> Comedies, which are the only genuine legitimate Entertain-
> ments of the Stage.[9]

Addison, too, would have us understand that the term might be
used in connection with stage entertainments. The *Spectator* Number
14, entitled "Letters from the Lion—from an Under-sexton on the
Masquerade—Puppet Show" contains four letters of which the first is
addressed by the lion from "My Den in the Haymarket," while the
remaining three bear the superscription "Covent Garden." The last
of the four letters gives satirical reflections on the two leading diversions of the town in which Mr. Powell sets up Whittington and his
Cat against *Rinaldo and Armida.* The conclusion voices Addison's
satire against Dennis' play:

> "I shall observe only one thing further, in which both dramas
> agree; which is, that by the squeak of their voices the heroes
> of each are eunuchs; and as the wit in both pieces is equal,

---

[7] Webster's *New International Dictionary.* The *N. E. D.* does not recognize
"masquerade" as a term applied to stage performances in the 18th century.
[8] Anonymous, *The Conduct of the Stage Consider'd,* p. 42.
[9] J. Dennis, *The Stage Defended,* p. iv.

I must prefer the performance of Mr. Powell, because it is in our own language."[10]

That masquerades were often morally baneful to those who attended them is also attested by contemporaries,[11] and one of the most pertinent statements that we have in proof of the fact is given by the critic, John Dennis, who in his Dedication of *The Stage Defended* scathingly rebukes Law who had affirmed that masquerades were more innocent than the drama:

> ". . . [This] is a frontless Assertion, and the very Reverse of Reason . . . young Ladies run a greater Risk of Their Reputations by being familiar with Fools, than with Men of Sense; . . . So Masquerades having neither the Sense of the Drama, nor the Sound of the Opera, Persons of both Sexes may go to them either with no Design, or with a very vile one. To which I might add the late Remark of a wise and pious Prelate, which is, *That Masquerades deprive Virtue and Religion of their last Refuge, Shame;*"[12]

References to literature against "Plays and Masquerades" published between 1698-1726, follow: *The Freethinker Extraordinary, Number 4,* mentioned in *Of Plays and Masquerades* 1719, p. 21; *The Freethinker Extraordinary, Number 63,* mentioned in *Of Plays and Masquerades* 1719, p. 23; *The Freethinker Extraordinary, Number 68,* mentioned in *Of Plays and Masquerades* 1719, p. 27; *The Honest Gentleman, Number 4,* mentioned in *Of Plays and Masquerades* 1719, pp. 23-4; *The Inquisitor,* June 26, 1711; and *The Spectator,* Number 14, March 16, 1710-11.

---

[10] *The British Essayists,* 1819, VI, 64-70. *Rinaldo and Armida* was composed by John Dennis and first acted at L.-I.-F., 1699. The musical entertainments in it were composed by John Eccles excepting a chorus in the fourth act which is borrowed from Mr. H. Purcell's Frost Scene. D. E. Baker,, *Biographia Dramatica,* II, 307-8. Baker elsewhere makes comment on Addison's attitude toward Dennis: "As his [Dennis'] attacks were almost always on persons of superior abilities to himself, viz. Addison, Steele, and Pope, their replies usually turned the popular opinion so greatly against him, that, by irritating his testy temper the more, it rendered him a perpetual torment to himself." *Ibid.,* I, 123-4.

[11] Anonymous, *The Stage Condemned,* p. 61; Anonymous, *The Conduct of the Stage Considered,* pp. 39-40; Anonymous, *Of Plays and Masquerades,* pp. 1-28; *Spectator,* Number 8; Anonymous, *A Seasonable Apology for Mr. H-g-r,* pp. 1-26.

[12] J. Dennis, *The Stage Defended,* p. v.

CONCLUSION

The stage-controversy in England from 1698-1726 shows amazing fluctuations of storm and calm. From Collier's attack on the stage in the spring of 1698 till the close of the year we note greater activity than in any other one year of the dispute. Before summarizing our findings, however, it may be well to recall that when Collier published his *Short View*, reform was in the very atmosphere of England. A reaction to the licentiousness of the Court of Charles II was taking place; the Puritan element dominant from 1642-1660 was reasserting itself; William and Mary were inaugurating and enforcing reform measures; societies were being formed for reformation of manners and for propagating the gospel in foreign parts; King and Parliament were stimulating the activity of these societies by legislative measures, and the wealthy were contributing financially to make them successful.[1]

Collier, then, cannot be said to be altogether responsible for the stage controversy from 1698-1726. He, it is true, assumed the generalship and fired the shot which set things in motion in 1698, but even before 1698 there were literary attacks on the stage-poets by the reformers who blamed the stage for contributing to irreligion and immorality. Gould's satirical writings against the play-house,[2] Archbishop Tillotson's *Sermons*, especially those on the "Education of Children" and on "Corrupt Communication,"[3] Archbishop Usher's *Body of Divinity*,[4] and Sir Richard Blackmore's Preface to *Prince Arthur* published in 1695 are examples. Collier's *Short View* attacked the same two vices which had been the basis of the general reform measures from 1680 on, only it attacked them under a four-fold aspect: (1) "Indecency of Language, (2) Swearing, Profaneness, and Lewd

---

[1] Josiah Woodward, *An Account of the Rise and Progress of the Religious Societies*, pp. 15-120. [J. Woodward] *An Account of the Societies for Reformation of Manners* . . . 1699, pp. 11-162. J. Oldmixon, *History of England*, III, p. 192.

[2] *The Play-House, A Satyr*, pp. 161-185; Prologue to *Satyrs and Epistles*, pp. 131-134, published in 1688-9 in *Poems, Chiefly Consisting of Satyrs and Satyrical Epistles*.

[3] Archbishop Tillotson died in 1694. The first collected edition of Tillotson's works contain 54 sermons and the "Rule of Faith." 200 sermons were added in succeeding editions and edited in 14 volumes by Ralph Barker, 1695-1704. *D. N. B. XIX*, pp. 872-8.

[4] *A Body of Divinity, or the Sum and Substance of Christian Divinity, Catechistically Propounded and Explained*, 1670. In 1702 the 8th edition was published. *Term Catalogues*, III, p. 260.

Application of Scripture, (3) Abuse of the Clergy, and (4) Making the top Characters Libertines and giving them success in their Debauchery." The living stage-poets whom it called to task were Wycherley, Dryden, Congreve, Vanbrugh, and D'Urfey—of whom all but D'Urfey were considered among the best wits of the day.

The table on pages 296-7 summarizes several interesting facts concerning the controversy. First, of the twenty publications listed from April to December 1698, seven authors attack the stage-poets and the stage, twelve attack Collier and vindicate the stage, and one—Dryden—though not taking sides, expresses contrition for his scurrility and regret that Collier had misinterpreted the glosses of the poets. Further, of the seven attacks on the stage all but Meriton's and Collier's are anonymous; of the twelve vindications six are anonymous and six are not. In the latter group we find vindications by three of the attacked stage-poets—D'Urfey, Vanbrugh, and Congreve—but their work is, for the most part, beneath their literary ability both in argumentative and rhetorical force. Of all the 1698 vindications, that by Dennis is the most scholarly; it sanely attacks Collier from the firmest stronghold—the fallacy of destroying the stage when it is admittedly of benefit in recommending virtue and discountenancing vice, the folly of refusing plays to the English who, of all people are most in need of diversion, and the rashness of attacking the play-house when it is the least harmful of the four reigning vices of the town.

The author of *The Stage Condemned,* supposedly Ridpath, although approving of Collier's four-fold attack on the English stage adds new arguments. He attributes the low ebb of morals not only to the clergy who, he says, have encouraged the stage, but to the Sundays Mask of King Charles the First, to the Book of Sports by Archbishop Laud, and to the kind of education which the youth receive in the schools. The arguments, however, had very little influence upon the controversy except to evoke satire from such men as Tom Brown. Not even Filmer in his *A Defence of Plays,* 1707, refers to the eighty pages allotted by Ridpath to censuring *A Defence of Dramatick Poetry,* 1698.

Again it is interesting to note that the Thomistic arguments on the lawfulness of plays drawn up by the Theatine priest, Father Caffaro, are introduced early into the controversy by an Anglican divine and that these arguments are echoed for twenty-eight years either from Caffaro's viewpoint *in favour* of legitimate diversion, or from Bossuet's *against* the stage as a legitimate diversion. Caffaro's principal arguments are, first, that plays—provided there be no excesses in them—are legitimate inasmuch as they afford entertainment by means of divertive words and actions; second, that the silence of the Scriptures concerning plays indicates that reason is to be the guide in permitting or forbidding attendance at them; third, that the mind oppressed with business and worry needs unbending and that the enjoyment of the play-house—provided no excesses are committed there—offers a fitting way to relax; fourth, that the profession of an actor is not sinful; fifth, that the censure of the Fathers of the Church against plays was directed against the excesses committed in the play-house, and sixth, that persons who pay actors to divert them are not only not guilty of sin but are doing a virtuous deed provided they do not give away their whole estate to the actors.

In the second place, the chart reveals that the years 1698, 1699, and 1704 are the most prolific of publications. This is easily explained. The publications for the years 1698-9 followed Collier's initial attack and his first *Defence;* interest was keen, and antagonism on both sides, bitter. The pamphlets in 1704 were—most of them—evoked by the great storm of November 26, 1703 and these either precede, coincide with, or directly follow the special fast day decreed by the queen for January 19, 1704 for the purpose of appeasing Divine Justice.

A third interesting feature is that Collier thrice defends his *Short View* but that he does not defend attacks made on his *Defence,* his *Second Defence* or his *Dissuasive* although he quotes from them all in his *Farther Vindication.* Collier's method of counter-attack was caustic; oftentimes it was a retaliation for insults given him by the poets; frequently Collier dragged into the dispute matters intensely personal to them; very rarely did he admit himself in error, and his quotations nearly always humiliated his opponent in the attempt to prove him in error. This may account for many of the inane and anonymous vindications given and for the quickness and the finality with which most of the stage-poets departed from battle.

A fourth observation may be made in that Dennis appears in the ranks to vindicate the stage and the stage-poets whenever a major attack has been made. He does so in 1698 after Collier's *Short View* had appeared; again in 1704 after the *Dissuasive* had been published; then he defends the stage in 1706 when Bedford's *Evil and Danger* was in prominence; and again in 1726 in reply to Law's *Absolute Unlawfulness of the Stage Entertainment.* In all the available Dennis pamphlets we note practically the same reasons as had been given in the *Usefulness of the Stage* for upholding dramatic entertainment. Besides Dennis we find that Gildon and Brown are prominent champions of the stage but in Brown there is a regrettable abuse of undoubted talent.

Bedford, from his first anti-stage publication in 1705 through the following decade and a half shows himself uncompromisingly hostile to the profaneness and immorality of the stage and stage-poets. He was prominent in Bristol and in London and his position undoubtedly accounted for some of the pompousness which we note in his arguments. His works are, however, valuable only in so far as they give contemporary side-lights on the stage-poets, plays, and on the Collier stage-controversy.

Shortly after Bedford's exit from the controversy Law steps into the arena. It is just before the final curtain is drawn but even his brief stay proves him to be the most rigid of the declaimers of stage-plays, the most rabid antagonist of the stage-poets, and the most unyielding in the argument that plays are, in themselves, a sinful diversion, and that those who attend them are guilty of serious offence against the law of God.

Much has been written concerning the effect which Collier's attack has had upon the stage. On the whole, literary critics agree that the effect was immediate and far-reaching. W. Hunt,[5] S. A. Allibone,[6] J. Genest,[7] W. B. Macaulay,[8] W. Hazlitt,[9]—all attest to the wide influence of the *Short View* on English comedy. Among the more recent writers who are of the same opinion are H. T. Perry,[10] D. C. Taylor,[11]

---

[5] *D.N.B.*, IV, 799.
[6] *A Critical Dictionary of English Literature*, I, 409-411.
[7] *Some Account of the English Stage, From the Restoration in 1660 to 1830*, II, 123-135.
[8] *Critical, Historical and Miscellaneous Essays*, IV, 350-411.
[9] *Lectures on the English Comic Writers, Lecture* IV, pp. 133-176.
[10] *The Comic Spirit in Restoration Drama*, p. 10.
[11] *William Congreve*, p. 142. Mr. Taylor says, elsewhere, that "its [The Short View's] influence spread like a Plague of Egypt." p. 122.

Stage controversy chart, 1698–1707+ (each entry followed by its classification number [1], [2], or [3]):

1698	1699	1700	1701	1702	1703	1704	1705	1706	1707	17..
Some Remarks [2]										
A Defence of Short View [1]										
Immorality of Eng. Pulpit [2]										
Stage Condemned [1]										
Animadversions [1]										
A Letter to Mr.C [1]										
Amendments [2]										
The Campaigners [2]										
A Farther Defence [2]										
A Short Vindication [2]										
Usefulness [2]	Love and a Bottle [2]									
A Defence [2]	Second Defence [1]					Stage-Beaux [2]				
Occasional Paper [1]	Letter to Mrs.T [3]					Dissuasive Ed.II [2]				
Immorality [5]	Feigned F. [5]					Visits [2]				
A Vindication [2]	An Account [1]					Act at Oxford [2]	Preacher I [1]			
Letter to A.H. [2]	Translation [1]	Epilogue [3]				Some Considerations [1]	Esther [5]			
Letter to Motteux [3]	A Dialogue [4]	Preface [3]				Person of Quality's [2]	Letter [1]			
Beauty in Distress [2]	Antient [2]	Love Makes a Man [2]		Church C. [1]	Dis-suasive [1]	Concio Laici [2]	Comical View [2]		Preacher III [1]	
Phaeton [2]	Reflections [2]	Perjured Husband [2]		Letters [2]	Re-futation [5]	Representation [1]	A Second Adv [1]	An Essay [2]	A Defence of Plays [2]	
Short View [1]	Stage Acquitted [2]	Pacificator [1]	Jew of Venice [2]	Scourge [5]	Humble [1]	Some Thoughts [1]	Serious Reflections [2]	Evil and Danger [1]	The Stage Vind. [2]	A Fart Vi

[1] Attacks on the stage and on the stage-poets.
[2] Vindication of the stage and of the poets.
[3] Acknowledgment of indecent writing.

Chart Showing
the

STAGE-CONTROVERSY IN ENGLAND
from
1698 - 1726

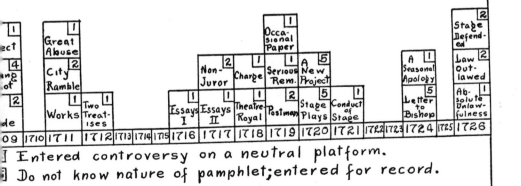

Ⅰ Entered controversy on a neutral platform.
Ⅱ Do not know nature of pamphlet; entered for record.

J. Ballein,[12] J. Krutch,[13] A. Nicoll,[14] and Montague Summers.[15] Mr. Summers is emphatic in his statement of the decisive effect of the *Short View* upon comedy. He declares:

> "The results of Collier's attack were immediate, and it is almost possible in English dramatic literature to draw a line of demarcation between the plays written before and after the spring of 1698."[16]

He asserts, further, that after Collier's attack the language of comedy was drastically revised and amended, that the more luscious descriptions were deleted or changed, and that lubric situations were glozed. He substantiates his assertion by stating that the most superficial acquaintances with the comedies of Cibber, Mrs. Centlivre, Steele, Taverner, Thomas Baker, Charles Johnson, Estcourt, Griffin, and C. Bullock would be sufficient to detect another and a chastened spirit.[17]

Mr. Perry writing in 1925 goes even further when he says:

> "the finest examples of English comedy are only just now recovering from the effects of their [Collier's and Macaulay's] disapproval and once more receiving unprejudiced attention."[18]

I agree with Mr. Summers that Collier's diatribe helped to produce immediate and far-reaching results, and even though I do not make the statement as regards the drama itself, (such criticism being left to specialists in that field), I do make it concerning the thought of the times personally expressed in prologues, epilogues, and dedicatory

---

[12] Jeremy Collier's *Angriff auf die englische Bühne,* pp. 202-4.

[13] *Comedy and Conscience,* Chapter VIII. Mr. Krutch evaluates the conflicting opinions of Whibley and Ward. The latter in his *History of English Dramatic Poetry* says "In truth, the position in which he [Collier] stood . . . had been proved impregnable. From this time forward a marked change becomes visible both in the attitude of the Court, Government, and of a section at least of the ruling classes, towards the stage." Whibley states in the *Cambridge History*: "The poets bowed their knee not an inch in obedience to Collier. They replied to him, they abused him, and they went their way. . . . The pages of Genest . . . make evident the complete failure of Collier's attack." p. 151.

[14] *Restoration Drama,* 1660-1770, p. 265.

[15] *The Restoration Theatre,* p. 9; p. 10; p. 90; p. 325. *The Complete Works of William Congreve,* pp. 47-48.

[16] *The Complete Works,* p. 47.

[17] *Ibid.,* p. 47.

[18] H. T. Perry, *The Comic Spirit in Restoration Drama,* p. 10.

epistles, as well as in contemporaneous pamphlets, history, literature, and critical writings. With him I censure Collier because he

> "belabours some harmless expression or innocent image with the same ungovernable indignation as he regards a light jest or wanton quip . . . [that] His weapon is the bludgeon and [that] he lays about him indiscriminately,"[19]

and with Mr. Genest I regret that at times Collier contended for victory rather than truth.[20]

On the other hand, Collier attacked the stage at a period when even its champions admitted ts profaneness and immorality; he attacked it when even they regretted its license. If he was successful in effecting reform, even his enemies will consider it justice to condone his faults.

---

[19] M. Summers, *The Complete Works of William Congreve*, p. 37.
[20] J. Genest, *Some Account of the English Stage*, p. 132.

BIBLIOGRAPHY

CHRONOLOGICAL BIBLIOGRAPHY

Collier, Jeremy, *A Short View of the Immorality, and Profaneness of the English Stage, Together With the Sense of Antiquity upon this Argument.* London, 1698. [xvi], 288 pp. (Easter, 1698).

Gildon, Charles, *Phaeton: or the Fatal Divorce. A Tragedy As it is Acted at the Theatre Royal in Imitation of the Antients: With Some Reflections on a Book call'd A Short View of the Immorality and Profaneness of the English Stage.* London, 1698. (April 30). The *Reflections* on Collier and the *Short View* comprise about three pages.

Motteux, Mr. [Peter], *Beauty in Distress. A Tragedy. As it is Acted at the Theatre in Little Lincolns-Inn-Fields. By His Majesty's Servants. With a Discourse of the Lawfulness and Unlawfulness of Plays, Lately written in French by the Learned Father Caffaro, Divinity-Professor at Paris. Sent in a Letter to the Author by a Divine of the Church of England.* London, 1698. (Published shortly after April 30). [ix-xxvi].

Dryden, John, "Poetical Epistle to Peter Motteux" on his Tragedy Called *Beauty in Distress.* London, 1698. 2 pp.

Anonymous: *A Letter to A. H. Esq.; Concerning the Stage.* London, 1698. 22 pp. Published shortly after Motteux's *Beauty in Distress.*

Anonymous, *A Vindication of the Stage, With the Usefulness and Advantages of Dramatick Representations. In Answer to Mr. Collier's Late Book, Entitled A View of the Profaneness and Immorality, etc., In a Letter to a Friend.* London, 1698. 29 pp. (May 17).

Meriton, G., *Immorality, Debauchery, and Profaneness, Exposed to the Reproof of Scripture and the Censure of the Law.* (May 19, 1698).**

Anonymous, *The Occasional Paper, Number IX, Containing some Considerations about the Danger of Going to Plays.* London, 1698. 23 pp. (May 21).

Anonyomus, [E. Filmer] *A Defence of Dramatick Poetry. Being a Review of Mr. Collier's View of the Immorality and Profaneness of the Stage.* London, 1698. [viii], 118 pp. (May 26).

Dennis, John, *The Usefulness of the Stage, to the Happiness of Mankind, To Government and to Religion. Occasioned by a Late Book, written by Jeremy Collier, M.A.* London, 1698. [viii], 144 pp. (June 6).

Vanbrugh, John, *A Short Vindication of the Relapse and the Provok'd Wife, from Immorality and Prophaneness, By the Author.* London, 1698. 79 pp. (June 8).

** Entered for record. I have not seen the pamphlet.

Anonymous, *A Farther Defence of Dramatick Poetry: Being the Second Part of the Review of Mr. Collier's View of the Immorality and Profaneness of the Stage. Done by the same Hand.* London, 1698. [viii], 72 pp. (June23).

D'Urfey, Thomas, *The Campaigners: Or, The Pleasant Adventures at Brussels. A Comedy. With a Familiar Preface Upon a Late Reformer of the Stage. Ending with a Satyrical Fable of the Dog and the Ottor.* London, 1698. Preface pp. 1-27. (July 9).

Congreve, Wm., *Amendments of Mr. Collier's False and Imperfect Citations etc. From the Old Batchelour, Double Dealer, Love for Love, Mourning Bride. By the Author of those Plays.* London, 1698. 109 pp. (July 12).

Anonymous, *A Letter to Mr. Congreve on His Pretended Amendments, etc. of Mr. Collier's Short View of the Immorality and Prophaneness of the English Stage.* London, 1698. 41 pp., 2 l. (September 2).

Anonymous, *Animadversions on Mr. Congreve's Late Answer to Mr. Collier in a Dialogue between Mr. Smith and Mr. Johnson. With the Characters of the Present Poets; and Some Offers towards New-Modeling the Stage.* London, 1698. [xxx], 72 pp. (September 8).

Anonymous [George Ridpath], *The Stage Condemned, and the Encouragement given to the Immoralities and Profaneness of the Theatre, by the English Schools, Universities and Pulpits, Censur'd. King Charles I. Sundays Mask and Declaration for Sports and Pastimes on the Sabbath, largely Related and Animadverted upon. The Arguments of All the Authors that have Writ in Defence of the Stage against Mr. Collier, Consider'd. And The Sense of the Fathers, Councils, Antient Philosophers and Poets, and of the Greek and Roman States, and of the First Christian Emperours concerning the Drama, Faithfully Deliver'd. Together with The Censure of the English State and of several Antient and Modern Divines of the Church of England upon the Stage And Remarks on diverse late Plays, as also on those presented by the two Universities to King Charles I.* London 1698. [viii], 216 pp. (September 16).

Anonymous, *The Immorality of the English Pulpit, as Justly Subjected to the Notice of the English Stage, as the Immorality of the Stage is to that of the Pulpit. In a Letter to Mr. Collier Occasion'd by the Third Chapter of his Book, entitl'd, A Short View of the Immorality of the English Stage.* London, 1698. 8 pp.

Collier, Jeremy, *A Defence of the Short View of the Profaneness and Immorality of the English Stage, etc. Being a Reply To Mr. Congreve's Amendments, etc. And to the Vindication of the Author of the Relapse.* London, 1699, [ii], 139 pp., [1] (November 10).

Cf. p. 138, N. 1 of present work concerning "1699."

Anonymous, *Some Remarks Upon Mr. Collier's Defence of his Short View of the English Stage, etc., in Vindication of Mr. Congreve etc., in a Letter to a Friend*. London, 1698. 18 pp. (December 6).

Anonymous, *The Stage Acquitted. Being a full Answer to Mr. Collier, and the other Enemies of the Drama, With a Vindication of King Charles the Martyr and the Clergy of the Church of England, from the Abuses of a Scurrilous Book Called The Stage Condemned. To which is added the Character of the Animadverter and the Animadversions on Mr. Congreve's Answer to Mr. Collier*. London, 1699. [iv], 185 pp. Jan. 1, 1698 is subscribed to Preface.

Anonymous [Oldmixon, J.], *Reflections on the Stage, and Mr. Collyer's Defence of the Short View. In Four Dialogues*. London, 1699. iv, 194 pp. (March 4).

Anonymous [Drake, James], *The Antient and Modern Stages survey'd. Or, Mr. Collier's View of the Immorality and Profaneness of the English Stage Set in a True Light. Wherein some of Mr. Collier's Mistakes are rectified, and the comparative Morality of the English Stage is asserted upon the Parallel*. London, 1699, [xxxii], 367 pp. (March 7).

Wright, J., *Historia Histrionica: An Historical Account of the English Stage; Shewing The Ancient Use, Improvement, and Perfection of the Dramatic Representations in this Nation. In A Dialogue of Plays and Players*. London, 1699. 28 pp.

Anonymous, A Translation of J. B. Bossuet's *Maxims and Reflections Upon Plays. (In Answer to a Discourse of the Lawfullness and Unlawfullness of Plays. Printed Before a late Play Entituled Beauty in Distress.) Written in French by the Bp. of Meaux. And now Made English. The Preface by another Hand*, London, 1699. [xvi], 118 pp.

Anonymous [J. Woodward], *An Account of the Societies for Reformation of Manners, In London and Westminster, And other Parts of the Kingdom. With a Persuasive to Persons of all Ranks, to be Zealous and Diligent in Promoting the Execution of the Laws against Prophaneness and Debauchery, for the Effecting A National Reformation*. London, 1699. [xxiv], 163 pp., [9] pp.

Anonymous, *Feigned Friendship, or the Mad Reformer*. London, 1699. (June 15). (Entered on the authority of *The Post Man* for June 15).**

Dryden, John, "To Mrs. Elizabeth Thomas, Jun." dated November, 1699. Letter XLII, *The Works of John Dryden*, edited by Scott and Saintsbury. XVIII, 166-7.

Collier, J., *A Second Defence of the Short View of the Prophaneness and Immorality of the English Stage, etc. Being a Reply to a*

** Entered for record. I have not seen the pamphlet.

Book, Entituled, The Ancient and Modern Stages Surveyed, etc. London, 1700. [iv], 142 pp. Nov. 26, 1699 is date of "To the Reader."

Farquhar, George, *Love and a Bottle.* London, 1699. Epilogue.

Defoe, D., *The Pacificator.* London, 1700. 14 pp. (February).

Centlivre, Susanna, *The Perjured Husband: Or, The Adventures of Venice. A Tragedy.* London, 1700. Preface.

Cibber, Colley, *Love makes a Man.* London, 1700. (Jan. 6). Dedicatory Epistle, iv. pp.

Dryden, J., "Preface Prefixed to The Fables," (1700). In *The Works of John Dryden,* edited by Scott and Saintsbury. Edinburgh. 1885. XI, 208-244.

Dryden, John, "Epilogue to the Pilgrim," 1700. In *The Dramatic Works of John Dryden,* ed. S. S. VIII, 502-4.

Granville, George Esq., Lord Lansdowne, *The Jew of Venice.* London, 1701. Epilogue.

Burridge, R., *Scourge for the Play-House, or the Character of the English Stage.* London, 1702**

Brown, Thomas; Ayloff, Capt., Barker, Henry Mr., *Letters from the Dead to the Living.* London, 1702.

Feild, John, *An Humble Application to the Queen, And Her Great Council, The Parliament of England, To Suppress Play-Houses and Bear-Baitings. With all Prophaneness and Immorality.* London, 1703. 15 pp. (Written Dec. 10, 1702).

Anonymous, *A Refutation of the Apology for Actors.* 1703.**

Collier, Jeremy, *a Dissuasive from the Play-House; In A Letter to a Person of Quality, Occasion'd By the late Calamity of the Tempest.* 1st edition. London, 1703. 16 pp. (Dec. 10).

Anonymous, [Josiah Woodward] *Some Thoughts Concerning the Stage in a Letter to a Lady.* London, 1704. 13 pp. (January 19).

Anonymous, *A Representation of the Impiety & Immorality of the English Stage, With Reasons for putting a Stop thereto: and some Questions Addrest to those who frequent the Play-Houses.* London, 1704. 24 pp. (Jan. 19).

Anonymous, *Concio Laici, Or The Layman's Sermon In order to an inward and sincere as well as an outward and formal Keeping of the Solemn Fast, Appointed to be Kept on January 1703/4. Shewing that Hypocricy, more than open Lewdness, is the crying Sin of the Nation; that it brought us into danger of the Calamity now impending over us, and that it keeps us from getting out of it.* February, 1704. Entered on authority of A. Bedford *Evil and Danger,* pp. 13-14.

Dennis, John, "The Person of Quality's Answer to Mr. Collier's Letter Containing a Defence of a Regulated Stage," II, 225-279.

** Entered for record. I have not seen the pamphlet.

1704. *Original Letters, Familiar, Moral and Critical*, 2 Vols. London, 1721.

Anonymous, *Some Considerations about the Danger of going to Plays*. London, 1704. 23 pp. (2nd ed. of *Occasional Paper, IX*, 1698).

Baker, Thomas, *An Act at Oxford. A Comedy*. London, 1704. Epistle Dedicatory, [xiv] pp.

Anonymous, *Visits From The Shades: Or, Dialogues Serious, Comical, and Political, Calculated for these Times* Between

I. *Jo. Haines's* Ghost, and the Reforming Mr. Collier. 11 pp.
II. Pryn, and The *Loyal Observator*.
III. *Nat. Lee* the Tragedian, and *Colly Cibber*, the Plagiary.
IV. *Pasquil*, and *Heraclitus Ridens*.
V. *Hobs*, and the Pious Mr. *Asgill*.
VI. *Ben Jonson*, and Mr. *Bak—r*, the Author of the *Oxford Act*.
VII. The Famous *Luxemburgh*, and Mynheer *Obd—m*.
VIII. *John Sobiesky*, and the present King of *P—d*.
IX. *Gustavus Adolphus*, and the present King of *S—n*. London. Easter, 1704.

Collier, Jeremy, *Dissuasive from the Play-House; in a Letter to a Person of Quality, Occasion'd by the late Calamity of the Tempest. To which is added, A Letter written by another Hand; in Answer to some Queries sent by a Person of Quality, Relating to the Irregularities charged upon the Stage*. 2nd edition. London, 1704. 32 pp. (June 9).

Brown, Thomas, *The Stage-Beaux toss'd in a Blanket: Or, Hypocrisie Alamode; Expos'd in a True Picture of Jerry - - - - A Pretending Scourge to the English Stage. A Comedy. With a Prologue on Occasional Conformity; being a full Explanation of the Poussin Doctor's Book; and an Epilogue on the Reformers*. London, 1704.

Bedford, Arthur, *Serious Reflections On The Scandalous Abuse and Effects of the Stage: In a Sermon Preach'd at the Parish-Church of St. Nicolas in the City of Bristol, on Sunday, the 7th Day of January, 1704/5*. Bristol, 1705. xxiii, 38 pp.

Bedford, Arthur, *A Second Advertisement concerning the Profaneness of the Play-House*. 1705. Bristol.**

Brown, Thomas; E. Ward: *A Legacy for the Ladies. Or, Characters of the Women of the Age. With a Comical VIEW of London and Westminster: Or the Merry Quack . . . . In Two Parts. The First Part by Mr. Tho. Brown: The Second Part by Mr. Edward Ward, Author of the London Spy, etc. To which is prefixt the Character of Mr. Tho.*

** Entered for record. I have not seen the pamphlet.

Brown and his Writings, Written by Dr. Drake, London, 1706. The Preface is dated Sept. 29, 1705.

Anonymous, [J. Collier] [J. Woodward], *A Letter to a Lady Concerning the New Play House.* London, 1706. (written September 29, 1705). 16 pp.

Anonymous, *Esther, A Sacred Tragedy from Racine.* 1705.**

Bedford, Arthur, *The Evil and Danger of Stage-Plays: Shewing their Natural Tendency to Destroy RELIGION, And introduce a General Corruption of Manners; In almost Two Thousand Instances, taken from the Plays of the two last Years, against all the Methods lately used for their Reformation.* London, 1706. [xiv], 227 pp., 2 l.

Dennis, J., *An Essay on The Operas After the Italian Manner, which are about to be establish'd on the English stage: With some Reflections on the Damage which they may bring to the Publick.* London, 1706. I, 444-471.

Anonymous, "The Stage Vindicated," A Satyr, by I. H. Esq., (In *The Muses Mercury* for July, 1707.) 10 pp.

Filmer, Edward, *A Defence of Plays: Or the Stage vindicated, From several Passages in Mr. Collier's Short View, etc. Wherein is offer'd The most Probable Method of Reforming our Plays. With a Consideration How far Vicious Characters may be allow'd on the Stage.* London, 1707. xii, 167 pp.

Collier, Jeremy, *A Farther Vindication of the Short View of the Profaneness and Immorality of the English Stage. In which the Objections Of a late Book, Entituled, A Defence of Plays, are Consider'd.* London, 1708, 46 pp.

D'Urfey, Thomas, *The Old Mode and the New. Or, Country Miss with her Furbeloe.* London, 1709. Prologue, Epilogue.

Anonymous, [J. Swift], *A Project for the Advancement of Religion, and the Reformation of Manners.* By a Person of Quality. London, Easter, 1709. 24 pp.

The Tatling Harlot, or, A Dialogue Between Bess O'Bedlam and her Brother Tom. Nos. 1 and 2. August 22, 1709, and August 26, 1709.

Bourbon, Armand de, Prince of Conti, *The Works of the Most Illustrious and Pious Armand de Bourbon, Prince of Conti. With a short Account of his Life, Collected and Translated from the French. To which are added some other Pieces, and a Discourse of Christian Perfection, by the Archbishop of Cambray, Never before Published.* London, 1711.

Anonymous [E. Settle], *The City-Ramble, or, A Play-House Wedding, A Comedy.* London, 1711.

** Entered for record. I have not seen the pamphlet.

Bedford, Arthur, *The Great Abuse of Musick. In Two Parts. Containing An Account of the Use and Design of Musick among the Antient Jews, Greeks, Romans, and others; with their Concern for, and Care to prevent the Abuse thereof. And Also An Account of the Immorality and Profaneness which is occasioned by the Corruption of that most Noble Science in the Present Age.* London, 1711. iv, 276 pp.

Cibber, Colley, *The Non-Juror. A Comedy As it is Acted at the Theatre-Royal By His Majesty's Servants.* London, 1718.

Anonymous, *The Theatre-Royal Turn'd into a Mountebank's Stage. In Some Remarks Upon Mr. Cibber's Quack-Dramatical Performance, called the Non-Juror.* London, 1718, 38 pp.

Bulstrode, Whitelocke, *The Charge of Whitelocke Bulstrode, Esq., to the Grand-Jury, and other Juries, of the County of Middlesex. At the General Quarter-Sessions of the Peace, Held April 21st, 1718, at Westminster Hall.* London, 1718. viii, 39 pp.

Anonymous, [C. Gildon], *The Post-Man Robb'd of his Mail: or, The Packet broke open. Being a Collection of Miscellaneous Letters, Serious and Comical, Amorous and Gallant. . . . In Five Books. By the best Wits of the present Age.* London, 1719. (IV, 212-219).

Bedford, Arthur, *A Serious Remonstrance In Behalf of the Christian Religion, Against the Horrid Blasphemies and Impieties which are still used in the English Play-Houses, to the great Dishonour of Almighty God, and in Contempt of the Statutes of this Realm. Shewing Their plain Tendency to overthrow all Piety, and advance the Interest and Honour of the Devil in the World; from almost Seven Thousand Instances taken out of the Plays of the present Century, and especially of the five last Years, in defiance of all Methods hitherto used for their Reformation.* London, 1719. xx, 383 pp.

Anonymous, *The Occasional Paper, Vol. III, Number IX. Of Plays and Masquerades.* London, 1719. 26 pp.

Anonymous, *Stage Plays justly Condemned.* 1720.**

Dennis and Gildon, *A New Project for Regulating the Stage.* 1720.**

Anonymous, *The Conduct of the Stage Consider'd, Being a Short Historical Account of its Original, Progress, various Aspects, and Treatment in the Pagan, Jewish and Christian World. Together with the Arguments urg'd against it, by Learned Heathens, and by Christians, both Antient and Modern. With Short Remarks upon the Original and Pernicious Consequences of Masquerades . . .* London, 1721, 43 pp.

Heydegger, *Letter to the Bishop of London.* 1724.**

Anonymous, *A Seasonable Apology for Mr. H-g-r. Proving the Usefulness and Antiquity of Masquerading from Scripture, and prophane History. With Observations on the several Species of Masks*

** Entered for record. I have not seen the pamphlet.

now in Use: And Likewise The Report from the Committee appointed to state and examine the Advantage arising from our present Masquerades. London, 1724. iv, 26 pp.

Law, William, *The Absolute Unlawfulness of the Stage-Entertainment Fully Demonstrated.* London, 1726. 50 pp.

Anonymous, *Law Outlaw'd: or, A Short Reply to Mr. Law's Long Declamation against the Stage. Wherein the Wild Rant, Blind Passion, and False Reasoning of that Piping-hot Pharisee are made apparent to the meanest Capacity. Together with an Humble Petition to The Governours of the Incurable Ward of Bethlehem to take pity on the poor distracted Authors of the Town, and not suffer 'em to terrify Mankind at this rate. Written at the Request of the Orange-Women, and for the Publick Good, by the impartial Pen of Mrs. S—O—, a Lover of both Houses.* London, 1726. 15 pp.

Dennis, J., *The Stage Defended, From Scripture, Reason, Experience, and the Common Sense of Mankind, for Two Thousand Years. Occasion'd by Mr. Law's late Pamphlet against Stage-Entertainments. In a Letter to * * * *.* London, 1726. xii. 34 pp.

GENERAL BIBLIOGRAPHY

Adams, W. H. Davenport, *Good Queen Anne; or Men and Manners, Life and Letters in England's Augustan Age,* 2 Vols. London, 1886.

Allibone, S. Austin, *A Critical Dictionary of English Literature and British and American Authors, Living and Deceased from the Earliest Accounts To the Latter Half of the Nineteenth Century. Containing over Forty-Six Thousand Articles (Authors) With Forty Indexes of Subjects.* 3 Vols. Philadelphia, 1891.

Alt, Heinrich, *Theatur and Kirchen in ihren gegenseitigen Verhältnitz.* Berlin, 1846.

Anonymous, *The Athenian Oracle, Being an Entire Collection Of all Valuable Questions and Answers in the Old Athenian Mercuries. Intermix'd with many Cases in Divinity, History, Philosophy, Mathematicks, Love, Poetry, never before Published. To which is added in each Volume, Alphabetical Tables for the speedy finding of any Questions.* 3 Volumes. London, Vol. 1, 1706; Vol. II, 1708; Vol. III, 1716.

Anonymous, [Daniel Defoe], *Dissectio Mentis Humanae: Or A Satiric Essay on Modern Critics, Stage and Epic Poets . . .* London, **1730.**

Anonymous, [D. Defoe] *The Storm: Or, A Collection of the Most Remarkable Casualties and Disasters which happen'd in the Late Dreadful Tempest Both By Sea and Land.* London, 1704.

Anonymous, *The Four and Twentieth Account of the Progress made in the Cities of London and Westminster, And Places adjacent, By the Societies for Promoting a Reformation of Manners; By furthering the Execution of the Laws against Prophaneness and Immorality and other Christian Methods.* London, 1719.

Anonymous, *The History of the Reign of Queen Anne Digested into Annals,* 11 volumes, London, 1703-14.

Anonymous, *Letters of Wit, Politics and Morality. Written Originally in Italian by the Famous Cardinal Bentivoglio; . . . Also Select Letters of Gallantry out of the Greek, . . . Done into English, by the Honourable H-H-Esq; Tho. Cheek, Esq., Mr. Savage, Mr. Boyer, etc. To which is added a large Collection of Original Letters of Love and Friendship written by several Gentlemen and Ladies, particularly, The Honourable Mr. Granville, Tho. Cheek, Esq.; Capt. Ayloffe; Dr. G—, Mr. B—y; Mr. O—n; Mr. B—r, Mr. G—, Mr. F—r, Mrs. C—l as Astraea; Mrs. W—n under the name of Daphne, etc.* London, 1701.

Anonymous, [Huddesford, William] *The Lives of those eminent Antiquaries John Leland, Thomas Hearne, and Anthony à Wood; With an authentick Account of their respective Writings and Publications from Original Papers,* 2 vols. Oxford, 1772.

Anonymous [Ralph, James; d. 1762.] *The Touch-Stone, or, Historical, Critical, Political, Philosophical, and Theological Essays on the Reigning Diversions of the Town . . . In which Everything Antique, or Modern, Relating to Musick, Poetry, Dancing, Pantomime, Chorusses, Cat-Calls . . . Circus, bear-garden, Gladiators, Prize-Fighters . . . is Occasionally Handled. By a Person of Some Taste and Quality. With a preface, Giving an Account of the Author and the Work—*London, 1728.

Arber, Edward, *The Term Catalogues, 1668-1709 A. D. with a Number for Easter Term, 1711, A. D.* 3 vols. London, 1903.

Brown, F. C., *Elkanah Settle His Life and Works.* Chicago, 1910.

Baker, David Erskine, *Biographia Dramatica, or a Companion to the Play house: containing Historical and Critical Memoirs, and Original Anecdotes, of British and Irish Dramatic Writers, from the Commencement of our Theatrical Exhibitions; amongst whom are some of the most celebrated Actors. Also An Alphabetical Account of their Works, the Dates when printed, and occasional Observations on their Merits.* London, 1782, 2 Vols. A second and enlarged edition was published in 1812.

Baker, Thomas, *Hampstead Heath. A Comedy. As it was Acted at the Theatre Royal in Drury Lane,* London, 1706.

Ballein, Johannes, *Jeremy Collier's Angriff auf die englische Bühne.* Marburg, 1910.

Barras, M., *The Stage Controversy in France from Corneille to Rousseau.* New York, 1933.

Beljame, Alexandre, *Le Public et les Hommes de Lettres En Angleterre au Dix-Huitième Siècle 1660-1744* (Dryden-Addison-Pope). Paris, 1897.

Bell, John, *The Poets of Great Britain, Complete from Chaucer to Churchill.* "The Poetical Works of William Congreve. With the Life of the Author." Edinburgh, 1778.

Betterton, Thomas, *The History of the English Stage from the Restauration to the Present Time. Including the Lives, Characters, and Amours of the most eminent Actors and Actresses With Instructions for Public Speaking; wherein the Action and Utterance of the Bar, Stage and Pulpit are Distinctly considered.* London, 1741.

Biographia Britannica: Or the Lives of the Most Eminent Persons Who Have Flourished in Great-Britain and Ireland, From the Earliest Ages, to the Present Times: Collected from the Best Authorities, Printed and Manuscript, and Digested in the Manner of Mr. Bayle's Historical and Critical Dictionary. The Second Edition with Corrections, Enlargements, and the Addition of new Lives; by Andrew Kippis, D.D., F.R.S. and S.A. Vol. IV. London, 1789.

Biographia Gallica, Or the Lives of the most eminent French Writers of Both Sexes, in Divinity, Philosophy, Mathematics, History, etc., From the Restoration of Learning under Francis I to the Present time. 2 Volumes. London, 1752.

Biographie Universelle, Ancienne Et Moderne, Ou Histoire, Par Ordre Alphabétique De La Vie Publique Et Privée De Tous Les Hommes Qui Sont Distingués Par Leur Ecrits, Leurs Actions, Leurs Talents, Leurs Vertus Ou Leurs Crimes. Ouvrage Entièrement Neuf, Rédigé Par Une Société De Gens De Lettres Et De Savants. 85 volumes, of which 52 volumes comprise the set proper, three volumes are devoted to mythology, and 30 volumes to the Supplement. Paris, 1812.

Broadside, *Proclamation by the Queen,* London, 1710.

Broxap, Henry, *The Later Non-Jurors,* Cambridge, 1924.

Burnet, Gilbert, *History of His Own Time:* From the Restoration of King Charles the Second to the Treaty of Peace at Utrecht, in the Reign of Queen Anne. London, 1883.

Butler, Samuel, *Satires and Miscellaneous Poetry and Prose* edited by René Lamar. Cambridge, 1928.

Catholic Encyclopedia. 15 Vols. New York, 1907.

Cibber, Colley, *An Apology For the Life of Mr. Colley Cibber, Comedian, and Late Patentee of the Theatre-Royal. With an Historical View of the Stage during his Own Time.* London, 1740.

Cibber, Colley, *The Dramatic Works.* 5 vols. London, 1777.

Cibber, C., *The Lady's last Stake, Or, The Wife's Resentment. A Comedy, As it is Acted at the Queen's Theatre in the Hay-Market, By Her Majesty's Servants*. London, 1708. Dedicatory Epistle, London, 1708.

Cibber, Colley, *Xerses: A Tragedy*. Prologue, London, 1699.

Cibber, Theophilus, *To David Garrick, Esq. With Dissertations on Theatrical Subjects*, London, 1759.

Collier, Jeremy, *An Ecclesiastical History of Great Britain, chiefly of England, From the First Planting of Christianity, To the End of the Reign of King Charles the II . . . New Edition with a Life of the Author, Embracing a few of his opinions, and those of the Nonjurors as a Body, by Thomas Lathbury, M. A*. 9 Vols. London, 1852.

Collier, Jeremy, *The Emperor Marcus Antoninus His Conversation with Himself. Together With the Preliminary Discourse of the Learned Gataker . . . Translated into English from the Respective Originals by J. Collier*. London, 1701.

Collier, Jeremy, *An Essay Upon Gaming, In A Dialogue between Callimachus and Dolomedes*. London, 1713; Edited by Ed. Goldsmid, Edinburgh, 1885.

Collier, Jeremy, *Essays Upon Several Moral Subjects. In Two Parts*. 2nd edition. London, 1697. Part III, London, 1705.

Collier, Jeremy, *The Great Historical, Geographical, Genealogical and Poetical Dictionary; Being a Curious Miscellany of Sacred and Prophane History*, 4 Vols. London, 1701-1721.

Collier, Jeremy, *Several Discourses Upon Practical Subjects. The Arguments of which may be collected from the Contents. 2nd Edition, with Enlargement*. London, 1726.

Concina, F. D., *De Spectaculis Theatralibus (Dissertationes Duae)*, Romae, 1752.

Congreve, William, *The Best Plays of the Old Dramatists*, edited by Alex C. Ewald, London, N. Y., 1903.

Congreve, William, *The Complete Works of William Congreve*, edited by Montague Summers. Soho, Westminster, 1923.

Congreve, William, *The Works*. 3 Vols. London, 1730.

Crane, R. S., and Kaye, F. B., *A Census of British Newspapers and Periodicals, 1620-1800*. Chapel Hill, N. C., 1927.

Croissant, DeWitt C., *Studies in the Work of Colley Cibber*, Lawrence, 1912.

Cushing, William, *Initials and Pseudonyms: A Dictionary of Literary Disguises*, 2 vols. New York, 1886.

DeBoissy, M. Deprez, *Lettres sur Les Spectacles Avec Une Histoire des Ouvrages pour et contre les Theatres*. Seventh Edition, Paris, 1779.

Defoe, D., *A Collection of the Writings of the Author of the True-Born Englishman*, London, 1703.

Defoe, Daniel, *Reformation of Manners, A Satyr*. London, 1702.

Defoe, D., *The Works . . . With A Memoir of His Life and Writings*, Edited by William Hazlitt. 3 vols. London, 1840.

Denman, John, *The Drama Vindicated*, Cambridge, 1835.

Dennis, J., *Original Letters, Familiar, Moral, and Critical, In Two Volumes*. London, 1721.

Dennis, J., *Select Works of John Dennis*. 2 vols. London, 1718.

DeRetz, John F. Cardinal, "Memoirs of Cardinal de Retz," [1614-1679] in *Courtiers and Favourites of Royalty Memoirs of the Court of France With Illustrations and Facsimiles of Documents Collected from the French National Archives*, by Leon Vallee. Paris, 1903.

Dictionary of National Biography, Edited by Leslie Stephen and Sidney Lee. 22 vols. with 6 supp. vols. New York, 1908.

Dodsley, R., *A Select Collection of Old Plays*. In Twelve Volumes. A new edition with Additional Notes and Corrections, by the late Isaac Reed, Octavius Gilchrist, and the Editor. London, 1825.

Dobrée, Bonamy, *Restoration Comedy*, 1660-1720, Oxford, 1924.

Dobrée, Bonamy, *Restoration Tragedy*, 1660-1720, Oxford, 1929.

Dottin, Paul, *Daniel DeFoe et Ses Romans*, Oxford University Press, 1924.

Downes, John, *Roscius Anglicanus, or an Historical Review of the Stage From 1660 to 1706*. Preface by Joseph Knight. London, 1886.

Dryden, John, *The Works of John Dryden, Illustrated With Notes, Historical, Critical, and Explanatory, and a Life of the Author*, by Sir Walter Scott, Revised and Corrected by George Saintsbury. 18 Vols. Edinburgh, 1885.

Dunton, John, *The Life and Errors of John Dunton, Citizen of London, with the Lives and Characters of more than a thousand contemporary divines, and other persons of literary eminence. To which are added Dunton's Conversations in Ireland; selections from his other works, and a faithful portrait of the author*. London, 1818.

D'Urfey, Thomas, *The Bath, or the Western Lass. A Comedy*. Epistle Dedicatory. London, 1701.

D'Urfey, Thomas, *The Modern Prophets: or, New Wit for a Husband. A Comedy*. Epistle Dedicatory. London, 1709.

D'Urfey, Thomas, *New Operas with Comical Stories and Poems on Several Occasions. Never before printed*. London, 1721.

D'Urfey, Thomas, *A Pill to Purge Melancholy or a Collection of Excellent New Ballads*. London, 1715.

Durham, Willard Higley, *Critical Essays of the Eighteenth Century. 1700-1725*. New Haven, 1915.

Encyclopaedia Britannica, A Dictionary of Arts, Sciences, Literature and General Information. 29 volumes, 11th Edition. Cambridge, 1910.

Enciclopedia Italiana, Di Scienze, Lettere ed Arti. Publicata Sotto L'Alto Patronato Di S. M. Il Re D'Italia. 1933.

Etherege, Sir George, *The Works of Sir George Etherege,* (Plays and Poems) edited with critical Notes and Introduction by A. Wilson Verity, London, 1888.

Evelyn, John, F. R. S., *Diary and Correspondence. To Which is Subjoined The Private Correspondence between King Charles I and Sir Edward Nicholas,* . . . edited from the Original MSS. at Wotton, by William Bray, Esq., F. R. S. 4 Vols. London, 1881-1887.

Garnett and Gosse, *English Literature* in Four Volumes. New York, 1923.

Garnett, R., *The Age of Dryden,* London, 1895.

Ferguson, James, Esq., editor of *The British Essayists;* to which are prefixed Prefaces Biographical, Historical, and Critical: . . . 45 volumes. London, 1819.

Genest, John, *Some Account of the English Stage, from the Restoration in 1660 to 1830,* Bath, 1832, 10 Volumes.

Gildon, Charles, *"An Essay On the Art, Rise, and Progress of the Stage in Greece, Rome, and England,"* in Vol. VII of *The Works of Mr. William Shakespeare.* London, 1710. (Printed for E. Curll).

Gildon, Charles, *Examen Miscellaneum, consisting of Verse and Prose.* London, 1702.

Gildon, Charles, *The Lives and Characters of the English Dramatick Poets. Also an Exact Account of all the Plays that were ever yet Printed in the English Tongue; their Double Titles, and Places where Acted, the Dates when Printed, and the Persons to whom Dedicated; with Remarks and Observations on most of the said Plays.* First begun by Mr. Langbaine, improv'd and continued down to this Time, by a Careful Hand. London, 1697.

Gildon, Charles, *Love's Victim or the Queen of Wales*—Preface. London, 1701.

Gildon, Charles, *Measure for Measure, or Beauty the Advocate.* Prologue. London, 1700.

Goezen, J. M., *Theologische Untersuchung der Sittlichkeit der heutigen deutschen Schaubühne.* Hamburg, 1770.

Gosse, Edmund, *English Literature,* 4 Vols. London, 1892.

Gosse, Edmund, *A History of Eighteenth Century Literature,* 1660-1780. London, 1891.

Gosse, Edmund, *Life of William Congreve,* London, 1888.

Gosse, Edmund, *Seventeenth Century Studies.* London, 1885.

Gosson, Stephen, *Stephen Gosson's Schoole of Abuse, Containing Pleasant Invective against Poets, Pipers, Players, Jesters, etc. with an Introduction Regarding the Author and his Works.* London, 1841.

Gould, R., *Love given over: Or, A Satyr Against the Pride, Lust, and Inconstancy etc., of Woman, With Sylvia's Revenge, or, a Satyr against Man, in Answer to the Satyr against Woman. Amended by the Author. London,* 1709.

Gould, Robert, *The Play-House. A Satyr.* Written in 1685, and included in a volume entitled *Poems Chiefly Consisting of Satyrs and Satyrical Epistles, licensed in 1688-9.* London, 1689.

Graham, Walter, *The Beginnings of English Literary Periodicals.* (1665-1715) New York, 1926.

The Guardian, 3 vols. Ed. by Chalmers, London, 1808.

Halkett, S., and Laing, John, *Dictionary of Anonymous and Pseudonymous English Literature.* New and Enlarged Edition, by Dr. James Kennedy, W. A. Smith, and A. F. Johnson, 7 vols., Edinburgh and London, 1926.

Halifax, Lord Marquis of, [Sarile, George], *Miscellanies.* London, 1704.

Hazlitt, William, *Lectures on the English Comic Writers.* London, 1819.

Hearne, Thomas, *Remarks and Collections Edited Under the Superintendence of the Committee of the Oxford Historical Society.* 11 Volumes. Oxford, 1906.

Horneck, Philip, *The High-German Doctor. With many Additions and Alterations. To which is added, a large Explanatory Index.* 2 Volumes, London, 1720.

Hoadley, Benjamen, *A Preservative Against the Principles and Practices of the Non-Jurors Both in Church and State, or, An Appeal to the Consciences and Common Sense of the Christian Laity.*

Hoey, Mrs. Cashel, *France Under Louis XIV (Le Grand Siècle). Its Arts, Its Ideas.* From the French of Emile Bourgeois. New York, 1897.

Hughes, John, *A Complete History of England: With the Lives of All the Kings and Queens Thereof; From the Earliest Account of Time, to the Death of His late Majesty King William III, Containing a Faithful Relation of all Affairs of State—Ecclesiastical and Civil.* 2nd ed. 3 Vols. London, 1719.

Jerrold, Walter and Clare, *Five Queer Women.* London, 1929.

Johnson, Dr. Samuel, *The Works of the English Poets, From Chaucer to Cowper; Including the Series Edited, with Prefaces, Biographical, and Critical: . . . The Additional Lives by Alexander Chalmers.* 21 Volumes. London, 1810.

Johnson, Samuel, *The Works of Samuel Johnson, LL.D.* 12 Volumes. To which is prefixed an Essay on his Life and Genius, by Arthur Murphy, London, 1820.

Jones, Rev. William, *The Scholar Armed against the Errors of the Times, or a Collection of Tracts on the Principles and Evidences of Christianity, The Constitution of the Church, and the Authority of Civil Government.* 1726-1800. London, 1800.

Kennett, W. *A Register and Chronicle Ecclesiastical and Civil: Containing Matters of Fact Delivered in the Words of the most Authentick Books, Papers and Records, Digested in Exact Order of Time, With Proper Notes and References. Towards discovering and connecting the True History of England, From the Restauration of King Charles II.* London, 1728.

Ker, W. P., *Essays of John Dryden,* In Two Volumes. Oxford, 1926.

Ker, W. P., *The Collected Essays of W. P. Ker;* Edited with an Introduction by Charles Whibley. 2 Volumes. London, 1925.

Krutch, J., *Comedy and Conscience After the Restoration,* New York, 1924.

Langbaine, Gerald, *An Account of the English Dramatick Poets or some Observations and Remarks on the Lives and Writings, of all those that have Publish'd either Comedies, Tragedies, Tragi-Comedies, Pastorals, Masques, Interludes, Farces, or Operas in the English Tongue.* Oxford, 1691.

Lathbury, Thomas, *A History of the Nonjurors: Their Controversies and Writings; With Remarks on Some of the Rubrics in the Book of Common Prayer.* London, 1845.

Lenz, Hermann, *John Dennis Sein Leben und Seine Werke; Ein Beitrag zur Geschichte Der Englischen Literatur im Zeitalter Der Königen Anna.* Marburg, 1913.

Lodge, Thomas, *A Defence of Poetry, Music, and Stage-Plays, . . . to which are added by the same author, an alarum against usurers. And the Delectable History of Forbonius and Prisceria. With Introduction and Notes.* London, 1853.

Lodge, Thomas, *A Reply to Stephen Gosson's Schoole of Abuse, in Defence of Poetry, Musick and Stage-Plays.* London, 1580.

Luttrell, Narcissus, *A Brief Historical Relation of State Affairs from Sept. 1678 to Apr. 1714.* 6 Vols. Oxford, 1857.

Macaulay, W. B. Lord, *Critical, Historical and Miscellaneous Essays.* With a Memoir and Index. In Six Volumes, New York, 1862.

Mackworth, Sir Humphrey, "Peace at Home: or a Vindication of the Proceedings of the Honourable the House of Commons on the Bill for Preventing Danger from Occasional Conformity." 2nd ed. London

1703, in *Tracts from 1660-1758,* a collection of 24 political treatises.

Milbourne, Mr., *Notes on Dryden's Virgil. In a letter to a Friend. With an Essay on the Same Poet.* London, 1698.

Moliere, J. B. P., *The Dramatic Works Rendered into English and edited by Henri Van Laun.* Edinburgh, 1878.

Notes and Queries, A Medium of Inter-Communication For Literary Men, General Readers, etc. Third Series. Vol. IV. July-Dec. 1863. London, 1863.

Notes and Queries, A Medium of Inter-Communication for Literary Men, General Readers, etc. Third Series, Vol. V. Jan. 1864. London, 1864.

Nicoll, Allardyce, *A History of Restoration Drama* 1660-1700, Cambridge, 1923.

Nicoll, Allardyce, *A History of Early Eighteenth Century Drama,* 1700-1750. Cambridge, 1929.

Oldmixon, John, *The History of England During the Reigns of King William and Queen Mary, Queen Anne, King George I. Being the Sequel of the Reigns of the Stuarts.* In 3 Vols. London, 1735.

Otway, Thomas, *The Works of Thomas Otway: Plays, Poems and Love Letters,* edited by J. C. Ghosh. Oxford, The Clarendon Press, 1932.

Overton, J. D., D.D., *The Nonjurors, Their Lives, Principles and Writings,* London, 1902.

Overton, John H., and Relton, Fred, *The English Church, From the Accession of George I to the End of the Eighteenth Century. 1714-1800.* London, 1906.

Overton, J. H., *William Law, Nonjuror and Mystic,* London, 1881.

Palmer, Samuel, "Index" to the *Times Newspaper,* Hampton Wick, 1934.

Pamphlets. A Collection of twenty-three pamphlets printed between the years 1699-1704.

Perry, Henry T. E., *The Comic Spirit in Restoration Drama.* Studies in the Comedies of Etherege, Wycherley, Congreve, Vanbrugh, and Farquhar. London, 1925.

Political Tracts. 3 Vols. Vol. I, 1700-1703; Vol. II, 1711-1714; Vol. III, 1715.

Prynne, William, *Histrio-Mastix, The Players scourge; or actors tragaedie, divided into two parts, wherein it is largely evidenced, by divers arguments—that popular stage-plays are sinful, heathenish, lewd, ungodly spectacles, and most pernicious corruptions—and that the profession of play-poets, of stage-players together with the penning, act-*

ing, and frequenting of stage-plays, are unlawful, infamous, and mis-beseeming Christians. London, 1633.

Paul, H. G., *John Dennis, His Life and Criticism,* New York, 1911.

Rapin, Rene, *The Whole Critical Works, Newly Translated into English by several Hands.* 2 Vols. London, 1706.

Rymer, Thomas, *A Short View of Tragedy: It's Original, Excellency, and Corruption. With Some Reflections on Shakespeare and other Practitioners of the Stage.* London, 1693.

Scoones, W. Baptiste, *Four Centuries of English Letters.* Edited and arranged by W. B. Scoones, London, 1893.

Secretan, Rev. C. F., *Memoirs of the Life and Times of the Pious Robert Nelson, Author of the "Companion to the Festivals and Fasts of the Church."* London, 1860.

Settle, Elkanah, *The Life and Works,* by F. C. Brown, Chicago, 1910.

Spence, Rev. Joseph, *Anecdotes, Observations and Characters of Books and Men. Published from the original papers, with Notes, and a Life of the Author by Samuel Weller Singer.* London, 1820.

Spingarn, J. E., *Critical Essays of the Seventeenth Century,* 3 Volumes. Oxford, 1908.

Stonehill, C., Block, A., and Stonehill, H. W., *Anonyma and Pseudonyma,* 4 Vols. London, 1926.

Strachey, Lytton, *Portraits in Miniature and Other Essays,* New York, 1931.

Summers, Montague, *The Restoration Theatre,* London, 1934.

Talfourd, T. Noon, *Critical and Miscellaneous Writings,* Philadelphia, 1846.

Taylor, D. Crane, *William Congreve,* London, 1931.

Thomas, Mrs. Elizabeth, Jun., *Pylades and Corinna: or Memoirs of the Lives, Amours, and Writings of Richard Gwinnett Esq.; . . . and Mrs. Elizabeth Thomas Jun.* London, 1731.

Thompson, Elbert N. S., *The Controversy between the Puritans and the Stage,* New York, 1903.

Traill, H. D., Editor of *Social England, A Record of the Progress of the People,* by various writers. New York, 1895.

Tutchin, John, *The Observator, or, A Dialogue between a Country Man and a Landwart School-Master* Nos. 6, 7, 8, or May 16, 1705, June 11, 1705, and June 27, 1705. London.

Urbain and Levesque, *Correspondance de Bossuet,* Nouvelle Édition Augmentée de Lettres inédites et Publiée Avec des Notes et des Appendices Sous Le Patronage De L'Académie Française. Paris, 1912.

Vanbrugh, Sir John, *The Complete Works of Sir John Vanbrugh. The Plays edited by Bonamy Dobrée; the Letters edited by Geoffrey Webb.* 4 Vols. Bloomsbury, 1928.

Vanbrugh, Sir John, *The Best Plays of the Old Dramatists,* edited, with an Introduction and Notes by A. E. H. Swaen, London, 1896.

Voiture, Monsieur, *The Works of Monsieur Voiture, A Member of the Royal Academy at Paris, compleat, containing his Familiar Letters to Gentlemen and Ladies with three Collections on Friendship, and Several Other Occasions: Written by John Dryden Esq.; Mr. Dennis, Dr. ——; William Wycherley, Esq.; William Congreve, Esq.; Mr. Thomas Brown; Mr. Edward Ward.* London, 1705.

Ward, A. W., *A History of English Dramatic Literature to the Death of Queen Anne.* 3 Vols. London, 1899.

Ward and Waller, *The Cambridge History of English Literature,* Vols. VI, VII, VIII. Cambridge, 1910, 1911, 1912.

Watt, Robert, *Bibliotheca Britannica; or A General Index to British and Foreign Literature* . . . In Two Parts:—Authors and Subjects. Volumes I, II, Authors; Volumes III, IV, Subjects. Edinburgh, 1824.

Whibley, Charles, *Literary Studies,* London, 1919.

William and Mary Tracts, 56 pieces. London, 1688-1693.

Wood, Anthony, M.A., *Athenae Oxonienses. An Exact History of all the Writers and Bishops who have had their Education in the most Antient and Famous University of Oxford, from The Fifteenth Year of King Henry the Seventh, A.D. 1500, to the Author's Death in Nov. 1695.* 2 Vols. London, 1721.

Woodward, Josiah, *An Account of the Rise and Progress of the Religious Societies in the City of London, etc. And of the Endeavours for Reformation of Manners Which have been made therein.* 2nd ed. London, 1698.

Wright, James, *Country Conversations, Being an Account of some Discourses that happened in a Visit to the Country last Summer, on Divers Subjects, chiefly of Modern Comedy, of Drinking, of Poetry, of Painting, etc.* London, 1694.

Wycherley, William, *The Best Plays of the Old Dramatists,* Edited, With an Introduction and Notes by W. C. Ward. London, 1888.

Wycherley, William, *The Complete Works,* Edited by Montague Summers. Soho, 1924.

II. Pamphlets and Periodicals

Blackwood's Edinburgh Magazine, Edinburgh and London, 152 Vols. Continued in 1906 (Vol. 153) as *Blackwood's Magazine;* Vol. VII, (July, 1820): "On Jeremy Collier and the Opponents of the Drama."

Gentleman's Magazine, London, Jan. 1731-Sept. 1907, by S. A. Clerk, 303 Vols.

History of the Works of the Learned. Or An Impartial Account of Books Lately Printed in all Parts of Europe. With a Particular Relation of the State of Learning in Each Country. Done by Several Hands. London, 11 vols. 1699-1710.

The Philological Quarterly, Iowa, (VII, 17-26), (1928). "Jeremy Collier and Francis Bacon," E. Freeman.

The Post Man, and the Historical Account. London, 1698.

Publications of the Modern Language Association, Baltimore, Volume XXXI, "Congreve's Plays," Henry S. Canby.

INDEX